THE JEWISH QUARTER *of* PHILADELPHIA

A History and Guide, 1881 – 1930

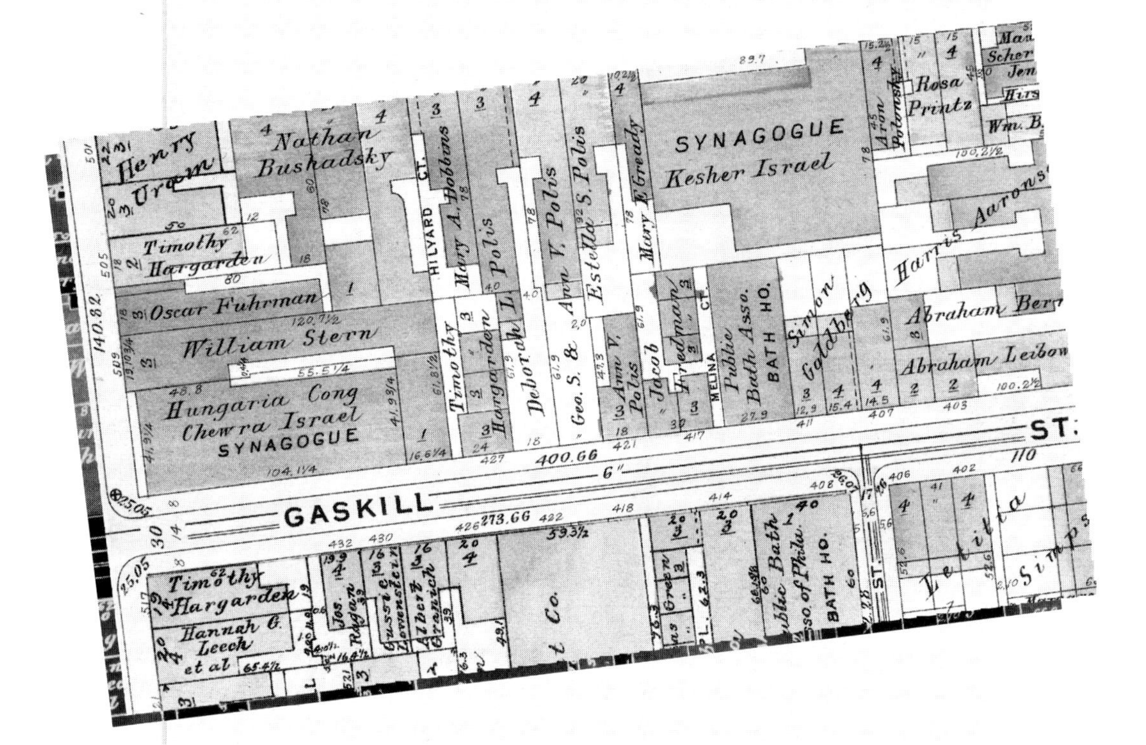

HARRY D. BOONIN

The Story of the east European Jews who settled in the area of Society Hill & Queen Village
with PHOTOGRAPHS *of* YIDDISH THEATRES, STEAMSHIPS, IMMIGRANT BANKS, RABBIS, SYNAGOGUES, WEDDING HALLS, BATHHOUSES, *and* LEADERS *of the* IMMIGRANT COMMUNITY.

JEWISH WALKING TOURS OF PHILADELPHIA, INC.

Grateful acknowledgment is made for permission to reprint from the following:

The Education of Abraham Cahan by Abraham Cahan, pp. 206, 330, and 395. Copyright ©1969 by The Jewish Publication Society of America. Reprinted by permission of The Jewish Publication Society of America. *The Downtown Jews* by Ronald Sanders, pp. 68, 69, and 94. Copyright ©1969 by Ronald Sanders (New York: Harper & Row, Publishers, Inc., 1969). Reprinted by permission of Georges Borchardt, Inc., for the author. *My World as a Jew: The Memoirs of Israel Goldstein* by Israel Goldstein, pp. 17, 19, and 20. Copyright ©1984 by Israel Goldstein (Cranbury, New Jersey: Cornwall Books, 1984). Reprinted by permission of Julien Yoseloff, for the author. American Jewish History, Journal of the American Jewish Historical Society, Waltham, Massachusetts; various issues. Copyrights, American Jewish Historical Society. Reprinted by permission of Michael Feldberg, Executive Director.

Cover and book design by Barbara Anderson.

Photo credits are given under the individual photographs. Cover photograph: Frank "Favel" Kushner's Tailor Shop, located at the corner of Marshall & Ritner Streets, South Philadelphia, circa 1919. The poster on the right is an advertisement for the play, "Back to His People." On the left, "The Sound of the Shofar." *Courtesy of Lois Sernoff.*

For information, address: Jewish Walking Tours of Philadelphia, Inc., P.O. Box 52160, Philadelphia, PA 19115

Reader's comments, photographs, and additional information are welcome.

Atlases: *Atlas of the 5th, 7th, & 8th Wards of the City of Philadelphia*, Compiled & Published by Elvino V. Smith, C.E., (Philadelphia, 1908, Buildings Revised to 1914), Plate 7; *Atlas of the 2nd, 3rd, 4th, & 30th Wards of the City of Philadelphia*, Compiled & Published by Elvino V. Smith, C.E., Philadelphia, 1917), Plate 4; and *Atlas 5th to 10th Wards of the City of Philadelphia*, Compiled & Published by Elvino V. Smith, C.E., (Philadelphia 1927), Plate 8. Photographs of atlases by Will Brown, Philadelphia.

Publisher: Jewish Walking Tours of Philadelphia, Inc., P.O. Box 52160, Philadelphia, PA 19115

First Edition

Library of Congress Catalog Card Number: 99-90015

ISBN 0-9669884-0-X

וקראתם דרור בארץ לכל ישביה

Proclaim liberty throughout the land unto all the inhabitants thereof
Leviticus 25:10

THE JEWISH QUARTER *of* PHILADELPHIA

A History and Guide

Acknowledgments

In 1992, after taking a walking tour of the immigrant Jewish East End of London, I questioned why more was not known of the old Jewish quarter of Philadelphia – streets surrounding the eastern end of South Street – since more than traces of the east European Jewish experience in this part of Philadelphia have survived.

Upon my return from England, I started to give tours of the Jewish quarter of Philadelphia. After a year or so I jotted down a few notes and hoped to produce a small pamphlet to accompany the tour. I did not produce the pamphlet; instead, my scramblings grew into this book. It is divided into two parts: a history and a street-by-street guide. For those who want to use the book solely as a guide for walking excursions, I suggest you start with the guide section. For those who intend to read the historical background, I say to you, *a gezint af dayn kop*, a blessing on your head.

The number of people who helped me is truly amazing. Thanks are due in great measure to a number of families that helped found the Jewish quarter of Philadelphia: Blitzstein, Charsky, Cohen, Englander, Erschler, Kratchman, Magil, Medoff, Oser, Plumer, Rosenbaum, Sarshik, Shapiro, and Spivak. Descendants of these pioneers graciously and enthusiastically shared family photographs, unpublished memoirs, and cherished memorabilia.

A word of special gratitude goes out to Peter P. Russial, Jr. and Mark Alsher, friends of many years. Both read the typescript and heroically attempted to overcome my many language shortcomings (in English and Yiddish). Accordingly, if this book does not measure up to the readers' standards, the blame lies squarely on the shoulders of my two linguistic mentors who obviously have left stones unturned.

I would like to thank Susan Babbitt, Stephen Frank, and Arthur Kiron for reading chapters or sections and offering many fine suggestions.

To Lulla Adler Rosenfeld I owe many thanks. Through our conversations she drew me into the Yiddish theatre world I never knew. She was my link to the family of Jacob P. Adler, the great Yiddish actor. Special thanks are due to Barbara Anderson who so beautifully handled the layout of the book, the cover, and the integration of the photographs into the text.

To the many others who helped, acknowledgment of thanks may be found in the notes next to the contributions they made.

I want to thank my wife, Ruth, not only for her gallant efforts in editing, but for introducing me to Yiddish, a delightful language of my own people. Over many years it has been a special bond between us. The only words of Yiddish I knew when Ruth and I married were: *"gey avek!"* Go away! These are the words I remember my grandmother saying to me often as a young boy.

Thanks are due to the librarians and archivists at The Free Library of Philadelphia; the Philadelphia Jewish Archives Center; the Balch Institute; the Center for Judaic Studies (formerly Dropsie College); the National Museum of American Jewish History; The Library Company of Philadelphia; the Philadelphia Historical Commission; the Archives of the City of Philadelphia; Independence National Historical Park-Library; Urban Archives, Paley Library, Temple University; The Historical Society of Pennsylvania; the Archives of the University of Pennsylvania; the American Philosophical Society; the Library at Gratz College; the Hebraic Section at the Library of Congress; the Archives of Yeshiva University, the Jewish Theological Seminary, New York Public Library, and YIVO Institute for Jewish Research in New York; the American Jewish Historical Society in Waltham, Massachusetts; Rocky Mountain Jewish Historical Society in Denver; American Jewish Archives in Cincinnati; and the Merseyside Maritime Museum, in Liverpool, England.

To my daughters, Sarah and Jessica, who are two generations removed from the immigrants, I owe my fatherly adivce (given at no extra charge): May you always cherish the gift of freedom that was given to you by your grandparents.

Harry D. Boonin

B'nai Abraham Synagogue, 521-527 Lombard Street. Photograph taken on the day of dedication, Sunday, April 3, 1910. Bunting can be seen on the lateral stairwalls and above the portico. The massive centered dome and the stair-tower domes pictured here were destroyed in a fire in 1926.

Courtesy of the Historical Society of Pennsylvania, Philadelphia, Pennsylvania

Philadelphia
December 1998

INTRODUCTION

The Jewish quarter of Philadelphia (1881–1930) cannot be found on any map, but its borders are marked out in contemporary writings of the period. Stretching from Spruce Street on the north to Christian Street on the south, and from South 2nd to South 6th Streets on the east and west, the checkerboard quarter was the heart of immigrant Jewish Philadelphia for two generations. These borders, like all borders, changed as time passed; and, like all Jewish borders, they changed faster than most.

Although residential streets were located throughout the quarter, the heart of the settlement was South Street. In 1887, the *Public Ledger* wrote: "On South Street many 'neat' stores have been built and indications point to the further improvement of that old down-town avenue of retail trade." In Russia, three out of four Jews made a living as small traders or artisans. Retail trade was their bread and butter. When they came to Philadelphia, they flocked to South Street and were called "South Street people," whether they had a store on South Street or on 4th Street. They were the business people of the Jewish quarter, ran the business of the synagogues, and were the leaders of the community. After closing their stores on Saturday night, South Street people gathered like royalty at Bershad's or Kratchmans' bathhouses to drink *schnops* (whiskey) and play a little poker.

Orthodox synagogues were located on every block. The leading rabbis in the Jewish quarter, Nathan Brenner, Simon J. Englander, Abraham H. Erschler, and Bernard L. Levinthal battled daily against what Rabbi Brenner called "the new thought." What was the new thought? And where did it start? And how did it start? Rabbis trained in Eastern Europe at yeshivas like the one at Volozhin were not prepared for America. Few east European Jews were prepared for the American experience that began at different times for different immigrants. For some it began on the ship coming over. Before the ship docked at the foot of Washington Avenue, boys and girls had already spent moonlit-nights on deck together and, whether chaperoned or not, these hushed meetings, with young hearts beating wildly, signaled an end of *shtetl* life and the beginning of American Judaism.

But whatever their religious beliefs, the immigrants had to earn a living and most did so in sweatshops. To enter a sweatshop on Lombard, Bainbridge, Monroe or South 4th Streets was a singular experience. It was described as a place where residence and workshop were identical, often consisting of only one room. The occupants lived and labored, year by year, enduring the most unvarying, unprofitable, and unenviable kind of life. By one account, in 1895 there were six hundred sweatshops within one mile of the Spruce Street Baptist Church (418-426 Spruce Street). Indeed, few were the joys of the immigrant. Tired from hunger and want, the helpless and wretched tailor allowed himself to be enslaved in the sweatshop by the boss tailor, sweating and toiling for sixteen hours a day at the *katerinka* (sewing machine) or forged to the old twenty-pound iron press. There were jobs, however, taken by even the very young, that were not in sweatshops.

One of the most delightful stories I was told during my research involved a downtown bathhouse. Looking back to when she was an eight-year old, an elderly woman described her job at the mikvah: "Each time a woman would be fully immersed under the water [*t'vila*], it was my job to yell out: *'ko-sher!'*" And when the elderly woman said that one word in two elongated syllables, her whole being became alive, and she was once again that eight-year-old immigrant from years ago.

Yet not every joy was denied to the immigrants. Yiddish theatre meant Dramatic Hall, 5th and Gaskill Streets. And no play was more popular with the first immigrants in the Jewish quarter of Philadelphia than *The Spanish Inquisition*, a piece that starred a very young Boris, and an even younger Bessie (Kaufman) Thomashevsky, later known as the "Sweethearts of the Yiddish Stage." We are told that the name of the play alone was enough to bring the *Yidn* (east European Jews) streaming into the theatre. And in the blackness of Dramatic Hall, the sweet voice of Boris Thomashevsky drew the immigrants back to their childhood and to parents whom they would never see again. Before their eyes they saw a youthful prince defend Jewish honor with sword and song. In the play Thomashevsky saved his people from burning fires. As he sang, surely many in the audience heard only the songs their mothers sang in the *shtetl*, songs that vividly portrayed the crackling of wood as Jerusalem burned. As the immigrants walked out onto Gaskill Street after a performance and headed back to hovels hidden in blind courts and alleys, something was stirred deep within their souls. The youth who sang before them promised what they wished for when they left the *shtetl*; he held out for them and their American-born children – freedom.

And the idea of freedom is nowhere more dramatically symbolized in America than in Philadelphia at the Liberty Bell. In 1896, when Zvi Hirsch Masliansky, the famous Zionist and the most eloquent and influential *matif* (preacher) then on the American scene, visited Philadelphia, the Liberty Bell was housed in Independence Hall. Children of the immigrants who lived in the neighborhood often played at the Liberty Bell. Masliansky entered Independence Hall:

The Liberty Bell inside Independence Hall, Philadelphia, early 20th Century.

Courtesy of Independence National Historical Park, Philadelphia, Pennsylvania

> I approached the Liberty Bell, observed it with respect and read the inscription in English, translating the verse from Leviticus: "Proclaim liberty throughout the land unto all the inhabitants thereof." Here the splendid little verse from our holy Torah, engraved upon the young Liberty Bell which is only a little over one hundred years old awakened in me my old Jewish national pride, the holy feeling that "Thou hast chosen us." The heroic, young American nation wanted to immortalize its freedom proclamation and did not find any holy, strong expression in the Muslim Koran, nor in the Christian New Testament, but in our old holy Five Books of Moses.

Jews lived in the area in large numbers for a short time. Although a "remnant of Israel" still remains today, most have left. As few photographic records were made of the east European Jewish settlement in Society Hill and Queen Village, what proof do we have that the Jews set down here? As quickly as they came, they were gone, like a migratory flock, stopping on a long flight, eating of the rich grass, and taking flight again. Who saw them land?

And who were they? The young leaders of the Jewish quarter in Philadelphia came from a remarkable generation of former yeshiva and *gymnasia* students from Russia who were born in the euphoric period immediately following the coronation of Czar Alexander II (1855-1881). Reforms swept through the open plains and steppes of Russia and through the *shtetlyekh* (towns).

Never again in Russia would there be a Jewish generation so splendidly trained. The future leaders of American east European Jewry not only received traditional Jewish educations, many of them received secular educations as well. After receiving the best that Russia had to offer, however, no room could be found for these Jews to breathe and grow in the lands of Tolstoy and Chekhov. Under the repressive regime of Czar Alexander III (1881-1894), they fled the land of their birth, and the United States became home to a new kind of immigrant: the Russian Jew.

Throughout this book I use the terms Russians and Russian Jew. I do not mean to slight or ignore the history of Ukrainian, Romanian, Polish, Hungarian, Lithuanian or Galician Jewry. I have done this for two separate, but connected reasons. First, most immigrants who settled in the Jewish quarter of Philadelphia (and later in South Philadelphia) came from the Imperial Russian Empire, an empire that included a part of historic Poland, Ukraine, Galicia, Hungary, and Romania, and all of Lithuania. Second, the newspapers of the period often referred to the immigrants as Russians or Russian Jews.

Within the Jewish quarter everyone was a Zionist, or at least it seemed that way. I could find no examples of anti-Zionist positions taken by inhabitants of the Jewish quarter. Rabbi Bernard L. Levinthal, a committed Zionist, led the community during these years, and he taught no one better than he taught his own children. The youth of the Jewish quarter grew up with Zionism. They were born at the same time. Many of the leaders, such as Rose Magil and Israel Levinthal, were active in the Zionist movement at tender ages. And from this small quarter measuring just a handful of blocks of Philadelphia, came two of America's foremost Zionists, Judge Louis E. Levinthal and Rabbi Israel Goldstein. Levinthal and Goldstein led the ZOA (Zionist Organization of America) during the 1940's, it's most critical period.

For forty-three years east European Jewish immigrants settled in Philadelphia by the thousands. By 1940, there were 235,000 Jews living in Philadelphia, most of them Russian Jews who had come since 1881, or the children of these recent arrivals. Russian-Jewish emigration before World War II can be divided into three periods: (1) from 1881 to 1890; (2) from 1891 to 1918; and (3) from 1919 to 1924. During the first period, leaders of the community, many of whom were young, came to Philadelphia via the New Jersey agricultural colonies. It was the second period that saw the arrival in Philadelphia of the greatest numbers of Russian Jews. Most came after the terrible pogroms of October 1905, specifically between 1906 and the start of World War I. The last group came in the third period, which was prior to the enactment of legislation by the United States Congress that halted virtual free access to these shores.

Every writer has a story to tell. This is the story of the east European Jews who settled in the Jewish quarter in Philadelphia at the turn of the century. It is the story of a time and a place. For two generations the quarter had strong leaders. It throbbed with a life-pulse that promised a bright tomorrow. And it is to that time and place we turn to learn of the youth, vigor, and new beginnings which sang through its streets.

Table of Contents

A History of the Jewish Quarter of Philadelphia

I. Before They Came;

Philadelphia 1880

There were about fifteen thousand Jews in Philadelphia in 1880, most of whom were born in Germany or were first-generation American Jews born to parents who had emigrated from Germany. Many came to the United States in the years immediately preceding the Civil War and lived in or near Northern Liberties, an area of the city north of Independence Hall. The Spanish and Portuguese Congregation Mikveh Israel, the oldest Jewish congregation in Philadelphia, located on N. 7th Street, was ready to celebrate the 100th anniversary of its first synagogue on Cherry Street. Reform Congregation Keneseth Israel was located at N. 6th & Brown Streets in Northern Liberties, and Dr. Marcus Jastrow, who would soon become a valued friend of the east European immigrants, was the rabbi at Rodeph Shalom Congregation, Broad & Mount Vernon Streets. The Philadelphia branch of the Alliance Israélite Universelle had been organized years earlier. The main branch, established in Paris in 1860, was founded as a central organization to protect Jewish interests wherever they were threatened.

Fifteen years after the end of the Civil War, few Jews lived in the neighborhood immediately to the south of Independence Hall. Known as Society Hill during the years of British and Quaker settlement and growth, it had been the place where the elite of the colonies gathered. George Washington danced at the Georgian mansion of Samuel Powel, 244 S. 3rd Street, but during the ensuing years the Powel House, along with other historic city houses in the area, deteriorated. And who could have foreseen what the coming year would bring? By the end of 1881 strangers from across the sea, wandering Jews from Eastern Europe, began to settle in the former Society Hill. Who lived here just prior to the coming of the east European Jews, or as it was called at the time, the Jewish invasion?

The best place to find an answer is in the federal census. Looking through the 1880 census schedules, street-by-street, alley-by-alley, one is struck by the lack of reference to east Europeans, Jews or non-Jews. Most residents, descendants of English pioneers and Irish immigrants, had been born in Pennsylvania. Lifting our eyes from documentary history and looking onto the streets, farmers' wagons would have been seen loaded with produce bound for the South Street curbstones or the shambles on Bainbridge Street. Market shopping was done daily, and commerce and residential life mixed easily together. Tracks in the old cobblestone streets which criss-crossed busy intersections carried horse-drawn trolleys. The stalls at the New Market on 2nd Street bustled with farmers from south of the city and New Jersey. In the summer the smell of wet corn and horses filled the air. Wagons of the stallholders on 2nd Street were scattered about in nearby alleys and courtyards. Nearer the waterfront, along Front Street from Pine south, the area had long since been abandoned to sailor boarding houses.

Dotted with decaying properties, the area was poor; it was populated by whites. Blacks lived in thick settlements west of 6th Street. Oyster houses on Pine Street, Passyunk Avenue, and S. 5th Street advertised oysters in every style: raw, stewed, panned, and fried. Oysters were sold everywhere. And saloons were on almost every block. In 1876, going from north to south along the 500 block of South 5th Street, one would have seen: Chas. Jackel's (503), Lager Beer Saloon; Wm. Pilbrow (505), a dealer in tobacco, cigars, and snuff; Wm. Adams (509), "Best for Hot Whiskey Punches"; William Tunger (510), Merchant Tailor, seller of watch chains; Frank Holzman's Saloon (514), advertised as opposite "the Wheatley"; Jacob M. Jacobs (516), a dealer in fine cigars; and J. Richie (526), a French steam scourer and dyer who cleaned kid gloves daily.

South Street, the old southern border of the city, was a crowded thoroughfare. Earlier in our history during the colonial period, horse-drawn coaches charged up Darby Road from the south, crossed the Schuylkill River at Gray's Ferry, ran east on Federal Road to Passyunk, darted up Passyunk to Cedar Street (as South Street was called), clamored east on Cedar to Delaware 2nd or Front Street, and then flew north upon the old King's Highway onto New York. In the early 1880's, the

Snellenberg family, 318 South Street, had been in the men's clothing business for over a quarter of a century; Jacob Levy, 535 South Street, sold peach and apple brandy; and Joseph Polak, 711 South Street, had a confectionery business. As early as 1853, at least three members of the B'nai Israel Synagogue, 5th & Catharine Streets (which disbanded several years before the east European Jews came) lived on Cedar Street.

II. EAST EUROPEAN JEWISH IMMIGRATION AND SETTLEMENT IN THE JEWISH QUARTER OF PHILADELPHIA 1881 - 1930

A. THE RUSSIAN AND POLISH POGROMS - 1881

After the assassination of Alexander II, the czar of Russia, on March 1, 1881, mysterious emissaries of Alexander III, the new czar, appeared in the larger cities of southern Russia, and plans were carefully laid for pogroms to occur during Passover. Although the role played by Jews in the murder of Alexander II was insignificant at most, Jews nevertheless became the target of the new czar. The first of hundreds of pogroms broke out in Elizabetgrad, an expanding industrial town 150 miles north-northeast of Odessa. The tragedy began on the fourth day of Passover when a Jewish tavern owner attempted to eject a Russian. The drunken man called for help. Several workers from nearby taverns rushed to the man's rescue and a fight broke out. This was the spark that ignited the conflagration.[1] Unknown to the Jews of Elizabetgrad, the fight was planned. Soon not only was the town caught up in the pogrom, the entire southern area of Russia was engulfed in flames. The pogroms spread to Odessa, Kiev, and hundreds of other towns and villages.[2] Immediately Jews, especially the young, began to leave Russia in number.

Classified in Brody, a Galician town on the Russian-Austrian border, the most able-bodied were selected to be shipped to Lemberg, the capital of Galicia, as a first step on their trip to America. In Lemberg, a second selection was made, and doubtful cases were set aside for absorption in Austria. Trains of about three hundred refugees selected for emigration were dispatched three times a week from Brody to Hamburg. From Hamburg the emigrants departed by steamer for Hull, West Hartlepool, or Grimsby on the East Coast of England and from there proceeded in convoys by rail to Liverpool.[3] By September, Russian Jews began arriving at Castle Garden emigrant depot at the port of New York, and the next month the Hebrew Emigrant Aid Society began shipping them to Philadelphia. In early November 1881, one hundred immigrants arrived in Philadelphia by train from New York. Two days later they were taken to an unidentified hall where the care and welfare of these starvelings fell to members of a committee of the Philadelphia branch of the Alliance Israélite Universelle.

Most of the first arrivals were hired to work in the workshops and factories of committee members.

Waterfront along the Delaware River, Philadelphia, circa 1888.

Courtesy of the Library Company of Philadelphia, Philadelphia, Pennsylvania

Among those on the committee were Messrs. Sinzheimer & Deutch, owners of a shirt factory at Walnut Street above Main Street in North Wales, described by the immigrants as being "three stops" from Philadelphia. Twelve of the one hundred immigrants who arrived in November were hired by Sinzheimer & Deutch at $4.00 a week, but when they learned that for the same work American-born workers were paid $8.00 a week, eight of them quit.[4] The pogroms threw Russian Jews into the arms of their American brothers. Neither camp was ready for the struggle ahead, but while the Philadelphia branch of the Alliance Israélite Universelle may not have been prepared to receive those who came by land (from New York), the same cannot be said for the first who came directly by sea to the busy port of Philadelphia.

B. THE AMERICAN STEAMSHIP COMPANY

Iron shipbuilding was developing by colossal proportions upon the Delaware River in the early 1870's. At the same time immigrants were needed by the factories and coal mines of the new, post-Civil War United States. Tying these two elements together was the Pennsylvania Railroad, which saw opportunities to attract transatlantic emigrant trade and once in Philadelphia to transfer great numbers of immigrants by rail to the Midwest. To move ahead with its plans, the Pennsylvania Railroad created the American Steamship Company. William Cramp & Sons Ship and Engine Building Company of Philadelphia was commissioned to build four ocean steamers for the newly formed steamship line: the *Pennsylvania, Ohio, Indiana,* and *Illinois* - named for the states through which the Pennsylvania Railroad ran to Chicago.

In 1873, the American Line, as the American Steamship Company was called, began service between Liverpool and Philadelphia, employing both steam and sail.[5] Almost immediately the advantages of the port of Philadelphia and the American Line were praised in the Hebrew press of Eastern Europe. The Pennsylvania Railroad was touted – in *Hamagid* (The Preacher), a learned Hebrew journal printed in Lyck, Eastern Prussia, but distributed throughout the Pale of Settlement (the area in western Russian where Jews lived) – as "the best and most reliable for emigrants who are going to the American West."[6]

Poster, American Line in Liverpool, circa 1875.

Courtesy of the National Museums & Galleries on Merseyside, Liverpool, England

On any given day the port of Philadelphia hummed with trade, and the spars and rigging of moored sailing vessels could be seen up and down the Delaware River. For example, on Saturday, December 9, 1876, a total of 149 vessels were loading, unloading or in ballast. In port that day were fourteen steamships, forty-four barks, ten brigs, seventy-six schooners, and five other ships. The Christian Street pier, where the ocean-going steamers of the American Steamship Company were docked, and the emigrant wharf of the Pennsylvania Railroad were contiguous, and cars of the railroad could be backed down onto the wharf itself.

When the Russian pogroms erupted, the steamship service of the American Line was well established with sailings twice a week between Liverpool and Philadelphia. The first ship to arrive at the port of Philadelphia carrying refugees from the pogroms was the *Illinois*. Approximately two weeks before its arrival, an Associated Press report was received, stating that the steamer *Illinois*, with three hundred Russian

Liverpool, England, circa 1910. Queens dock through to Wapping Dock. *Courtesy of the National Museums & Galleries on Merseyside, Liverpool, England*

refugees, had left Liverpool bound for Philadelphia. German Jewry in Philadelphia secured an old depot of the Pennsylvania Railroad at 32nd & Market Streets to temporarily house the arriving strangers. It made arrangements to clothe the immigrants, find them employment, and care for the sick. The mayor of Philadelphia, Samuel G. King, was engaged in the effort and he sought to tap the philanthropic and benevolent nature of the citizenry. The Pennsylvania Railroad promised to have a number of cars and a locomotive standing at the wharf prepared to transport the immigrants to the depot. All was ready.

On Thursday afternoon, February 23, 1882, the steamer *Illinois* came to her moorings at the Christian Street pier, bringing 329 Jewish refugees from Odessa, Kiev, and Warsaw, the first refugees to arrive at the port of Philadelphia after the pogroms. Making their way from the steamer to the wharf, the immigrants were met by Dr. T. J. Ellinger of the Committee of Physicians. "During the examination of their few effects the Jews formed in an irregular line several ranks deep along the pier, and waited with exemplary patience, though they felt the cold severely, throughout an interval, the tediousness of which, especially the weary women, many of them with babes in their arms, and the little children, was greatly increased by an unexpected delay in the arrival of the train that was to transport the party to West Philadelphia."[7] Eventually the immigrants were landed and cared for by the Alliance.[8]

C. THE ASSOCIATION OF JEWISH IMMIGRANTS OF PHILADELPHIA

Early in September 1884, an interrogation of arriving Jews at the Christian Street pier convinced Jews in Philadelphia that the newly arriving immigrants needed the help of the established Jewish community. The incident began in New York some months earlier when twenty-eight Jewish emigrants from Romania were not permitted to land, a decision that was based on the action of the Commissioner of Emigration who was reportedly aided by Superintendent Hirsch of the New York United Hebrew Charities. The emigrants were denied admittance to New York on the basis that they were paupers and were sent back to Hamburg, Germany, on the steamer *Westphalia*.[9]

Several weeks later the United States Consul in Hamburg informed the Treasury Department in Washington, the department responsible for administration of the immigration laws, that paupers, supposedly the same Jews who had been returned to Germany, had somehow managed to secure passage to Liverpool and in Liverpool had boarded the steamer *Pennsylvania*. The Acting Secretary of the Treasury notified the Emigrant Commissioners; in turn, they notified Deputy Collector Smith at Philadelphia, who notified Peter Wright & Sons, the agents for the American Steamship Company, that the paupers were about to attempt to land again, this time in Philadelphia. With officialdom duly notified, the might of the United States government, its agencies, and affiliated private interests stood ready to confront the paupers, or those thought to be the paupers who were denied admittance into the United States at the port of New York some months earlier.

The U.S. officials, however, were not the only ones awaiting the arrival of the steamship *Pennsylvania*. At the wharf to greet the steamer were three Jews: the Rev. Sabato Morais, the very popular Minister-Chazan of Mikveh Israel; Simon Muhr, a Philadelphia German Jewish philanthropist and owner of the imposing Muhr Building, Broad and Race Streets; and Jacob Judelsohn. None of these men were born in the United States, and all played a major role in assisting the new arrivals settling in this country. The least known of the three was Judelsohn, the only one from Eastern Europe. Born in Marionpol, Russia, in 1855, Judelsohn came to this country in 1879 and settled in New York City. He

S.S. Indiana, owned by the American Steamship Company and launched March 25, 1873 by William Cramp & Sons Ship and Engine Building Co.

Oil Painting by Robert S. Austin, 1878. Courtesy of the Independence Seaport Museum, Philadelphia, Pennsylvania

below:
Poster, American Line in Philadelphia, circa 1875.

Courtesy of the Independence Seaport Museum, Philadelphia, Pennsylvania

became secretary of the "Jewish Immigration Society, New York," perhaps, the Hebrew Emigrant Aid Society of the United States. Moving to Philadelphia, Judelsohn became the Philadelphia representative of H. Bernstein & Co. of New York, a banking exchange and insurance business dealing in foreign coins, drafts, and money orders. Judelsohn had an office in Northern Liberties, but he soon moved to 510 S. 5th Street. After a short time Judelsohn left Bernstein and went into the exchange business for himself at the S. 5th Street address.[10]

Of the 538 steerage and intermediate passengers (those in the poorest classes of passage) aboard the *Pennsylvania* when it docked at the pier of the American Line near the foot of Christian Street on Monday, September 8, 1884, eighty-two Jewish men, women, and children were corralled off on the deck and were not allowed to land with the other passengers. Inspector Rodgers informed the captain of the ship that no Polish or Romanian Jew was to be permitted to leave the vessel until proof was given that he or she was not a pauper, nor likely to become one.

When the other passengers had been landed with their bags, Count Peter Wodzicki, the interpreter for the American Line, began interrogating the Jews individually. When asked the amount of money they had, many drew up their shoulders and innocently responded: "*Ich habe kein Geld* [I have no money]." When they were told that paupers with no money would have to

be returned to Europe, "there was considerable whispering, after which, from the most unexpected places, were drawn five, ten and twenty mark notes." These were unrolled from folds of dirty linen, taken from the bottom of trunks, or produced, after much trouble, from bootlegs.

Through the efforts of Muhr and Judelsohn (Judelsohn spoke Romanian, Russian and Yiddish), the immigrants, except for a mother and her child who requested to be returned to Jossi, Romania, were permitted to land; the mother and child were eventually landed also. Whether the immigrants aboard the *Pennsylvania* were the same paupers who had been refused admittance in New York was never established. Muhr pointed out to the authorities that although a number of the immigrants had the same names as those denied admittance in New York, it was not uncommon in the old country for many persons from the same place to have identical names.[11]

Judelsohn, not willing to let the methods practiced upon his coreligionists go unchallenged, called a meeting to discuss the protection of Jewish immigrants at the port of Philadelphia, distributed circulars at different synagogues, and requested Sabato Morais to be present.[12] At Wheatley Dramatic Hall, the idea of forming an association for the protection of Jewish immigrants in Philadelphia was proposed. Word of Judelsohn's ideas quickly reached the established Jewish community of New York and Philip Cowen, the publisher of the influential *American Hebrew*. In a letter to Henry S. Morais, the son of Sabato Morais, Cowen wrote: "Judelsohn has turned out to be a great mischief maker. He tried it here but could get no countenancing and now his head has been so completely turned that he is crazed."[13]

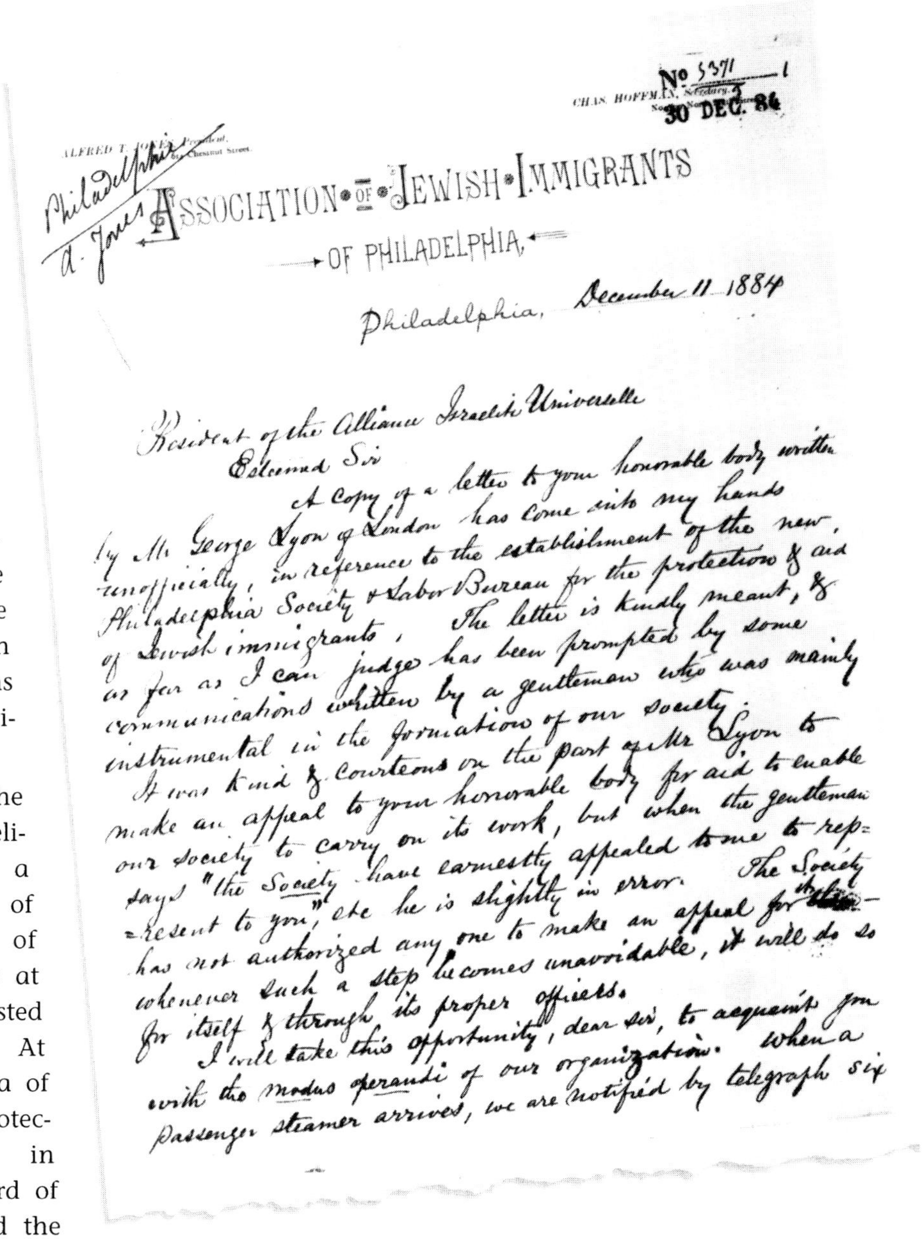

Letter from Alfred T. Jones, president of the Association of Jewish Immigrants of Philadelphia to the president of the Alliance Israelite Universelle, Paris, France, dated December 11, 1884.

Courtesy of Bibliothéque et Archives de L'Alliance Israelite Universelle, Paris, France

The letter reflected the thinking of many American and German born Jewish leaders in America at that time. The active encouragement of east European Jewish immigration was viewed with great alarm. Jewish leadership in Philadelphia was already supporting the Jewish Hospital, the Jewish Foster Home, the Jewish Education Society, the Young Men's Hebrew Association, the United Hebrew Charities of Philadelphia, and other worthy causes. They also supported recently arrived Russian immigrants with food, clothing, coal, money for rent, *matzo* for *peysekh* (Passover), sewing machines, etc., and while the Jewish community readily assumed a duty toward immigrants already landed here, a similar duty was not envisioned toward those still in Russia. That was where the community drew the line.

Judelsohn may have gotten word of Cowen's opposition (Henry S. Morais and Judelsohn lived in Philadelphia and corresponded with one another) because Judelsohn advised the elder Morais that efforts were being made to thwart his, Judelsohn's, plans to found a society devoted to assisting Jewish immigrants at the port of Philadelphia and helping them find work. In a letter to Sabato Morais, Judelsohn wrote: "In order to prevent the interference of shortsighted, ignorant and prejudiced parties to disturb us in our movement, with the display that we are going to burden our charities with an Immigration and Labor Society, I found it necessary to publish a part of my yesterday's communication to Geo. L. Lyon, Esq."[14]

Judelsohn wrote to Lyon, the Secretary of the Jews' Emigration Society in London, that although the immigration movement in Philadelphia was strong, the Philadelphians were already overburdened. Judelsohn begged Lyon to communicate with the Committee of Hamburg and urge them to send no emigrants to Philadelphia until a regular organization could be established, estimated by Judelsohn to be in a few months.[15] At a subsequent meeting in Wheatley Dramatic Hall, which was attended by over four hundred recent arrivals from Eastern Europe, the Association of Jewish Immigrants of Philadelphia was founded.

Judelsohn's pivotal role in the establishment of the organization not only confirmed in Cowen's mind the belief that Judelsohn was crazed but also convinced Cowen that Judelsohn was dangerous. Writing to the younger Morais, Cowen stated:

> As to Judelsohn, he is no riddle. I did not wish to give you any instructions about him as I preferred not hampering you. But you will find him a meddlesome, troublesome individual who is never so happy as when in his zeal he gets others in hot water. It has been a marvel to me that your best men should have been led around by the nose by a person who has neither ability, standing or influence, nor anything else to recommend him, except that he was opposed to the methods of New York because he had not the brains to grasp the situation, and it pleased Phila. to do anything to show its olden hostility to us.[16]

Who were the best men who were led around by the nose by Judelsohn? Elected president of the Association of Jewish Immigrants was Alfred T. Jones, the respected Jewish editor of the *Jewish Record*, 1875-1886. Other best men included Simon Muhr; Charles Hoffman, a lawyer and one of the founders and first editors of the *Jewish Exponent*; Abraham Kessler and Lieb Levine, founders of Chevra B'nai Abraham; and many other community leaders.

Judelsohn refused to accept a position in the Association of Jewish Immigrants of Philadelphia and returned to New York. He became an accountant, kept abreast of matters in Philadelphia, contributed articles to the *Jewish Exponent*, and continued to correspond with Sabato Morais. He remained deeply interested in immigration matters, testifying before a sub-committee of the Joint Congressional Committee on Immigration in New York City. Several years later, on December 15, 1891, at the age of thirty-six, Jacob Judelsohn died of pleuropneumonia.[17]

The Association Judelsohn helped to start, however, began to flourish immediately. By November 28, 1884, the Association rented a twelve-room house for newly arrived immigrants. A total of 1,076 Jewish immigrants arrived at the port of Philadelphia by steamer during the Association's first year, but of this number only 145 persons remained in Philadelphia. The majority left the city within days after their arrival for final destinations in other cities.[18] In a letter to the headquarters of the Alliance Israélite Universelle in Paris, the president, Alfred T. Jones, explained the workings of the Association of Jewish Immigrants of Philadelphia:

> I will take this opportunity, dear sir, to acquaint you with the *modus operandi* of our organization. When a passenger steamer arrives, we are notified by telegraph six hours before it reaches the wharf. Our agent (the only paid officer) is thus enabled to be on the spot, & is duly empowered by the U.S. Commissioners of Immigration to board the ship to confer

with the immigrants. He superintends their conveyance to the Railroad trains of all who are destined for other cities, thereby expediting their departure & saving them from the exaction of illegal charges or other impositions practiced on strangers in large cities, & also notifies their friends, if they have any, of their departure. Those who remain in this city are provided temporarily with lodging & meals in a large house rented and furnished by us for the purpose (for which we have engaged a man & wife as superintendents in which also the office of our Labor Bureau is established).

We then seek homes for the families that remain, saving them from drifting into the slums of the city, & from herding together. Employment is sought for all old enough to work, & for some, tools or machines are provided, where we think it is necessary & the recipients worthy, although to find work in the present depressing state of the manufacturing & mercantile interests is most difficult. Besides this we are often compelled to furnish articles of clothing & assistance towards the purchase of furniture.[19]

Three years later the house was closed and the Association rented facilities when needed. The organization continued to expand, grow, and aid immigrants at the port of Philadelphia, but it suffered a reversal when Jones, the staunchest American-born ally of the Russian immigrants in Philadelphia and throughout the country, died on October 3, 1888. At the time Russians began to arrive in Philadelphia in large numbers, Jones, in editorials in the *Jewish Record*, zealously supported their efforts.

Few in the established Jewish community of Philadelphia thought that the Russian Jews would continue to arrive, and most hoped that things would soon return to normal. The first years of east European Jewish immigration saw relatively few of the newcomers settle in Philadelphia. Most were transmigrants on their way west or south and for them, Philadelphia was the penultimate haven on a long journey. But some did stay and make Philadelphia their home.

D. THE JEWISH QUARTER

East European Jews began to settle around the eastern end of South Street in the early 1880's. Surprisingly, the boundaries of the area were defined early. In "Our Philadelphia Letter" for August 20, 1886, a regular column of the *American Hebrew*, the Jewish quarter of Philadelphia was described as "...bounded by Third and Eighth and Lombard and Christian Streets." As the years passed, the quarter grew slightly to the north, taking in Pine and Spruce Streets, and it shifted slightly to the east. Until the turn of the century, Jewish immigrant communal life did not spill south across Washington Avenue, although isolated pockets of Jewish residential life sprang up early in South Philadelphia. This book focuses on an area bounded by Spruce Street on the north, Christian Street on the south, 2nd Street on the east, and 6th Street on the west. Several other nearby blocks and properties are included.

When east European Jews began to settle in the area around South Street, German Jews described as "uptown" the area in which they lived to distinguish it from the area where the east European Jews were settling, which was "downtown." Market Street, the main east-west thoroughfare which runs from the Delaware River to the Schuylkill River separated the two camps, uptown being north of Market Street and downtown, south of Market Street. In the English-language newspapers of the day, the area where the immigrants settled south of Market Street was described as a slum district, and in truth it was. Since so many Jews settled here, it did become a *de facto* ghetto, although few referred to it as such. But however others referred to it, the east European Jew simply called the area, in Yiddish, the Jewish quarter.

East European Jews not only put down roots around South Street, they settled elsewhere in the city, notably, on North 2nd Street and streets surrounding it in Northern Liberties, in isolated areas of South Philadelphia, and in "Jew-town," the area around Tulip and William Streets in Port Richmond. When writers wanted to describe these non-contiguous areas where Russian Jewish immigrants settled, they sometimes referred to them collectively as the Russian colony, a term used to describe the vast settlement of Russian Jews throughout Philadelphia. We will focus our attention on only one part of the larger settlement, the Jewish quarter. Unlike Jewish quarters in the Old World, in Philadelphia a wall did not surround the quarter and there was no *Judengasse* (Jew Street). Or, was there a wall in the minds of the immigrants? And was South Street, Jew Street?

East European Jews were called *Yid* (singular) or *Yidn* (plural). The word carried with it a pejorative connotation for those who wanted it to, but when used by east European Jews themselves, like the famous Yiddish actor Boris Thomashevsky, the word *Yid* was spoken and written with much love, affection, and humor because the east European writer or speaker knew all that was wrapped up in those three letters. The words *Yid* and *Yidn* clearly differentiated the newcomers from the *Yahudi* (singular) or *Yahudim* (plural) who were the Jews from uptown, that is, the German Jews. *Yidn* could sometimes be seen in caftans, with *peyes* (side curls). Some women wore the flowing skirts and *fatsheyles* (shawls) of the *shtetl.* The *Yahudim* dressed exactly as non-Jewish Philadelphians but could be distinguished from non-Jewish Philadelphians by the fact that they were members of the Mercantile Club and could be seen entering the beautiful temples of the city.

Why did Russian Jews settle in the Jewish quarter of Philadelphia? David B. Tierkel, editor of the Yiddish newspaper, the *Philadelphia Jewish American*, addressed that question as early as 1908: "Twenty-five years ago when Jews came from Russia in masses, they found South Street to be the most prominent business street in South Philadelphia. Several German Jews had businesses on South Street. The Russian Jews could talk to them and the new arrivals began to settle around South Street." Tierkel added that rent for houses in the small streets surrounding South Street was just a few dollars, and these properties were located only five or six blocks from Strawberry and Bank Streets where many of the immigrants were employed in the garment industry. (Strawberry and Bank Streets, many of whose commercial buildings have been preserved and put to more modern uses today, are found outside the old Jewish quarter in the square bounded by Market and Chestnut Streets on the north and south and 2nd and 3rd Streets on the east and west.) Unstated by Tierkel, but surely a major reason for settling in the Jewish quarter, was the location of the area, only several blocks from the Emigrant Depot on the wharf at Christian Street and the Delaware River.

The immigrants were hemmed in on all sides. To the south was Washington Avenue. In the early years there were not thick settlements of Russian Jews south of Washington Avenue, as there would be after the real estate boom of 1900. To the first generation of east European Jewish immigrants, Washington Avenue was a border. Those who wandered south of Washington Avenue were subjected to random beatings. A Jew was wary of crossing that wide-open street on which the trains ran. To the north, above Spruce Street, commercial property values were high and there were few residential buildings. East of 3rd Street the Polish and Irish did not flee upon the Jewish invasion. Living in a narrow bandwidth of streets that ran down to the docks at the Delaware River, they stayed and often singled out for abuse Jews who stumbled across 2nd Street. West of the Jewish quarter were African Americans in the northern streets and Italians in the southern streets. The scant evidence that has come down to us on Jewish African American and Jewish Italian relationships on this western border fails to picture the hostilities that existed between Jews and other ethnic groups.[20]

E. AT A CROSSROAD - 1888

Within weeks after the death of Alfred T. Jones, the Association of Jewish Immigrants of Philadelphia issued its annual report, and a little over a week later, on November 4, 1888, the fifth annual meeting of the Association took place at the recently opened schoolhouse of Rodeph Shalom Congregation on 8th Street, below Girard Avenue. Both in the report and at the meeting basic questions were raised concerning the purpose and aims of the Association. The leadership was squarely in the hands of the German Jewish community, the east Europeans being pushed to the background. When Jones died, not only was the immigrants' chief supporter taken from them, but the Association itself brought the very need for an immigrant society into question.[21]

If large numbers of Russian Jews continued to come to the United States, asked the Association of Jewish Immigrants of Philadelphia, what should its position be? In November 1888 the Association and the community were at a crossroad. Every Jew recognized that there was a Jewish question in Russia: What should be done with the Jews of Russia? On the one hand, the

Association did not want to encourage immigration. It cost too much to support the Russians, and German Jews of Philadelphia questioned whether the Russians were "our concern."

To address the issue of discouraging further immigration, the Association requested that an article be placed in the Hebrew press of Eastern Europe - *Hatsefira* (The Dawn), a moderate weekly published in Warsaw, and *Hamagid* - advising the penniless and the incompetent not to come. By the publication of notice giving the true state of conditions in the impoverished immigrant communities in Philadelphia, the Association also attempted to counteract the effect of alluring advertisements posted in Europe and the work of immigration agents who were bent on increased usage of railway and steamship transportation.[22] On the other hand, the Association could have said much more than it did. It could have written in the Hebrew press of Eastern Europe: *Do not come!* (As other local American Jewish immigrant organizations did.) The Association of Jewish Immigrants of Philadelphia, by discouraging the penniless and incompetent, merely stressed the importance of what the law already stated.[23]

Clearly, German Jews, who made up the leadership of the Association, did not want to sacrifice their high standard of living, earned in their youth by the sweat of their brows, to attempt to solve a problem in far-off Russia. Many in the German Jewish community were immigrants themselves. They had come to the United States penniless, peddled during the years before the Civil War, and by the immigrant-decade they were relatively secure. Philadelphia Jewry knew that Russia was an enormous country with the world's largest Jewish population. What if they all wanted to come!

The greatest surprise by far in the report was the call by the Association for the construction of an immigrant depot at the port of Philadelphia, similar in character to Castle Garden at the port of New York. It is not only surprising that the idea was proposed, even more surprising is the fact that the proposal found its way into the Association's report. If the Association did not truly support increased immigration, it would not have sought to gain the community's support to build an immigrant depot at Philadelphia. Mixed signals were being sent by a society and a community in doubt as to how to solve the "Jewish Question" in Russia.[24]

The report concluded with an ominous two-page essay entitled: "The Immigration Society and its Work. The Question of its Continuance." The thrust of the conclusion questioned the commitment of the entire Jewish community of Philadelphia to support further Russian immigration. It stated that the purpose of the Association was misunderstood by the community, that "its labors had been largely decried as fostering the influx of an undesirable population," and that monies raised to support the Russian immigrants had come from a very limited number of "our citizens." It asked whether the work of the Association of Jewish Immigrants should be abandoned. The report ended on that note.

Jews in Russia, however, knew nothing of the malaise that paralyzed the Philadelphians. They were stirred to emigrate not by action or inaction in Philadelphia but by family decisions made in the *shtetl*. From preserved accounts we learn that the immigrants themselves proved most resolute. Early immigrants who came to Philadelphia via the port of New York and the emigrant station at Castle Garden came not only through organizational help, but also on their own. The story of Charles (Judah) Cohen is typical.[25] Born in July 1879 in Gadyach, Poltava, Ukraine, ten-year-old Cohen came to America in August or September 1890 with his parents, younger brother, and three sisters. After a twenty-one-day crossing of the Atlantic, the family was held at Castle Garden for ten days. Later the boy learned the authorities held the family because they were afraid Mr. Cohen would desert his wife, a common occurrence in those years. Released from Castle Garden, the family arrived in Philadelphia in September, just after Rosh Hashanah (the Jewish New Year). At three o'clock in the morning the Cohens were let off the train at the immigrant station at 9th & Spring Garden Streets, a barn-like structure with no accommodations for passengers.

After the Cohens showed the address they had, they were told to take the 7th Street car to Pine Street.[26] Getting off the streetcar at Pine Street, they could not find the house they were looking for. "Sister Beckie was only 7 and brother was only 3," wrote Cohen in his memoirs. "Sister Anna was just 9 months. So mother carried Anna on one hand and a bundle of our baggage in the other. Father was loaded down with most of our hand baggage and I took care of brother. He walked part of the time holding my hand. He was so tired and sleepy that I had to carry him the rest of the time. Fannie and Beckie held on to mother's skirt. We traveled that way for more than two hours."[27]

During the summer of 1890, stories appeared in the general press in Philadelphia, describing threatened expulsions of the Jews of Russia from their long-time homes. At the same time rumors reached the Jews of Russia that Baron Maurice de Hirsch, the wealthy French industrialist and one of the outstanding Jewish philanthropists in modern history, had established a fund of $120,000, the income of which was to be employed to help Russian Jews reach America. While it was true that Baron de Hirsch had established a fund, it was not true, at least at this time, that the income was to be used to assist Jews to leave Russia.[28] Rather, the fund was established to assist Jews who had already left Russia or who were in the United States. The fine distinction made by the Trust was obviously lost on the *shtetl* Jews of Russia as well as on their anxious relatives here. To clarify the matter in Russia, Louis E. Levy, the new president of the Association of Jewish Immigrants of Philadelphia; Charles Hoffman, secretary; and George Randorf, agent, wrote a letter to the editors of *Hamagid*.

Published as a warning, the letter began by saying that in the "lands of Russia and Poland" a rumor had spread that the great amount of money that Baron de Hirsch gave to establish a fund for Jews in these countries had been earmarked to help exiles reach America. It continued:

> To remove the responsibility from Baron de Hirsch and to remove the barrier from the path of the downtrodden in Russia and Poland, lest they think they will truly hope to find assistance in America, the Association, founded several years ago for the good of the exiles, deems it a holy obligation to notify our brothers there that the rumor is baseless and to warn them that they should not lean on a "thin reed [II Kings 18:21]," for the money of the philanthropist has not been earmarked for the exiles from there, but rather to educate the sons and daughters of our brothers from Poland and Russia who have already settled in the land [the United States], to learn a trade and the language. Anyone who does not listen to our words and comes to America is risking his life.[29]

The letter from the Association of Jewish Immigrants reflected a change in attitude toward immigration. For the first time the Association recognized that an entire people might be on the move, and no American Jewish charity could afford the expense to care for an entire people. At this time the two most influential Jewish immigrant organizations, the Alliance Israélite Universelle and the Baron de Hirsch Trust, took similar positions. The fear that the established Jewish communities of the West would be looked to for financial support from an entire people was real, but what these organizations did not fully grasp was that the great wave of mass emigration had started and nothing, neither fear nor reason could stop it. (By the summer of 1891, however, the eyes of most had been opened wide and the gravity of what lay ahead was understood.) Jewish communal organizations could not control who left Russia on the long and dangerous journey to the *Goldene Medine* (United States). Because of the anxiety caused by the threats of expulsion from Russia and because of the belief, right or wrong, that help from Baron de Hirsch was forthcoming, emigration from Russia increased dramatically beginning in the summer of 1890. Unlike the first years of Russian emigration when the young and idealistic left the *shtetl* for a better life, now everyone wanted to leave.

F. THE JEWISH ALLIANCE OF AMERICA - 1890

The dilemma facing the Philadelphia Jewish community was not how to control or stop mass Russian immigration. Rather it was: how could the great masses of immigrants be helped once they arrived? The first organization to recognize this basic fact, the first to be composed of leaders from the established and immigrant communities, the first to be national in scope, and the first to embrace mass immigration as a reality was the Jewish Alliance of America, founded in Philadelphia in August 1890 by two of the city's most popular young immigrants, Bernard Harris and Dr. Charles David Spivak.[30]

Bernard Harris, a great great grandson of the Vilna Gaon and one of the first lawyers to arise from the ranks of the late 19th century Russian Jewish community in Philadelphia, was born in Vilna on November 26, 1862. He attended a yeshiva and *gymnasia* in his hometown; he studied Hebrew, German, French, and Russian, but left for England in 1883 when his political activities became known to the authorities. Born Ber Olkenitsky, Harris, like many immigrants, changed his name upon entering the English-speaking world. In England, where many Russian exiles had gathered, he studied the English classics and languages before coming to Philadelphia in 1888. Here he secured a position as bookkeeper with the Levytype Company, a printing firm owned by Louis E. Levy.

Harris was a tall, solidly built Jew with full aristocratic cheeks. He wore gold-rimmed glasses. His imposing figure, calm demeanor, and the manner in which he spoke, which was as a true gentleman, set him apart. He quickly became acquainted with Mayer Sulzberger, the great Philadelphia lawyer and judge.[31] Through Sulzberger's help, Harris secured a position in the Hebrew Education Society where he taught the immigrants in the evening school at Touro Hall, 10th & Carpenter Streets. In the early 1890's, Harris was associated with the *Jewish Exponent* and published *Der Volks-Vechter* in Philadelphia, a Yiddish newspaper that soon was sold to a New York daily. Harris, who was one of the most popular speakers in the Russian colony - the only speaker more popular was Spivak - entered the University of Pennsylvania and was graduated with a law degree.[32]

Much more is known about Spivak, one of the giants of the Jewish people. Through his work with the Jewish Consumptives' Relief Society in Denver, Colorado, between 1904, after he left Philadelphia, and his death in 1927, Spivak became known to American Jewry.[33] In Denver, with boundless energy and merciful understanding, he treated advanced cases of tuberculosis at a time when the disease was the scourge of the ghetto. While his work with tuberculosis would occupy most of his adult life, his early years were spent in Philadelphia where his restless energy was already evident. Spivak's ten-year stay in Philadelphia, which helped prepare him for his life's work, is told at this point and throughout this book.

Wedding photograph of Dr. Charles D. Spivak and Jennie Charsky, March 1893, studio of F. Gutekunst, Philadelphia.

Courtesy of Charlesa Feinstein

Dr. Charles David Spivak dreamed as few immigrants dreamed. Obstacles were there to be leaped over. Not only did he skip like a ram, not only did he lead by nature, not only did he work for the betterment of Jewry and mankind, he did all these things with humility and a smile. The Jewish people have produced few men like him. He was the young leader of the Russian colony in Philadelphia from almost the day he arrived. "Everyone knows him. And were he not so modest, much more would be known about him. To know him is to love him. There is no lovelier nor more beautiful person, not in America nor in the old country." These tender words of lofty praise by Abraham Cahan, the founder and longtime editor of the *Jewish Daily Forward*, were written about Spivak upon his 60th birthday.[34]

Born Chaim David Spivakovsky on December 25, 1861, in Kremenchug, Russia, Spivak received a traditional Jewish education and learned a number of languages, including Russian, French, and German. Involved in revolutionary activities from an early age, he was forced to flee Russia. In the border town of Brody he met Abraham Cahan. From there he traveled to Lemberg, Austria, attached himself to the *Kiev Am Olam* (Eternal People) group under the leadership of Nikolai Aleinikoff, and came to New York in May 1882.

Within less than a year, Spivak found himself in Maine: "In New England, in the cold 'Siberian' state of Maine, in the small town of Lisbon Falls, forty-three years ago [written in 1927], we met each other working in the Morris Woolen Mills, I [Moses Freeman] as a wool washer and he [Spivak] as a wool sorter. Young, healthy, and handsome, always lively and witty, he was the illuminating star, the heart and soul of the colony of Russian Jewish intellectual *Am Olam'niks* who were sent or perhaps it is better to say, banished from the New York immigrant society to work in the woolen mill, far from the immigrant center in New York." Educated in American ways there, Spivak had a good word for everyone. He worked in Maine for a little over one year, taking the best from that Yankee culture. In a letter to the editor of the Village News, the local paper in Lisbon Falls, Spivak wrote: "It will never fade from my memory the politeness of the kind people of your village when conversing with me; I never perceived an offending smile on their faces while I was delivering a speech in the English language which was anything but English. They encouraged me by saying 'Well, you talk English pretty well.' Yes, Lisbon Falls was my introductory school. There I learned the language and the habits of the people of the greatest Republic on earth."[35]

Upon his return from Maine, Spivak worked in New York for a short time and then took a teaching position at the Jewish agricultural colony in Vineland, New Jersey. While in Vineland he obtained, through the recommendation of Michael Heilprin and Myer S. Isaacs of New York, the position of librarian of the Young Men's Hebrew Association in Philadelphia, and he came to the City of Brotherly Love.[36] The position of librarian at the YMHA not only gave Spivak time to prepare to enter medical school and time to study and write, it also gave him the opportunity to meet the city's German Jewish leadership. In fact, he was one of the few Russian immigrants who moved easily in German Jewish circles.

Spivak had blond, almost red hair and "wise-smiling" eyes. His mustache was a thick reddish-blond and his laughter was ever present. He settled amongst the socialists and anarchists of immigrant Jewish Philadelphia and lived the communal life of "bread and tea." And if there was not enough money for bread and tea, he worked on hides in a factory. As Moses Freeman stated: "Chaim Spivak, the Jewish scholar and Talmudist, had in fact learned: 'it is better to flay a carcass in the marketplace than to become dependent on people's charity. [Pesachim 113a]'" Unlike those around him, however, Spivak did not believe in anarchism. In a good-natured manner he laughed heartily at anarchistic pleas and arguments. He was a moderate Social Democrat who did not forget the lessons of *kheyder* (elementary religious school) nor the wisdom of *yiddishkayt* (Jewish way of life).

Almost immediately upon his arrival in Philadelphia, Spivak was asked to address the newly formed Hebrew Literature Society, described in the press as a Russian society, the most important east European Jewish immigrant society formed in Philadelphia during the entire period. Reporters for the newly founded *Jewish Exponent* were taken with the peals of laughter that would rise from the audience when Spivak spoke. The immigrants clamored to hear him, whether he spoke in Hebrew, Russian, or Yiddish - and whether he was scheduled to speak or not (when he was not scheduled to speak, the audience implored him to address them). He began writing for the *Jewish Exponent* almost upon the founding of the newspaper.

In the fall of 1887, Spivak entered Jefferson Medical College.[37] During his years at Jefferson, he taught Hebrew with Sabato Morais at School No. 3 of the Hebrew Education Society, 2856 Lark Street, Port Richmond. Morais, the Minister-Hazan of Mikveh Israel, was in his middle sixties and Spivak was a twenty-seven-year-old medical student but despite their age difference, a fast friendship quickly developed. When Michael Heilprin, the most beloved east European Jew in the United States at that time, died in New York, it was Spivak who took the lead in Philadelphia, requesting Morais to honor Heilprin: "Rev. Dr. S. Morais. Dear Sir. The friends of the late Michael Heilprin propose to hold a memorial meeting on Sunday evening May 27th at the Rooms of the Y.M.H.A. Your presence, Reverend Sir, would add to the solemnity of the occasion, and a few words from you, as one who knew him so well would be timely. In behalf of many Russian friends of the illustrious dead, yours in אבלות [mourning] Ch. D. Spivak."[38]

The two friends not only taught together, they traveled together. Spivak accompanied Morais to the Carmel agricultural colony in New Jersey to check on its progress. A talk given by Morais to the immigrants in a large communal room was reported in the *Exponent*: "In it were assembled nearly all the male adults among the colonists, who listened to words of exhortation and encouragement spoken by Dr. Morais and explained by Mr. Spivak." At age twenty-seven and while still a student, Spivak was seen by the *Exponent* reporter as being called upon to explain the words of Morais, one of the greatest Jews of the time.[39]

But whatever role Morais assigned to Spivak, that of translator or a wider role, it is clear that great confidence was already placed in Spivak by Morais and by the *Exponent*.

Spivak studied at Jefferson Medical College for three years. To complete the curriculum, he was examined by Dr. Lewis W. Steinbach who certified that Spivak was "of good moral character and by April 1890 will have read the various branches of medicine at least three years." In the records of the college, Spivak is identified as "Charles D. Spivak of Russia." He graduated from Jefferson with two other Jewish students: Ludwig Loeb "of Germany," with whom Spivak opened a little dispensary on Lombard Street the following year, and Daniel G. Golding "of Nebraska." Spivak was awarded a gold medal for the best essay on a subject pertaining to obstetrics.[40]

At the beginning of August 1890, when the Philadelphia press ran lead stories concerning the threatened expulsion of Jews from their long-time homes in Russia, Spivak had been in his offices at 338 Spruce Street for several months. Immediately, Spivak realized that an organization national in scope was needed. He believed that plans should be made to disperse the immigrants throughout the country rather than have them congregate in a few large cities on the East Coast.[41]

Spivak's thinking was formulated a few years earlier and is reflected in an essay published on the first page of the *Jewish Exponent*. After discussing the benefits of a cooperative plan being followed in the Lasker Colony in Kansas, Spivak turned his attention eastward:

> "The second colony in the East is the Alliance near Vineland, N.J., the greatest and most prosperous of all. The success of this colony may be ascribed principally to the location. As the soil of Vineland is fit only for small fruits, and fruit plants yield the first crop after four or five years, the colonists had to find means for subsistence. Being situated near Philadelphia, they make a nice and comfortable living by sewing on machines for certain houses in Philadelphia.
>
> Colonization en masse can be made efficient when it is based on firm business principles," he continued, "either as in the Vineland colony which is in fact a settlement of city laborers with the advantage over the city laborer that they hope in the near future to be able to devote their energies solely to agriculture; or the adoption of the cooperative plan like the noble Lasker colonists have done, which of course, requires from the settlers themselves a certain amount of intelligence and a firm conviction that in unity and mutual aid lies the power of self-help.

In addition to advocating the twin ideas of combining business and agriculture, and of employing mutual aid, Spivak emphasized that commitment had to come from American Jewry as a whole. In a report Spivak delivered at the formal founding of the Jewish Alliance of America, he expressed this idea in the following words: "The American, the German, the Hungarian, the Portuguese and Russian Hebrews have come together for the first time; they have found the platform which unites them all."[42] The bringing together of many diverse Jewish views was a strength that was to mark Spivak's career. He believed that all Israel was one, and his early Philadelphia experiences prepared him for struggles ahead in Denver.

Spivak, and probably to a lesser degree Harris, was able to convince a number of Jewish leaders in the United States of the wisdom of their plan. Simon Muhr, from Philadelphia; Hon. Simon Wolf, from Washington, D.C.; B. H. Hartogensis, and Rev. Dr. W. H. Schneeberger, from Baltimore; and others quickly embraced the principles of the Jewish Alliance of America.[43] Harris and Spivak devoted the late summer and fall to bringing the immigrants and the established Jewish communities together.[44] Their efforts bore fruit, and on February 15, 1891, the first convention of the Jewish Alliance of America was held in the Hall of the Young Men's Hebrew Association, Eighth Street below Green, in Philadelphia.[45] Representatives from the German and Russian communities assumed positions of leadership and although the two groups had worked together before, they had never attempted to do so on such a grand scale. Altogether several hundred delegates attended.

The stage at the YMHA was covered with green trees thickly placed together with American flags. Over an arch were the letters JAA in white immortelles and to the left was the Hebrew phrase "For the time has come." On an easel was a large framed placard with the Hebrew inscription: "Lo! the voice of the cry of the daughters of my people is from a far-off land. [Jeremiah 8:19]." Spivak read the major address and Simon Muhr was elected president.[46]

The national makeup of the organization was marked early. Several months before the convention, the mayor of Charlottesville, Virginia, Samuel B. Woods, wrote and encouraged Spivak to send Russian Jews to Albemarle County, Virginia, where Woods stated there were thousands of fertile acres.[47] At the convention Mr. Bernhard Marks of California spoke and explained how colonization of Russian immigrants was feasible and proper. A branch of the Jewish Alliance of America was formed in the colony of Alliance, New Jersey. During the spring two meetings were held in Baltimore and although the word was beginning to spread across America, time was running out. At the second Baltimore meeting Muhr announced that it would take a membership of fifty thousand before the Jewish Alliance of America could begin carrying out its projects.[48] While American Jews talked and planned, however, the Russians were already on the high seas.

During July 1891, nothing was heard from the Jewish Alliance of America, but in an open letter to the readers of the *Exponent* one month later, signed by Bernard Harris as secretary, we learn that the anticipated influx of Russian Jews had already stormed ashore in New York.[49] Harris referenced a circular the Jewish Alliance of America had received from the Alliance Israélite Universelle, which in turn quoted from a communication it had received from the Executive Board of the Baron de Hirsch Trust. The circular called on the fledgling Jewish Alliance of America for its "earnest and effective cooperation."

The quoted portion of the circular from the Executive Board of the Baron de Hirsch Trust contained the heart of the matter. It advised that eight thousand "Russian-Hebrew" immigrants had landed at the port of New York during July, and seventeen hundred had landed in early August. It pointed out the utter impossibility of distributing the immigrants in the usual manner, and advised that the Trust deemed it its duty to address the Alliance Israélite Universelle for the purpose of learning to what extent the Alliance was ready to arrange for the distribution of immigrants throughout the United States to points where a welcome and work awaited them.

The huge influx of Russian Hebrews caused permanent changes in the thinking and the direction of the Alliance Israélite Universelle and the Baron de Hirsch Trust, and, indirectly, led to the demise of the Jewish Alliance of America. Both older immigrant organizations realized, perhaps for the first time, that Russia itself did not hold the answer to the Jewish question in Russia. This was a major shift in the thinking of the leadership of western Jewry. Samuel Joseph, the historian of the Baron de Hirsch Fund, saw the summer of 1891 as a "crisis" and Zosa Szajkowski, the great Jewish historian of this period, saw all these events as "a turning point in the history of the Alliance Israélite Universelle."[50] From this time on, the uplifted arm of the Statue of Liberty in New York Harbor not only signaled a welcome to those arriving, it also beckoned to those still in Russia.

In his letter to the *Exponent*, Harris exhorted *Exponent* readers to take immediate and determinative action. He urged them to proceed to the organization of committees at once: "There will certainly be found among your members men whose experience will be of great value in carrying out the purposes of our Alliance." The desperation can almost be heard in Harris' voice. But it was too late for the Jewish Alliance of America to help. The Trustees of the Baron de Hirsch Fund called a conference to discuss the subject of increased immigration. But in reality it was called to allow the organization with the soundest financial backing to take charge so that economic aid could be handled in a manner most beneficial to the immigrants. Organizations that sent representatives, in addition to the Fund, were the United Hebrew Charities, the Independent Order of B'nai Brith, the Free Sons of Israel, the Union of American Hebrew Congregations, and the Jewish Alliance of America. Thus was formed the American Committee for Ameliorating the Conditions of the Russian Exiles.[51]

At this critical juncture, Spivak decided to further his medical career with post-graduate studies in Berlin, and the Jewish Alliance of America, although in capable hands, faltered without him. By September 1891 Spivak was in Paris. From there he proceeded to Berlin where he studied for a year. When he returned to Philadelphia, the Baron de Hirsch Fund had assumed the responsibility for Russian Jewish immigration. Nothing more was heard from the Jewish Alliance of America. Its greatest achievement was its attempt to have the Russian and German Jewish communities in the United States work together, and there is no indication that fraternal strife caused its downfall.[52]

G. YEARS OF HEAVY IMMIGRATION - 1891 TO 1914

Beginning in the winter of 1891, and throughout the following spring and summer, immigration increased dramatically into the United States and into Philadelphia. Typical of arrivals was that of Leon Kobrin, the future Yiddish author and playwright. Kobrin's ship docked at the "foggy port" of Philadelphia early in the morning of January 5, 1892. Although moored at the pier, the immigrants could not leave the ship until the doctor examined their arms for evidence of vaccination. With a mist upon the Delaware, the men put on their *taleysim* (prayer shawls) and *tfiln* (phylacteries) and began to pray. They *shoklt zikh* (rocked back and forth) and Kobrin tells us "prayed with great fervor." The women also rocked back and forth in prayer over *sidurim* (prayer books) and *korbn-minkhes* (the prayer book for Jewish women). The same spirit overcame the youngsters who earlier when the ship docked had run throughout the vessel screaming.

In the fall of 1892, immigration was temporarily halted because of the discovery of a few cases of typhus in the United States and an outbreak of cholera in Germany.[53] At the end of that year immigration resumed but at reduced levels, and it remained fairly constant over the balance of the last decade of the 19th century. In the first year of the new century, Romanians in great numbers started the long trek to the *Goldene Medine*, and they were followed, after the *Kishinev* pogroms, by increased Russian Jewish immigration.

News of the *Kishinev* pogroms drew the immigrants of the Jewish quarter in Philadelphia together for the first time. Mass meetings to aid the victims of the slaughter were hastily called. "The pathetic scenes enacted in the Kesher Israel Synagogue, Fourth and Lombard streets, last Sunday, when men and women arose in their seats and lamented the loss of parents and sisters and brothers, were repeated with distressing frequency."[54] The lamentations were the first of many to come.

Vorwärts

פארווערטס

New York and Philadelphia Wednesday November 29 1905 — Price One Cent

דער טרויער-טאג
אין פילאדעלפיא

יוניאָנס לאָדזשעס, סאָסייעטיס, חברות, פעראיינען, אידישע סטודענטען און אלע אי-
דען פון פילאדעלפיא װעלען זיך פעראייניגען אין דעם גרױסען שװאַרצען
מאַרש צו טרויערען נאך די געפאַלענע העלדען אין רוסלאַנד.

Front page of the *Jewish Daily Forward*, November 29, 1905. "The Day of Mourning in Philadelphia"

On October 17, 1905, liberal elements in Russian society were strong enough to force the czar to issue a manifesto guaranteeing limited rights to the subjects of Russia.[55] Stronger and better organized, another segment of the general population of Russia with ultraconservative ideas, the *pogromschiks*, determined that the czar had gone too far. They included Black Hundreds (members of a militant, anti-Semitic, quasimilitary organization), the *narod* (workers and peasants), troops, police, hooligans, and recently released prisoners. They were embarrassed that the czar was forced to act against his will, horrified that the absolute authority of the czar had been challenged, and, as always, they were bent on slaughter.[56] Spontaneously and as planned, wild mobs turned the full might of mayhem and butchery against the Jewish nation in Russia. During the last two weeks of October 1905, over six hundred pogroms took place, mostly in southern Russia.[57] Although the death toll was not as high as it would be for the pogroms following World War I, word of the pogroms, coming so unexpectedly, produced a gloom over the city of Philadelphia and over all centers of Jewry throughout the world.

Because the 1905 pogroms occurred mainly in southern Russia, and because a great part of the Russian Jewish population of Philadelphia came from that area, there was hardly a family in Philadelphia untouched by the murder and terror.[58] Within two weeks after word of the pogroms reached Philadelphia, $55,000 was raised to send to Russia. The money came from Jew and Christian alike. Italians and Hungarians, as well as other nationalities, gave generously. The horror of the pogroms touched all, from the mayor on down. On one day, more than one hundred meetings were held in Philadelphia for the purpose of raising additional funds for the thousands of victims.

Floating roadway leading from Princes Landing Stage, Merseyside, Liverpool, circa 1910.

Courtesy of the National Museums & Galleries on Merseyside, Liverpool, England

Jews met at Emunas Israel-Oheb Sholem; Judge Mayer Sulzberger addressed a huge gathering at Kesher Israel. Mass meetings were held at B'nai Reuben, New Auditorium Hall, and other halls and synagogues in the Jewish quarter.

Two weeks later the gloom of the city was given expression in a march of mourning. On Wednesday, November 29, 1905, Philadelphia witnessed what was described in the *Press* as "perhaps the saddest sight which has ever been seen in the streets of this city and one which made the profoundest sort of an impression on those who gathered to see it pass."[59] Ten thousand men and women, each with a black flag in hand, marched under great banners of dull black. In a line that formed on S. 3rd Street near Bainbridge, the march began. A band accompanied the marchers and played "unspeakably sad, minor harmonies." Although it rained all day, some of the older women had no head covering and only scant protection for their feet. At 4th and Catharine Streets labor unions joined. Small black flags hung from almost every house in the Jewish streets. The mourners proceeded to Pennsylvania Hall at 6th & Carpenter Streets, where over two thousand Zionists joined. The music of the Zionists and a self-defense society band spoke of revolt. And the march continued. From there it went through the Italian quarter. The Italians crowded on the sidewalks of their narrow streets to watch the men, women, and children pass by. Many of the Italians, after the custom of their country, doffed their hats as the symbols of mourning were carried by. In the center of the parade was a chorus of forty men who at intervals sang folk songs of Russia. "At times the effect was like a great organ, and the quiet which prevailed on the streets was like that of a vast cathedral."[60]

The victims of the pogroms and their families began to stagger into every part of Philadelphia where Russian Jews lived. This was not a migration. This was a veritable flight. They came, not as before in ones and twos, but as whole families, not wanting to leave anyone behind. By 1908, the Russian colonies of Philadelphia were overflowing with recent arrivals. And still they came, by the thousands.[61] The emigration of Leon Boonin and his young sisters and brothers into the port of Philadelphia is typical of this period of heavy immigration.[62] In 1910, the children had been left orphans in Russia and wished to be united with two older brothers in Philadelphia, Mendell and Abraham. The brothers in Philadelphia sought the advice of Isadore Joseph Cooper, confidant, advisor, and ticket agent who had offices near the Washington Avenue immigrant station on Pier 53.

Cooper assured the family safe passage and arrival. As part of his service, Cooper wrote letters of introduction. This is the letter that Cooper mailed to the family of Mendell and Abraham in Russia (Linderman is not further identified):

My dear Mr. Linderman:

Kindly see that the bearers of this note are well cared for during their voyage. They are orphans and are bound to an uncle and two brothers, which relatives are personal friends of mine. Any courtesy shown them will be greatly appreciated by yours truly

I. J. Cooper

Cooper suggested that the family travel in the summer, as winter crossings of the Atlantic were not favored, especially for young children. He urged that tickets be bought for a sailing direct from Hamburg so that the North Sea did not have to be crossed in a smaller vessel. The family did travel in the summer, but did not take Cooper's advice concerning the North Sea passage and paid dearly, as they crossed to Grimsby, England, in rough weather on a small boat - all very sick. The family's tickets were via Liverpool, England, to Philadelphia on the American Line. Mendell and Abraham believed that a direct sailing from Hamburg might mean a landing in New York and an examination at Ellis Island, something the family wanted to avoid, if possible. One of the children had a limp, and it was feared, based on rumors in the immigrant community, that an examination at Ellis Island would be more strict. Many favored inspections at immigrant stations other than Ellis Island[63] In his *Memoirs*, Leon wrote:

> We reached Hull, England [in the beginning of August, 1911] and traveled by train to Liverpool. There we were obliged to load our own baggage into large express wagons because of a strike of the longshoremen. Some of our baggage was very heavy. We had two large sacks each of which required two men to handle, and also a number of heavy

suitcases. We were all taken, together with our baggage, and brought to a poor section of the city and deposited in a large courtyard shaped like a horseshoe with only one large entrance gate. The large yard was paved with cobble stones, the buildings were old and had corrugated iron awnings in front of them, which gave the whole place a dreary and shabby appearance.

While in Liverpool, shipping officials tried to get the immigrants to sail to the port of New York (because a strike then in progress affected sailings to Philadelphia) but Leon, and most of the Philadelphia-bound immigrants, would not change their minds. Within several weeks, however, the strike was settled and the six brothers and sisters boarded the *S.S. Dominion* of the American Line, bound for Philadelphia.

After an exhilarating voyage, the younger children had free run of one of the decks and their older brothers and sisters met members of the opposite sex unsupervised on moonlit decks,

S.S. Dominion of the American Line (1909–1915). Sailed between Liverpool and Philadelphia.

Courtesy of the Steamship Historical Society Collection, University of Baltimore Library, Baltimore, Maryland

...[w]e entered the Delaware River early in the morning and were sailing up it all day. Everyone was on deck and all were in good spirits. The sight of land and the realization that we were, at last, approaching our goal, served as a tonic to our strained nerves. We were now in a holiday mood and all very talkative. My own knowledge of the geographic location of Philadelphia was very poor and I kept wondering why we were traveling so long in sight of land and had not as yet reached port. This, together with my subdued anxiety of our approaching final contact with the immigration authorities, somewhat dampened my spirits.

The *S. S. Dominion* docked at the foot of Washington Avenue late in the afternoon and the immigrants, after an inspection conducted on board ship, began to disembark. Families with questionable entrance credentials were made to wait. Darkness fell, inspections stopped, the anchor was raised, and the ship made for the open river. Leon wrote:

Again we felt greatly disturbed and disappointed. The fact that many of our immigrant passengers were already admitted gave those of us who now remained on board a feeling of sadness and jealousy mixed with fear; and no matter how we all tried to maintain our composure, that sullen feeling prevailed. I was especially disturbed at the thought that the day's excitement might affect the children's sleep and cause them to appear tired and, in particular that their eyes might not be fully rested when confronted with the immigration examiners.

The next morning the ship again was docked at the Washington Avenue landing. Leon was on deck early. He felt much cheered as a man who introduced himself as the person delegated by Mendell and Abraham to go over the immigration process contacted him.

Everything went smoothly, however, and the children were admitted. Leon concluded the story:

We disembarked at Front and Washington Avenues and joined Mendell, Abe., Uncle Goldberg and Fanny who were awaiting for us. After the exchange of greetings we all marched on foot up Washington Avenue to Fifth Street, and up Fifth Street to Carpenter Street where Uncle Goldberg and his family lived. There we spent part of the afternoon and proceeded by streetcar to our new residence at Seventh and Snyder Avenue where brother Abe. had his drug store.

Until the very beginning of World War I, *shtetl* Jews continued to make plans to leave Eastern Europe as they had for almost two generations, but the war immediately choked off immigration. After four long years of battle, much of it fought in the heartland of Polish and Russian Jewry, the war ended - but not for the Jews. In the month of November 1918 there were pogroms of varying dimensions in hundreds of towns and townlets in Poland. Shops were plundered, houses looted, synagogues desecrated, and Jews assaulted and killed.[64] Pogroms broke out in Lemberg, Przemysl, Kielce, Brzesko, and Chrzanow. On November 11, 1918, World War I ended, but for the Jews of Poland pogroms erupted that same day after the authorities disarmed the Jewish militia.[65]

Regular ocean transportation of passengers was not immediately resumed after the war's end, but of more immediate concern to east European Jewry was overcoming the difficulties of leaving Poland and the newly forming Soviet Union. At this time immigration into the United States remained basically unrestricted, but Jews of the former Russian Empire who wanted to leave faced terrifying obstacles in the lands of their birth.[66] What was the reaction in Philadelphia to the pogroms in Poland? An editorial in the *Public Ledger* stated: "Civilization will be a mockery and democracy a delusion so long as any nation tolerates or permits the sort of treatment which has been meted out to the Jews of Poland." Outrage was expressed that such things could happen. Very little public outrage in Philadelphia, however, was aimed directly at the Poles themselves. Convinced that no more could be done, the Jews of the city planned a march.

On Monday, June 2, 1919, Jewish working men and women of Philadelphia were released from their jobs at noon. School children were dismissed after the morning session. Jewish businesses throughout the city closed. Hundreds of stores along South Street displayed cards explaining that they were closed because of the protest against the massacres in Poland. Men, women, and children gathered on S. 5th Street at Washington Avenue, for by that time the heart of immigrant Jewish Philadelphia was located south of Washington Avenue. And from Washington Avenue representatives of the Jewish population, under the general leadership of the Philadelphia Federation of Ukrainian Jews, gathered and reached south to McKean Street. Mourning garb was worn by all. Women wore black skirts, white waists (blouses) and crepe arm bands. Men were dressed in dark clothing. In uniform, recently discharged servicemen who had just returned from France were numerous, a surprised reporter for the *Evening Bulletin* wrote: "The number of soldiers, sailors and marines in the parade was a revelation of the contribution made by local Jews to the winning of the war. The veterans marched excellently, despite the heat."[67] Twelve hundred Jewish soldiers, sailors and marines marched together. Wounded veterans rode.

Aquitania at Princes Landing Stage, Merseyside, Liverpool, circa 1915.

Courtesy of the National Museums & Galleries on Merseyside, Liverpool, England

A total of forty thousand Jews began to march up 5th Street through the old Jewish quarter. First came the veterans. Next, three thousand members of the "Ladies' Waistmakers Union," most probably the International Ladies' Garment Workers' Union, followed; and after them came representatives of three hundred lodges of Brith Sholom and two hundred lodges of the *Arbeiter Ring* (The Workmen's Circle). The Blue and White Flag of Zion was carried by hundreds of marchers. Others bore American flags.[68] (Additional organizations in the march are found in Appendix A.)

Fifth Street from Washington Avenue to Walnut Street was jammed from curb line to house wall. From there the marchers wound their way to the Metropolitan Opera House on North Broad Street where speeches were made. The *Public Ledger* reported that in none of the speeches was there a word of malice or ill feeling towards the hopes and aspirations of the new Polish republic. "The speakers simply demanded that the leaders of that state be made to understand that they could not expect to stand shoulder to shoulder with civilized nations in the new order of things so long as any minority under their government was to be subjected to murder and denied fundamental rights because of its religious professions."[69]

Kosher Food Riot, Philadelphia, February 1917.

Courtesy of the Urban Archives, Temple University

H. THE DOORS CLOSE - 1919 TO 1924

The movement of east European Jewry into the port of Philadelphia, halted for over four years by World War I, did not resume immediately. On January 30, 1919, the *Haverford*, identified by four masts and a "too outrageously tall" funnel, arrived at the foot of Washington Avenue on its first sailing after the armistice, carrying returning soldiers from Europe. On the next sailing from Brest, the *Haverford*, the solitary survivor of the American Line, carried 2,084 troops on board.[70] Regular sailings resumed from Liverpool that year and in the summer the ship not only began bringing immigrants to the port of Philadelphia, it also brought war orphans and French brides.[71]

Despite the per centum limit law of 1921, immigration continued unabated into Philadelphia, but three years later the great movement of emigrants into the United States came to an end with the passage of the Quota Act of 1924.[72] Summer sailings of the *Haverford* had to be cancelled and, although the *Haverford* did make a sailing in September, it was to be its last. On September 29, 1924, the last immigrant ship to bring passengers to the port of Philadelphia, the *Canopic* of the White

S.S. Haverford, White Star Line, Philadelphia. Last voyage to Philadelphia, September 10, 1924. Being docked at Washington Avenue Pier.

Courtesy of the Urban Archives, Temple University, Philadelphia, Pennsylvania

Star Line, docked at the Washington Avenue Immigrant Station.[73] Losing $35,000 on this sailing alone, the *Canopic* carried 127 cabin passengers, but only 91 steerage passengers. Regular emigrant passenger sailings into the port of Philadelphia were abandoned.

Forty-three years of immigration had split the east European Jewish community. Those that made it to the New World were more than geographically separated from those left behind. The American half of east European Jewry was to know relative prosperity and security in the years ahead, while European Jewry, often barred from leaving the countries of their birth and refused asylum by the world at large, was to know fear, darkness and death. The grand experiment in the United States was over. The doors were closed.[74]

The immigrants settled around South Street and many opened shops there and on surrounding streets. Life was difficult but few would have traded places with their relatives in Eastern Europe. The years passed quickly. The 1920's were prosperous, a time to save a little money and perhaps move to one of the neighborhoods away from downtown. The stock market crash of 1929 did not hit the immigrants immediately, but the following year their world came crashing down.

I. THE BANKS CLOSE – 1930

Throughout the morning of Tuesday, December 23, 1930, and as a consequence of the closure of another bank the prior day, desperate immigrants ran to withdraw their life's savings from M. L. Blitzstein & Co., popularly known as the Blitzstein bank, located on the northwest corner of 4th & Lombard Streets. The bank attempted to meet the demands for cash, but it could not do so. Early in the afternoon a small note was post

Blitzstein building, northwest corner of 4th & Lombard Streets, 1959. The bank, designed by Philadelphia architect J. Horace Frank in 1919 and built of Indiana limestone, ran 45' along Lombard Street and 27' along S. 4th Street. It had pilasters and a pedimented entrance on S. 4th. Street. The interior featured a mezzanine. A 1930 expansion added the three northern bays along S. 4th Street. *Courtesy of Urban Archives, Temple University, Philadelphia, Pennsylvania*

ed on the bank door: "Because of the unusually large withdrawal of deposits we are compelled to close our doors in order to protect the interests of the depositors."[75] Immediately a crowd gathered outside. When asked if it was true, two policemen from the 3rd & Delancey Street station who were posted at the door nodded their heads and comforted the shocked depositors. The news spread quickly through the old cobblestone streets and immediately the telephones at the *Yidishe Velt* (Jewish World), the only Yiddish daily newspaper then printed in Philadelphia, began to ring. Callers asked the same question: Is it true? No one could believe the bank had closed, and despite the wind and the cold, merchants, shopkeepers, and nearby residents came and stood for hours. In the evening many more came.

Established in January 1891 by Marcus and Anna Blitzstein as a ticket order and money exchange office, M. L. Blitzstein & Co. thrived. When Marcus died in 1897, Anna, known in the family as *Babushka*, managed the exchange and eventually converted it into a successful, private, unregulated, immigrant bank. In the first decade of this century, Congress established a Commission to look into the subject of immigrant banking:

> The Immigrant Bank is an institution which flourishes in every part of the United States where immigrants from southern and eastern Europe are gathered in any considerable numbers. These banks bear little resemblance to regular banking institutions. They are without real capital, have little or no legal responsibility, and for the most part are entirely without legal control. Immigrant bankers, as a rule, are also steamship-ticket agents, and usually conduct some other business as well. Consequently the "banks" are, for the most part, located in groceries, saloons, or other establishments which are natural gathering places for immigrants.
>
> Besides handling the savings of his patrons, the immigrant banker performs for them many necessary services. He writes their letters, receives their mail, and is their general adviser in what to them are important affairs.[76]

Immigrant banks, found in poster-bedecked offices of the immigrant representatives of steamship companies, cared for the overnight deposits of countrymen, and transmitted money abroad. Jewish immigrant bankers spoke Yiddish. Almost all immigrant banks were unincorporated and individually owned. The term "& Co." and other terms of a corporate nature frequently appeared in the names of these establishments but were meaningless in a majority of cases as far as indicating any distribution of ownership. The terms were used in the belief that they added a certain dignity to the firm. Immigrant banks were easy to identify. Advertisements adorned the windows, walls, and signboards. Available space in the office was filled with steamship posters, money-changing notices, and many-colored placards.

Anna Blitzstein and Moses (Marcus) Lionel Blitzstein, owners of the Blitzstein Bank.
Courtesy of Laura Goldsmith

The Blitzsteins were the passage agent for the American Hamburg Packet and other steamship lines. Anna Blitzstein, perhaps the first woman banker in Philadelphia and one of the first women bankers in the country, was known for her wise advice. In the early years of the 20th century, efforts were made by federal and state authorities to regulate banking, including immigrant banking. When the Commonwealth of Pennsylvania passed the private banking act of 1911, Anna was able to continue to run her private bank without state interference or regulation, being grandfathered under exemption six of the act.[77] Anna eventually outgrew her first bank.

The second Blitzstein bank, and the first built as a bank, was located on the northwest corner of S. 4th & Lombard Streets (the first Blitzstein bank stood on the northeast corner of the same intersection).[78] During the 1920's the bank prospered and assumed a central role in the area's commercial life. It was, however, dealt a setback upon the death of its founder, Anna Blitzstein.[79] The new owners - Anna's son, Samuel Blitzstein, and a son-in-law, Constantine B. Voynow - recovered quickly. In the fall of 1930, they expanded the bank north along S. 4th Street and almost doubled its size.[80] At the time the bank closed, it had six thousand depositors, many of whom were local merchants.

On Monday morning, December 22, 1930, the day before the Blitzstein bank closed, another Philadelphia bank, Bankers Trust Company, composed of nineteen branches with 135,000 depositors and over $45 million in deposits, closed its doors. The Pennsylvania Secretary of Banking, Peter G. Cameron, closed Bankers Trust Company to prevent the disastrous results of a run on the bank and stated that the closing would have no effect on any other bank in the city. The banking community, however, sensed disaster. In an effort to prevent runs on other banks, a statement was issued by a Clearing House committee that same afternoon: "We [the leading bankers in the city] believe that the financial situation in Philadelphia is basically sound and there is no occasion for depositors in other banks and trust companies to become alarmed on account of the closing of the Bankers Trust Company."[81]

Notwithstanding this assurance, on the afternoon of December 22nd, a run began on another Philadelphia bank, the Franklin Trust Company, which had deposits of $37 million. At the close of the business day the city was in turmoil. That evening, the mayor of Philadelphia went on the radio and urged the people to be calm and not precipitate a run on any bank. But the mayor's words hardly calmed a frightened populace. In fact his words did just the opposite; they added to the panic, at least among the immigrants. The run on the Blitzstein bank began the next morning.[82] And within less than twenty-four hours of the mayor's broadcast, the Blitzstein bank shut its doors.

Upon the bank's closure, crisis meetings were held at the family home. The Blitzsteins were a close family and even the children participated in these tense gatherings. A granddaughter remembers hearing the oft-repeated outcry: "Thank God, *Babushka's* dead."[83] But no matter how traumatic the bank's closing was for the family, depositors understood the Blitzstein bank was an "innocent victim of the panic created by the closing of the Bankers Trust Company."[84] Three days after the Blitzstein bank closed, a throng inside the nearby large hall of the Brith Sholom building, 506-508 Pine Street, selected a committee of fifteen to represent depositors in upcoming court battles. Later in the day over two thousand persons gathered in front of the bank to pour their hearts out to anyone who would listen. At one point someone shouted: "Let's go to the *Yidishe Velt!*"

Soon the business offices of the newspaper were filled with hundreds of Russian Jewish immigrants, but neither the *Yidishe Velt* nor the courts could help. After 1930, the Depression widened and Jews who lived in the South Street area, like most Americans, struggled to put bread on the table. Real estate held by the bank as security for mortgage loans was impossible to sell, and cash on hand was inadequate to fully repay the immigrant-depositors. Overnight, the Blitzsteins and local shopkeepers awoke to the reality of the Depression. The Blitzstein bank never opened again.[85]

The closing of the bank was painful to the Blitzstein family. But in a larger sense, the closing signaled the beginning of the end of an era. Other signals abounded. As we have seen, immigrant shipping at the port of Philadelphia stopped in 1924. Fresh, new east European immigrants no longer replaced long-time residents of the South Street area when these residents moved to outlying sections of Philadelphia. Even though the Depression and World War II postponed the exodus, immigrant Jewish life was coming to an end. Two generations of east European Jews had settled around South Street, made a *bisl gelt* (some money) and then, like Joshua, they moved on to the promised land: Strawberry Mansion.

Der Peddler *(The Peddler)* by Eliakum (Eliokum) Zunser, circa 1890. Written by Zunser to support the ideals of the Jewish Alliance of America.

III. IMMIGRANTS AT WORK

A. PEDDLERS AND SWEATSHOPS

East European Jewish immigrants exhausted most of what little money they had on the long journey to America. Some ran out of funds at the dock in Hamburg or Rotterdam and by the time they reached Liverpool, they had to borrow money. It was not uncommon for immigrants to arrive in Philadelphia with less than $25, all of it borrowed from fellow passengers during the voyage. Of those immigrants who planned to settle in the City of Brotherly Love, most sought refuge with a relative. The *greener* (greenhorn) was welcomed, and the American relatives eagerly listened to the latest gossip from the *alte heym* (the old country). Exhausted, the newly arrived immigrant was given a clean bed and the host-relative slept on the floor. In the morning the new arrival began to look for work. Peddling and cigar factories provided many jobs. The most popular work was in the tailor trade.

Peddling was a common calling, particularly among the Jews who came from Lithuania. The *litvak* (Lithuanian Jew) would spend his last $10: $5 on a peddler's box, $3 or $4 for goods, and $1 for a basket in which to put his goods. He would place the box on his back and answer the call: "Be on the march, you Lithuanian!"[86] Lucien Moss, a leader of the established Jewish community in Philadelphia, visited a school of the Alliance Israélite Universelle in Port Richmond and the nearby surrounding dwellings of the recently arrived Russian immigrants, and in a letter to Sabato Morais, wrote, "Ask any of those children in number at the school, what does your father do, and the invariable answer is, he peddles."[87]

Not only was peddling a part of the working life of the immigrant, it was part of the intellectual life as well. On the evening of Thursday, October 31, 1890, the Russian Jewish folk poet, Eliakum Zunser, recited his own works from the stage of Dramatic Hall. Zunser, one of the most beloved Jews of that era, arrived from Russia the previous year. Lullabies, sung to the immigrants by their mothers in Russia, were not folk songs handed down from generations past, but in many cases were the beloved recent works of Zunser. Few immigrants knew until years later, after they had already left their *Yiddishe Mama*, that songs, like *Di Blume* (the Flower), were not ancient songs of their people, but fresh new melodies from the heart of one man, Eliakum Zunser.

That evening Zunser appeared with a pianist, a violinist, and a bass viola player. He chanted his own poetry as he kept time to the music with the beat of his foot. The musicians, playing before a packed house, accompanied his readings of his own original musical score. "One of his poems," reported the *Jewish Exponent*, "is the Peddler, in which he describes the position of the Russian-Jewish peddler living a miserable existence, and advised that he leave basket and strap and his miscellaneous array of things for the green fields and the pure air, amid which he may labor in happiness with ploughshare and mower and reaper."[88] In addition to peddling, the immigrants entered factory life. In the Centennial decade and earlier, work in cigar factories required a great deal of training and a definite skill. Soon, however, modern machinery (bunchers and rollers) allowed unskilled hands to do the same work.

But by any measure it was the needle trade that attracted the Jewish immigrant. Almost everyone was a presser, baster, buttonhole maker, or sewing machine operator. Later the immigrants also became cutters. They worked at home, in sweatshops or in small factories located on Bank and Strawberry Streets.[89] The finest Jewish tailors were those who formerly toiled for the Russian Army making uniforms for the officers. Young girls were experienced with the needle before they left the *shtetl*. After arrival in the United States, almost everyone acquired a *katerinka* (jocular American Yiddish for a sewing machine). In 1892, when there was fierce competition for jobs and work in the sweatshop involved long hours, from seven in the morning till the evening meal, the sweatshop system itself came under the scrutiny of a committee of the United States House of Representatives. One of the witnesses who testified before the committee was familiar with conditions prevailing in Philadelphia:

Q. What do you understand by the "sweating system"?

A. The sweating system is a system under which work is given out to a contractor by the manufacturer, and by the contractor sublet to a workman who makes their work...

Q. Which of these cities named would you consider first in the extent to which the business is carried on?

A. Philadelphia.

Q. Take Philadelphia. Will you kindly give a succinct description as in your opinion puts most clearly before the committee the condition of things there?

A. Well, in Philadelphia there are a large number of Italians, emigrants engaged in this business, I mean as employes of the sweaters, and also a large number of Russians, who are also employed.

Q. Is the business almost exclusively in the hands of these particular classes at that place?

A. Yes, Sir; and you will find a contractor will go to one of the manufacturers, and we will say that he contracts for a garment at $2. The employes who make that garment will, perhaps get $1.25, or possibly in some cases $1.50, and the contractor himself gets the balance of it. The sanitary conditions are such that I know a number of places on different streets in Philadelphia where there will be working in a room, not as large as this, certainly not any larger, 20 people. Some of you who are familiar with Philadelphia know the old style of houses, and possibly in a room 18 feet by 12 feet you will find 20 people working under this system...

Q. And what would characterize, as you have suggested, one-half the business in Philadelphia. That is a fair basis to put it on.

A. Well, the places are decidedly unclean. These old houses have very poor plumbing arrangements and the conditions with the sewers are miserable and the houses are just as unclean and untidy as it is possible to be for that class of people and they seem to like dirt about as well as anyone I know of, and you will find them in these rooms, where they will have their work benches and many of the employes when they lie down to sleep will lie right down on the bench, and their closets, to which the women and children have to retire if they wish to use a closet, in many cases is directly connected with the same room or in a hall where the - well, the stench and conditions are horrible.[90]

To understand the men's clothing industry in Philadelphia, it is necessary to go back to 1835, the year that marks the beginning of ready-made clothes. Prior to that time only slops for sailors (cheap clothing) and slaves' clothes were ready made, but inside of twenty years ready-made men's clothing replaced traditional home sewing. By 1857, manufacture of men's clothing was divided into thirty-nine operations, some of which could be learned easily in a few weeks. No language skills were needed and children as young as seven years old could work long hours.

At the beginning of east European Jewish immigration into Philadelphia, the clothing industry was centered in the Fifth and Sixth wards of the city, east of 7th Street, between Vine and South Streets:

Clothing. This industry in the Fifth ward is large, employing 516 persons in 17 establishments on men's clothing, and 71 persons in 10 establishments on women's clothing. But in the Sixth ward it is the leading industry, employing 17,450 persons in 127 establishments on all forms of men's clothing, and 1,974 persons in 38 establishments on women's clothing. This employment is not conducted wholly or even most largely in the buildings occupied by the establishments, the work being given out for men's clothing to persons and families who work at their homes in various parts of the city, but chiefly in Kensington and the northern wards.[91]

This was the state of affairs in 1882, but it would soon change. As Jewish and Italian immigrants poured into Philadelphia, the center of "home work" in the needle trade shifted south from Kensington, to Lombard Street, to Monroe Street, and farther south into the heart of South Philadelphia. The sweating system included three parties: the manufacturer, who gave out the cloth and contracted to have it made into garments; the sweater, or small contractor who hired the laborers; and the sweated, or the working tailors.

Itinerant Peddlers, Pennsylvania, 1886.

Courtesy of the Philadelphia Jewish Archives Center, Philadelphia, Pennsylvania

The manufacturer was known as the wholesale clothier or the clothing house and their role in the sweating system was the most clearly defined. The principal and sometimes the only manual work done on the premises of the manufacturer was the cutting of cloth. The leading clothiers hired the best talent in their cutting rooms. When the east European Jews came to Philadelphia, cutters were not Jewish. A typical wholesale clothier had offices and salesrooms on the premises.

In the 1880's, wholesale clothiers in Philadelphia were divided into two major exchanges: the German Merchant Tailors' Exchange (non-Jewish) and the Philadelphia Clothing Exchange (Jewish), organized at a meeting at Mercantile Hall on November 6, 1882.[92] The latter was established to obtain the recognition of Philadelphia as a center relating to the clothing trade.[93] When the immigrants first arrived, clothing factories and sweatshops were located on Bank and Strawberry Streets. Beginning in 1892, we also find Russian clothing houses on these two streets. (Appendix B contains two listings: (1) the names of members of the Philadelphia Clothing Exchange in 1886, located on two blocks of Market Street and the block of N. 3rd. Street between Market and Arch Streets, and (2) the names of Russian wholesale clothiers on Bank and Strawberry Streets.)

The second party to the triumvirate was the contractor or sweater. The contractor agreed to sew the cut material into a garment for a fixed price. The following description is typical of a contractor's shop in the Jewish quarter of Philadelphia:

> We enter a sweatshop on Lombard, Bainbridge, Monroe or South Fourth Street. It may be one of several floors in which similar work is going on. The shop is that of the so called contractor - one who contracts with the manufacturer to put his garments together after they have been cut by the cutter. The pieces are taken in bundles from the manufacturer's to the contractor's. Each contractor usually undertakes the completion of one sort - pants, coats, vests, knee pants, or children jackets.[94]

The contractor was the person who sweated the profits out of the immigrant. The contractor or sweater was also known as the "boss tailor" (translated into Yiddish as the *shnayder boss*). Tailors were divided into two groups, the working tailors and the boss tailors. Some contractors worked alongside their employees and sewed the garments; others did not. Most contractors, recent immigrants themselves, were adventurers, risk takers with little or no capital, running their operation at any location where work could be done and a profit quickly made.

The third party to the arrangement was the immigrant tailor. Always under the thumb of the boss tailor, men, women, and children tailors quickly sank into poverty. Two fears haunted the immigrant: one was lack of money and the other was consumption (tuberculosis). Having to work with others suspected of already being infected with tuberculosis was constantly on the mind of the immigrant. When it could be arranged, sweatshops operated outdoors in the summer, to the rear of the city houses of old Society Hill. New arrivals to Philadelphia from the towns and small villages of rural Russia who had not been exposed to tuberculosis could succumb quickly to the disease. At the end of the immigrant period, Moses Freeman looked back to the early years of east European Jewish immigration into Philadelphia:

> Tired from hunger and want, the helpless and wretched tailor allowed himself to be enslaved in the sweatshop by the boss tailor, sweating and toiling for sixteen hours a day at the *katerinka*, or forged to the twenty pound iron press. The tailors, the old time sewing machine operators, finishers and pressers, they all superhumanly toiled and bled in dark, stuffy and polluted tailor shops for slave wages. Instead of saving money with which to help himself and free himself from hard work in the shop, the operator, presser or finisher, after a few years bleeding in the sweatshop, saved up the workingman's gift, the White Plague, the most terrible of terrors, the "con," as they called it here, shortened in America from "consumption."[95]

B. THE UNIONS

The hours in the sweatshop were long, the work was tedious, the air - foul, the danger to health - real, the salary - deplorable, and the future - dark. But since tailoring was the main source of work, east European Jews struggled tenaciously to protect the right to earn a living as a tailor. Many felt joining a union best protected the right. Based on scant evidence available, Russian Jewish tailors formed or joined unions upon their arrival in Philadelphia.

The Tailors' Employes' Protective Association was formed about 1880 or 1881 (Jewish membership included German Jews and east European Jews from Port Richmond). For the years from 1881 to 1885 nothing is learned about Jewish participation in union activity in the men's clothing industry in Philadelphia.[96] In February 1886, the Tailors' Employes' Protective Association merged into an assembly of the Knights of Labor, thereafter known as Operators' and Basters' Local Assembly No. 5274. Another local of the Knights of Labor was Pressmans' Local Assembly No. 8002. Both locals had Jewish membership. Two months after the merger, a strike was called. Concessions from a manufacturer were secured, but much of the Locals' treasury was depleted during the strike. The concessions cost the tailors dearly, and they wondered if membership in the larger organization was worth the price.

Further actions of the Knights of Labor caused the two locals even more pain. In October 1886, boss tailors were admitted into the Knights of Labor as a local under the fiction that the boss tailors were employees of the manufacturers; in reality they were the employers of the immigrants. When boss tailors gained access to the confidential deliberations of Locals 5274 and 8002, the Locals withdrew from the Knights of Labor and reorganized the defunct Tailors' Employes' Protective Association. At a meeting attended by more than seven hundred tailors, Mark Cohen, a member of the reorganized protective Association, pointed out that when they did not belong to the Knights of Labor their wages ranged from $12 to $25 weekly; after joining the Knights, wages averaged $10 to $12 a week.[97]

But Cohen could not see all the factors affecting the earnings of the immigrant tailors, and it was easy for the membership to draw simple conclusions. Immigration into the country was at record levels. Labor was cheap and getting cheaper. The immigrants were part of a huge movement of people from one continent to another, from one world to another, and being part of it, it was difficult for the immigrants to see much beyond their own lives - nor would it have helped if they could have seen beyond the Jewish quarter. During the last half of the decade of the eighties, immigrants continued to arrive in great numbers and by 1890 there were 5,000 east European Jews living in the Jewish quarter and as many as 10,000 in the City of Philadelphia.

At this time the American Jewish press discovered the sweating system but saw it as something far away. The editors of the *Jewish Exponent* decried the evils they saw in England: "We are told openly in the House of Lords and in the *London Times*, that it is through this low-priced labor that a large export trade, amounting to 4,000,000 pounds annually, is kept in England..." *The Exponent* concluded: "We earnestly hope that the evils of the sweating system may never take firm hold in this free land." A letter from the Merchant Tailors of New York to the *American Hebrew* was to the same effect: "In England, the suffering among the employees of tailors and clothiers [sweating system] was so great that Parliament appointed a special commission to investigate the same, and it was then proved that leading merchant tailors in London had their work (which competes with ours) done at such low prices as to arouse universal indignation." As late as 1888, the *Exponent* saw the sweating system as a product of England, far removed from Lombard and Monroe Streets in the Jewish quarter of Philadelphia. The Jewish press, however, would quickly learn that it did not have to look to England to find evils. Like the tailors, it did not see the fast-paced changes occurring.[98]

The first Jewish labor federation in Philadelphia was formed as the Jewish Federation of Labor, with nine branches. One branch was Cloakmakers' Union No. 1, with a total membership of 1,500, the largest branch. Unions that made up the Federation were comprised of feuding socialists and anarchists, among others, with most trying to outdo the other for leadership and recognition. Manufacturers of ladies' cloaks were the largest industry employing Jewish immigrant labor in America. When the cloakmakers' strike of 1890 began in the spring (after Passover) in Philadelphia, striking Russian Jews, identified as being in the country from three to five years, stated that, if the strike were not settled by the following Monday, they would demand the abolishment of the sewing machine. Dealing with these unrealistic demands on behalf of Sabato Morais, who had been urged to enter the strike and try to settle it, was George Randorf, one of the young Russian immigrants to lead the colony in the early years.[99]

Randorf, born in Odessa about 1861, was educated as a chemist. Unlike many of his Jewish brothers in Russia, he sought to enter the Russian military, but was denied admittance because he was Jewish. He attended a conference in Berlin, the aim of which was to establish an agricultural colony in Oregon, and it was with this group that he immigrated to the United States. Unsuccessful in his attempts to reach Oregon, Randorf entered the printing trade in New York. While there, he became deeply involved in the early Yiddish theatre. He left New York, became a teacher at the night school in Alliance, New Jersey, and came to Philadelphia in 1888. His abilities were quickly recognized, and soon he was working for the Association of Jewish Immigrants of Philadelphia.

In the summer of 1890, the cloakmakers quickly exhausted strike benefits, and desperation set in almost immediately. Randorf's office at 616 Spruce Street "was always packed with poor Jews who sought 'help and comfort' from the compassionate man." Randorf worked painstakingly to counter the powerful forces of anarchism. One method Randorf used was to attend regular weekly anarchist lectures. At one lecture, after "Professor" Thomas Garside finished his speech, Garside challenged anyone in the audience to refute his statements. Randorf rose and in a quiet manner, although surrounded by anarchists, stated that he strongly disapproved of a theory of social rule without government. Randorf, like Harris and Spivak, was a natural leader and did not shrink from advancing unpopular arguments in hostile settings.[100]

The cloakmakers' strike, which had been going on for over two months, turned violent in early August. Men hired to replace the strikers were attacked in their homes. In a little courtyard running off 6th Street, just above Lombard, a group of strikers standing before a small dwelling behind a home on the 600 block of Lombard Street, attacked three workers who lived there. The police took sixteen of the attackers into custody. The next day, Max Staller, president of the Cloakmakers' Union and secretary of the Jewish Federation of Labor, and Isadore Prenner, manager of Cloakmakers' Union No. 1, two of the strike leaders, were arrested after speaking at Dramatic Hall.

Morais' role in the settlement of the strike is well known.[101] Randorf wrote to Morais, stating that a man who was to accompany Randorf to a "house of sufferers, could not come because he had been put under arrest."[102] Three days later Randorf advised Morais that the wife of one of the strikers who lived on the 300 block of S. 6th Street was still sick and, though she needed medicine, she would not go to the Society of the United Hebrew Charities of Philadelphia "as she had been once refused on the ground that her husband had joined the strike."[103] In the same letter Randorf advised Morais that a family on Catharine Street had two children, one of whom was coughing and both had hardly more than bread and jelly for days. At the residence, Randorf observed there were no signs that the stove had been recently used. Morais, through the use of all his persuasive powers, was finally able to bring the parties together. This, in part, was due to the diligence of Randorf, Morais' Sancho Panza, who kept Morais advised of the true facts in the Jewish quarter.[104]

Within less than one year after the settlement of the cloakmakers' strike, another tailors' strike began. About six or seven hundred Jewish tailors struck on June 15, 1891, the union being Tailors' Union No. 1, of the Jewish Federation of Labor.[105] The strike was quickly settled but, unknown to the industry, the most difficult years still lay ahead.

In 1891 and 1892, immigration into Philadelphia almost doubled each year.[106] To ascertain how the increased immigration affected the life of the working-poor in Philadelphia, a special investigation into sweatshop work was ordered by Robert Watchorn, Esq., the Chief Factory Inspector in Harrisburg. During the hot summer of 1894, Deputy Factory Inspectors Mary O'Reilly and John O'Keefe were instructed to personally inspect, door-to-door, the area known to the Factory Inspector as the slum district, an area that included the Jewish quarter. In her special report, O'Reilly summarized her findings:

> The fact is, that a large number of presumably reputable tailoring establishments, send out work, and all such work is invariably sent out because it is cheaper than to do it on their own premises, and this cheapness constitutes the sweating system, the reduced price being "sweated" out of the unfortunates who secure the cheap work.
>
> A sweatshop is a place where both residence and workshop are identical, often consisting of only one or two rooms where the occupants live and labor, year by year, the most unvarying, unprofitable and unenviable kind of life. Hope well nigh extinguished, ambition all but dead, and life a real burden. In such a place as this (where cleanliness is unknown, all the laws of health violated with impunity, and disease and death are prevalent) wearing apparel is made and sent to the stores, and I have no doubt it often happens that such clothing is the means of spreading the diseases which undoubtedly are originated and cultivated there. There are in Philadelphia 648 sweatshops, where, in normal times, not less than 6,000 men, women and children live and toil.[107]

Going house to house on the streets of the Jewish quarter, O'Reilly and O'Keefe found as many as five or six sweatshops on blocks of Monroe and Lombard Streets and, while some were conducted under clean and wholesome conditions, most were not. Even though the Commonwealth of Pennsylvania went to the expense to learn the conditions then prevailing, little, if any, action was taken based on the findings in the report. The years that followed brought further strife in the men's clothing industry in the Jewish quarter.

On May 3, 1895, three thousand machine operators, basters and bushelers in Philadelphia struck at noon.[108] Most were Russian Jews. Among the tailors, the strike - the largest at that time in the men's clothing industry in Philadelphia - was regarded as a protest against the sweating system. The newspapers reported that from forty to fifty clothing firms, including all the large establishments, would be affected and that six hundred contractors, many of whom were sweaters, would be crippled in their operations.[109]

About this time the United Garment Workers of America (UGWA), chartered in 1891, made its appearance in Philadelphia. The UGWA maintained its organization for the benefit of cutters and a handful of more skilled workers and had little use for the ordinary Jewish tailor. On May 9, 1895, a representative of the UGWA denied contemplating bringing UGWA workers to Philadelphia from Baltimore to take the place of the striking Knights of Labor. Happily, within the next few days the strike was settled and all but five hundred of the striking workers went back to work.[110] In explaining the role the Knights of Labor played in the settlement of the strike, a Knights' representative stated to the press that

> the success of the present garment makers' strike did not mean that all the sweat shops in the city would be abolished, the strikers in the present instance being for the most part Russian Jews. It was among these latter chiefly, Mr. Traphegen said, that the sweat shops had been abolished. There were still a number of Germans in the upper portion of the city, and of Italians in the lower portion, who were still forced to work in sweat shops under very great hardships, and it was the aim of the Knights of Labor, he said to ultimately liberate these also from the conditions under which

they are suffering, as it had just succeeded in elevating the condition of the Russian Jews.[111]

Just how high the condition of the Russian Jew was elevated is uncertain, but not uncertain is the marked change in direction charted by the men's clothing industry from this time. Just as the sweatshop was coming under an all-out attack from many directions, the clothing factory began its ascendancy. When the Russian Jews first came here, clothing factories existed, but they more closely resembled large workshops than factories. Beginning about the middle 1890's, massive plants and huge factories began to be constructed.[112]

Immigration into the United States from Russia in 1906 and 1907 increased to record levels, never to be exceeded. A total of 125,234 Jewish immigrants entered the United States from Russia in 1906. The year 1907 saw only slightly fewer enter. The effect of this increased immigration on the Philadelphia labor market was marked unemployment. By the winter of 1907-1908, the United States was in the grip of an economic crisis, and in South Philadelphia the number of Jewish immigrants exceeded seventy thousand, many of them recent arrivals. Economic conditions had not improved when Rose Pastor Stokes, wife of millionaire socialist and philanthropist J. G. Phelps Stokes, addressed the Ladies' Waist Makers' Union, Local No. 15, on December 4, 1909, at the Hebrew Literature Society, 310-312 Catharine Street.[113] Stokes told her hungry listeners of the conditions in New York, where a waist makers' strike was in progress, and urged them to vote on a strike, which they had not been prepared to do before she spoke.[114]

At her urging, the women voted 350 to 15 for a strike, which began on December 20, 1909, and may have involved as many as fifteen thousand young women and girls in Philadelphia. Many in Local 15 were recent Jewish immigrants from Russia. One does not have to look far for proof that a large number of the young women and girls were Jewish. The strikers gathered each day at popular meeting halls in the Jewish quarter (four of the halls were in the 200 block of Pine Street); in addition, strike meetings were addressed in Yiddish. Furthermore, on the first morning of the strike when 5,000 girls gathered at one of the halls and outside on the street, the *Press* reported: "They were divided into little groups, and most of them spoke Yiddish, for fear that some spies might listen to their conversation."[115]

The waistmakers' strike of December 1909, which lasted four months, was unlike previous strikes because of its size and because the strikers were women. With respect to the size, it was perhaps the largest strike involving Jewish workers ever to take place in Philadelphia. Moreover, some of the feminist themes, which would appear more often during the following decade, were raised before large and sympathetic audiences. For example, on Christmas Day, 1909, a large meeting held at New Auditorium Hall, 747-753 S. 3rd Street, in the heart of the Jewish quarter, was addressed by Mary Charsky, one of the strike leaders. She blamed the men for the low wages paid to women and girls: "If the women are responsible for the short wages, the men alone are to blame." She added: "First the men take their sisters and daughters to work with them, then they condemn them for doing so, at the same time accusing them of reducing the wage scale. While the men can meet the demands of the boss individually, the girls are forced to accept lower wages."[116]

In 1914, the Amalgamated Clothing Workers of America (ACWA) was formed as a national organization and quickly, several UGWA locals in Philadelphia joined. The leadership of the ACWA was almost exclusively Italian and Jewish. From this point on the ACWA picked up the struggle of the working tailor. The largest and most important battles were yet to be fought, but since these struggles occurred outside the Jewish quarter, they are not included in this book (see, however, 431 Pine Street in the guide).[117]

IV. SYNAGOGUES

When Jews arrived in what would become the Jewish quarter, they found no east European synagogues. If they had *yahrzeit* (the observance of the anniversary of the death of a loved one), they had to walk or take a horsecar to Jew-town, an area of the city of Philadelphia located in Port Richmond, five miles northeast of the Jewish quarter. It was settled in the 1870's by a few families from Suvalkia and Kovno provinces of Russia. They founded Chevra B'nai Israel and opened a synagogue on the corner of William and Tulip Streets in 1876.

In 1881, the only site for prayer in the Jewish quarter

was the small prayer house of Beth Elohim, 417 Pine Street, but services were held in German and only on *Shabbes* and festivals. Therefore, one could not *daven shakhris* (say morning prayers) here. The immigrants could have said *Kaddish* (the memorial prayer for the dead) at Beth Elohim, but there is no evidence they did. So strongly were the immigrants tied to the *shtetl* life of Russia, they would rather walk five miles to Jew-town to say *Kaddish* in familiar surroundings, than honor the memory of a loved one in a nearby, but unfamiliar prayer house.[118]

As more east European Jewish immigrants came to Philadelphia, however, *chevrahs* (societies or associations) were formed. Also spelled *chebra* in the English-language press of the day (*chebroth* in the plural), *chevras* were formed as basic fraternal, burial, insurance, and philanthropic societies. *Chevras* were also formed for the purpose of prayer, and chevras formed for other purposes often conducted prayer services as well.

Among the immigrants themselves, a synagogue was called a *shul* or a *shil* (pronounced sheel), depending on where they came from in Eastern Europe. An immigrant who came from Lithuania, White Russia, and parts of northeastern Poland was called a *litvak* and prayed in a *shul*. A person who came from Galicia, an area to the south of Lithuania was sometimes called a *galitsyaner* and prayed in a *shil*. In the Jewish quarter, *chevras* were formed by former residents of the same area in Eastern Europe or the same *shtetl*, or by those who used the same *nusach* (rite) in prayer, or by members of an American *landsmanschaft* (beneficial association), or by friends, or businessmen on the same block. As alien-residents and in some cases as citizens, east European Jews believed they had the right to establish their own *chevras* but surprisingly this belief was challenged.

The established Jewish community did not look favorably upon the existence of *chevras* that could proliferate quickly and seemed to exist without organization or control. Condemned because of what was viewed as its slavish adherence to tradition, the *chevra* was thought by some to be better left in the ghetto of Eastern Europe than brought to the shores of America. Sabato Morais, the best friend the immigrants had, was initially opposed to the *chevra*. In a sermon preached at Congregation Mikveh Israel, Morais referred to *chevras* that "infested" the Jewish quarter, stating that they were no benefit to themselves and worked positive injury to the larger and more influential congregations. Morais described the forms and ceremonies of the *chevras* as a disgrace and as being full of absurd superstitions. "He thought that it was the clear duty of the congregations to take the important matter into their hands, and use every means to break them up."[119]

Not only the established Jewish community decried the ancient traditions, habits, and customs of the recent arrivals from Eastern Europe, members of the local Presbyterian Church did also. Ironically, the indictment of the Presbyterians contained a certain grudging respect and awe for tradition, something noticeably missing from the words of the Jews themselves. James B. Thompson, of Old Pine Street Presbyterian Church, 4th & Pine Streets, in Old Pine Street Church News, wrote:

> The laws of Moses are expounded in a dialect constructed on a Tower of Babel model, and known as Yiddish, in the former Presbyterian Church edifice at Fifth and Gaskill streets, the Universalist Church, and the African Methodist; and to these houses of prayer each Saturday morning, all through the slum districts, from garret and cellar, through alleys choked with garbage and from courts reeking with vile odors - themselves not cleanly by our standards - come a people who, rather than have one jot or tittle of their traditions changed, would go once more to the uttermost parts of the earth, and starve, or die by violence, if must be; but change? Never![120]

In addition to Morais and the Presbyterians, in 1887 the *Jewish Exponent* wrote on the *Chebra* question, but it took a different approach. The *Exponent*, which did not support a call to break up the chevras, recognized that not all men could become members of "fashionable and expensive" synagogues:

> The *Chebroth* are divided up into small bodies, each with its petty salaried officer; and none attaining either importance, influence, or dignity; none attaining or retaining a fair or proper support; so that they are rendered almost powerless for good, made instruments of evil incentives to ostentatious pride; the giant that is pinioned to the earth by many pygmies.
>
> The remedy for this, and the step forward upon this point, are not in a union or consolidation of the *Chebroth* - a thing that will never be accomplished - but in their confederation for certain specified purposes.
>
> The experiences of all Jewish institutions in America teach us the wisdom of concentrating our strength; and the principle is elastic enough to be applied to the *Chebroth*. If

the *Chebroth* all joined hands here they might be able to obtain the services of a learned and intelligent Rabbi; a man who would be able to elevate, instruct, lead, and direct, in the right direction, the foreign Jews, whose numbers of late years, has been so largely on the increase.

The substance of what the *Exponent* wrote about confederations was undoubtedly true, but the words chosen (i.e., petty salaried officer, ostentatious pride), showed little understanding for fellow Jews subjected to generations of anti-Semitism, uprooted from their long-time homes, and thrust into a foreign land whose culture and ways were strange to them. Since few east European Jews at the time subscribed to the English-language press, the editorial may not have been read by them, but within two years of the publication of the *Exponent* editorial, three *chevras* did pool their resources and they were able to bring Rabbi Eleazar Kleinberg, the Vilna *Moyre Hoyroeh*, to the Jewish quarter. After the death of the *Gaon* of Vilna, the rabbis of Vilna bore the title *Moyre Hoyroeh*, a Hebrew term meaning an authorized teacher or rabbi. And not only were *chevras* not broken up, they thrived and expanded. In the end, the massive number of immigrants and their need for a place to pray and congregate determined the outcome.

There were eight large synagogues in the Jewish quarter: B'nai Abraham, Kesher Israel, Roumanian American Congregation, the Vilna Shul, Anshe Shavel, B'nai Reuben, the Hungarian Synagogue, and the Neziner Congregation. These eight synagogues or *chevras* are described in the guide. There were also numerous smaller *chevras* in the Jewish quarter:

> Outside of the dozen or less larger synagogues and temples, there were scores of smaller chevrahs, usually occupying the second floor of some store, often a grocery store. Cleanliness was not next to Godliness in some of these synagogues. The prayer books were greasy and torn. In the daily services, exclusive of Shabbos, the worshippers came in smelly working clothes. Some elderly people even slept on a bench in the synagogues because they had no homes. Toilets were usually out of order. Members sometimes openly fought among themselves, indulging in caustic oaths in Yiddish. Yet these impoverished synagogues were the social centers and the life of the poorer Jews.[121]

Little is known about these smaller synagogues (see APPENDIX C).

V. THE YIDDISH THEATRE

No matter how difficult life was in the sweatshop, no matter how little the family earned, money was found for the Yiddish theatre.[122] The language was *mame-loshn* (mother tongue, i.e., Yiddish) and life portrayed on the stage was followed with great intensity, the action drawing audible responses and comments from the audience as if they too were participants. The Philadelphia correspondent of the *American Hebrew* put it this way describing the early Yiddish theatre in Philadelphia: "The grocers complain that less eatables are sold on account of the housewives and family being in a constant hurry and flutter to get in time to the theatre, cheating their stomachs with dry cold lunches."[123]

In Philadelphia in the late 1880's the stars were in alignment in the world of Yiddish theatre. Plays were written in a night. The plots of some plays were stolen in a night - from the gallery in a competitor's theatre. A song that played well in one show was sung out of context in another because it was a good song and, perhaps, the actor's favorite. The most-loved prayer of the Jewish people, *Kol Nidre* (All Vows), was chanted to bring the immigrants to tears - whatever the plot. Not all of the lines were written out in advance, and for dramatic effect, good actors provided their own lines; great actors provided immortal ones. In these early years the best actors and actresses quickly rose to the top, some in a matter of months. The immigrants loved *shund* (popular Yiddish theatre). And they loved no actor more than Boris Thomashevsky. Then a youthful six-footer with dark curly hair, he was adored by fans who gathered after a performance to see him exit onto Gaskill Street, a public passageway little wider than an alley.

Early Yiddish drama (to 1890) was produced at two halls and three theatres in Philadelphia. The two halls were located within the Jewish quarter, and the three theatres were located just outside of the quarter. All five are described, however, since each one played a part in the beginnings of the Yiddish theatre. After the nineties, mainstream Yiddish drama was produced outside the Jewish quarter and this broader history is beyond the scope of this book. (Three buildings used for Yiddish theatre within the Jewish quarter after 1890 are described in the guide portion of the book: the Princess Theatre, 508 South Street; New Auditorium Hall, 747-753 S. 3rd Street; and the old firehouse at 512 S. 3rd Street).

GERMANIA THEATRE 532 N. 3RD STREET

Originally known as Ladner's Military Hall, the Germania Theatre was located in the District of Northern Liberties, in the heart of German Jewish Philadelphia. During the Civil War many volunteers were recruited here.[124] After the war it became a popular pleasure resort in this mostly German neighborhood. In German the hall was called Ladner's *Militärhalle*. New management took over the hall in 1877 and renamed it the Germania Theatre, a name it retained for the next twenty-five years. The theatre was closed in April 1880 and rebuilt. It opened as a German theatre for the new season on September 15, 1881. The following description of the theatre was written two decades later:

> The Germania from the outside looks like anything but a theatre. Were it not for the uniform coating of white paint one would imagine the theatre was a row of dwelling houses. Inside, however, is a pretty little auditorium and a number of refreshment rooms.

Two Germans, Concied and Herrman, previous managers of the Thalia Theatre in New York, took over the management of the Germania on September 18, 1882, and they put it under the direction of Alexander Kost.[125] Not much is known of Kost. Judging from his actions, he appears to have been a man willing to take a chance, but one who did not accept failure graciously.

While under Kost's management, the first Yiddish show in Philadelphia, *Brendele Kozak*, was produced here by the Thomashevskys.[126] The entire Thomashevsky family was active in the Yiddish theatre. In a larger sense, the Thomashevskys were the Yiddish theatre in early immigrant Jewish Philadelphia. Pinchas, the father, wrote material and Chaya Baila, his wife, re-wrote it. The Thomashevsky girls performed on the Yiddish stage on Saturday evenings and sang in meeting halls in the Jewish quarter on Sunday afternoons. Max, or as he was known in the Yiddish theatre world, Mike, a younger son, became a theatre manager in Philadelphia. But it was Boris Thomashevsky, the oldest son, who brought fame to this immigrant family. Since Boris was only a teenager[127] when the first performance was put on at the Germania, we can assume that Pinchas played a larger role in that effort than the role assigned to Pinchas years later by Boris in his memoirs.[128] The ticket selling was left to Alexander Kost and he, thinking that the actors were to put on a performance about Jews in the German language, advertised in the local German neighborhood, the streets surrounding the Germania. Playbills, and presumably handbills, were distributed.[129]

Kost's marketing scheme was successful and the theatre was packed for the first performance. Given before an audience of Germans and German Jews, a non-Yiddish speaking audience, the performance was a total failure. The only Russian Jews in the theatre, a few immigrants who lived at the boarding house where the Thomashevskys stayed, were seated in the gallery. Fifteen minutes before the curtain rose, Kost said, "Hear, you Jewish comedians, do you do your roles in German?" Boris answered that the troupe was a Jewish community theatre and that "we play in Yiddish." Kost yelled "To the devil. Don't you understand, we have a German audience." Somberly, Boris asked his father, "What will happen?" Pinchas answered: "Try to talk a little German."[130]

Before the first act was over, the audience, made up of men in formal wear and women wearing ball gowns, walked out. The Thomashevskys finished the show for the few east European Jews in the gallery. When the performance ended, Kost said to the Thomashevskys: "Hear me, you know nothing! You are no actors! Go peddle!" We owe much to Pinchas Thomashevsky for not following Kost's amusingly misguided advice. But the family quickly left the City of Brotherly Love. After performing in Boston, Pittsburgh, Baltimore, and other east-coast immigrant havens, the Thomashevskys returned in 1886, and for the next four years they played Philadelphia often. For a short time the Thomashevskys made Philadelphia their home, as some of the younger children went to school here and Pinchas ran a newspaper agency on S. 3rd Street.

After the Thomashevskys left Philadelphia, Kost continued as the manager of the Germania until April 30, 1885, when the management was turned over to Alexander Wurster. Under Wurster's leadership the Germania attained an excellent reputation in the German Jewish community. Plays continued to be produced here in German until about 1901. By that time many east European Jews had settled in the neighborhood.[131] Seizing the opportunity, Max Thomashevsky, renamed the building the New Columbia Theatre, and he opened it as a Yiddish theatre.[132] One of the early stars who was raised at the theatre was Molly Picon (her mother worked here as a seamstress). Yiddish plays were put on regularly at the New Columbia until the winter of 1908-1909 when the little theatre became too small for the thousands of east European Jews pouring into Philadelphia, and Max Thomashevsky moved his company around the corner to the Arch Street Theater. The New Columbia Theatre was converted into a garage and several years later the structure was torn down.

THALIA THEATRE
417-427 CALLOWHILL STREET

Before the Civil War, the first floor of Ashton & Company's City Museum, 417-427 Callowhill Street, in Northern Liberties, was a museum of curiosities and a "temple of Science." The second floor, Star Hall, opened as a legitimate theatre on Saturday evening, September 9, 1854. Renamed the Atlantic Garden Theatre, it was destroyed in a spectacular fire on the evening of November 25, 1868.[133] In the 1870's, a new theatre was built at this location; it was named the Concordia Theatre. Amateur German Jewish dramatic and literary groups used it for entertainments and hops. A barbershop, confectionery, and other stores were located on the ground floor. On the upper floor, the theatre had an orchestra circle and a gallery; it could seat 800 people. The bi-level proscenium boxes were fronted with a balustrade, and two freestanding Ionic columns framed the upper box. In front of the theatre, a market shed ran through the heart of Callowhill Street, extending from Crown Street to 6th.

Thalia Theatre, 417-427 Callowhill Street, 1939.

Courtesy of Urban Archives, Temple University, Philadelphia, Pennsylvania

Later, it became an operetta house where Gilbert and Sullivan was produced in German. Alexander Kost, the former manager at the Germania Theatre, took over the management of the Concordia, and the name was changed to the Thalia Theatre.[134] Plays in the German language were produced under Kost's management at the Thalia for less than a year before the theatre closed on March 22, 1886. For the new season that fall, the Thalia opened as a Yiddish theatre under the direction of Boris Thomashevsky.[135] As a very young man, Thomashevsky, a resonant baritone, wrote plays, was a sweet singer, managed the family's acting company, looked after his younger brothers and sisters, and in the late 1880's married a sixteen year old shop *meydl* from Baltimore, Bessie Kaufman.[136] Thomashevsky played the Thalia, on and off, over the next two years.

The theatre was used by other Yiddish troupes, including another acting company from Philadelphia, the Jewish Operetta Company under the direction of Jacob Gartenstein (Hartenstein), an impresario and actor from Russia. As a lessee and manager of the Thalia, Gartenstein produced at least seven plays here in the fall of 1887.[137] A number of reviews appeared in the press commenting upon the talents of Gartenstein when he played the Thalia.[138] It is not known if Yiddish theatre was produced at the Thalia during the winter of 1887-1888, but in March 1888 Boris Thomashevsky's Jewish Opera Company returned to the Thalia.[139] During the month of March 1888, Thomashevsky put on six performances of three different plays: *The Terrible Dream; Chaluza,* and *The Life of Rothschild.* [140]

Productions staged at the Thalia by Boris Thomashevsky did not go unnoticed by the *Jewish Exponent*: "Mr. Thomashevsky, be it said to his credit, spares neither pain nor expense to ensure a perfect suc-

Thalia Theatre, interior 1939. Detail of proscenium arch.

Courtesy of Urban Archives, Temple University, Philadelphia, Pennsylvania

below
Thalia Theatre, interior 1939. The proscenium arch of the old theatre and the "curved sweep of the gallery railing" can be seen.

Courtesy of Urban Archives, Temple University, Philadelphia, Pennsylvania

cess. The actors, as well as the orchestra, the leader of which is Professor Lemish, who has made quite a mark in the musical field, are sufficient guarantee as to the future success of Mr. Thomashevsky's enterprise."[141] In an 1889 letter written to the *Exponent* by George Randorf, previously the rægisseur of one of the first Yiddish theatre companies in New York, he looked back to 1882: "The talent of the then young Boris Thomashevsky could not be mistaken as to its future influence on the destiny of the Jewish stage - he is now director of the Oriental Theatre of this city [Philadelphia], 511 S. 5th Street."[142] Thomashevsky's talents as a director, manager, and producer were recognized early. Oddly, the press of the late 1880's did not carry stories about Thomashevsky's acting and singing abilities.

At this time, the great Yiddish comic actor, Sigmund Mogulesko, convinced Thomashevsky to invite him and his troupe, the Roumanian Opera Company, to Philadelphia.[143] Mogulesko not only convinced Thomashevsky to invite his troupe to perform at the Thalia Theatre, he prevailed upon Thomashevsky to lend the troupe money for train fare. Mogulesko came to the Thalia on a Friday evening and produced *Coquettish Ladies*, which had been a colossal success in New York. Philadelphia's Jews had heard much about the play and ran to buy tickets. Each performance sold out. The troupe, which included David Kessler and Sigmund Feinman, proclaimed, "What do we want from New York! Who needs New York! Philadelphia is a great city and Thomashevsky is a great director!"[144] Upon Mogulesko's arrival at the Thalia, Thomashevsky took Bessie Kaufman to her family in Baltimore and left Philadelphia to Mogulesko. When Thomashevsky returned to Philadelphia to start a new season, he was shown posters announcing that Mogulesko would take over Market House Hall, 735 Christian Street and compete with him. Just as an incipient theatre struggle between the two friends erupted, Mogulesko decided to return to New York.

At the Thalia in early September 1888, Thomashevsky produced *The Murdered Brother* and *Koldunye* but soon began to divide his time between the Thalia and Wheatley Dramatic Hall. In December, Gartenstein, identified as the lessee and manager of the Thalia, presented Max Karp in *Dr. Almasada*, perhaps the last play presented at the Thalia.[145] Plays produced by Thomashevsky, Gartenstein and Mogulesko were hits from the pens of "Professor" Moyshe Hurwitz and Joseph Lateiner, popular early Yiddish playwrights, and from the pen of Abraham Goldfadn, sometimes called the father of the Yiddish stage.[146]

In February 1889, city officials closed the Thalia because it had no fire escapes. The next year the building was sold and absorbed into the nearby rambling John F. Betz Brewery complex. For fifty years bottling machinery filled its lower floors. In August of 1939, the theatre building was sold at auction, and for the next thirty years furniture was warehoused here. The building was torn down in 1971.

WHEATLEY DRAMATIC HALL 511 S. 5th STREET

The centerpiece of Yiddish theatre in the Jewish quarter was Wheatley Dramatic Hall, located on the northeast corner of 5th & Gaskill Streets. The formal names were Wheatley Dramatic Association Hall and Literature Hall (William Wheatley was a local theatre manager and actor). From 1884 to 1889 it was called Dramatic Hall, although the name Wheatley continued to be associated with the building. When the Thomashevskys played here, their troupe was known as the Oriental Theatre Company, a name that was painted on the front and side walls of the building. Boris Thomashevsky remembered the hall by various names, among them, the Gaskill Street Opera House, an almost comic reference since Gaskill Street is little wider than an alley.

The building's use as a theatre goes back to just after the Civil War. The Wheatley Dramatic Association, an energetic American amateur acting group formed in 1860, acquired possession of the property, converted it to a theatre, and fitted it up in grand style: "Private boxes, new scenery, finely ornamented proscenium drop-curtain, and everything appertaining to make it a first-class place of entertainment, has been provided. The comfort of the audience has been taken into consideration, and seats are furnished that will please the most fastidious."[147] The new theatre was dedicated on April 17, 1867, *She Stoops To Conquer* and *The Live Indian*, being the first plays presented. For the next thirteen years, the Wheatley Dramatic Association offered plays here regularly each season. Between 1880 and 1887 the hall was used sporadically by the Association but not thereafter.

On the evenings of September 30th, October 3rd and 4th, 1887, Jacob Spivakovsky, identified in the Yiddish press as the "world-renown artist Herr J. Spivakovsky," produced selected scenes from a number of Goldfadn's most popular plays *(Shulamis, Dr. Almasada, and Bar Kochba)*. These were the first Yiddish performances given at Wheatley Dramatic Hall.[148] Although Gartenstein also used the hall, apparently the performances by Spivakovsky were wake-up calls for Boris Thomashevsky because about this time, or in a slightly later period, Thomashevsky began to look for a centrally located theatre within the Jewish quarter:

> Here in Philadelphia I did not feel as strong as in Baltimore. Here I did not have my fans. Another thing, we had to perform in the German area of the city, far from the Jewish quarter. The *Yidn* had to take two cars to see me in the theatre, but the house on Christie [Christian] Street was right in the heart of the Jewish quarter where all my fans lived. We had to think it over. I took counsel with my father and with the entire family. We decided that we had to search for a place downtown in the Jewish quarter. We found a hall, the Dramatic Hall, which was located on the corner of 5th & Gaskill Streets, in the middle of the Jewish quarter, much closer to the Jews than Christie Hall and announced that on Friday and Saturday we would play in Thomashevsky's Dramatic Hall and in the middle of the week at the Thalia Theatre on Callowhill Street. We killed two birds with one stone, playing uptown for the German Jews and for our Jews who had to take two cars; but on Saturday and Friday we played only for our Jews. We did a good business at both theatres.[149]

Boris Thomashevsky became the proprietor of the Oriental Theatre Company, and he performed at Dramatic Hall regularly from the autumn of 1888 through the winter of 1889. In the beginning of 1889, Louis Silverman was the business manager, ticket seller, and general supervisor of the front of the theatre.[150]

Much of what we know about Dramatic Hall comes from an article in the *Times-Philadelphia*, a popular newspaper of general circulation. An unknown reporter has left a remarkable description of the hall when the Oriental Theatre Company performed *Two Jolly Cavaliers* on Friday evening, January 18, 1889. The headline stated: "THE JEWISH THEATRE." Underneath was written: "STRANGE DRAMAS, ACTORS AND AUDIENCES AT FIFTH AND GASKILL STREETS. AN OPPRESSED NATION'S ART. SOME RUSSIAN JEWS OF THIS CITY FORM A DRAMATIC COMPANY - GOLDFADN, THE JEW SHAKESPEARE."

Stretching our imagination, we can picture ourselves, prosperous Main Line Philadelphians, spreading out the Times-Philadelphia before breakfast on Sunday morning, January 20, 1889, and being drawn into the body of the article: "The long-cherished desire of the Polish and Russo-Hebrew population of this city has at last been realized in the establishment of the Oriental Theatre at Fifth and Gaskill Streets, which is more popularly known as the Jewish Theatre. It is the old Wheatley Dramatic Association Hall."

Our reporter takes us by the hand and magically we enter that theatre of long ago."The scenery, the singing, the acting and the audience were all foreign to anything ever seen in Philadelphia." There were about five hundred men, women and children in the theatre, Russians, Poles, Austrians, Germans and Hungarians. The women sat in the first rows. The gallery was packed. Children played in the aisles and men and women got up and walked around when they got tired of sitting. The opera was "apparently" very funny, for the audience applauded vociferously. There was very little handclapping. Men and women stamped their feet. "When the gallery gods kept up the applause too long they were hissed by the audience in the parquet."[151] And the reporter continued:

"Manager Silverman had his hands full before the show began. He sold gallery tickets for 15 cents. Seats in the rear of the parquet were 25 cents and 35 cents, and the front row

Wheatley Dramatic Hall, circa 1890.

Courtesy of the National Museum of American Jewish History, Philadelphia, Pennsylvania

Boris Thomashevsky

Courtesy of American Jewish Archives, Cincinnati, Ohio

Bessie (Kaufman) Thomashevsky

Pinchas (Philip) Thomashevsky

Courtesy of New York Public Library, New York

seats were sold for half a dollar. Tickets were printed in English and they were the only thing English about the place. Whenever a patron got to his seat and found it was not in a desirable location, he went back to the ticket office and kicked to Manager Silverman, who remarked to the reporter that a manager's life was not a happy one."

Our keen-eyed reporter paid particular attention to detail and no more splendid picture of the early Yiddish theater in Philadelphia has survived:

> There was a furious rush for the front seats in the gallery. Nobody talked English. Manager Silverman said that very few of the patrons of the theatre could talk or understand any English. At the foot of the stairs leading to the parquet was an applestand lighted by two tallow candles. There were pop beer, peanuts, sour balls, apples, pretzels and other refreshments on sale, which were bought by the audience between acts. Manager Silverman took in about a half peck of pennies and nickels. The most important patrons were two women, who bought one of the two proscenium boxes. There was very little light in the theatre outside of the stage. The orchestra used tallow dips set in tin cans.

We see how the Yiddish theatre appeared to an American reporter who went down to the Jewish quarter but, however the theatre looked to reporters, grocers, the audience, and the business manager, it was viewed differently by the actor and director. In 1909, Boris Thomashevsky looked back to the late eighties in Philadelphia and wrote:

> We played every night. That was what was announced on the posters. But we did not have such luck as to play every night. A few times each week it rained. A few times each week there was an exalted *bris*, or an exalted wedding. So the *Yidn* did not come and it was necessary to cancel performances. But God had pity on us. Friday and Saturday it was not nice outside and the *Yidn* could not go visiting, so they took a walk to Gaskill Street Dramatic Hall and haggled over the price of a ticket. They paid 15¢ for a 25¢ ticket and saw a play.[152]

Boris Thomashevsky's three sisters were also in the troupe, Mrs. Greenberg, Mrs. Epstein, and Miss Emma Thomashevsky. "The latter [Emma} is a very clever little comedienne, quite pretty and full of dramatic promise. Boris Thomashevsky's two brothers-in-law, Messrs. Greenberg and Epstein, are also in the company. There is another brother-in-law actor - Louis Levitsky. Mrs. Boris Thomashevsky is leading lady."[153]

Comparing stages, Boris Thomashevsky wrote: "In the Thalia Theatre I had a large stage with all the comforts. In my small theatre, in Dramatic Hall downtown, I also had a beautiful stage but it was small."[154] Dramatic Hall was not maintained in good repair after the Wheatley Dramatic Association left (Thomashevsky decried the mud and dirty steps), and

Bessie Thomashevsky, his sixteen-year-old child bride, wrote: "Our 'theater' Dramatic Hall was on the second floor. The stage was small, with an uneven floor that was dirty and slippery. One had to pay attention so as not to trip over the footlights [candles] and fall into the orchestra. The dressing room was made of narrow boards and the ceiling leaked. When it rained, we put pots and pans around the floor to catch the water, or else the stage would float away."[155] But neither rain nor mud kept the actors or the *patriotn* (fans of a particular actor or acting company) away. Bessie wrote: "We took Dramatic Hall and made a Concert Hall from it for the summer; this means that some people sold ice cream with soda *vasser* in bottles which shot out the stopper with a *'knock'* [crack or snap] while others performed in the theatre. The audience *'knocked'* with the bottles and the actors *'knocked'* with their lines."

Plays produced at Dramatic Hall during the autumn of 1888, when Boris Thomashevsky was twenty, were enthusiastically received by a people who had forsaken home, country, and parents, for a new life, freedom, and security. In the United States, hopes were sometimes dashed. Anti-Semitism and the poverty of the *shtetl* were replaced by the reality of the sweatshop. Still, escape in the Jewish quarter of Philadelphia was only blocks away. Among the performances at Dramatic Hall were: *Dr. Almasada, Antiochus in Jerusalem, Elilas Dom (Blood Accusation),* and *Joseph in Egypt*. They were historical melodramas designed to appeal to the highest values of the Jewish people.[156] Other works were also produced, such as the comedy *Yankel the Rascal,* written by Pinchas Thomashevsky before he left Russia, and *Opera with Music.*[157]

The Spanish Inquisition, a popular piece in the Thomashevsky family repertoire at Dramatic Hall, is the only early Philadelphia production described in detail. In Spain, a Jewish maiden (Bessie Thomashevsky) fell in love with a Spanish prince (Boris Thomashevsky). The prince turned out to be a Jew (First Act). The Jews of Spain were told that they must stop lighting Friday night candles and become Spanish. They were taken away (Second Act). The Jews wept and cried, *Sh'ma Yisroel* (Hear, O, Israel). Just as the Jews were about to be thrown into a fire, the Spanish prince, who had fallen in love with the Jewish maiden, appeared. Thomashevsky took out his sword, killed the enemy and saved the Jews (Third Act). "Just in time" (the words of Bessie Thomashevsky) it was Yom Kippur. The prince chanted *Kol Nidre*, but on his way home from synagogue the prince was caught and put upon the gallows. A rope was placed around his neck. At this point the Jewish maiden appeared on horseback, grabbed a dagger, cut the rope, and saved the prince (Curtain). This was the play, as written. As performed, however, things did not work out this way. Bessie tells us that everything was fine until she had to ride the horse (they used a real horse on the tiny stage at Dramatic Hall). While struggling to grab the knife, the horse squashed her foot against the scenery and Bessie cried out: *"Gevalt!* Save my foot!" And she left Boris with the rope around his neck. The audience, thinking that Boris was being sacrificed on behalf of all Jewry, loved the ending better than the one Pinchas had written.[158]

A fantasy, *The Spanish Inquisition* was extremely popular with the first wave of immigrants, the name of the play alone being enough to bring throngs streaming into the old hall. Not only was the thematic material highly emotional, just as emotional was a feud between father and son, Pinchas and Boris, over the writing of the piece. Pinchas left three manuscript sheets blank, and at the bottom of the third sheet wrote: "Curtain falls." After staring at these pages, Boris questioned his father: "Why haven't you written down how to finish the act? Why are three sheets empty?" Stung, Pinchas, in classic Jewish tradition, responded with his own set of questions: "Well, are you still an actor? Let me see how you will finish the act. Must I write down everything for you?"[159]

The Thomashevskys and the entire troupe stayed at Mrs. Levitt's private boarding house. While they enjoyed theatrical successes, financial rewards did not always follow. The actors often went hungry. Bessie tells us the troupe had to rely on others for food; but food or no food, visitors came to pass the time with them, day and night. Guests included Gartenstein, Spivakovsky and a primadonna Drozdovich; Mr. Silverman, the gabbai at B'nai Abraham; Mr. Strauss; an unidentified "Jewish banker"; Gellis, remembered by Boris Thomashevsky as "the greatest meat-magnate from the State of Pennsylvania," and Bogdanoff, a jeweler who regularly fed the actors. For Boris Thomashevsky, this was the time of his life. Living on top of starving tailors, underpaid cloakmakers, and others who, like the Thomashevskys, spent much physical effort but saw little financial reward in return,

Boris Thomashevsky still knew good times. And times were to get even better.

Thomashevsky read in a New York Yiddish newspaper of a dispute between the manager of the Thalia Theatre in New York, Maurice Heine (Haimovitch), and the legendary Yiddish actor, Jacob P. Adler, a dispute that led to Adler's discharge.[160] Adler, who had come to New York from London the previous summer with his second wife, Dina Shtettin (a star in her own right), may have become too popular for Heine. In addition, Heine had personal reasons for wanting to discharge him. Adler had not only become the rægisseur, he had taken up with Heine's wife, Sonia, a lovely creature described by Bessie Thomashevsky as the most beautiful woman then on the Jewish stage. Sonia had already lost her heart to Adler (Sonia would later marry Adler and use her Hebrew name, Sara).

Young Boris Thomashevsky, the astute businessman, quickly grasped the possibilities the New York rift between Heine and Adler offered for him. He decided to go to New York and invite Adler to perform in Philadelphia. Unknown to Thomashevsky, for Adler, whose wife Dina had recently given birth to their daughter Celia, an invitation to Philadelphia was nothing less than a *matone* (gift) from heaven. Thomashevsky asked his mother to sew his torn Prince Albert suit. He borrowed a necktie from a brother-in-law, cleaned his stovepipe hat with kerosene, shined his shoes with stove polish, and borrowed a few dollars from Gellis, the butcher. Gellis had just repaid Thomashevsky $2 from a prior over-due loan, and now it was the actor's turn to borrow from the butcher.

Thus attired, Thomashevsky caught a train for New York. At this point, Thomashevsky and Adler had never met. Adler lived in the Occidental Hotel on the Bowery, at the corner of Broome Street. Thomashevsky knew the hotel, as he had stayed there:

> Adler, the great Adler, with his wonderfully beautiful, intelligent, large eyes, with his majestic figure, in a torn silk robe and crooked old slippers, was cracking jokes. He made us all laugh. I felt, however, that in his jokes his heart was bitter. The wise Dina, his then wife, sighed and sighed. I understood that the sigh was not from pain, but that she could not stand Adler's joking and talking nonsense at a time when they were in such a tense situation. The new mother finally could not contain herself and in a weak voice she cried out: Yakobshi, what is the use of joking? Mr. Thomashevsky has come from Philadelphia on business.[161]

And they got down to business, the starving twenty-two-year-old stage manager from Philadelphia and Adler, the Great Eagle (Adler means eagle in German).

What could Thomashevsky offer Adler to entice him to come to Philadelphia? Thomashevsky concluded that an offer to work with a talented cast would be a convincing argument. The talented cast, in young Boris' eyes, meant his own family.

מיסטער אדלער,

Jacob P. Adler, 1887

Thomashevsky began. He stated that one of his sisters was a primadonna and a second sister was a dramatic actress. Little Emma danced the *Kamarinskaya* (a popular lively Russian dance). Continuing in this vein, he said that one brother-in-law was the best Count in *Capricious Daughter*; the other brother-in-law spoke French, and Bessie, his wife, was also a primadonna. Thomashevsky saved his best argument for last:

> And as for me, Mr. Adler, you need ask nothing. The entire theatre is at my fingertips. If I need a play, overnight there is a drama. In a few hours, a comedy, in a day and a half, an opera with music, songs and dances. I paint the decorations myself. We do not have costumes, but in Philadelphia we borrow. And that which we still need that will we get. You should come to perform in my Dramatic Hall. Money will be as mud. Philadelphia awaits you.

It is doubtful that Adler listened to much of this speech. After Thomashevsky finished, Adler - who had been toughened on the back streets of Odessa and seen much in his thirty-seven years replied: "Young man, I believe everything you say, but I want to know what I will get for 'shackles and dying'?"

"What does that mean?" asked a surprised Thomashevsky. Adler answered: "I shall have $100 a night." Thomashevsky's reaction was: *"Finster iz mir gevorn in di oygn!* [Everything went black before my eyes!]" Recovering quickly from what Thomashevsky initially viewed as an outrageous demand, he agreed to pay Adler $100 a night for two Friday and two Saturday evening performances and $50 a performance for two Saturday afternoon shows, for a total of $500. Adler continued to press his advantage, overwhelming the younger Thomashevsky. He stated that he wanted to perform in Carl Getzkov's famous drama *Uriel Acosta.*[162] Thomashevsky readily agreed to this request. To seal the bargains, Adler suggested they go to a Jewish restaurant on Canal Street and dressed in a handsome coat and top hat, an outfit not lost on young Boris, Adler led the way. In the restaurant Thomashevsky learned more: "I must take Sonia Heine-Haimovitch with me to Philadelphia," Adler said, "I have no one else to play Yehudis (Judith) in *Uriel Acosta*, and the role is a big one. Sonia Haimovitch is the appropriate actress for the role and she has the right figure. She plays the role excellently."

Thomashevsky, loyal to his own family and surely not fully understanding all of Adler's motives at first, protested. Thomashevsky stated members of his family had performed in *Uriel Acosta*, knew the parts, and these roles should go to members of his family, especially to his wife, Bessie, or his sister, Mary Epstein, both of whom had played Yehudis, the leading female role in the play. But Adler would not budge. With an almost boyish charm, not lost through the years or through translation from one language to another, Thomashevsky observed: "From his talk I understood that Adler was not indifferent to Sonia." Adler concluded the discussion: "Sonia Haimovitch must play Yehudis."

When Thomashevsky returned to Philadelphia and announced that the Great Eagle and Sonia Heine-Haimovitch were coming to play at Dramatic Hall, there was a run on tickets. Posters and handbills announced that Adler was being brought to Philadelphia "with much effort and at great expense." The box office was open from 10 o'clock in the morning until 10 o'clock at night, but only for several days. Tickets for all the performances were sold quickly and speculators made handsome profits.[163] The good news was telegraphed to Adler in New York.

Adler was not satisfied by the telegraphic notice and requested that Thomashevsky wire him two hundred dollars in advance. Thomashevsky, however, did not want to wire the money. He wanted to deliver the money in person. He bought a new Prince Albert suit, a top hat, and a thick cane with a gilded bamboo top, and took a train to New York. He thought to himself: "Let's see some respect for the Philadelphia director!" Thomashevsky went straight to Adler's room in the Occidental Hotel, did not even remember knocking, pulled out a rolled-up ball of money, counted out two hundred one-dollar bills, laid them on the table, and without a word but with a wink, said to Adler: "Come to Philadelphia!"

And Adler and Sonia came to Philadelphia on a Thursday evening in the spring or summer of 1890,[164] the night before the first performance. They took separate rooms in Nadler's Jewish hotel on Pine Street.[165] Things could not have worked out better for Adler. Joy was in his heart and everyone around him sensed it. That first evening he was invited to eat at Nadler's restaurant. Boarders, those who ate regularly at Nadler's and who knew that Adler was in town, banged on their plates with their forks as he entered. "Women, girls, Jews and scamps" stood by the door. The restaurant had a large window through which one could see apple *knishes* (a kind of cake baked with butter or fat), tomatoes, cucumbers, and radishes. Everyone pushed into the store to get a glimpse of the Great Eagle. Adler was in excellent spirits and had a good word for everyone. With respect to the owner of the restaurant, Adler joked: "Why is he called Nadler, it sounds like Adler."

During dinner, Adler wanted to know if the props, a *Torah*, a *talis*, and prayer books, had been secured for the performance of *Uriel Acosta* the next day. Thomashevsky responded: "What a question! Everything is here. There is a *Torah*, a *talis*, prayer books, one cannot complain. *Yidn davenen zeyer veynik in Filadelfia, un di sforim valgern zikh arum* [In Philadelphia Jews pray very little and prayer books lie around neglected]." Adler also wanted to know if the other actors knew their lines and Thomashevsky assured him they did, ending the conversation by stating: "Rehearsal is tomorrow morning at 11:00 o'clock."

The next morning the Thomashevsky family who made up most of the cast waited anxiously at Dramatic Hall for Adler's first rehearsal in Philadelphia. The clock struck eleven. The family sat like statesmen on the stage. The Thomashevsky women were "showily dressed" *(oysgepitz in esik un in honik)* in feathers from a tailor, with Thomashevsky's child bride, Bessie, adorned in a dress she had sewn from her wedding trousseau.

The orchestra, the first Yiddish theatre orchestra in Philadelphia, was composed of two fiddlers and a bass player. It was ready. All were members of the Lemish (Lemisch) family: a father, Selig Itzik; his son, Milo (violin); and a grandson, who had to stretch on his tiptoes to reach the strings. They played on old Romanian instruments. Selig Itzik, who played with the Thomashevskys as early as 1882, had been a Kappelmeister in the Austrian Army and may have also been in the Crimean War. Selig Itzik evidently made quite an impression on the Yiddish theatre world because Jacob Gordin, the famous Yiddish dramatist, wrote a play dedicated to him, entitled *Selig Itze, the Klezmer.*

Noon came. A half-hour passed. And Adler had still not come. Not being able to wait any longer, a *patriot* (fan), was sent to Adler's room. The patriot returned and announced, "Adler is still sleeping." In a rage one of the family members went to Adler's room and shortly the family learned that "Adler was coming." The prompter cleared his throat, wiped his glasses, and rolled up his sleeves. From fright, the prompter could not find the words in the script. Such things happened during the rehearsal, but the performances at Dramatic Hall took Philadelphia by storm. The young *patriotn* waited for Adler outside the theatre alongside Gaskill Street.

Adler quickly became acquainted with the beautiful women and girls who came to see Thomashevsky. Soon some of them came especially to see him. Adler was handsome, interesting, and Thomashevsky states approvingly "remarkably effective." Adler knew how to create joy with his stories and jokes. He was also an excellent dancer. He knew all the dances of the Odessa playboys and the young women and girls of Philadelphia quickly learned the dances. Thomashevsky wrote: "Every day and night there were revelries and these were held in secret. This meant that we would go about 'as if' on business."[166] In short it was a happy and joyous time! Thomashevsky continued: "Later, in his older years, when Adler would speak to me about that time when he acted with me in Philadelphia, he would recollect those happy evenings and days, and expressed a longing for that time."

But, as Thomashevsky stated, then trouble came. In New York, the "wise" Dina Adler heard rumors and came to investigate. At this time Dina had already separated from Adler, but she would never forget him and would continue to act with him and his family for years. When she got to the Jewish hotel on Pine Street, Dina did not find Adler in his room. Thomashevsky wrote: "She encountered what she suspected." Adler left in the middle of the night.[167] Thomashevsky left at this time also. Both spent the balance of 1890 in Chicago.

It does not appear that Adler performed again in Philadelphia before 1893, at which time he put on a profitable benefit performance at the Academy of Music for the Hebrew Literature Society. Dramatic Hall was converted into the Hungarian Synagogue in the summer of 1891 (see 511 S. 5th Street in the guide).

MARKET HOUSE HALL 735 CHRISTIAN STREET

The hall at this location was known as Market House Hall, or Kelly's Hall; Thomashevsky called it Christie Street Hall. Prior to 1888 plays were produced downstairs in a large open room; later, performances may have been put on upstairs. When the first floor was used for the Yiddish theatre, the hall had no permanent seats and the stage was quite small. Tickets were sold for 15¢, 25¢ and 35¢, but since the chairs could be moved, the *patriotn* bought the least expensive tickets and simply moved the chairs to the foot of the stage.[168] How the building got the name Kelly's Hall and who Kelly was is not known.

Jacob Gartenstein produced Yiddish plays here, perhaps as early as 1886. For a period of three or four years during the early 1890's, famous stars of the Yiddish stage performed here. For example, before the 1893-1894 season opened in New York, Albert (Abba) Schoengold played here in *The Greenhorns* on October 21, 1893. During that season, a Yiddish handbill announced that Mr. Fishkin from Chicago would be performing at Kelly's Hall on February 23, 1894.

Not only out-of-town professional Yiddish performers appeared here, local talent did also. One of the most popular actresses of that day was a local shop *meydl* by the name of Madame Sofia Friedman. Called the first primadonna of the Yiddish theatre in Philadelphia, she had a beautiful voice and people loved to hear her sing, but acting was difficult for her and little is known about her. The hall was torn down in 1906.

STANDARD THEATRE 1126-1134 SOUTH STREET

Located slightly to the west of the Jewish quarter, the

Standard Theatre played a major role in the early history of the Yiddish theatre in Philadelphia. In 1888, the former Presbyterian Church at 1126-1134 South Street was converted to a theatre and at the end of June 1890, the Oriental Opera Company of Boris Thomashevsky played here. Bertha Tanzman starred in the role of Dina in Goldfadn's opera *Bar Kokhba* on the 27th, and as Esther the Queen in Goldfadn's operetta *Ahasuerus* on the 28th. The next month, Thomashevsky's Company produced *King Solomon* at what was advertised as "popular summer prices." The Standard was a large theatre and a regular stop for New York troupes in 1893 and in 1894. David Kessler, Abba Schoengold, and Sigmund Mogulesko played here. It was a good place to perform after the theatre season, before the season and if things were slow in New York, during the season. Yiddish companies used the Standard intermittently during this early period.[169]

From 1899 to 1907, the Standard was managed by Darcy & Speck, a stock company that produced plays in English, but which actively sought the immigrant business. Darcy & Speck advertised regularly in the Philadelphia edition of the Yiddish-language *Jewish Daily Forward* and produced plays with immigrant themes. Beginning on September 17, 1906, with matinées every day, *Rachel Goldstein* was presented, a piece set on the Lower East Side of New York. Rachel Goldstein, the heroine, had just landed in America; the melodrama was well received as it was repeated the following year. The motto of the theatre under Darcy & Speck was: "Go to the Standard, Sing and be Happy." Yiddish theatre was also produced during this period but on a sporadic basis. At some point during 1908 the Standard was converted to the "Standard Vaudeville and Picture Theatre," and motion pictures, a wonder to the new arrivals, competed with live theatre.

The flood tide of east European Jewish immigrants heard much from their American cousins about Yiddish theatre in America, and they wanted to see it themselves. To satisfy an increasing demand in Philadelphia in the winter of 1909, Max Thomashevsky relocated his Yiddish theatre troupe to the stately Arch Street Theater where Yiddish shows were soon produced nightly, with two shows on Saturday. But this move did not satisfy the demand. In fact, business was so good at the Arch Street Theater that the news traveled quickly to New York. By March

Opened as a theatre in 1888, the Standard was also called the Thalia and the Adler, photograph, circa 1934.

Courtesy of YIVO Institute for Jewish Research, New York

1909, a syndicate nominally headed by S. A. Horowitz, but squarely under the control of Jacob P. Adler, made plans to buy the Standard Theatre, convert it into a Yiddish theatre, and compete with Max Thomashevsky for the lucrative Philadelphia Yiddish theatre trade.[170]

Adler intended his theatre for classic Yiddish drama. In September 1909, the name of the Standard was changed to the Thalia Theatre and on the weekend of September 10th and 11th, the Thalia opened with Tolstoy's *Kreutzer Sonata*, *Shulamis*, and *Ben HaDor* (The Son of the Generation). Jewish organizations were offered discounts if they purchased large blocks of seats for benefit performances, but the discounts did not help and the Thalia, which operated here for only several weeks, closed.

By the end of October 1909, the name of the theatre was again changed, this time to the Adler Theatre. It was then that Sara and Jacob P. Adler, by this time married for many years, came to Philadelphia to perform. The theatre "came to life" when the Adlers arrived.[171] Shows were produced before packed houses. One of the shows advertised at the Adler Theatre was *Selig Itze, the Klezmer,* perhaps put on the billing by Adler to honor the memory of Selig Itzik Lemisch, the old klezmer who played for Adler when he performed in Philadelphia in 1890.[172] Adler's nightly performances on South Street were magical and brought throngs running. His name was on the lips of immigrant-Jewish Philadelphia, and his brand of magic was not restricted to the theatre itself. The sidewalks of South Street could be a stage, as demonstrated by Adler on at least one occasion.

During the week of November 15, 1909, Adler directed the distribution of handbills, announcing plays at the Adler Theatre. Gallery prices were 15¢ and this was the price charged for a gallery ticket for a weekday performance. On Saturday evening, November 20, 1909, however, Adler, without prior notice, decided to produce and perform in *The Merchant of Venice.* Since Adler would star in his most famous role, that of Shylock,[173] he wanted a "whole quarter" for a gallery ticket. The huge crowd, which stood in a long line, protested the last-minute price increase and when protests did not help, screams of Bluffers! and Swindlers! were heard. Soon there was a full-scale riot on South Street.[174]

Adler, dramatic artist to the core, responded with a telephone call to the local police station. The police arrived and began to make arrests. Out of this melee, a cease-fire was somehow negotiated. Those arrested were set free, but not before the crowd agreed to pay 25¢ for a gallery ticket. Upon payment, everyone rushed to witness the performance. Inside, the mood of the crowd changed quickly, and roaring applause arose from the gallery every few minutes. As the crowd was leaving the theatre, the protesters were asked why they had caused such a brawl. Each said that he did not do it. "Those other ones, the coarse youth did it, but he is always glad to pay a quarter for a gallery ticket when Mr. Adler plays Shylock."

November and December 1909 was the high-water mark for the Yiddish theatre in Philadelphia. Performances were given at the Arch Street Theater and Adler's Theatre seven days a week and twice on Saturday. Over the next twenty-five years, the Arch Street Theater would sparkle with popular Yiddish drama, *shund,* and vaudeville. The Adler Theatre, however, quickly faded, replaced by the Gibson, an African American venue made famous by many great performers.

In the late 1920's, the Gibson closed. The theatre was once again converted into a movie house and it again took the name, the Standard. On October 15, 1954, during Hurricane Hazel, a section of the building's ceiling collapsed; later the building was torn down.

OTHER THEATRES

The Arch Street Theater, the most famous and most beloved of all the Yiddish theatres in Philadelphia, was not located in the Jewish quarter and its rich history is beyond the scope of this work. After World War I, Yiddish theatre was produced in Northern Liberties at the American Theatre, Franklin Street and Girard Avenue, later called the Astor, and at Max Thomashevsky's Garden Theatre, 8th & Race Streets. Other theatres, including the Walnut Street Theatre and the Academy of Music, were used often.

The Arch Street Theatre, 613 Arch Street, 1935. Opened as a legitimate theatre in 1828. *Courtesy of the Library of Congress, Washington, D.C.*

AMATEUR THEATRE IN THE JEWISH QUARTER

Early amateur theatre, beginning in 1888, was performed in Russian, not Yiddish. The first group of east European Jews to produce amateur plays was the Russian Dramatic Circle (in Russian, *Russkii Dramaticheskii Kruzhok*). Early Russian settlers in Philadelphia included idealistic young men and women who had immigrated to America as part of *Am Olam* and other similar movements. Called *Am Olam'niks,* they used the theatre to express their love of the Russian language which many of them had studied before fleeing Russia. Russian Jews made a basic distinction between the Russian government and the Russian people. They believed that the Russian people were a beautiful people who spoke an exquisite language. Their quarrel was with the Russian government: the czar and his robber-band of officials.

The first play produced by the immigrants, Gogol's *Zhenitba (The Marriage),* was put on at Dramatic Hall on Wednesday evening, October 24, 1888, for the benefit of sufferers of a fire in the Bowery.[175] The play was a financial as well as an artistic success. "Besides the language, which was faultless and genuine Russian, for the first time performed in Philadelphia, the costumes and scenery were Russian to the core." The male lead in *The Marriage* was played by Charles D. Spivak, at the time a medical student, and the female lead was played by seventeen-year old Jennie Charsky. *The Exponent* reviewer, mildly laudatory of the acting of Spivak, "played the role with effect," wrote glowingly of Charsky's performance, "aroused the audience by her vivacity and verbosity."[176] The next play, *The Career,* by the Russian playwright Kroloff, was produced in May 1889. The profit made from that performance was used to benefit the Hebrew Literature Society. During the depression of 1893, the Russian Dramatic Circle gave a benefit performance at Kelly's Hall for the starving immigrants. The cost of that performance (but not the name of the play) has come down to us. Receipts taken in totalled $141.85. Expenses included rent for the hall - $15; advertisements - $8; rouge, powder and decorations - $7.07; circulars printed in Russian - $4.40; costumes - $2; copying the scripts - $2, and other costs. The profit was $92.99.

The leadership of the Russian Dramatic Circle or Club gradually shifted to Elias Goldensky. He was born in 1867 in Radomsyl, a small town near Kiev in Ukraine, but he spent his boyhood years in Kremenchug, in eastern Ukraine. Goldensky emigrated to Philadelphia in 1891, and within ten months of his arrival he was working at the studio of the dean of American photographers, Frederick Gutekunst.[177] After Goldensky's arrival, he and Spivak collaborated on amateur performances. The Russian Dramatic Club, begun at the time Spivak and Jennie Charsky came to Philadelphia, ceased to exist about 1896, the year the Spivaks (they married in 1893) left for Denver.[178] At the end of the last century, the Star Specialty Club, a group that put on performances at the old firehouse at 512 S. 3rd Street, presented non-professional theatre for several years.

Rebecca M. Goldsmith, 1896. Member of the Russian Dramatic Circle. Goldsmith acted with Spivak and Goldensky in *Zhenitba (The Marriage)*, Kelly's Hall, April 25, 1894.

Courtesy of Charlesa Feinstein

During the early years of the 20th century, members of a younger generation, many of whom were born in this country, would visit each other on Sunday to partake of a musical afternoon of singing or playing the piano. Certainly this experience was quite different from that of recent immigrants, escaping with their lives from the *pogromschiks* of 1905. In 1907, a new dramatic society was formed in the Jewish quarter called the Progressive Dramatic Circle, and plays were produced at New Auditorium Hall, 747-753 S. 3rd Street. In 1908, the name of the troupe was changed to the Jacob Gordin Dramatic Society in honor of a visit that Jacob Gordin made to Philadelphia just before his death *(see, Hebrew Literature Society, Catharine Street).*

With the lone exception of the old firehouse at 512 S. 3rd Street, the places where Yiddish theatre was performed in the Jewish quarter, both professional and amateur, have been torn down. No monuments or plaques have been erected in the area to record for future generations the glories of the beginning of the Yiddish stage in Philadelphia.

VI. SOCIETY HILL, SOUTHWARK, & QUEEN VILLAGE

East European Jews settled in that part of Philadelphia previously known as Society Hill and Southwark. The Free Society of Traders, a joint stock company chartered by William Penn in 1682, was conceived to aid in the settlement and economic development of Pennsylvania. Under a deed from Penn, 20,000 acres of land were conveyed to the Society, including a lot extending from Spruce Street to Pine Street and from the Delaware River to the Schuylkill River, nearly one hundred acres. Near Front and Pine Streets, south of Dock Creek, there was a hill that became known as the Society's hill, soon changed to Society Hill, a name once used to describe the region south of Pine Street down to Swedes' Church. The name Society Hill quickly fell into disuse, and by 1857 it had been "discontinued for the last sixty-eight or seventy-eight years."[179]

Although the term Society Hill was not in use when the Jews settled here, in the 1950's the name was revived to spark sluggish real estate sales. The Chairman of the City Planning Commission in 1957, Albert M. Greenfield, was in favor of redeveloping the area but did not think much of the name Society Hill. Greenfield, concerned that the name Society Hill would create the wrong impression, suggested that the name "Old City Urban Renewal Area" might be more appropriate.[180] With no discernible support for Greenfield's awkward phrase, the reborn name of Society Hill quickly took hold. It is used today as if it had not fallen out of favor for over one hundred and fifty years.

The historical boundaries of Society Hill are somewhat vague, although many believe boundary markers delimit the area precisely. Society Hill today is found in the northern section of the old Jewish quarter. In Candid Shots, a regular column in the *Evening Bulletin* in the 1950's under the byline of Paul Jones, the general area containing historic Society Hill is described: "If you walk east on Chestnut street from Independence Hall, turn down Second as far as South, and then make a circling return to Washington Square, you will have cast a loop that includes Society Hill."[181] Jones did not pinpoint where inside the loop Society Hill begins and ends, and perhaps rightly so. It adds to the charm of Society Hill that its boundaries remain somewhat vague and mysterious.[182]

Southwark is an area immediately south of South Street and east of Passyunk Avenue. Prior to 1854, the District of Southwark was a separate governmental body. The southern section of the Jewish quarter was located in this old District. Today, the National Registry District of Southwark includes an area bounded generally by South Street on the north, Washington Avenue on the South, 5th Street on the west and the Delaware River on the east. Queen Village, another term used today, is bounded by almost the same streets.

---

opposite page:

Atlas of the 5th, 7th, & 8th Wards of the City of Philadelphia, Compiled & Published by Elvino V. Smith, C.E., (Philadelphia, 1908, Buildings Revised to 1914), Plate 7

A Guide TO THE *Streets* OF THE *Jewish Quarter* OF *Philadelphia*

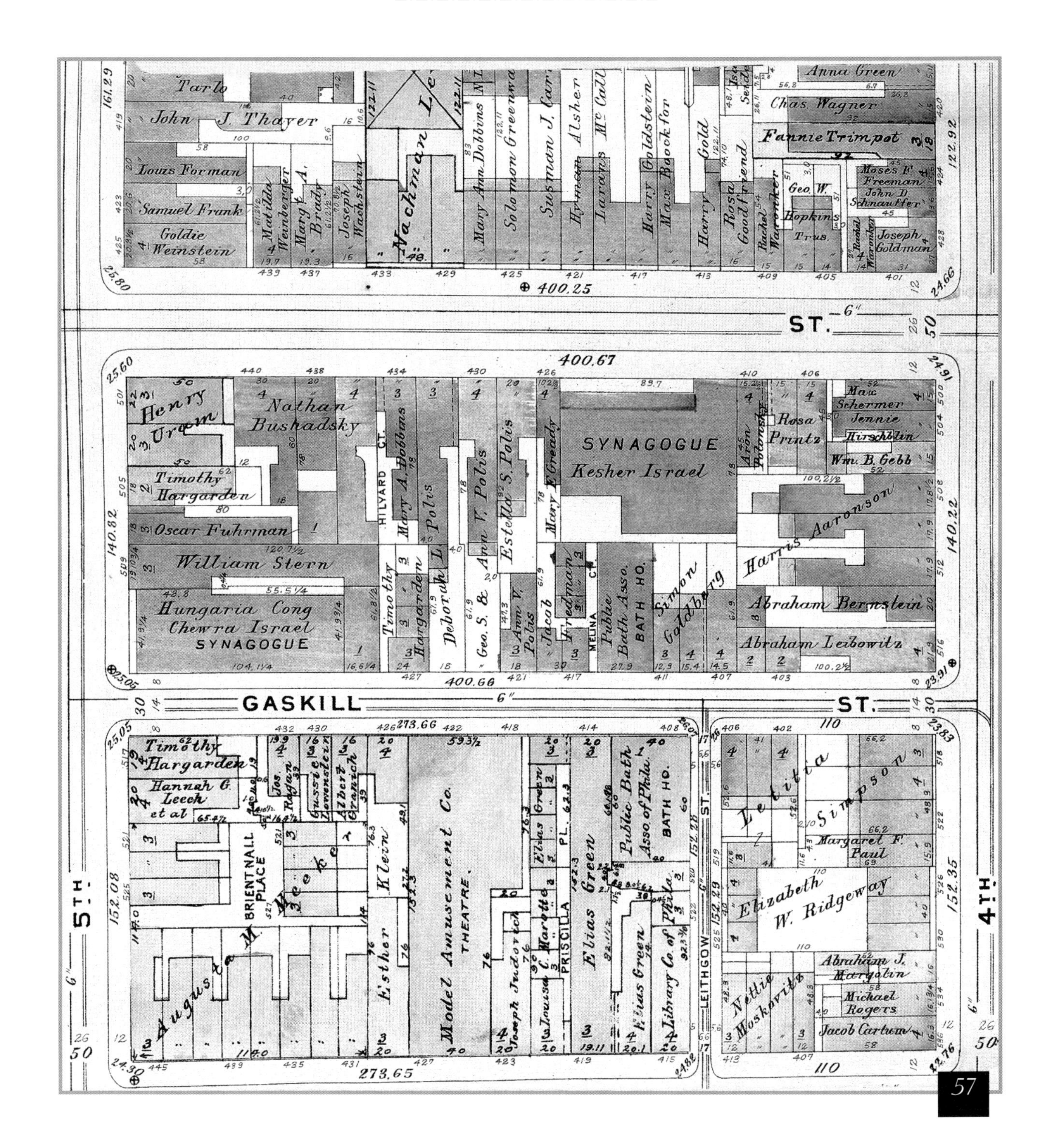

The Guide

The guide is arranged by streets. The first section includes east-west streets, bounded by Spruce and Christian Streets. The second section includes north-south streets, bounded by S. 2nd and S. 6th. The guide follows the pattern of east to west and north to south. Central streets in Philadelphia, including those described here, were laid out in 1682 by Thomas Holme, surveyor to William Penn. Other than High Street (now Market Street), the original names of the east-west streets were taken from the names of plants and trees. Streets south of High, those that two centuries later became part of the Jewish quarter, were named for trees. Cedar Street (now South) was the most southern street in Penn's plan. The guide also includes streets south of South Street, namely: Bainbridge, Monroe, Fitzwater, Catharine, and Christian.

The major north-south streets are numbered. Originally, the streets were numbered from and named for the Delaware and Schuylkill Rivers, the natural east and west borders of Penn's "greene country towne." For example, 6th Street was called Delaware 6th. West of Broad Street, numbered streets were preceded by the word Schuylkill. On December 8, 1853, the Common and Select Councils dropped the river names and renumbered north-south streets consecutively from the Delaware River. For example, east of Broad Street, the word Delaware was dropped, and Delaware 6th became 6th Street. Delaware 5th became 5th Street, and so on. West of Broad, Schuylkill 8th became 15th Street, Schuylkill 7th became 16th Street, and so on. The numbered streets below Market Street are preceded with the letter S. for South, indicating that the location is south of Market Street. Numbered streets north of Market Street are preceded with the letter N. for North.

In 1951, the voters of Philadelphia elected Joseph Sill Clark mayor of the City of Philadelphia. Under his administration, and in harmony with newly enacted federal legislation, formative plans were made to redevelop Washington Square East, an area extending from the south side of Walnut Street to the north side of Lombard Street, and from the Delaware River to 8th Street. Clark's successor, Richardson Dilworth, moved the idea forward. The aim of the project, known as "Redevelopment," was to restore the area to its colonial and federal beginnings. Completed in time for the Bicentennial, Redevelopment not only brought about the rebirth of colonial and later properties, it also indirectly encouraged the private restoration of the east European Jewish experience, especially on streets not located within the confined area of the Washington Square East Redevelopment site. For example, the attractive buildings of the Hebrew Literature Society and the Central Talmud Torah, located on the 300 block of Catharine Street, have been preserved, converted to residential use, and designated as historic by the Philadelphia Historical Commission.

No attempt has been made to identify every organization or property that was significant to the Jewish quarter. For example, there were many landsmanschaftn, or home town organizations, but only two are described: the Elizabetgrad Beneficial Association and Boslover Beneficial Association, both named for towns in the southern part of czarist Russia. On the other hand, I have tried to identify all the Yiddish theatres, halls, synagogues, and Yiddish newspapers found in the Jewish quarter. The Yiddish theatres are identified in the history section and in the guide. The larger synagogues, the halls, and the Yiddish newspapers are identified in the guide and in the appendices. The smaller synagogues are identified in the appendices. Clothing houses, although not located in the Jewish quarter, are nevertheless identified in the appendices since they played such a major role in the early Russian Jewish settlement.

Today, brick sidewalks and cobblestone streets add a special charm to the area. South Street is a mix of shops and restaurants. Art galleries are found slightly north of Society Hill in Olde City. Antique shops are located on Pine Street west of the old Jewish quarter and in the city's fastest growing collectibles district around S. 6th & Bainbridge Streets. To the east at the Delaware River is the new Independence Seaport Museum. Jewish delis can be found on South and S. 4th Streets.

Society Hill, located in the northern part of the old Jewish quarter, and Queen Village, located south of South Street, tree-lined and picturesque year-round, are most magnificent in the spring. That is when the lilac breaks through the dark gray of winter, and blossoms appear in Independence Park, which is located just several squares north of Society Hill. Each spring owners in the area, in coordination with Friends of Independence National Historical Park, open the doors of the most beautiful homes to the public. As part of "Philadelphia Open House Tours," an opportunity is afforded the visitor and resident alike to see the best of Society Hill and Queen Village.

SPRUCE STREET

Original Georgian, Federal, and Greek Revival homes can be found here and along surrounding tree-lined streets and walkways. The street is rich in history and lovely for walking.

First medical office of Dr. Charles D. Spivak, 338 Spruce Street (second property from right), circa 1951.

Courtesy of Independence National Historical Park, Philadelphia, Pennsylvania

The First Medical Office of Dr. Charles D. Spivak: 338 Spruce Street. Known as the Williams-Hopkinson House, this landmark Federal town house (a private residence today)[1], built between 1785 and 1791, was the setting for the founding of the Jewish Alliance of America.

On August 1 and 2, 1890, the Philadelphia press carried stories of threatened enforcement in Russia of the czar's Temporary Rules under which Jews in the Pale of Settlement would be deprived of long-time basic rights of residence and business. Charles D. Spivak realized the gravity of the threats immediately. He called a meeting, held here on the evening of August 6th, and turned his medical office into a place of public assembly. Spivak sensed, as few did at the time, that whether the czar and his *chinovniks* (governmental clerks) followed through with their threats or not, Jews would leave Russia. Anticipating mass flight, Spivak sought to convince fellow Jews in Philadelphia that a new wave of immigrants from Russia should not be settled in the large cities on the East Coast of the United States. This was the first instance of "public activity" (support for the wide distribution of new arrivals throughout the country) by the Russian Jewish community in the United States.

Attending the meeting were representatives of immigrant lodges, beneficial associations, and eight Russian congregations: B'nai Jacob, B'nai Abraham, Rodef Zedek, B'nai Reuben, Anshe Nezin, Kurlander, B'nai Israel and Anshe Shavel. Sabato Morais also attended the meeting; he had been interviewed by a reporter for the *Inquirer* on the same subject several days earlier and was somber regarding his assessment of the eventual outcome. Also present were Bernard Harris; Charles Hoffman; Moses Klein, the former agent of the Association of Jewish Immigrants of Philadelphia; Reuben Kanevsky, the founder of Chevra B'nai Reuben; Louis E. Levy, the new president of the Association of Jewish Immigrants of Philadelphia; R. M. Reibstein, of B'nai Abraham; and other leaders of the immigrant community. Spivak summed up his ideas for dealing with the crisis in one sentence: "Agriculture is the *auchor-sheet* [sheet-anchor] of Israel."

Within a week an outline of the plans and purposes of the Jewish Alliance of America were published. The preamble contained noble language and grand principles:

> The persecutions to which our brethren in Russia are at present exposed give every indication that a large number of them will seek refuge from unbearable hardships on the free shores of America. To secure their welfare in this country, the one great means that is now presented is the cultivation of the soil and kindred industries therewith connected; thereby they will escape the dangers and the hardships connected with existence in the overcrowded cities on the seacoast and in the interior; they will be reared amidst healthful surroundings, both moral and physical, and will be developed into men and women honorable at once to their adopted country and to their religion. [1]

East European Jewish immigrants did not see the United States as their country, but as their adopted country. Eight days after the first meeting, Spivak wrote to Morais, advising him that circulars would be sent to all Jewish congregations, lodges, and synagogues, soliciting delegates to attend a larger meeting to be held on August 20, 1890, at 203 Pine Street.[2] Spivak advised Morais that a plan of organization was to be laid before the gathering and ended his personal note to Morais

[1] Unless otherwise noted, buildings are private residences.

with these words: "We hope you will grace us with your presence." Although Spivak quickly turned his boundless talents and full time to the founding of the Jewish Alliance of America, he did not ignore his medical practice.

Spivak's reputation brought him patients from every walk of life. Soon after the fiery Leon Kobrin - later a popular author and playwright - immigrated to Philadelphia in 1892, he hurt his hand in a sweatshop accident and was brought to Spivak's office for medical attention. During a series of visits, Kobrin, the youthful revolutionary, tried to convince the cheerful doctor that only in an anarchistic society could mankind reach its true potential. Spivak, ever the practical doctor, and *mentsh*, who could not wait the two hundred years the anarchists pledged it might take to bring about utopia, put his hand on Kobrin's shoulder and turned his laughing eyes on the intense, future writer:

> *Milii yu'nosha!* [Dear young man! Kobrin was twenty years old; Spivak, thirty-two]. God willing, in a few hundred years from now - if we live so long - whether the socialist revolution will come and be victorious, we will talk about it then, about what kind of society you and I will build for mankind. But in the meantime, we should ask the Social Democrats to help us improve conditions of life for mankind that live in today's society. Yes, yes, dear young man, what's worse is not better, as your anarchists babble, but what's better is better. Familiarize yourself with the literature of the Social Democrats.[3]

Spivak took the improvement of life for mankind as a personal charge - a responsibility he saw as his lot. The secretary of the *Hakhnosses Orkhim* (Hospitality to Strangers) in Philadelphia in early 1896, David G. Kratzok, put it another way when describing Spivak's work there: "He [Spivak] bound himself" to attend to the sick among the immigrants at the *Hakhnosses Orkhim*, 218 Lombard Street. Kratzok was right. No one else bound Spivak to do this. Spivak was trying to find a way to give medical care to those who needed it the most, but resolution of his own inward struggle would have to wait until he settled in Denver.

The Society Hill Synagogue; 418-426 Spruce Street. Three Jewish congregations have occupied the old Spruce Street Baptist Church building: Beth Hamedresh Hagodol, Nusakh Ashkenaz (the Great House of Study, the Ashkenazi Rite), 1911 to 1915; Roumanian American Congregation, 1916 to 1967; and Society Hill Synagogue, 1967 to present.

The massive northern facade of the building dominates this residential block. During the immigrant period, the Roumanian American Congregation was a long-time occupant here and the congregation was known as the Great Roumanian Shul. Located at the southwest corner of Lawrence Court, the building adds much grandeur to a street lined with stunning historic homes.

SPRUCE STREET BAPTIST CHURCH.

The 16-foot-wide tripartite front - consisting of a basement of Connecticut granite, a principal story flanked by two square projections and penetrated by twenty-foot great entrance doors, and an attic story - was designed in 1849 by Thomas U. Walter (1804-1887), the celebrated 19th-century Philadelphia architect.[4] The cornerstone to the original building was laid on September 28, 1829, on behalf of a dissident faction of the First Baptist Church of Philadelphia. Built on a lot 73' x 102', with the north wall set back from the Spruce Street building line, it was completed in 1831, and in 1836 took the name of the Spruce Street Baptist Church. From 1851, tower cupolas, rising to a total height of ninety feet above the pavement, adorned and finished the Spruce-Street front. Today the cupolas have been removed.

The most prosperous period in the history of the Spruce Street Baptist Church was under the pastorate of Rev. Dr. J. Wheaton Smith from 1853 to 1870 when contributions for all purposes aggregated $40,000 a year and more than seven hundred persons comprised the congregation. But upon the Jewish onslaught, attendance declined sharply, and the Baptists set their sights on a more affluent neighborhood further west on Spruce Street. The building here was abandoned in 1908. It stood vacant for almost three years before it was purchased by Beth Hamedresh Hagodol, Nusach Ashkenaz, a downtown synagogue.

The beginnings of the synagogue are not well understood. It was identified as the Beth HaMedresh Hagodol Synagogue, or the B'nai Jacob Congregation, or "Beth Hanedrosh [*sic*] Shoulum." The rabbi of the synagogue was Rev. Moses Rivkind (also Riffkind). Rivkind told the *Exponent* that the property cost $30,000 and that he planned to expend about $8,000 on alterations.[5] No synagogue in the Jewish quarter promised as much at its beginning. But underneath the surface there was conflict and strife. The synagogue was dedicated in the midst of a bitter kosher butchers' strike when the city divided itself into pro-Levinthal and anti-Levinthal camps (Rabbi Bernard L. Levinthal was then the unofficial chief rabbi of Philadelphia). Supporters of the synagogue do not appear to have been Levinthal people.

To understand the frenzy that accompanied the consecration of this house of worship, it is necessary to go back to early 1911 when the kosher butchers' strike was called. The butchers wanted to buy meat from any kosher source, but the *Vaad Hakashruth* (The Board of Kashruth) would not approve the purchase of Chicago-dressed meats. Rabbis Levinthal and Joseph Grossman supervised the *Vaad*. Mixed into the dispute, in addition to the *Vaad*,[6] the rabbis, the butchers, and the housewives, were two Philadelphia wholesale dealers who controlled meat prices. Included in the price for meat was a mark-up charged by the dealers, arguably to cover charges they paid to the *Vaad Hakashruth*. Undoubtedly, *Vaad* costs were passed on to the consumer. Less clear was what percentage of a recent consumer-price increase was attributable to *Vaad* costs.

Disputes involving the price of kosher meat were nothing new to the Jews coming from the Pale of Settlement. The Russian government collected taxes from the person who won the governmental right to sell kosher meat in each city. In some cities in Russia a single person controlled this right, called the *korobka* (basket tax). True, profits were made from the sale of kosher meats, but great risks were involved as much capital was needed for the salaries of transport workers, the use of slaughterhouses, and the payment of stamp fees and

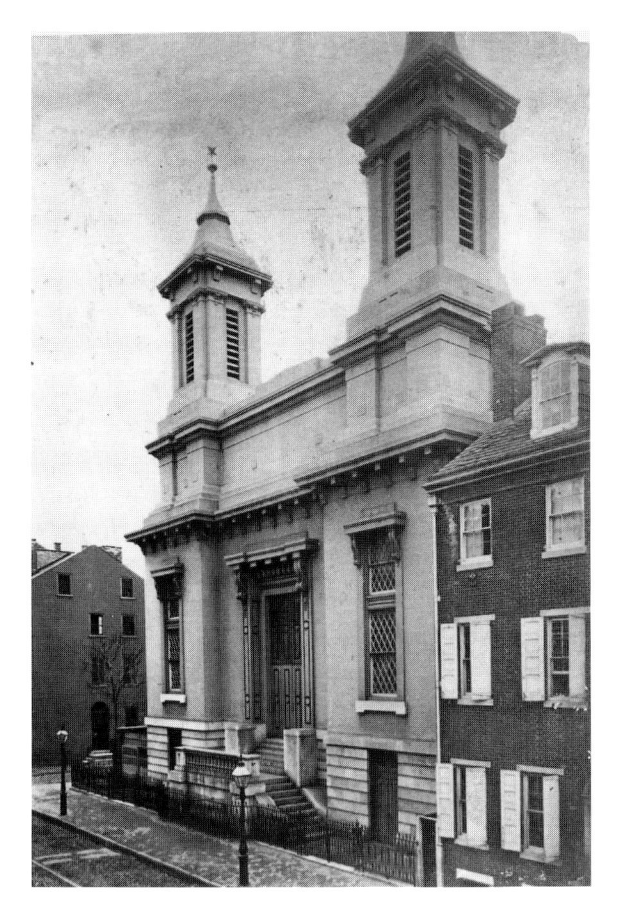

Spruce Street Baptist Church, 418–426 Spruce Street.
The 16' front designed by Thomas U. Walter,
the celebrated 19th centruy architect
from Philadelphia, circa 1878.

Courtesy of The Library Company of Philadelphia

licenses. Excess profits in some Russian cities were returned to local charities. In other places the individuals who made them kept excess profits. Abuses were frequent but do not appear to have been the rule.[7]

With Russian history fresh in the minds of the immigrants, it was easy to convince a segment of Philadelphia's Jewish community that excess profits had been made from the sale of kosher meat. On the surface, Rivkind championed the concept of cheaper kosher meat for Philadelphia's immigrant Jewish community. To him the solution was simple: Rivkind started his own *Vaad HaKashruth Hakelloli* (the General Organization of Kashruth). Begun by Rivkind at Beth Hamedresh Hagodol, the new *Vaad* stood for the proposition that it would provide cheaper kosher meat: "The *Vaad Hakashruth Hakelloli*, the Rabbi [Rivkind] said, will be a *Vaad HaKashruth* without politics, without advertisement and without any special interest to represent. Our main purpose is to see that the meat served to the Jews of this city is kosher, irrespective of whether it comes from Chicago, St. Louis, Philadelphia or any other city."[8] The year 1911 saw the depth of Jewish poverty in Philadelphia. Wages were at the bottom. Although the huge shirtwaist makers' strike had been settled early the previous year, the working immigrant saw little benefit. Every penny was precious, especially to the masses that had arrived since the turn-of-the-century pogroms.

It was against this background that the dedication of Beth Hamedresh Hagodol took place on September 8, 1911. According to the non-Jewish press, more than six thousand men, women, and children marched through the downtown streets to the synagogue. So great was the throng that sought admission to the building to witness the consecration that the marchers formed into a line extending for an entire city block. After each speaker, the crowd in the building was let out and a new group was admitted to hear the next speaker and see the festivities. A more grand beginning cannot be imagined but, quickly, the underpinnings collapsed.[9]

By the next summer, riots in the synagogue were making front-page news in the Philadelphia press. The *Inquirer* reported a riot at Beth "Hanedrosh Shoulum." According to the *Inquirer*, Rabbi Rivkind was approached while he was preaching and commanded to stop speaking. A scuffle ensued. In the general excitement, Mayer Catler, a member of the congregation, was struck on the head with a water pitcher. Members of the Board who had recently been impeached were ejected from the building following a strenuous argument with Rivkind. Afterwards, charges were made that Rivkind had, without the knowledge or consent of the Board, inserted provisions in a so-called agreement of appointment that made him absolute owner of the personal property of the synagogue. Accusations concerning misappropriation of funds flew back and forth.[10]

In early September 1912 a peace meeting was held. Two factions, one supporting and one opposing Rivkind, came to agreement on issues such as who should handle the money received for the coming High Holy Days. Several minor points which the disputants were unable to resolve were referred to Dr. Cyrus Adler, then president of the Kehilla (the Jewish Community of Philadelphia). Notwithstanding the peace resolutions, however, the promise of Beth Hamedresh Hagodol quickly faded and within a year the sheriff had to be called in to sell the building.[11]

The second Jewish congregation here was the Roumanian American Congregation.[12] Its roots go back to two smaller congregations. Notwithstanding the large Romanian-Jewish population in Philadelphia, although it never approached the size of its Russian counterpart, only three small Romanian synagogues existed in the Jewish quarter in the early years: Congregation Porath Joseph, located at 754-756 S. 3rd Street; Or Chodosh, 429 Lombard Street, and Agudas Achim, 512 S. 3rd Street. In the summer of 1916, Or Chodosh and Agudas Achim merged, moved here, and adopted the name, the Roumanian American Congregation.[13] For years this Spruce Street location was headquarters for Romanian Jewry in Philadelphia.

Few changes were made to the building during the years that the Roumanian American Congregation occupied it. Beginning in the mid-1920's, membership began to decline as immigrants moved out of the neighborhood. The years of the Great Depression were difficult, but in 1940 the leaders of the shul, Joseph Weintraub, Abraham Leibowitz, Jack Segal, Harry Gitman, and Harry Spier, undertook an arrangement where the "mortgage could be redeemed at a discount of 50 per cent." Based on this favorable arrangement, the congregation was able to use some of its money to install a new oil burning heating system. And just five years later, on Sunday, June 10, 1945, the synagogue celebrated its "Golden Jubilee and the Burning of its Mortgage."[14]

The burning of the mortgage, however, was a bittersweet victory because in the years immediately following the end of World War II, American-born youth of the congregation continued to disperse and the *nakhes* (sweet joy) of being able to transfer a debt-free building to a new generation of observant Jews was denied to the surviving members of the congregation. In May of 1960, talks commenced to combine the Roumanian American Congregation with the Hungarian Synagogue at 5th & Gaskill Streets. The mood at that time was to sell the Hungarian Synagogue and move the Torahs, plaques, and other objects to the Roumanian American Synagogue, which would then assume the name of the Society Hill Free Synagogue. But the merger never took place.

The old building was in desperate need of repair. Three times during the winter of 1960-1961 water pipes burst because there was no money to buy oil to heat the building. The exterior and interior were badly in need of paint and it was the opinion of congregants that the woodwork and windows had to be replaced immediately. The fate of the synagogue rested on the outcome of a special meeting of the congregation called for Sunday, May 7, 1961. At the meeting, a motion was made to appoint a committee to negotiate for the sale of the building. The motion was unanimously defeated. In a second motion, Morris Segal, the *gabbai*, urged the congregation to borrow between $15,000 to $25,000, money needed to preserve the building. The motion was approved unanimously, and the trustees of the synagogue agreed to endorse the loan and become personally responsible for repaying the debt created. At the same special meeting, it was also voted that the name of the synagogue should be changed to the Roumanian Congregation of Society Hill.

In 1967, the name Society Hill Synagogue was adopted. Thereafter extensive restoration work was carried out in 1968, 1972-1973, and 1978. In 1995, a splendid new bimah was built. While significant and extensive restorations have been carried out over the past thirty years, the Yiddish lettering done so lovingly years ago - די גרויסע רומענישע שוהל - (The Great Roumanian Shul) remains above the massive entrance doors. It is a tribute to the current leadership of the Society Hill Synagogue that it has chosen not to disturb this prominent remembrance of another era.

לשמוע אל הרנה ואל התפלה
די גרויסע רומענישע שוהל

איינלאם קארטע צו נאטעס דינסט פאר
סליחות, ראש השנה ויום כפור
שנת תשי״ח 1957 הבע״ל
אין אונזער פראכטפאלער שוהל
426 ספרוס סטריט
וואו עס וועט פארבעטען דער באוואוסטער
חזן שלמה קאלטער

15 | מזרח רעכטס | $10,00

Roumanian American Congregation, 418–426 Spruce Street.
Ticket for High Holy Days, 1957.
Courtesy of YIVO Institute for Jewish Research, New York

The popular religious leader at this Conservative synagogue is Rabbi Ivan Caine. For information concerning membership and services, contact the synagogue office.

The Second Medical Office of Dr. Spivak: 511 Spruce Street. Dr. Charles D. Spivak moved his medical practice to this handsome city house in 1893 (a private residence today). Although he was only thirty-two years old, Spivak headed the clinic of gastrointestinal diseases at Philadelphia Polyclinic, 1822 Lombard Street. His widowed-mother, Deborah Spivakovsky (Dorfman), who in quieter moments lovingly called her son "Chaim'noo," lived here with him. She was the president of a society of women called *Malbish Arumim* (Clothing the Naked), a society that provided garments to needy children of the Talmud Torah. In addition, Deborah was the honorary recording secretary to the *Hakhnosses Orkhim*, which she helped to found on Lombard Street.

The observant mother and the liberated son, although housed under one roof, lived in different worlds. When Spivak was called upon to speak in Philadelphia, his mother often came to hear him. Gatherings in the Jewish quarter were heavily attended by anarchists and radicals. At one meeting, Deborah Spivakovsky wore her *fatsheylke* (kerchief), under which she wore a *sheytl* (wig). Easily identified as an Orthodox Jewess, Deborah was denied entrance to the hall. After making a disturbance, she gained admittance, rushed to the platform where her son was lecturing and exclaimed: "Chaim, they would not admit your mother. Leave the hall immediately!" Spivak stopped the lecture, walked down to where his mother was standing, embraced her warmly, kissed her tenderly, escorted her to the platform, sat her on a chair - and continued his lecture.

During his last three years in Philadelphia, Spivak continued to speak out in favor of Russian Jewish causes. In 1893, Spivak told an audience at Association Hall "packed from pit to gallery," that he opposed a pending extradition treaty with Russia, whereby the Russian government would be able to reach out to any part of the United States for the "reclamation of any of her citizens who may have left Russia by means of false passports and taken refuge in this free republic." Spivak told how his compatriots in Russia, behind barred doors and with watchers on guard, read translations of the American Declaration of Independence and the Constitution. What drew revolutionaries to clandestine meetings in fields and woods on the outskirts of the *shtetls* of czarist Russia were not only the writings of Marx and Engels, but the writings of an American, Thomas Jefferson.[15]

Rabbi Brodsky of B'nai Jacob married Spivak and Jennie Charsky on March 27, 1893. Born on September 24, 1871, in Poltava, Russia, Jennie Charsky came to America with her two younger sisters, and was reunited with her father in Rosenhayn, New Jersey, a Jewish agricultural outpost near the larger Alliance colony. She was involved in intellectual activities at a young age, and it is possible that she and Spivak met when he taught at the Alliance colony in 1885. If so, although still a youngster, she already knew what she wanted. In 1888, we find her in Philadelphia acting with Spivak in amateur theatre performances.

From this time on, through remarkable determination and surely supported by Spivak, Jennie struck out on her own. In September 1889, Charsky registered as a full time student at West Chester Normal School, West Chester, Pennsylvania, just outside of Philadelphia, the first Jewess to attend the school. She made her religion known only to the Dean. While at West Chester, she was interviewed by a reporter for the local West Chester newspaper concerning revolutionary movements in Russia. Where did a poor immigrant girl get the money to go to a school of higher education? Before enrolling, Charsky met with Mayer Sulzberger and William Hackenberg of the Baron de Hirsch Trust Board and requested that they lend her money from Trust funds for tuition. Either she or Spivak devised a plan to convince Sulzberger and Hackenberg to give her the needed money on the condition that she repay the Trust after she became a teacher.

Charsky remained at West Chester until the summer of 1891. When Spivak left for Germany, she transferred to the University of Pennsylvania and enrolled in biology. Being one of the few women at Penn, she was hazed by the men, not for being a Jew, but for being a woman. After one year of unmerciful teasing, Charsky left Penn. Spivak returned from Germany in the summer of 1892, and in September Charsky again transferred schools, this time enrolling as a law student at Cornell. After one successful semester, she returned to Philadelphia to marry and raise a family.[16] Charsky was also active in the communal life of the Jewish quarter. She founded the Daughters of Israel, a society organized so that Russian Jewish women could help alleviate the poor condition of their coreligionists. At this time she also taught English to the immigrants. In the early 1890's, Spivak and Charsky led the way for a new generation of young Philadelphians who had recently escaped from Russian *shtetl* life, but who had not yet set upon their own path in the New World.[17]

Dr. Charles Spivak and Jennie Charsky. Written on the reverse side by Spivak, "Taken on Monday, Sept. 26th, 1892, the day of the departure of the lady of my heart for the Cornell University."

Courtesy of Charlesa Feinstein

The Jewish Maternity Hospital: 532-536 Spruce Street. The Jewish Maternity Hospital was founded to assist poor Jewish married women during pregnancy and delivery. In the later years of the hospital, infants up to one year of age were cared for. Obstetric and other services were provided to the poor free of charge.

In 1914, during a speech at the dedication of a new building here, the president, Millard Merz, remarked that the hospital was "doing the greatest amount of obstetric work in Pennsylvania, that is, of any one institution, and in our new hospital, we expect to do still more."[18] But the hospital was about much more than obstetrics. It was run by women from the German Jewish community, and nowhere was the principle of *gemilus kheysed* (the performance of acts of loving kindness) more evident.

Founded on November 1, 1873, as the *Ezrath Nashim* (Helping Women), in its early years it rendered aid at the residences of its charges. "How modestly, how quietly, the few who organized it, began their labors! The Women's Society, *Ezrath Nashim*, was the name it bore for more than a few years, when the tide of empire had not yet taken its course far westward. But conditions changed, numbers increased, and soon the work of this single institution brought it to the front among charities in our midst."[19] In 1891, the name was changed to the Jewish Hospital Association and in November of that year the property at 534 Spruce Street, formerly the home of Mr. & Mrs. Samuel Snellenberg, was acquired for a hospital.[20]

Dedicated during the week of January 11, 1892, flowers were sold to passers-by despite the cold weather. Inside, rooms were decorated with bunting and flags, and the orchestra of Frederick Grimes provided music. Physicians' offices were on the first floor, and convalescent and lying-in rooms were on the second and third floors.[21] In 1898, the medical staff consisted of sixteen doctors, almost half of whom were women. The permanent physician and superintendent was Dr. Sarah Vasen. When she took ill, Dr. Rosalie M. Blitzstein, a daughter of the owner of the Blitzstein bank, was placed in charge. Others were Drs. Clara T. Dercum, Helen Kirshbaum, Eleanor C. Jones and Anna E. Broomal. Also on the staff were Dr. Benjamin L. Gordon, who founded the first Zionist organization in Philadelphia the previous year, and Dr. Ludwig Loeb, who along with Spivak, founded the Maimonides Clinic on Lombard Street in 1891.[22]

In 1898, almost 95 percent of the patients were foreign born, approximately 90 percent coming from Russia. Most of the women confined in the hospital had other children at home, 38 percent having five or more children already at home and 5 percent having ten or more. The women were encouraged to remain in the hospital after giving birth, where the newborn were cared for in the nursery and the mothers were given a clean bed in pleasant surroundings. The average length of stay was two weeks.

In March 1901, the Jewish Maternity Association acquired the next-door property at 532 Spruce Street, and for the next twelve years the institution continued to grow as immigrants poured into Philadelphia. Significant alterations were made to the properties. In 1906, the roof was raised and the attic squared up. The nurses then occupied the attic. Three years later, a one-story addition was added. Andrew J. Sauer was the architect for these improvements.

The Federation of Jewish Charities, which took over responsibility for the hospital from the Association in 1912, pledged $40,000 toward the erection of a new hospital and the former town houses located at 532-534 Spruce Street were torn down. The Philadelphia architectural firm of Hewitt and Granger designed a three-bay, four-story maternity hospital on this otherwise residential block of Spruce Street. Architecturally, the new building featured monumental pilasters. Today, the first floor of the building, which is no longer used as a hospital, has been altered. As built, the second story was most prominent. Balustraded sills enhanced the windows of each bay, the center sill framing the top of the first-floor door surround. In the presence of five hundred people, dedication exercises were held on June 10, 1914.[23] The following year, Dr. Ludwig Loeb was elected as the Medical Director, and five years later the small property at 536 Spruce Street was acquired. Because maternity services were also provided at Mount Sinai Hospital, the Jewish Maternity Hospital was closed in the twenties.

The next occupant was the Rebecca Gratz Club.[24] Architects Silverman & Levy designed extensions for the building. In July 1928, the property at 536 Spruce Street was torn down and the lot was used for a garden. The Club, founded in 1907 to provide a home for poor single immigrant Jewish girls, had been located in Northern Liberties and on the 700 block of Catharine Street. The building here was used for the

Club for almost forty years. The words "Rebecca Gratz Club," can still be seen above the portal leading to the courtyard. At the present time, the building is a multi-family dwelling.

Library Hall, 203 Pine Street, circa 1870. It was built in 1867, and meeting rooms on the second and third floors of this Italianate style building were used often by the immigrants. The first floor was occupied by the Sixth National Bank from 1867 to 1933.

Courtesy of the Historical Society of Pennsylvania, Philadelphia, Pennsylvania

PINE STREET

Today, Pine Street is upscale and residential. Semi-circular fanlights, elaborate door trim, and splendid dormers greet the visitor. Stroll along the historic blocks of Pine Street. In the summertime many residents of the 500 block can be seen watering their brightly decorated flower boxes.

Meeting Rooms (above the Sixth National Bank): 203 Pine Street. In 1867, the Italianate style three-story Sixth National Bank was built on the northwest corner of 2nd & Pine Streets.[25] The cast-iron arcaded first floor was identified as 350 S. 2nd Street. The second and third floors, constructed of brick with white marble dressings, were identified as 203 Pine Street. The rooms on these two floors were designed as society meeting rooms and a number of Jewish immigrant societies met here, such as the Tourgenieff Club. Named for the famous Russian writer, Ivan Turgenev, it was a popular intellectual society. Speakers addressed the membership in Russian. The fifth lecture on American History (Thomas Jefferson) was to be delivered here on Saturday, April 12, 1888.[26] Many meetings were attended exclusively by the recent arrivals, and English was rarely heard.

On Wednesday evening, October 5, 1887, the Hebrew Literature Society hosted a gathering for an evening's entertainment. Upward of 100 to 125 people attended. The gathering consisted mainly of young men, all of foreign birth. Founded two years earlier for the purpose of encouraging the study of Hebrew, English, and Yiddish Literature, for maintaining a library, and for sponsoring lectures, the Hebrew Literature Society grew quickly. Pictures of Montefiore, Mendelssohn, other eminent sages and rabbis, and a picture of Jerusalem, hung on the walls. To rent the rooms, described as "cheerful apartments" (and called Library Hall), the Society paid $11 a month. The *Exponent*, acting as overseer of the immigrant community, expressed its pleasure at the direction the Society was taking: "It is gratifying to note that none of those rabid socialistic or unbalanced anachistic elements were to be met with among the large audience."[27]

Soon, devout members of the Hebrew Literature Society wanted to convert it into a strictly religious organization. While those advocating a religious direction eventually left, their aims divided and weakened the Society for a number of years. During this time and later, the Hebrew Literature Society was sometimes identified as a socialist society; but while socialist ideas were certainly a part of everyday life in the Jewish quarter, evidence to prove that the Society was a socialist society is sketchy. The extant evidence points in another direction and pictures an intellectual and literary society. The education of its members was the overriding goal of its leaders.[28]

In 1889, anarchists were also headquartered here and met on Sunday afternoons. Other intellectual societies and landsmanshaftn met here. The Elizabetgrad Beneficial Association, founded in 1893, met in 1900 and continued to meet here for the next twenty years, until it acquired its own property at 715 Pine Street. Landsmanshaftn, like the one from Elizabetgrad, accumulated funds from contributions and dues and used these funds to aid members and their families who were sick or otherwise in distress. These organizations purchased cemetery grounds, paid death benefits, and provided aid for surviving families.

Eastern end of the 200 block of Pine Street, north side, circa 1905. Shops occupied the first floors of these colonial and federal homes.

Courtesy of the Philadelphia City Archives

The Sixth National Bank was forced to close for the Bank Holiday of February 28, 1933. It never reopened. In 1937, the building, along with two adjoining properties and 207 Pine Street, was sold to the South Philadelphia National Bank for $45,700. The second and third stories of the Sixth National Bank building were taken down in recent years. Today, only the cast-iron arcaded ground floor remains.

The Stamper Mansion: 224 Pine Street. Built in 1752 or 1753 by John Stamper, mayor and alderman of Philadelphia, the three-story mansion that stood here was fronted with red and blue glazed brick. It had a columnar doorway and its cornice and dormers were fine specimens of ancient woodwork. It was also called the Blackwell Mansion, after the Rev. Dr. Robert Blackwell, who married a descendant of John Stampers.[29]

By 1905, a fire escape was placed on the front of the building, often a sign that the property was no longer being used as a one-family residence. In August 1907, Jacob Sork, a local property owner, converted the colonial mansion into a meeting house by taking out brick walls between two rooms on the first floor and erecting a fire escape at the back of the property.

Union gatherings dominate the Jewish history of Sork's meeting house. On a breezy October evening in 1909 a handful of Jewish men met here to lay the foundation for the Cutter's Branch, Local 15, of the International Ladies' Garment Workers' Union (ILGWU). Although most cutters were not Jewish when the immigrants first came to Philadelphia, after a number of years this most lucrative branch of the tailor trade fell into Jewish hands.[30]

Not only cutters met here, but shirtwaist makers also turned to this classic 18th century city house as a meeting place. Two months later, at the beginning of the famous shirtwaist maker's strike, when thousands left their sewing machines and cutting boards, meetings of the Association of Ladies' Garment Workers (ALGW) were called at nine locations throughout immigrant Philadelphia. The Executive Board of the ALGW met here during the two-month strike, and general meetings were called here every morning. At this time, there were fifteen thousand shirtwaist operators in the city of Philadelphia, and thirteen thousand were claimed to be union members. Within a short time, most of these strikers became part of the powerful ILGWU.

In 1913, the *Philadelphia Jewish Herald* contained a directory of weekly meetings of landsmanschaftn, unions, and beneficial associations. Meeting here at that time were the Ladies' Waist Makers' Union and the Bakers' Union, Local 201. Founded in 1900, Local 201 of the Bakers' Union met every Friday at 2:00 P.M., a time convenient for those who rose early for work, but who could still hurry home to observe the Sabbath. Bilingual broadsides, printed in Yiddish and English, noticed a special meeting here of the Children's Coats and Sailors' Jacket Makers Local 249, on Saturday, June 17, 1916. The notice provided that trade questions were to be discussed, a minimum scale of wages was to be adopted, and a system of work was to be marked out.

By 1920, the building had been converted to a cigar factory, and in 1921 the Stamper Mansion was torn down. The property located here today is a private residence.[31]

Forward Hall: 200 block of Pine Street. This federal townhouse was erected between 1838 and 1840 as a private residence. On May 8, 1892, single Jewish women from uptown opened the new home of the Young Women's Union here. The YWU was an organization formed in 1885 (at 238 Pine Street) to care for the young of the Russian immigrants while their mothers were at work.[32] It began as a small kindergarten with the primary object of teaching the children English. In 1892, the kindergarten and a day nursery occupied the first floor. A meeting room, library, dormitory and playroom were on the second floor. By 1897, the day nursery was perhaps the largest in the city. The average daily attendance was thirty-four. The cost of maintaining a child was 7¢ a day.

In 1906, six years after the Young Women's Union moved to its permanent home on Bainbridge Street, Jacob Sork (the owner of the Stamper Mansion) acquired this property and he converted the first floor into Forward Hall. During a particularly bitter kosher butchers' strike, a large number of Jewish women from the southern section of the city met here on Wednesday, July 24, 1907 (the butchers met at Washington Hall on S. 4th Street). The women declared they would not buy beef until prices were reduced. The price of beef, 9¢ a pound, had been raised by 1¢. The women pledged themselves to use all possible efforts to influence other Jewish women to join the movement. A temporary organization was effected, and a strike committee of more than thirty women was appointed.[33]

In 1908, the Ladies' Maternity Society met here; it had 900 members. Fraternal and beneficial organizations met here regularly, among them were the Hebrew American Beneficial Association, the First Roumanian Bucharest Beneficial Association, and Theodore Roosevelt Lodge No. 15 of the Independent Order of Brith Sholom.

Mount Sinai Dispensary: 236 Pine Street. This Federal style city house was erected in 1834, but it was not until 1900 that its short Jewish history began. While no Jewish hospital operated in the Jewish quarter at this time, three Jewish dispensaries were opened, one at 419 Lombard Street, one at 238 Pine Street and one here. The Franklin Free Dispensary, which had been located at 238 Pine Street since 1898, and the Beth Israel Hospital Association joined together under the name of the Mount Sinai Hospital Association, and it opened a little dispensary here at the end of June 1900. After being open for only three weeks, it was already a busy place. Downtown Jewish doctors here - some of them recent immigrants themselves - saw seventy-five patients a week. No fee was charged for medical services. The staff included doctors proficient in dermatology, dentistry, surgery, neurology, pediatrics, and "genito-urinary." Long lines of the poor crowded the pavement outside the dispensary every morning waiting for the doors to open at nine o'clock. The staff included Benjamin L. Gordon; Max Staller; Henry D. Shmookler, founder and long time supporter of the Mount Sinai Hospital, and Rosalie Blitzstein. When the Mount Sinai Hospital opened at 5th & Wilder Streets in March of 1905, the dispensary was no longer needed, and it closed. This property has been a private residence for many years.

Knights of Pythias Hall: 238 Pine Street. In September 1880, a dwelling here was torn down and construction was started on the Knights of Pythias Hall. Completed in early 1881, this hall - used extensively by the immigrants, beginning several years after their arrival - was opened for inspection to the public on February 22, 1881. Built four-stories high and towering over its next-door neighbors, the hall had an upper floor fronted with Mansard-roof windows. The building was faced in pressed brick with ornamental brick belt-courses. The front door was corniced with light stone. On the first floor were a reception room and a long dining hall suitable for meeting purposes. A broad stairway, with balustrade finished in light and dark woods, ran the height of the building. On each floor was one large lodge room, connected with committee and waiting rooms. The lodge rooms were richly finished.

The Young Women's Union of the Hebrew Education Society was founded here on March 1, 1885, with a small kindergarten class of fifteen children.[34] Fanny Binswanger, the founder and inspirer of the Young Women's Union, opened the kindergarten as its working head. She was assisted by Misses Alice Jastrow, Martha Winstock, Bella Feustman, Martha Goldstein, Nellie Bachman, Gertrude Hahn, Rose Goldsmith, Esther de Casseres, Ida Espen, Rosena Fels, and Nettie Guggenheim, each one of whom gave one morning a week. Also founded here in 1885 was the Roumanian-American chevra, Or Chodosh (Society of New Light), which in 1891 had 125 members. After a number of moves it merged with Agudas Achim in 1916 and moved to 418-426 Spruce Street.

Not only did children use this most attractive and comfortable hall, it was used as a meeting place during strikes. During the cloakmakers' strike in the summer of 1890, Sabato Morais addressed the strikers here. The next year during the strike in the men's clothing industry by members of Tailors' Union No.1 of the Jewish Federation of Labor, the Boss Tailors met here in June. Abraham Simon presided and Bernard Weintraub acted as secretary. Seventy-three boss tailors formed the Tailors Employers' Protective Association here on June 15, 1891, and they resolved not to yield to any demand of the strikers. Such resolutions normally lasted for a week, but rarely longer.

The Phipps Institute, founded and endowed by the financier and philanthropist Henry Phipps, opened here on February 3, 1903, for the study, treatment, and prevention of tuberculosis. Although the Institute was not a Jewish organization (the rules for patients were printed in English, Italian and Yiddish), Jewish tubercular patients took advantage of the Institute, especially prior to the opening of the Jewish Consumptive Institute in September 1910. When located here, the Institute had fifty beds on the upper floors, with the clinics on the street floor. As part of the treatment for tuberculosis, milk and eggs were consumed by the patients at the "ideal ratio" of eight glasses of milk to four eggs per day. The property was torn down in the early 1960's.

House of Zion, Pine Street. Yiddish poster for a "Concert and Literary Evening" at the House of Zion, December 27, 1908.

Courtesy of the Philadelphia Jewish Archives

House of Zion: 200 block of Pine Street. Erected between 1823 and 1824, this Federal townhouse was acquired on November 17, 1902, by Dr. Benjamin L. Gordon, Solomon Frank, and Herman Krueger, as trustees of the Zion Association of Philadelphia. Known as the House of Zion, or the Zion Institute, or Beth Zion, the property was headquarters for the Zionist movement in Philadelphia for eight years. Among the organizations that met here were the Aids of Zion, Young Workers of Zion, and the Maccabean-Zionist Society. The Institute had a library, a reading room, and classrooms. Lectures and concerts, given in support of Zionist causes, were held here.[35] During a national Zionist gathering in Philadelphia, the House of Zion was headquarters for the leadership from around the country.

In 1910, the property was sold to Agudas Achim, Lodge No. 156, Independent Order of Brith Abraham, which held the property for ten years. During this period other organizations also met here. The Elizabetgrad Beneficial Association, an organization composed exclusively of men, expressed concern over the fact that when a member died the organization lost contact with the widow and orphans and suggested that a Ladies' Auxiliary be established. The newly formed Auxiliary, which held its third meeting here on November 9, 1915, was to prosper for a number of years.

"Lower Part" of Spruce and Pine Streets: In 1914, Elizabeth Pennell, an experienced traveler and a zealous champion of patriotic Philadelphia families, described what she identified as the lower part of Spruce and Pine Streets:

> And what did I find it?-- A slum, captured by the Russian Jew, the old houses dirty, down-at-the-heel; the once spotless marble steps unwashed, the white shutters hanging loose; the decorative old iron hinges and catches and insurance plaques or badges rusting, and nobody can say how much of the old woodwork inside burned for kindling; Yiddish signs in the windows, with here a Jewish Maternity Home, and there a Jewish newspaper office; at every door, almost every window, and in groups in the street, men, women, children with Oriental faces, here and there a man actually in his caftan, bearded, with the little curls in front of his ears, and a woman with a handkerchief over her head, and all chattering in Yiddish and slatternly and dirty as I remember them in South-Eastern Europe, from Carlsbad to Prague to those remote villages of Transylvania where dirt was the sign by which I always knew when the Jewish quarter was reached. A few patriotic Philadelphians have recently returned hoping to stem the current, and their houses shine with cleanliness. In Fourth Street the dignified Randolph House, which the family never deserted, seems to protest against the wholesale surrender to the foreign invasion. In Pine Street, St. Peter's, with it green graveyard, has survived untarnished the surrounding desecration. But I could only wonder how long the church and these few houses will be able to withstand the triumphing alien, and I abandoned hope when, at the very gate of St. Peter's, a woman with a handkerchief tied over her head stopped me to ask the way to "Zweit und Pine."[36]

How ironic that Pennell's virulently anti-Semitic description of the Russian Jew of Philadelphia is also one of the most detailed.

The Russian Jewish Invasion: On the south side of Pine Street, in the 400 block, stands the stately Third Presbyterian Church. Built in 1768, it is called Old Pine Street Church and is surrounded on three sides by a well-kept churchyard. Among the many heroes buried here is William Hurry, who rang the bell at the State House (Independence Hall) when liberty was declared in July 1776.

In Philadelphia on October 11, 1881 (approximately six months after the first wave of pogroms spread throughout the southern part of Russia), the Pastorate of Hughes Oliphant Gibbons, the Eighth Pastor of Old Pine Street Church, began. The early years of Dr. Gibbons' ministry passed peacefully.

> Then, in the early nineties came the Russian Jewish invasion, which has increased year after year steadily and invincibly. For a decade many members of Old Pine Street withstood it; but there were removals every year. In the last four years [written in 1905] it has been a case of "get out of the neighborhood as soon as you can sell your house." Today it is hard to find a Protestant family in the vicinity of Old Pine Street Church; and Catholics are by no means plentiful.[37]

The invasion was viewed by the Presbyterians with alarm. They took flight, running from the Jews, who themselves were running from the Russians.

Headquarters of the Amalgamated Clothing Workers of America: 431 Pine Street. Erected between 1839 and 1840, the building was purchased by the ACWA on July 21, 1921. Upon acquisition, the clothing workers built a three-story addition in the rear, a fire tower, and converted the building to meeting rooms. By the following year, the union was ready to take on the Men's Clothing Manufacturers of Philadelphia, a successor to the Philadelphia Clothing Exchange. But whether they were ready to take on Judge Rogers of Common Pleas Court, No. 2, was another matter.

Jousts with outspoken Judge Rogers revealed how fragile the immigrant's place was in their adopted country. During a hearing on a request for injunctive relief brought in Common Pleas Court No. 2 on July 31, 1922, in connection with a strike in the men's clothing industry, Judge Rogers ordered officers and agents of the ACWA to remain in the courtroom while documents were reviewed. Among other things, Rogers wanted to know how many members of the union were naturalized American citizens. Referring to members of the union as foreigners, Rogers silenced William A. Gray, counsel for the garment workers, with a wave of the hand when Gray sought to interrupt. Rogers' strident language reflected a mood in the country in 1922: "Such agitators [Jews and Italians] should be driven out of America and such organizations should not be tolerated under law." After further confrontation between the judge and counsel for the union, Rogers demanded the production of union records. When told that they were at 431 Pine Street, Rodgers directed the sheriff to Pine Street to "seize all records and literature of the organization [the ACWA] found there." In response to a comment made by Gray that the officers and agents of the union would not run away, Judge Rogers said: "No. The court has fixed that with the superintendent of police. We will see that the attention of the police department and the federal immigration officials is called to this un-incorporated body in the investigation of its purposes and methods and its general make up."[38]

In May 1928, the ACWA moved and the building was bought by the Independent Order of Brith Abraham, a New York-headquartered benevolent organization, identified in the press as the "largest Jewish organization in the world."[39] Less than two years later, at the beginning of the Depression, it was sold by the sheriff. Notwithstanding the sale, Brith Abraham continued to meet here as a tenant. On March 22, 1933, over seven hundred people gathered to condemn Hitler's rise to power. In the fifties, the building was used as a restaurant, and in 1959 it was the Rosenberg Caterers. The next year Louis Silverman wanted to convert the building into a small theatre where Shakespeare could be performed, but the local citizenry, fearful that Shakespeare would draw "hippies" to the area, convinced the Zoning Board not to approve such use, and the building was quickly torn down.

Independent Order of Brith Sholom: 506-508 Pine Street. In 1919, two tenements here were acquired by the Independent Order of Brith Sholom. These buildings were torn down, and a new three-story lodge and office building designed by Edwin Rothschild was constructed. Its architectural embellishments included pilasters.

Brith Sholom, the only national Jewish fraternal membership organization headquartered in Philadelphia, was founded in 1905 at 509 S. 5th Street. At its seventh annual convention, held at Labor Lyceum Hall, N. 6th & Brown Streets in Philadelphia, there were 800 delegates. By 1913, it had 40,618 members in 309 lodges in ninety-three cities. In a letter dated March 18, 1935, to Martin O. Levy, Grand Secretary of Brith Sholom, Dr. Cyrus Adler lauded the vision and objectives of the organization:

> "In fact Brith Sholom, to my mind, has done what it could and what of course all Jews ought to do - endeavor to promote Jewish religion and Jewish education. I have also been gratified at the association that I have had with Brith Sholom through its affiliation with the American Jewish Committee and I have found its representatives to be among the thoughtful and sober people who are devoted to the service of the Jewish people and not concerned about the aggrandizement of their own organization. I have particularly and in many ways worked together with your Grand Master, the Honorable William M. Lewis, and have learned to esteem him highly as a man to whom no Jewish cause is alien."[40]

Judge Lewis, speaking before Brith Sholom on its 20th anniversary in 1925 said: "Brith Sholom was the inspiration of forty-four men who wanted to counteract the tremendous prejudice that existed against their race by good deeds and a good will to the world." In addition, Brith Sholom offered the immigrants and their families insurance in the form of sick and death benefits.[41] Before Social Security, the Jewish community, and not the federal government, provided these benefits.[42]

The Brith Sholom building on Pine Street was torn down during Redevelopment. The properties located here today are private residences.

Vilna *shul*. Interior, 1994. The only rowhouse *shul* remaining in the old Jewish quarter.

Photograph by Fred Wagner

The Vilna shul: 509 Pine Street. Abraham Aba Ben Yehuda Shapiro founded the Vilna shul in a rented building on Parkside Avenue in 1904, and it is the only synagogue founded in a remote part of the city that moved to the Jewish quarter. From Parkside, it moved to 10th and South Streets, then to 5th & South, and in 1917, to the

300 block of Lombard Street.[43] Shapiro was born into a middle-class family in the small town of Malat, Lithuania, in 1842 and was trained at the yeshiva at Volozhin. He became a hardware merchant, taking on a prominent role in the communal life of Malat, and at one time occupied the position of town elder. At the age of thirty-three, Shapiro moved to Vilna where he remained until 1904, when he emigrated to the United States and settled with his sons in Philadelphia.

His desire was to found a synagogue where people from Vilna could pray and meet for various communal functions. The synagogue, through its trustees, found it difficult to attract new members to the *shul* when it was located on the 300 block of Lombard Street. Therefore, Shapiro established an interest-free loan program, and announced it in the newspapers. Poor peddlers, push cart operators, and other itinerant sellers accepted Shapiro's offer and joined the *shul*. Membership, however, was not restricted to persons from Vilna. As long as a worshiper was a *litvak*, he was welcome to pray here. After Shapiro's death on December 7, 1917, his son Bernard dedicated his residence at 509 Pine Street as the permanent site for the synagogue in memory of his father.

In 1922, a two-story 19' x 25' rear addition was built onto the former row house at 509 Pine Street. The main room was not large enough to place the *bimah* in the center, so it was located on the north wall, along with a wooden, hand carved *ornkoydesh* (the Torah is read facing the congregation). Two rows of twelve stained-glass windows were built into the rear addition, each row running from one side of the addition, across the back, to the other side. In an article in the *Jewish Exponent*, April 27, 1990, Evey Ruskin presented a "little bit of Europe set down in a Society Hill row house." In a beautiful tribute to the Vilna shul, she wrote:

> It [the Vilna shul] is a little jewel; a women's balcony, horseshoe-shaped and bordered by a graceful banister; an enormous Colonial-style brass chandelier that drops down from the two-story front section of the large rectangular-shaped main room; brightly colored stained glass windows; and a Torah ark topped by large lions with light-bulb eyes and embellished with trompe l'oeil gilded carvings that resembles a border of drapes.

At the dedication on September 10, 1922, several rabbis, including Rabbis Levinthal (see B'nai Abraham), and Max D. Klein, the religious leader of Adath Jeshurun Congregation, made speeches. In 1927-1928 approximately 375 children of the Isaac Leeser School, divided into fourteen classes, met at the Vilna shul. The superintendent was Morris W. Koladner. In the fifties and sixties, the rabbi was Joseph Hillel Snapir (for *Snapir*, see *Kesher Israel*). On January 19, 1941, the congregation celebrated its Silver Jubilee.

Rabbi Joseph Hillel Snapir, the rabbi at the Vilna shul and Kesher Israel, circa 1940.

Courtesy of Moishe Snapir

In the late 1980's membership declined. At this point Rabbi Menachem Schmidt came to the Vilna *shul*. That was ten years ago and Rabbi Schmidt continues to lead a youthful, enthusiastic congregation of Orthodox worshipers. Since the dedication in 1922, few changes have been made to the building. The pastoral murals on the east and west party walls done by Morris Balk, the same artist who did similar scenes of ancient Israel in other synagogues in the area, have been added, but little else has changed. During the immigrant period many row houses in the Jewish quarter were converted into synagogues, but "Vilna" is the only survivor. The dark heavy wooden benches, the pressed tin ceiling, the chandelier, the wooden *ornkoydesh*, beckon to the visitor and worshiper alike. The *Ezras Noshim* is no longer used. Women sit downstairs, separated from the men by a *mikhitsa*. Life at Vilna is as close as one can get in the last decade of the 20th century to the sweet life that the *frume Yidn* in the immigrant generation knew in the Jewish quarter of Philadelphia. *Simkhas* (joyous occasions) are celebrated with friends with whom one prays everyday. A special warmth is found here, a *nakhas* not soon forgotten. For information about membership or prayer services, contact the synagogue.

A Jewish Foundling: 500 block of Pine Street. During the short time B'nai Abraham was located here in the early 1880's, one Sunday evening a knock was heard at the front door. A bundle was found containing a baby wrapped securely in a shawl. Accompanying the child was a bottle that was still warm. A letter written in Yiddish, pinned to the child's dress, read:

"To the President and Brethren of the Society B'nai Avrohm, Anshe Russia.

Brother President and Brothers. By this means I make you honored brothers acquainted with my most unfortunate position. Maternity reached me in the greatest poverty and on account of this poverty, I am forced to do this great act of cruelty, having no one to advise, and none to whom I could confide my sorrow. To rid myself of my child, with no other remedy at my disposal, I place it in your hands, hoping and trusting that you will extend your merciful charity over him and make of him a true Israelite, which alas! it was impossible for me to do, for I could not even fulfill the rite of circumcision. I beg that you will rear the child into Israelitish ways, for you will thereby do honor to our faith, and God in his mercy will extend his lasting blessings to you and the brotherhood of the Society and your names will be praised. If there is any chance to give the child a Hebrew wet nurse, pray do so, for he came from respectable Hebrew parents. When God will relieve me of my great poverty, I will call for my child and satisfy the Society; and I sincerely hope and pray that you, brother President, Mr. Stone, and brothers, will fulfill the wishes of my letter and allow the child to receive the name of Lieb ben Reb Jacob [...........]."[44]

A local doctor examined the baby. He knew a women who could nurse, and the child was given to her. B'nai Abraham made arrangements for the bris. The four-story building located here was torn down, but it is unclear when this occurred.[45]

National Preparatory School, 515 Pine Street, circa 1920.

Courtesy of the YIVO Institute for Jewish Research, New York

The Third and Last Office of Dr. Charles D. Spivak: 529 Pine Street By the time Spivak moved his family to this Federal style townhouse in May 1895 (it is a private residence today), he was the most popular member of the Russian colony in Philadelphia. But for reasons of his wife's health, Spivak made known that he intended to move his family to Denver, Colorado.

On the evening of February 28, 1896, upon only a few hours notice, nearly a "half-hundred" friends gathered outside to surprise the Spivaks and toast their departure. Among those attending were Dr. Rachel Skidelsky, who worked with Spivak at his first dispensary on Lombard Street, and her husband, Simon, who wrote for the Philadelphia papers; Elias Goldensky, later to become a world-famous art photographer, who performed in the theatre with the Spivaks on more than one occasion; David Apotheker, theatre critic, writer for the *Volks-Vechter* and publisher and editor of the *Gegenwart*; members of the Blitzstein family, Harry and Jennie Blitzstein, Sophie Blitzstein Voynow, and C. B. Voynow; and other doctors and friends.[46]

The guests showed up at the front door with a train load of provisions and took the house by surprise: "After possession had been acquired, the amiable host and hostess resigned their rights in favor of the invaders and willingly agreed to take their places as the only guests of the evening." The "invaders" brought in herring purchased from an unidentified famous caterer on Lombard Street. Sandwiches, pfeffernuss, pretzels and tarts - the tarts being obtained from the "great confectioner of Gillis Alley"[47] - were also set out. "Overtopping all, hissing and steaming, stood the mighty 'Samovar' so dear to the hearts of all assembled." Hidden away in the kitchen was a keg of beer, out of whose "bung [bunghole]" gushed a stream of foaming liquid. Also obtained for the festivities were wines from Spain and whiskey from Ireland. Short speeches followed. "Everyone expressed the great regret in losing from our colony so active and energetic a member - a man who filled a part no other one could take." The hours passed in song and dance.

Soon after this festive evening, the young Spivak family left for Denver. Eight years later Dr. Charles D. Spivak helped to found the Jewish Consumptive Relief Society (JCRS), a sanatorium for advanced cases of tubercular patients, arguably for two generations one of the best-loved Jewish institutions in the United States. The JCRS had supporters in every Jewish community in the country, and the name Dr. Charles D. Spivak was known to American and European Jewry.[48] In 1920, as part of a Medical Commission, which was part of the American Army, Spivak volunteered to go to Poland to ascertain the conditions existing there after the preceding six years of mayhem and murder. Although almost sixty years old and a world-renowned physician, Spivak chose to serve, in what was a military organization, as a private, refusing any special consideration. He insisted on being treated as one of the boys. He was the oldest volunteer.[49]

Dr. Charles D. Spivak, the bright star of the Russian colony in Philadelphia for ten years, died in Denver, Colorado on October 16, 1927. Four days after Spivak's death, Moses Freeman wrote a memoir about the great man. Although Spivak left Philadelphia thirty-one years before, it is one of only two memoirs found in Freeman's two-volume history of immigrant Jewish Philadelphia. Freeman's concluding words are given here: "But Dr. Chaim Spivak is no more! Gone from us is the people's friend and lifesaver. Gone from us is one of the true intelligent Jews of the olden generation who lived and worked for his fellow man and for his people. He did his holy work modestly, without honor seeking, and without artificial publicity. Who will take his place from the new generation of American Jews? Who will fill the vacuum that remains empty, empty. Sleep in peace dear unforgettable friend! There is a person who earns his portion in the world in one moment. You have earned your place. May you rest in peace."[50]

Isaac Sion (1866–1939), circa 1894. Sion won a scholarship to the Law School of the University of Pennsylvania. He was graduated in 1894, one of the first east European Jews in Philadelphia to turn to the law. He practiced at 507 and 521 Pine Street for 45 years, and was the secretary to the Russian Consulate in Philadelphia for over 20 years under Czar Nicholas II. Sion was a scholar of languages and literature.

Courtesy of Charlesa Feinstein

Boslover Hall: 701-703 Pine Street. The hall here was one of the most popular halls in the area. It was used as a hall for forty years.

Former residents of Boguslav, or Boslav, a town located in the south of Russia met at 615 S. 3rd Street in 1902 to form a *fareyn*. Over the years the Boslover society grew, and in 1925 it acquired the properties at 701-703 Pine Street, converted them into clubrooms, and added on a three-story rear addition at a cost of $25,000. Boslover merged with other societies, and by the early sixties it was known as Boslover Ahavas Achim Belzer

Association. It had about one thousand members - most of who were over sixty-five years old. The building was used for meetings and was rented for other functions, including weddings and Bar Mitzvahs. On the surface it's future looked bright.

During Redevelopment, a plan was submitted to City Council and approved on May 6, 1963, which provided for the continued occupancy of the property by Boslover. Immediately, Boslover at great expense improved the hall. These improvements were required to be made by various municipal and other agencies. But the Redevelopment Authority of the City of Philadelphia had a surprise for Boslover. It tendered a proposed agreement that Boslover was required to sign which included the following language: "The Owner (Boslover) agrees that the uses permitted on subject premises will be restricted to functions sponsored by or on behalf of duly elected members of the Boslover Association. The owner further agrees that subject premises will not be used, leased or rented to nonmembers of the Association or for meetings, gatherings, parties, dances or functions at which nonmembers will be present."

The provision could be read to mean that a nonmember could be the Bar Mitzvah boy or the wife or other relative of a member and that a nonmember, even the Bar Mitzvah boy, could not enter the hall. Boslover brought suit. The Supreme Court of Pennsylvania, in a 4-3 decision, ruled against Boslover on a narrow point of civil procedure. Without the income from Bar Mitzvahs and weddings, Boslover could not afford to operate the building, and the hall was torn down. The lot has been vacant for over 30 years.[51]

Elizabetgrad Beneficial Association: 715 Pine Street. In December 1923, the Elizabetgrad Beneficial Association (EBA) gave up its rooms at 203 Pine Street and bought this three-story town house, which it kept until after World War II. The former residential property was converted into meeting rooms in 1924, and at one time the letters EBA could be seen on the marble lintel above the doorway.

In the early years of the EBA, balls were very popular social events and were well attended by the membership. The larger *landsmanschaftn*, like the one from Elizabetgrad, had sister organizations in other cities, mainly New York. Representatives of the Philadelphia EBA often went to New York to attend their balls and the New Yorkers came to Philadelphia. There was great camaraderie in these affairs.

Many *landsmanschaftn* were connected in some way with a synagogue, but the one from Elizabetgrad had no strong connection. Elizabetgrad itself had no famous yeshivas and it was not known for having produced renowned religious scholars. The absence of extreme piety was common to many places in southern Russia. Towns like Kremenchug, Odessa, Ekaterinoslav, Elizabetgrad, Nikolayev, Kherson - towns that populated Philadelphia with its former residents - were not primarily settled by ultra-religious Jews. In fact, just the opposite was true. *Litvaks*, eager to escape from what they viewed as Jewish religious domination of their lives in the early part of the 19th century, anxious to be assimilated in the general Russian population, and driven to make a better economic life for their families and themselves, left the northern part of Russia from 1810 to 1860 to settle in the frontier towns of the south of Russia and, while synagogues and houses of study were built in the new towns of the southern parts of Russia, traditional religious practices did not stifle those who sought a more assimilated way of life.

But neither Jewish religious practices on the one hand, nor the anti-religious attraction of assimilation bound the immigrant members of the Elizabetgrad Beneficial Association together. Rather, the doing of *maysim toyvim* (good deeds), learned by members in their youth, bound such organizations tightly together. Fund raising for the poor, needy, sick, and elderly, in the United States and in Russia, and the performance of acts of loving kindness, were viewed by the brotherhood of the EBA, and other brotherhoods and ladies' auxiliaries, as the reason for their existence. This was especially true during World War I, the Russian Revolution, and the breakdown of law and order in the Soviet Union following the Revolution.

The meeting rooms for the EBA were places where one could go in his loneliness. It was a place where one could joke and cry in Yiddish, although by 1928, on its thirty-fifth anniversary, members of the Elizabetgrad Beneficial Association were already having a difficult time recreating the enthusiasm of the early years.[52] In more recent years, the EBA sold burial plots to three Philadelphia cemeteries. The members paid dues for years so that they would be assured of a place amongst the brotherhood. The EBA sold the property here on

Pine Street in 1960, and merged with two other chevras to form the UJO (United Jewish Organization), a weak confederation of former vibrant *landsmanschaftn*. Today, the property is a private residence.

The Home of Rabbi Levinthal: 716 Pine Street. The town house of Rabbi Bernard L. Levinthal, the unofficial city hall of the Jewish quarter, was erected between 1808 and 1809. The Beth Harov Association gave this city house to Rabbi Levinthal on June 27, 1900, and the gift was celebrated in a week-long ceremony. Every evening the new home was filled with visitors who came to congratulate the young rabbi and wish him the best. In the early years of this century, the Levinthal home was the center of immigrant Jewish religious life in the city of Philadelphia.

Levinthal's grandson has left us a description of the house and of his famous grandfather:

> Although grandpa lived in the house, and the house was in a residential section of Philadelphia, it had assumed the character of a public building - a small town city hall wherein a group might meet informally in one room and another group conduct an arbitration proceeding across the hall. Adjacent to the living room was what once must have been the dining room. It was in this room that grandpa held court. Beyond this room was a slightly smaller room in which there was a large table covered with a cloth and on the table there was always a large salad bowl, bread and butter and condiments, including *chrane* [horseradish] for gefulte fish. It was here that Philadelphia could boast of a dining table that was open to all, seven days a week. At least eight or ten chairs were set around the table, and anyone wishing to eat had but to seat himself and a rotund, good-natured cook named Mollie would emerge from the kitchen and inquire in Yiddish what she should serve.[53]

Louis Feinberg, a Philadelphia rabbi, wrote about his youth. One Sunday morning, the busiest time of the week for a rabbi, Feinberg chanced to visit Levinthal's home in company with another member of the Aids of Zion. The office was filled with people who came on all manner of business - litigants, travelers, *shokhtim*, authors, prospective bridegrooms, etc.:

> Yet the Rabbi greeted us heartily. "Have you read such and such an article in Ha-Zefirah?" he asked. We told him we had not. "You ought to read it; it is excellent," he said, and hurried into another room and brought the paper in question. My friend and I took the paper and began to plow through the recommended article, which was written in typically modern Hebrew. We were making fine headway but the rabbi was not satisfied to stand aloof. He moved closer to us, translated a rare word here, explained a difficult passage there, and kept up an illuminating running commentary all through. For more than a half hour he sat with us in the large dining room, while impatient litigants in the office were sitting on the edges of their chairs, nervously tapping the floor with their feet and biting their lips with impatience. Several times the rabbi's factotum tip-toed into the room to see what was keeping the rabbi, but he dared not interrupt. To give us an informal lesson in modern Hebrew literature stood above regular business.[54]

Manuel F. Lisan, a young Zionist who recently arrived in Philadelphia, invited Rabbi Levinthal to be the first Friday evening lecturer at the Zion Institute for 1904-1905. The announcement that Rabbi Levinthal would speak was a delightful surprise to the young Zionists. Lisan went to Levinthal's home to escort him to the Zion Institute on Pine Street: "To our embarrassment we came to Rabbi Levinthal's home, when the family and their guest, Rabbi Brodsky from Newark, N.J. were in the midst of singing Zimiros, having a real Oneg-Sabbath. The familiar melodies touched my heart, reminding me of the Zimiros we sang at my parents table on Friday evenings." The rebbitzin came out from the dining room and asked the boys to join in, but they were reticent to do so and declined the offer. "We slowly began to retire into the living room, however, Rabbi Levinthal heard my voice. He immediately came out asking me to wait a few minutes when he will be ready to accompany us to the Zion Institute."[55]

Rabbi Levinthal's son Israel has also left a loving remembrance:

> Our home was a focal point for most of the rabbis in the country. As soon as a rabbi arrived in America, before he settled in any post, he would come to our home, to get father's advice and guidance. There was no Jewish hotel and no kosher restaurant in Philadelphia, so our home was their hotel and their restaurant. It was a veritable hachnosas orchim, a wayfarer's house, where a warm welcome was offered to everyone who came. I cannot recall a time when the door of the dining room was not wide open, or the tablecloth removed. A warm invitation *"kumt essen,"* [come, eat] greeted all who entered.[56]

The Levinthal family sold the property on January 12, 1952. It is a private residence today.

LOMBARD STREET

Abraham's Hotel: 218-220 Lombard Street. In the early years, immigrants disembarked from steamers at the foot of Christian Street or Washington Avenue and, unable to find lodging in town, or afraid to attempt to go into town, some simply slept with their few belongings at the wharves on the river front. Four Jewish women from the immigrant population, Clara Levitsky, Sima Ginz, Deborah Spivakovsky (the mother of Dr. Charles D. Spivak), and Chasya Levitsky, shocked that the newly arriving immigrants had to sleep at the wharves, established what was called in Hebrew, a *Hakhnosses Orkhim* (Hospitality to Strangers), or in English, a Wayfarer's Home. The home was chartered at 430 Lombard Street on April 29, 1891, and was known as Abraham's Hotel. It was a place where the newly arrived immigrants could lay their heads until friends or relatives could be located or until arrangements could be made to obtain railroad tickets to bring them to their final destination in the United States. Y. L. Malamut, the historian of the Jewish quarter in the 1940's, identified Abraham's Hotel as "[t]he most beloved [Jewish] institution in Philadelphia." In 1902, 500 "old-fashioned, kind-hearted, Yiddish-speaking, sheitel-crowned mothers" of the neighborhood ran it.[57]

Abraham's Hotel moved here next to a fish and meat market in the summer of 1891 and remained until 1908. Transients numbered from three to sixty a day. To obtain food for the starvelings, women volunteers started out each morning pushing a cart: "They would comb the streets where Jews lived and solicit fish, kosher meat, bread, and other necessities from Jewish bakers, grocery store owners, and butchers. Once the push carts were loaded, they hurried back to their headquarters at 218 Lombard Street where their hungry guests waited."

Over ten thousand free meals were served during the first two years. At first, the *Hakhnosses Orkhim* occupied but one floor; later it occupied the entire building; and finally it occupied 218 and 220 Lombard Street. Dr. Spivak attended the sick, and David Moses, 305 Gaskill Street, a *mohel*, performed marriages and circumcisions. Meals were served in the basement dining room. On *Shabbes* long tables were covered with clean white tablecloths, and scrubbed benches were placed at each table. A synagogue occupied the greater part of the first floor, and services were held three times a day. The long-time superintendent and reader at the synagogue was David G. Kratzok. The rooms on the upper floors were used as bedrooms. The larger rooms contained six single iron bedsteads, and clothes were hung on hooks.

In 1898, Anna Blitzstein, the owner of the Blitzstein bank, founded a *Moyshev Zkeynim* (Old People's Home) here. She served as president of both the Old People's Home and the Wayfarer's Home, known collectively as the Sheltering Homes, in the years 1897-1898, 1900, 1905, 1915 and 1916. With the financial backing of Wolf Klebansky, the Sheltering Homes moved to 315-317 S. 3rd Street in 1908.

During Redevelopment, the entire 200 block of Lombard Street was torn down to make way for new buildings and parking lots.

Congregation Kesher Israel: 412-418 Lombard Street. Pressed between two city houses stands the crown jewel of the Jewish quarter. No building described in the guide can compare to it in historical importance.

On July 30, 1793, a plot of ground west of Delaware 4th Street on Lombard was deeded in trust to seven Universalists, believers in universal salvation, for the erection of a meeting house. One of the trustees was Israel Israel (1745-1822), the High Sheriff of Philadelphia for four years. Israel was the son of Michael Israel, a Jew, and Mary J. Paxton, a member of the Episcopal Church.[58] Soon after the purchase, members of the Universalist church began to erect the building seen here today, but in the autumn of the year yellow fever struck and 10 percent of the population of Philadelphia died. The epidemic and "money troubles" caused work on the church to be suspended and the building was not completed for three years. Laid out laterally along the south side of Lombard Street, the pulpit - made by a "mast-maker and a shoemaker" - was placed on the south wall (by 1836 the pulpit had been moved to the west wall). As built, the church had no galleries. A cellar under the entire building, used as a place for storage of liquor and groceries in general, yielded revenue for the newly formed congregation. The walls were without plaster and the seats were plain benches. The entrance was by two doors on Lombard Street near the west end. It is not known if the building was free-standing as built.[59]

Joseph Priestley (1733-1804), the world-famous English scientist (who in 1771 isolated oxygen) and a Unitarian theologian, immigrated to America and settled in Northumberland in northern Pennsylvania. He

Congregation Kesher Israel, 412–418 Lombard Street, circa 1940. Northern wall roughcast directly over brick along Lombard Street, with four stained-glass windows. The J. Franklin Stuckert Romanesque/Colonial Revival Pompeian entrance (left) was added in 1896.

Courtesy of the Historical Society of Pennsylvania, Philadelphia, Pennsylvania came to Philadelphia and learned of the little Universalist church on Lombard Street. On Sunday morning, February 14, 1796, not being admitted to preach Unitarian theology anywhere else in Philadelphia, he began a series of lectures here at the new, but not yet dedicated, building of the Universalists. The press stated that he delivered a "most excellent discourse" before a congregation that was so numerous the church building could not contain them, so that "many were obliged to stand as sit, and even the doorways were crowded with people."[60] The capital of the United States was then in Philadelphia and among Priestley's regular attendants was Vice President John Adams.[61] Priestley himself described the audience as respectful and attentive and stated that he was told the "greater part of the members of Congress are my hearers and intend to continue so."[62] The following year he began a second series of discourses, but by this time the Unitarians had moved their place of worship to the Chapel of "the University" (the University of Pennsylvania, 4th and Arch Streets) and there is no evidence that Priestley again used the Universalist Church.[63]

In 1834, the Universalists erected a Sunday School here and, several years later, the name of the church was changed to the First Universalist Church. The highlight of the 1830's was a speech given here by Joseph Smith, the founder of the Mormon Church. Speaking here, Smith "astounded" and "electrified" his audience.[64] Further improvements continued to be made until the late sixties ; but, beginning in the Centennial decade, the building fell into disuse.[65]

The first Jewish congregation to use the building was Chevra B'nai Jacob. On November 28, 1887, the Universalists received an offer from B'nai Jacob to buy the building, including a small burial ground on the south side of the property. B'nai Jacob requested that the bodies buried on the grounds be removed.[66] After the request was satisfied, the Jews took possession of the building and B'nai Jacob was dedicated on Sunday, June 9, 1889. Sabato Morais opened the ceremonies with prayer and made a few remarks. Rev. Iliowizi, the newly elected rabbi at Adath Jeshurun, addressed the congregation in German; Rabbi Israel Moses Sachs from B'nai Abraham spoke in Yiddish; and Jacob Singer, Esq., later the Register of Wills of Philadelphia (1901-1904), spoke in English. "The membership of the congregation is one hundred strong, all from Russia."[67]

"Notice. It is made known with the knowledge of the president and the trustees of Kesher Israel. Whoever has *yahrzeit* and is not a member must give 50 cents to the synagogue. Also, it is made known that no one may go up to lead a service without the permission of the *gabbaim* or the sexton. House Committee."

Photograph by Fred Wagner

Rabbi Chaim Shraga Brodsky, one of the first Zionist rabbis to emigrate to the United States from Eastern Europe, was chosen rabbi at B'nai Jacob. Born in Slonim, White Russia, in 1853, he studied in the yeshivas of his hometown and afterwards at Volozhin. He became a jewelry merchant but was not successful at this work. Blessed with a talent for preaching, he went from town to town, eventually coming to the United States and to B'nai Jacob.[68] The cantor at B'nai Jacob was Mordecai Schatz. At this time Brodsky and Rabbi Levinthal founded the Talmud Torah and the Chevra Kadisha. In 1894, B'nai Jacob and Rodeph Tsedek-Anshe Szager merged and took the name Kesher Israel. Upon the merger, Brodsky left to become the editor of the *Stadt-Zeitung*, 710 S. 3rd Street.[69]

Less than two years later, the well-known architect J. Franklin Stuckert was retained by Kesher Israel to make extensive exterior and interior renovations. At the eastern end of the building the present Romanesque Revival entrance with Pompeian brick and a stair-hall pavilion were added. Separate doors were provided for men and women within the arch of the entranceway. Immediately inside the building, the women used the stairway to reach the gallery. Also added was a pressed metal minaret on the roof "influenced by Moorish design." The exterior bricks were covered in roughcast. A two-story schoolhouse was constructed on the adjoining lot.

Inside, the main sanctuary received a pressed tin ceiling. A large centered gas-lighted brass and crystal chandelier and four smaller chandeliers were decorated with glass pendants and ornaments. A curved *Ezras Noshim* (women's gallery) was added and the front was decorated with gilded wreaths. The entire interior was redecorated in pale green and buff and the seating capacity was increased to 600 downstairs and 250 upstairs.[70] "At the front of the synagogue is a platform raised about two and a half feet above the main floor. It is surrounded by an iron fence railing four feet high, and contains the altar, reading desk, chairs and tables. Back of the altar is placed against the wall the cabinet containing the parchment copies of the Ten Commandments, covered with red velvet with gold ornamentation, above this is a cluster of five lights, the center one having a red globe, surmounted by a star-shaped reflector. The windows are of stained glass with Hebrew inscriptions."[71]

Congregation Kesher Israel was dedicated on Sunday, January 24, 1897. On the bimah was Rev. Dr. Sabato Morais, beginning the last year of his remarkable life.[72] No Jew in the established Jewish community of Philadelphia in the last two decades of the 19th century gave more of himself or herself to the east European Jewish immigrants than Morais. The Rev. Dr. Marcus Jastrow, emeritus rabbi of Rodeph Shalom Congregation addressed the huge throng in German. Zvi Hirsch Masliansky, the famous *matif* from Slutsk, Russia, who spoke in Yiddish, followed him.

At the turn of the last century and during the early years of this century, two rabbis were associated with Kesher Israel: Zvi Hirsch Masliansky and Bernard L. Levinthal. Masliansky was invited to be the main speaker at the dedication with the thought given to inviting him to become the rabbi. He was a great advocate of Zionist causes his entire life, had a commanding presence, and his fiery rhetoric was well known to the immigrants of Philadelphia before he immigrated in 1895. He was in the United States about a year when he made his first trip to Philadelphia. Unlike other immigrants, who viewed Philadelphia as a port city and left within a day or two, or settled here and made it their home, he visited the city and saw it as a tourist.

And as a tourist he visited the most important places of interest to a Jew in 1896, including the Court of Common Pleas, No. 2, of Philadelphia County. "I became inspired," he wrote, "when my same friend [Levinthal] led me into the courthouse. He did not explain to me beforehand who the judge was. He told me he only wanted to show me an American Judge, how he sits and dispenses justice." Masliansky continued: "I considered the judge as he sat in his justice robes upon the high bench. I noticed the judge's eyes. They were large, clear, black; his round head covered with dark, black curly hair, the lovely grace on his brown countenance, the small smile on his lips, the keen, wise glance each time on the man who stood before him to answer questions. This lively picture made me very curious and quietly I asked: *'Zogt mir nor, ikh bet aykh, iz der rikhter nit a yid?'* [Just tell me, I beg you, is the judge not a Jew?]"

"I was waiting for you to ask this question," answered Levinthal with a smile: "I wanted to see if you, as a newly arrived Jew from dark Russia, a land in which a Jew is forbidden to be a postman, or an official street sweeper, would recognize a Jew in a judge's robe sitting on a judge's bench? Yes, my friend, you did recognize him, the judge is really a Jew and what a Jew! A great religious scholar and a great scholar in Jewish studies who is interested in all Jewish matters! He studies a page of Talmud and writes Hebrew. He has one of the greatest Jewish libraries and generously assists Jewish writers, poor religious scholars and poets 'with a full hand.' I believe you must have heard his name while still in Europe, Judge Mayer Sulzberger."[73]

Within the Zionist movement, Philadelphia was one of the first cities to develop a following, and Kesher Israel was the central focus of that early development. Not only was Kesher Israel the leading Zionist synagogue in Philadelphia, during its early years, it was used as the principal meeting hall for the larger Zionist gatherings. A rally here in October 1897 on behalf of the newly formed Ohavei Zion (Friends of Zion) was called to review the proceedings at the first Zionist Congress at Basle, Switzerland, six weeks earlier and to enlist new members.[74] Speakers at the rally included the Rev. Dr. S. Schaffer of Baltimore, a delegate at Basle, who advocated creating a national fund for the purchase of land in Palestine, and Masliansky, who spoke in what the *Exponent* described as "pure Hebrew." At Masliansky's urging, three hundred new members were enlisted at the meeting. At a late hour, Kesher Israel was vacated and "five score Zionists" escorted the two guests, Schaffer and Masliansky, to the *sukkah* (booth) of Rabbi Levinthal, where a "lunch" was served and where Hebrew-Zionistic songs were sung (Levinthal then lived at 534 Pine Street, directly to the rear of B'nai Abraham). The enthusiastic assembly of young Zionists lasted until four o'clock Sunday morning.

One hundred and seven years after Philadelphians crowded the doorway of the building to hear Dr. Priestley speak, and sixty-four years after Joseph Smith, the founder of the Mormon Church, drew 3,000 followers, Abraham Cahan, the beloved editor of the *Jewish Daily Forward*, addressed one of the first mass meetings of east European Jews in Philadelphia here. "The audience was so large that many could get no farther than the pavement, the building being jammed to the doors." This meeting was called on Sunday, May 3, 1903, to hear the news of the recent pogroms in Kishinev. Besides Cahan, Rabbis Levinthal, Masliansky, and Abraham H. Erschler (the rabbi at Anshe Shavel), spoke. Abraham Cahan said: "He [Cahan], the leader of the socialists, known as the infidel, the heretic, stands now in an orthodox synagogue and preaches from the same pulpit with Rev. Masliansky and Rabbi Levinthal."[75] Just over one year later, the immigrants were again brought together here in tragedy.

On July 4, 1904, the day after Theodor Herzl died, a special meeting of the Council of Zionists in Philadelphia was held at the Zion Institute. Delegates from local Zionist societies called for a memorial meeting to honor the memory of Herzl. The following Sunday, approximately five hundred members of the Young Workers' of Zion assembled at the Institute on Pine Street and, bearing American and "Zionist" flags, they marched to Kesher Israel. Inside the synagogue, the crowd was so great that the aisles were a solid mass of humanity. The platform was draped and at the front of the synagogue was a large portrait of Herzl.

Although Masliansky did not have any formal connection with Kesher Israel after 1899, he kept close ties, even after he agreed to give regular Friday evening sermons at the Educational Alliance in New York. The speech he gave at Kesher Israel on Sunday, January 24, 1909, is an example of his devotion to the synagogue and Zionism. The United Zionists of Philadelphia, including representatives of the Ohavei Zion, Keneseth Zion, Aids of Zion, and the Maccabean Zion Society called the meeting. Chaired by David B. Tierkel, the editor of the *Philadelphia Jewish American*, the meeting was addressed in German by Professor Max Margolis, who exhorted his listeners to be Zionists for the sake of their children; by Dr. Benjamin L. Gordon, who appealed to those present to purchase the shekel, the self-imposed national Jewish tax on every Jew in the world; and by the orator of the day, Masliansky, who declared that the country of the Jews was not a nation, but something far more exalted: an international republic.

Rabbi Bernard L. Levinthal, who is remembered as the rabbi at B'nai Abraham, was also the rabbi here. His affiliation came about as follows. In 1912, Kesher Israel was identified in the Philadelphia press as one of the most influential congregations of "Orthodox Hebrews" in the city. Although Kesher Israel had pursued Levinthal to become its rabbi for a number of years, Levinthal stated he would not accept the post unless it were offered to him unanimously. At that time Levinthal had jurisdiction over ten Hebrew congregations, the smaller ones being run by his appointees. During the kosher meat dispute in 1911, Levinthal championed the use of Philadelphia-dressed meats for the Jews of Philadelphia. This was a popular position with a large segment of the Jewish community and, based on Levinthal's unwavering stand, Kesher Israel unanimously chose him as its rabbi.[76]

In March 1939, the congregation of Kesher Israel voted to identify itself as a Conservative Synagogue, the first in the Jewish quarter (and in South Philadelphia) to join the Conservative movement. The following year, Rabbi Joseph Hillel Snapir (1892-1971) was engaged as the rabbi. Snapir, born in Warsaw and educated at yeshivas in Novo Minsk and Lomza, Poland, immigrated to the United States and settled in Brooklyn prior to coming to Kesher Israel. He was the rabbi at Kesher Israel for thirty years and brought the old building back to life. Snapir conducted the children's Hebrew school, served as the cantor and choirmaster, and taught adult Talmudic sessions weekday evenings. During the time that Snapir was at Kesher Israel, men and women prayed together except for those women who voluntarily chose to gather in the gallery. He was a member of the *Bet Din, Vaad Hakashruth*, and the Board of Rabbis of Philadelphia. During the years that Snapir was here, Morris Balk painted murals depicting the Exile in Babylon, the Return to Israel, and other scenes of ancient Israel. During the late seventies, a strong synagogue board of directors - Abe Mersky and his brothers, Harry Singer, Jack Miller and Professor Davinsky - led the congregation. They successfully staved off real estate developers who were hungry to turn the property into multiple housing units. It is truly remarkable that such a fragile treasure has survived.[77]

Rabbi Joseph Hillel Snapir.
The rabbi at Kesher Israel from 1940 to 1971.
Courtesy of Moishe Snapir

In more recent years there has been a renaissance at the synagogue, including the refurbishment of the building and its trappings. Among the leaders of the congregation are Dr. Michael Yaron, Norman Millan, Rick Millan, and Abe Mersky. A new pressed tin ceiling in cheerful blue and white colors was installed; artist Craig Britton reinterpreted the faded Balk murals; the brass chandeliers were brought to life with new crystals; a hardwood floor was added on the gallery level; the four towering stained-glass windows on the north wall were restored; and the walls and old-style wooden benches were refinished. The leadership was recognized by a proud congregation on Sunday, September 13, 1998, when the building was rededicated. Heartfelt speeches by Mayor Edward G. Rendell, Michael Yaron, and Abe Mersky highlighted the day.

Today, on Rosh Hashana and Yom Kippur, you will find the synagogue crowded with a new generation of observant Jews, worshipping in a building over two hundred years old. For information concerning services or membership, contact the synagogue.

Maimonides Clinic: 419 Lombard Street (North side). One month after opening across the street, the Maimonides Clinic (named for the 12th century Spanish rabbi, physician and philosopher) moved here to the second floor in June 1891. Charles D. Spivak and Ludwig Loeb opened the clinic to provide poor Jews with proper medical care. The clinic, open for both medical and surgical treatment, saw an average of fifty patients a week. When necessary, the doctors visited patients at their homes. A drug store on the premises dispensed drugs for 20¢ a prescription. In June of 1893, the clinic moved to the southeast corner of 5th & Spruce Streets.[78] The entire north side of the 400 block of Lombard Street was torn down in 1965.

Book Store of Moses Freeman: 429 Lombard Street. In 1888, Moses Freeman, the historian of the Russian Jews of Philadelphia, opened a bookstore here. Like another great Jewish historian of that time, Simon Dubnow, Moses Freeman not only wrote the history of his people, he lived it.[79] Freeman was born in Odessa, Russia, in 1859 and attended *kheyder* until the age of twelve. After witnessing the pogrom of 1871 in Odessa, Freeman's father sent him to the Hassidic Romanovka Yeshiva. He next attended the modern Groyse Yeshiva in Odessa. After his studies, he married at age nineteen and upon witnessing the pogroms following the assassination of Alexander II, he immigrated to America in May 1882 as part of the *Am Olam* movement. Freeman spent two years at the Vineland, New Jersey, agricultural colony and then came to Philadelphia. He stayed a short time and left in 1884 to work in a woolen mill in Lisbon Falls, Maine, where he met Charles D. Spivak. In the summer of 1886, Freeman returned to Philadelphia and, for the next fifty years, like his fellow immigrants, he struggled to make a living.

After a life spent in Philadelphia as a newspaper publisher, a storeowner on South Street and a representative of New York newspapers, Freeman wrote *Fifty Years of Jewish Life in Philadelphia,* the history of his people. His writings show a remarkable insight into the society of which he was a part. He understood the harsh reality of the early years in the New Jersey agricultural colonies; he knew the loneliness of a factory in Maine; he understood the jealousies of the South Street merchants; he knew the damage that the anarchists and other radicals caused to the Jewish religion, and he knew the magic that Boris Thomashevsky created at the theatre.

Bershad's Russian and Turkish Baths: 436-442 Lombard Street. Nathan Bershadsky, born in 1850 in Elizabetgrad, immigrated to the United States in 1886 with his large family. The Bershadsky (Bershad) family opened a Russian and Turkish bathhouse here in 1895, or possibly earlier, and different family members owned and operated it for many years. Inside, it was decorated throughout with blue and white tiles in the mosaic style.

Bathhouses were expensive to operate because repairs and renovations were constantly required.[80] In 1913, a chimney here had to be removed from the basement and a new one built. In 1914, a support for a 4,000-gallon tank had to be constructed and, in 1918, a two-story rear brick addition was added at an estimated cost of $3,000. In later years, Bershad's was a popular place for Jewish basketball players after a game at the Broadwood Hotel. Area businessmen used Bershad's, and it was a busy meeting place into the middle 1960's. A favorite at Bershad's, and at all the bathhouses, was poker and pinochle. It was played on Saturday late into the night. Shortly before it closed, the name of the bathhouse was changed to the Society Hill Baths. The bathhouse was torn down in 1970 or 1971. Today the properties are private residences.

B'nai Abraham: 521-527 Lombard Street. Chevra B'nai Avrohom Mi Russe (Society of Sons of Abraham from Russia) was founded by seventeen Lithuanian Jews on October 1, 1882.[81] Known in Yiddish as the *Russishe shul* and in English as B'nai Abraham, it was the first Russian *chevra* founded in the Jewish quarter. The immigrants came here to recite the *goyml* (prayer of thanks) after making safe passage across the Atlantic Ocean. Before there was a wayfarer's inn or a relief society in immigrant Jewish Philadelphia, B'nai Abraham fed the hungry; and the homeless, who came straight from the Christian Street wharf, found a place to lay their weary limbs. Later the immigrants gathered here to learn the fate of loved ones in the pogroms and the Russian Civil War. Occupying this site for 114 years in two buildings - the first, built as a church, and the present, built as a synagogue - B'nai Abraham was the soul of the Jewish quarter during the immigrant years, and today it is the center of a vibrant Orthodox way of life.

By the summer of 1885, B'nai Abraham had grown from seventeen original members to two hundred, and it made arrangements to rent Liberty Hall, 716-718 Lombard Street for the High Holy Days. The rent was paid in advance but a dispute arose with the owner of the hall, Mr. Still, over the use of a room and damage to furniture. When the landlord levied on the Torah scrolls as security for damage to the property, B'nai Abraham sued in Common Pleas court. Without waiting for the outcome of the litigation, the congregation agreed to purchase the First Colored Wesley Methodist Church, 521-527 Lombard Street.[82]

The beginnings of the first building used by B'nai Abraham at 521-527 Lombard Street go back to 1820. A splinter group of African Americans broke away from Mother Bethel around the corner on Delaware 6th Street and formed the Wesley Church.[83] A carpenter's shop on the lot was torn down and on September 13, 1820, work was started on a two-story "neat brick edifice." Except for the galleries, it was completed in several months and consecrated on Sunday, December 24, 1820. Galleries were constructed the following year. It was a freestanding structure that could seat 800 persons, fronting on and set back from the building line on Lombard Street.[84] The rectangular building, oriented lengthwise north and south, had lintel-type window heads, thin muntins, a smooth brick facade, and a classic frontispiece. The main architectural feature was a lunette (with tracery) in the south gable facing Lombard Street, perhaps containing stained glass. Because of the building's relatively large size and its importance within the AME Zion Church movement, it was used as the location of the Philadelphia Annual Conferences for almost thirty years. By 1885, the church had grown in membership. It turned its sights west of Broad Street, and the building was sold to B'nai Abraham, the first congregation of east European Jews south of Market Street to own a building.

At the dedication ceremonies, held on Sunday, December 6, 1885, President Silverman introduced Rev. Ingleblatt, who spoke in Yiddish, chanted the prayers, and was assisted by a male choir of eight voices. The joy of the membership knew no bounds: "Not one of them considered traveling to peddle in the country to earn their meager food. For an entire week, day and night, they danced and rejoiced continuously. Many of them slept in the building on the hard benches in order not to part from the synagogue which they bought with the money that they earned with their bloody sweat, peddling in the country with heavy packs of cheap wares."

The charter of B'nai Abraham, approved by the Court of Common Pleas on January 23, 1883, provides that the object of the synagogue is the "worship of Almighty God according to the orthodox ritual of the Jewish Church, the accumulation of a fund by dues and assessments from its members for their protection and benefit in case of sickness or disability, to provide for the interment of deceased members wives and children and the support of members during any period of mourning." To implement the charter, B'nai Abraham issued by-laws that provided the rules under which the synagogue operates.[85] These by-laws, as much as any contemporaneous document, help us understand the day-to-day life of our forefathers.

Meetings at B'nai Abraham were conducted in Yiddish. This rule was amended only recently. Rules governing admittance to membership were rigid. Every candidate had to have been in the country for at least six months and, if married, the marriage must have been performed according to Jewish custom. The prospective candidate had to earn a decent living for himself and his family. Candidates could be admitted if over twenty years of age, but not older than forty-five. Admission of candidates to membership was voted by secret ballot. Black and white balls were deposited in a small wooden box. If, after balloting, there were three black balls in the box, the prospective candidate was rejected, or "black-balled." He could apply again but first had to wait six months. If there were two black balls, the decision on admission to membership was referred to the president.[86]

Once admitted, a member could be fined for infractions of the rules. If a member were called to say *tehilim* (Psalms) at the side of a seriously ill member and he did not appear, he could be fined 25¢. If a gabbai was absent without a good excuse, he could be fined 25¢. The sexton was required to clean the synagogue and see that everything was in order; punishment for non-performance could be dismissal. A member who did not attend a general or special meeting could be fined 50¢. A member who did not attend a funeral could be fined $1.

The rules also addressed benefits. Sick benefits, payable at the rate of $5 a week, could be paid as long as the sickness was not caused by "drunkenness or other immoral behavoir." Assistance to sick members was provided by the brotherhood. Two *shomrim* (night watchmen or assistants) were to be on hand from 10 P.M. to 6 A.M. to say *tehilim*. When a child from six months to four years was sick, only one *shomer* was sent. Benefits from the *chevra*, though barely minimal, were the sole benefits the immigrant had for his family and himself upon sickness or death, and they were highly valued. But the average day was not spent receiving benefits or paying fines.

The average day was spent in prayer. Prayers were then, and still are, said three times a day at B'nai Abraham, evening prayers being said at dusk. During the immigration period, Yom Kippur services began at dawn and worshippers prayed in their stocking feet. The night of Yom Kippur was passed in the recitation of Psalms. On *Shabbes*, in several of the downtown synagogues, the buildings were packed an hour before services began. But B'nai Abraham, like all the synagogues, was used for more than a house of prayer.

When toughs assaulted Jews who lived near Washington Avenue, B'nai Abraham became a house of assembly.[87] At a meeting held here on August 15, 1891, Sabato Morais, serving as the leader of immigrant Jewish Philadelphia until Rabbi Levinthal arrived several weeks later, attempted to dissuade his Russian Jewish listeners from organizing societies and clubs for their own protection. Morais explained that the law of

The synagogue is not the "Sons of Jacob" as stated under the original of this 1890 photograph, but is the building of B'nai Abraham, 521–527 Lombard Street (1885–1909). The building was constructed in 1820 for the Wesley church and the church occupied it until 1885. It is the only known photograph of this vernacular Greek Revival building.

Courtesy of the National Museum of American Jewish History, Philadelphia, Pennsylvania

the land would protect them and afford them the same rights afforded to everyone else. Russian Jews, especially those coming from the southern part of Russia, were accustomed to forming their own defense forces because of the pogroms they experienced before coming to America.[88] They listened to Morais but were not convinced. At a second meeting on the same subject several weeks later, the building was densely packed. Premeeting circulars informed the immigrants that a society would be formed to protect the downtown Hebrews.[89] Attending the second meeting were Bernard Harris and Dr. Charles D. Spivak. When an advocate for self-defense became rash in his suggestions, Harris rose and demanded to be heard. He spoke with fervor and warmth, counseling the crowd that in America it was wrong to take up arms as a Jewish group. Harris advised the crowd that they were proceeding in the wrong direction, and he said that defense clubs and other such organizations solely Jewish were to be condemned. He advised the throng, however, to be careful in their honor as Jews, asking them to defend themselves when assaulted or insulted and not stand by and "experience that to which others would not submit."

Besides being a house of prayer and a house of assembly, B'nai Abraham was also a house of study *(besmedresh)*. The study house, attached to the synagogue building, was most likely the former Sabbath Sunday School of the Wesley Church. The first *chevra gemora* (Talmud study group) in the city was formed here. Before 1927, the entire Talmud was studied here three times under Rabbi Zelig Sacks and once under Rabbi Aaron Radin (it takes an average of seven and one-half years to complete the Talmud once, but this period can be increased or decreased depending on the rate of progress). There was also a *chevra mishnayes*, a group that studied the mishna, the collection of the oral law, the basis of the Talmud; a *chevra eyn Yaakov*, a group that studied the legends of the Bible; a *chevra mikra*, a group that studied the Bible, and a *chevra tehilim*, a group that recited Psalms. The last two groups met only on the Sabbath, but the others met every evening except Friday and attendance was large.

The first two rabbis of B'nai Abraham, Israel Moshe Sacks (1886-1889) and Eleazer Kleinberg (1889-1891), although chosen while they were still in their early fifties, died after serving the congregation for only short periods. On September 1, 1889, Kleinberg was also chosen to be the rabbi at B'nai Reuben and Ahavas Chesed-Anshe Shavel, thus bringing about the result suggested several years earlier in the *Exponent* editorial. At the bottom of page three of the *Jewish Exponent* in its edition of October 2, 1891, a small notice appeared announcing that at a special service at B'nai Abraham, the new rabbi, Baer "Lowenthal" (sic), who had arrived from Russia a few days before, delivered his first address in Jargon, the word used by the English-language press at the time to describe the Yiddish language. This is the first mention of Rabbi Bernard L. Levinthal in Philadelphia. In 1945, Rabbi C. David Matt wrote, "The story of Levinthal's ministry is the story of Philadelphia Jewry of the past fifty-four years and, in a measure, also of Orthodox Jewry throughout America."[90]

Rabbi Bernard L. Levinthal, 1906. Rabbi at B'nai Abraham from 1891 to 1952.

Courtesy of the Philadelphia Jewish Archives Center

Rabbi Bernard L. Levinthal was born in Srednick, Kovno, Lithuania, on May 12, 1865, although other dates are given for his birth. Known as an *ilui* (a young genius), Levinthal received his rabbinical diplomas from Rabbi Isaac Elhanan Spector and Rabbi Samuel Mohilever in 1886. The same year he married Minna Kleinberg, the daughter of Rabbi Kleinberg, the second rabbi at B'nai Abraham. From the time Levinthal arrived in Philadelphia, until his death in September 1952, he did everything he could to further the cause of Judaism and the interests of the Jewish people, in Philadelphia, throughout the country, and in Europe.

He was a superb organizer and as early as 1902 he founded, or helped to found, the following organizations: (in Philadelphia) the Hebrew Free School, the Home for Hebrew Orphans, the *chevra kadisha*, the Jewish Sheltering Homes, the Friends of Zion Society, the Mount Sinai Hospital, the Talmud Torah, and the Kosher Meat Association of Philadelphia; and (in New York) the forerunner of Yeshiva University and the American Conference of Orthodox Jewish Rabbis. He was also elected a vice president of the American Federation of Zionists. After 1902, he helped to found the American Jewish Committee, Brith Sholom, the American Jewish Congress, and other local and national organizations.

For over a half a century Levinthal battled assimilation. Wherever inroads into traditional Judaism were made, he was there to plug the hole, stem the tide, reverse the course. Whether it was the observance of *kashrus* (religious dietary laws) or the Sabbath, he was a relentless advocate of traditional Judaism in a world headed in another direction. If ever any Jew fought windmills, it was Levinthal. Today, Levinthal's outlook would classify him as "modern" rather than traditional. He advocated the teaching of secular subjects at the yeshiva, stressed the importance of political Zionism, and at his Hebrew High School, invited a conservative rabbi to teach. At best, it is difficult to put labels on a man of such breadth and vision.

On Rabbi Levinthal's 50th, 60th and 70th birthdays, gala celebrations were held.[91] He was recognized as the dean of the Orthodox Rabbinate of America. On his 80th birthday, celebrated in May 1945, Levinthal insisted that no celebration take place because the war was still in progress. From the day he came to Philadelphia from Kovno as a young rabbi, no person was better known to Russian Jewry in Philadelphia. His stance on kosher meat disputes early in the century lead to personal attacks against him by socialists and anarchists and even led to death threats, but he survived all challenges and today his name is held in the highest regard.

Of all the events that took place in the old church building between 1885 to 1909, none was more electrifying than a speech given by Zvi Hirsh Masliansky. The story is told by Dr. Israel Levinthal, a son of Rabbi Levinthal.

> I recall the night of his [Masliansky's] talk, and though I was only seven or eight years old, I accompanied my parents and the speaker to the Russishe Shul, where he was to speak. Though it was on a mid-week eve, we found the synagogue crowded to the doors. Men were standing in the aisles and on the window ledges - they even forced their way into the women's gallery. An admission fee was charged, and it is remarkable how so many of the audience who were poor paid the price so willingly in order to hear him. For almost two hours, Masliansky held the audience in a spell. Now he would have them laughing, and a few moments later they were sobbing. He was a master at picturing scenes and in extracting new meanings from Biblical tales. Young as I then was, I not only followed his address but was fascinated by it.[92]

B'nai Abraham, 1993. The synagogue is a hall with a gallery on three sides supported on six columns. A second tier of six columns carries a clerestory.

Photograph by Fred Wagner

By 1908, the *Russishe shul* wasn't large enough for the growing congregation. A design for a new building by Barnet J. Medoff, completed in December 1908, called for a brick structure, with stone trimmings, 48' x 80', in the Byzantine style of architecture.[93] These plans, if completed, have not survived, but even without the plans - and only from the proposed size of the building - it appears that such a building would not have accommodated the needs of a rapidly growing immigrant community. The reason the old building was finally torn down, however, was much more immediate. In early 1909, a part of the ceiling collapsed and services had to be conducted in the *besmedresh*, much to the discomfort of the worshippers and the study groups. A building committee was formed and on Monday, May 10, 1909, demolition work began. The old building was quickly torn down and a new building began to rise on the same lot. The corner laying ceremony for the new B'nai Abraham synagogue, the one standing today was held in sight of more than 1,200 people.[94] Congregants assembled at Poel Zedek Synagogue, 1011-1021 S. 5th Street, passed the other large synagogues as a body and, joined by delegations from these congregations, proceeded to march two abreast to 521-527 Lombard Street.

Dramatic in concept, the outstanding architectural features of the synagogue are the "Mogen David" rose windows on the north and south walls. Within the rose windows are tracery, geometric in design. Just as distinctive were a massive centered dome, mounted on a pedestal on the roof, and stair-tower domes (these were destroyed in a 1926 fire). High up on the Lombard Street facade, twin tablets of the law are set in the front gable. Designed by Charles W. Bolton,[95] the synagogue is modeled after the Pike Street Synagogue (Kalvarier shul, 15 Pike Street) in New York.[96] The Kalvarier shul and B'nai Abraham rise above a high basement. Both are fronted by twin lateral stairways leading to columned porticos, but the similarities end there. The Kalvarier synagogue had neither domes nor rose windows.

The new B'nai Abraham is 48' in width along Lombard Street and its east and west walls extend 135' to Addison Street. Twice as large as the old church, the new building was described as "Oriental in style of architecture" in one account and as "Romanesque, with an element of the Byzantine," in another, no doubt the domes and the rose windows accounting for the different style descriptions. The magnificent central dome dominated the building and the neighborhood. Inside, the hall on the second story is surrounded on three sides by a gallery, which is supported on six columns in the Doric Order.[97] A second tier of six columns supports a clerestory. The hall is divided and has two distinct seating arrangements. The front, or northern half, has benches running parallel to the side walls in the traditional style. Railing dividers front the first row of benches on either side. Benches in the rear half of the hall to the rear of the *bimah* run perpendicular to the side walls. The ark is on the northern wall, and the *bimah*, surrounded by dark wooden handrails and contrasting white-painted balusters, is in the center of the hall facing the ark. In 1910, the eastern wall was a party wall, and it therefore has no windows. The three-sided gallery can seat approximately four hundred women; a wooden balustrade that was curtained in the 1940's surrounds it.[98]

Funeral of Rabbi Bernard L. Levinthal, September 23, 1952.
Procession moving west on Lombard Street.

Courtesy of the Urban Archives, Temple University, Philadelphia, Pennsylvania

Built exclusively by Jewish workmen, the building was dedicated on Sunday, April 3, 1910. At the ceremonies, John E. Reyburn, mayor of Philadelphia and Dr. Cyrus Adler, president of Dropsie College, spoke. In his talk, Levinthal said:

> The B'nai Abraham Synagogue is the first and oldest Russian-Jewish synagogue in Philadelphia, founded twenty-seven years ago. In its early existence it served as an Hachnosos Orechim, a shelter for the immigrant and the stranger. Always has it stood for orthodox Judaism, the Judaism of our fathers. It is not only a place for prayer, but every evening there can be seen men, putting aside their business and professional interests, studying Talmud and the Midrash here in this building.[99]

Lightning during the early morning hours of July 25, 1926, started a fire on the roof of the five-story factory next-door, and the fire spread quickly to the synagogue. Thousands of people poured onto the narrow streets to watch even though lightning and a pelting rain continued. The domes, the galleries, and the chapel were severely damaged. Some thought the building should be torn down, but leaders of the community - Jacob Ginzburg, publisher of the *Yidishe Velt* and Martin O. Levi and Adolph Rosenblum of Brith Shalom - urged B'nai Abraham to remain on Lombard Street and rebuild. After raising $9,000 during the Yom Kippur appeal that year, including $5,000 from Joseph Nochem Suskin, the synagogue was rebuilt and rededicated on Sunday, April 3, 1927, seventeen years to the day from its original dedication.

Of special interest in the building are the *yahrzeit* boards in the social hall downstairs. Black-lettered carved sand-colored plaques surround the room. Made of glass from Carrara, Italy, and donated to the synagogue by the Perilstein family, these memorial plaques hold the names of the founding generations of the congregation. After Rabbi Levinthal's death in 1952, B'nai Abraham had no permanent rabbi for many years. Approximately seven years ago, Rabbi Shraga Sherman came to Philadelphia, and he is busy at B'nai Abraham continuing the work started so many years ago. Members of long-time B'nai Abraham families, such as the late Leon Wapner, devoted their lives to preserving a way of life based on the traditions and beliefs of their fathers and mothers. The synagogue is open for daily Orthodox prayer. Worshipers and visitors are welcome.

Liberty Hall: 716-718 Lombard Street. As a central gathering place for the African American community in Philadelphia for many years, Liberty Hall had seen many celebrations in its day, none more meaningful than the one that occurred on August 28, 1881. Several weeks prior to that date, Mayor King had appointed four African Americans to the police force, the first to be appointed in Philadelphia. That day the hall, including the stage and the aisles, was packed to hear speeches and recognize the four officers. The owner of the building, William Still, presided over the ceremony.

Jews started to use the hall as early as 1885. When Sir Moses Montefiore, the famous English Jew who sought to improve the life of the Jew in Russia through face-to-face meetings with Czars Nicholas I and Alexander II, died on July 28, 1885, at the age of one hundred, a memorial tribute was planned by B'nai Abraham. At this time B'nai Abraham did not have its own synagogue building.

> At Liberty Hall, last Sunday afternoon four glimmering candles threw their misty light upon the dusky faces of many Russian Hebrews. Ungrateful the Russian refugee is not, he even in his exile and poverty remembers that Moses Montefiore was his friend, and he lays his humble laurel, upon the brow of the noble and pious dead. The congregation of the Children of Abraham assembled in a body at No. 718 Lombard Street to hold a memorial service. The hall was fittingly decorated and among the many pictures, two of the great Jew were proudly conspicuous. Several hundred people were present. Men and boys and women sat silent and still, joining in the prayers or listening intently to the oration of Rabbi Harris Sall, who was engaged specially for the occasion. President L. Silverman brought him forward. He donned a high velvet cap and enfolded himself in the taleth, and then began an address in Yiddish which lasted three full hours.[100]

The Talmud Torah, organized by Rabbis Levinthal and Brodsky, purchased Liberty Hall and on Saturday evening, January 21, 1893, it was dedicated. The old hall was decorated with American flags and buntings, and Morais, Brodsky, and Levinthal spoke. The school provided lessons in the Hebrew language and the Jewish religion to poor boys of the Russian immigrants. The Talmud Torah, which at this time had the support of 350 patrons, held classes on Sundays from 10:00 A.M. till noon and from 2:00 P.M to 4:00 P.M. During the week, classes were held after public school from 4:00 P.M. till 7:00 P.M. every day except Friday.[101] The salary paid to the Hebrew School teachers was $12.00 a week. In 1911, the Talmud Torah erected its own building at 314-320 Catharine Street.

It is not known when Liberty Hall was torn down. The properties are private residences today.

GASKILL STREET

Bathhouse, 410–412 Gaskill Street.
Philadelphia Medical Journal, April 23, 1898

Public Bathhouses: 410-412 and 413-415 Gaskill Street. Bathhouses were located on the north and south sides of the 400 block of Gaskill Street. The bathhouse on the south side of the street at 410-412 Gaskill opened on April 21, 1898. It eventually became the men's bathhouse although it was built for men and women. The bathhouse on the north side of the street at 413-415 (a private residence) was built for women in 1903.[103] Provisions were also made in the women's bathhouse for the washing of clothes. By 1905, approximately 300,000 baths had been taken at these bathhouses.

Public bathhouses were opened at the turn of the century in major cities in the United States. In the early 1890's, public spirited individuals in Philadelphia believed that bathing and washing facilities were needed by the poor, especially the immigrant poor and to fill this need, the Public Baths Association was organized. A canvas of the neighborhood surrounding Gaskill Street disclosed that for nineteen hundred persons, there were eleven bathtubs and of these only four were in use for bathing. The others were utilized as woodbins and for general storage purposes. The bathhouse on the south side of the street, which was two and one-half stories, was built in accordance with a design prepared by Louis E. Marie, architect of the firm of Furness, Evans & Co. It was built of hard red brick laid in Flemish bond with dark mortar on a lot 40' X 60'. The men's apartment here had twenty-six showers and one tub and the women's apartment had fourteen showers and three tubs. For 5¢, each bather was given a separate room, a large towel, fresh soap, and plenty of hot and cold water. The women's building on the north side of the street remained open until the thirties. As late as 1933 or 1934, a woman could wash herself, her children, and her clothes for 5¢. All ethnic groups, religions, and races were granted access to the baths. They were not conducted under rabbinical supervision.

The officers and board members of the Association appear to have been forthrightly interested in the bathing habits of the Jews. After only six weeks of operation, the Association noted that the busiest day of the week was Friday: "This is probably due to the fact that a very large percentage of those living in the neighborhood are Jews, and for a few hours just before sunset on Friday, when the Jewish Sabbath begins, the number of bathers of this nationality is very large."

Franklin B. Kirkbride, the treasurer and a trustee of the Association, delivered a speech about the bathhouse at John Hopkins in Baltimore on December 1, 1898:

> It is surprising at times to find in what large numbers our Hebrew citizens patronize the baths, and to see how strict many of them are in observing the provisions of the Mosaic law in this respect. On Sept. 14, only 18 persons bathed; but two days later, the eve of the Hebrew new year, more than 400 Israelites presented themselves to take their New Year's bath, though the day was raw and cold and many of them clearly did not come from a mere sense of pleasure.[104]

When the newer bathhouse opened at 413-415 Gaskill Street, an announcement, circulated in Yiddish, read: "Baths for older women. Children with their parents who are under ten years old are free." Although the circular used the Hebrew word מקואות *(mikvahs)* for "Baths," the Jews must have understood that they were not "ritual" baths because the word kosher was omitted. The price of a private kosher bath, which cost 15¢ to 25¢ in 1914, was beyond the reach of many of the east European Jewish immigrants. However, rather than abandon the laws of immersion altogether, large numbers of those not strictly observant turned to public bathhouses.

WORLD — 6 — די אידישע וועלט

קויפט אלעס וואס איהר דארפט אויף סויטה סט.

פאַרגעניגט זיך

בעזוכט
גאָלדמאַן'ס שוה סטאָר
229 - 231 סויטה סטריט (קאָר. אמעריקאַן סט.)

נומע נייעס פאר דושון כלות
אוננעהייערע פוירניטשור בארגיינס
LOUIS E. WISER, 623 South St., Both Phones

קאַפּלאַנ'ס
דעפּאַרטמענט סטאָר
נ. א. קאָרנער פיערטע און סויטה סטריטס
ספּעשעל גרויסער סייל
CAPLAN'S Department Store
N. E. Cor. 4th & South Sts.

וויליאם ראטשילד'ס
415 סויטה סטריט
Wm. ROTCHILD, 415 South Street

מ. ליפּקאָוויטש און סאַנס
קלאָדיערס און העטערס
ס. א. קאָרנער דריטע און סויטה סטריטס
M. LIKPOWITCH & SONS
Clothier and Hatter
S. E. Cor. 3rd and South Sts.

פלעגנטי הייסע וואסער פריי
$15.00
$8.50
לואיס בינער
610 סויטה סטריט

ע. ווילף'ס
505 סויטה סטריט
E. WILF, 505 South Street

דייוויד ראמ'ס
סוטס
ד. ראם, 6טע און סויטה סט.
David Romm's Challenge Sal

ב. ב. בלאך
1% 2%
B. B. BLOCH

א. שליים
קלאוק און סוט סטאָר
519 סויטה סטריט
A. SCHLEY, 519 South Street

"Buy everything you need on South Street." Readers of *Di Yidishe Velt* were told that because the rent on South Street was low, savings could be passed along to buyers in the form of bargain prices.

Di Yidishe Velt, July 11, 1916

SOUTH STREET

Retail businesses dominated South Street: "From Second St. to Sixth St. the population is almost entirely Jewish, while South St. all the way to Broad Street and beyond is lined with Jewish stores. In these stores, as in most of those conducted by the Jews in this section, the proprietor and his family live in the rooms in the back of the store on the first floor while the upper floors are rented out as apartments. These store-front dwellings are therefore very profitable."[105]

Just how profitable they looked to the Jews themselves was another matter. Writing in 1934, and looking back over a quarter of a century spent in a clothing store on South Street, first at 413 and then at 301, Moses Freeman put it this way: "As hard and bitter as it is to be a worker, a servant to someone else and to have to answer to a boss, believe me that being a businessman, a storekeeper on South Street, is much worse. The worker has his hours of toil, but he has his evenings and his Sabbath to rest. To be a merchant, a businessman on South Street, that means bondage to his store, to his business. He is welded like a *katorzhnik* [a galley slave] to his wheelbarrow in Siberia...[d]ay and night, like mice in holes. One doesn't watch over his own business as much as he watches over his neighbor's business to see that his neighbor doesn't take in more than he does."[106]

Viewed by a worker, we get a different picture of these same business people. Workers and sweatshop people envied the storeowners of South and S. 4th Streets. The owners were seen as the people who controlled the life of the Jewish quarter. They decided which cantors would appear in concert and which cantors would get the best positions for the High Holy Days. Businessmen were seen as the ones who gave generously on Yom Kippur. In fact, their munificent gifts were announced out loud to the entire congregation and the announced amount of each Yom Kippur pledge by the businessmen plunged like a knife into the heart of the worker.

South Street was always changing. The following description of the South Street market comes from the memoirs of a Russian Jewish immigrant who came to Philadelphia as a boy in 1890: "At that time the farmers used to come in to South Street twice a week and line up along the curbing from 2nd to 6th. They would come in the night before. About daybreak they would open their wagons and display their wares. The big day was Saturday. It started about 5 a.m. and lasted till midnight."[107] For many years, New Jersey farmers brought their produce to sell along the South Street curbstones. While the farmers were in town, a favorite lodging spot was the old Farmer's Inn, 611 Annapolis Street, several doors below South Street, east of 2nd. On the same block was the huge market stable where the horses were kept while the farmers were in town. But after the turn of the century, farmers' wagons began to disappear, replaced by pushcarts along S. 4th Street. Permanent awnings, which had been a feature of South Street for years, covered wares displayed on the sidewalk in front of South Street stores, but in 1915 the awnings were ordered to be removed by the courts.[108]

The year 1908 was to bring great changes to South Street. In May, an application was made for a building permit to alter the building at 334 South Street to make it a moving picture amusement parlor. On June 10th, a riot occurred in another part of Philadelphia when three thousand Kensingtonians tried, all at once, to gain entrance to a motion picture show at Kensington and Cumberland Streets. A panic ensued, the police were called, and clubs were used freely before the crowd was subdued. Every Russian immigrant on South Street must have heard the story. By late that summer, Abraham L. Levis began negotiations with Nathan Snellenberg to buy 508 South Street and erect a new theatre. It opened as the Biograph later that same year, the first structure built as a movie house on South Street. In December 1908, plans were announced to build a theatre at 610-612 South Street, which later became the Hippodrome.

On the other hand, some things on South Street never changed. Men's furnishing stores that were here in number until well after World War II were the heart of South Street for many years. Customers were helped into these stores by "pullers-in," salesmen deftly trained at whisking an unsuspecting victim into such an establishment from the pavement in front of the store before the victim could object (other salesmen came by this talent naturally). In 1928, barkers, or "pullers-in," who had been part of South Street life for almost a half a century, were to go. But they did not go. In 1936, the elimination of the old-time barker or pavement salesman was sought, but they remained. And many adults today remember in the 1940's and 1950's being pulled into a clothing store on South Street and before they realized what had happened, they were already wearing a jacket, and perhaps more.

East European Jews took over South Street and they and their descendants have operated stores to this day. For the most part, these merchants have been omitted from this book. There were so many stores that a separate book could be written on the storekeepers of South Street. Several representative businesses will be described, however, because to fully omit any reference to the stores would leave a distorted picture of this "old downtown street of retail trade." By the 1920's, leadership of South Street was organized. In 1928, there was the Reliable Clothier's Association; in 1930, the South Street Booster's Association; in 1936, the South Street Business Advancement Association, and in 1946, the South Street Business Ass'n, Inc.[109]

M. Lipkowitz: S.E. Corner of 3rd & South Streets. South Street merchants advertised widely in the local Yiddish press. At the beginning of the 20th century, many immigrants had lived in the United States for years, knew the spoken English language, but had difficulties reading Latin letters. To address this problem, English words were sometimes printed using Hebrew lettering. An example of this use of Hebrew printing can be found in an advertisement by M. Lipkowitz in 1913. He advertised that he was an "Up-to-date CLOTHIER & HATTER," and in bold Hebrew lettering announced that מלך הקלאטהינג חי וקים *"The King of Clothing lives and abides!"* Other than the word "clothing," this was a phrase well known to the immigrants. The second word is the English word clothing, simply written in Hebrew letters.

Joseph Snellenburg: 318 South Street. Snellenburg's, a leading clothier in Philadelphia for several generations, was started here by the patriarch of the family, Joseph Snellenberg, in the 1850's.[110] The family remained at this location until 1882 when the Snellenburg manufacturing operations were moved to 40-42 N. 3rd Street where other German Jewish clothing houses were located. At the same time, the growing Snellenburg empire acquired the triangular property at the intersection of Passyunk Avenue, 5th Street, and South Street and opened the Snellenburg's Clothing Depot for the retail sale of its merchandise.

300 Block of South Street: In the 1910 census, a total of seventy-one persons were counted as living in ten adjoining properties on the 300 block of South Street. The adult-residents at these properties were born in Russia or Austria and gave Yiddish as their native language. All but two of the seventy-one adult residents identified Yiddish as the native language of their parents: one identified Polish as the native language of her parents (she was a servant), and the other gave German (she was listed as a "daughter-in-law.") Almost every parent of the adult residents listed was born in Russia. Those identified as being born in Pennsylvania were all children. Notwithstanding the 1912 Ph.D. study quoted above (which stated that multiple families occupied these buildings), many of these three-story, storefront properties were occupied by only one family.

Crystal Palace: 334-336 South Street. On May 2, 1908, an application was made to alter the existing building to a moving picture amusement parlor. This was the first motion picture parlor opened in the Jewish quarter. The Crystal Palace had a recessed fireproof front, "metal on metal frame" construction, and a rear emergency exit onto Kater Street (formerly Trout Street). The alterations cost the owner, Louis Lederhandler, $1,200, and it can be assumed that the Jewish residents of the neighborhood flocked to see moving pictures because within the next two years, three other theatres opened on South Street between 4th and 7th streets.

In April of the following year, the Crystal Palace was closed by the city and later that month a contract was awarded to build a new moving picture theatre here for Hirsch & Co. By July 1909, business was so good that William Menkot, the new owner of the Crystal Palace, spent $3,500 on a one-story front addition. Interior changes were also made to the new building. Although the name has changed, the building is still used as a theatre.

People's Bank: 410 South Street. From 1921 to 1923, a branch office of the People's Bank was located here. The history of the bank begins with Charles Lipshutz at Rosenbaum's bank on South 3rd Street.

Lipshutz, president of Brith Achim, the Vitebsker Benevolent Association, and the Jewish Consumptive Relief Society, was born in Mogeliev, Russia in 1872 and immigrated to the United States when he was seventeen. For a short time he worked for the Association for the Protection of Jewish Immigrants. With his father, he moved to a farming community in New Jersey, but soon left, as many of the immigrants did, and returned to Philadelphia where in 1890 or 1891 he started to work at Rosenbaum's immigrant bank, 609 S. 3rd Street. Lipshutz, who had a good understanding of languages, stayed with Rosenbaum until 1906 when he left to start the People's Bank with Maurice L. Wurzel. This bank was located in the heart of South Philadelphia for a number of years and later moved to 7th & Girard Avenue. When east European Jews continued to arrive in great numbers, Lipshutz and Wurzel expanded their operations and opened a branch office here on South Street in 1921.

די פיפעלס באנק

דיא גרעסטע און עלטעסטע אידישע באנק אין פילאדעלפיא

מיר שיקען געלד נאך יוראפ

7טע און דזשיראַרד עווע.

און 410 סויטה סטריט

טשארלס ליפשוץ, פרעזידענט, מאררים ל. וואורצעל, וויים פרעז.

People's Bank branch, 410 South Street, circa 1922.

Courtesy of the YIVO Institute for Jewish Research, New York

When the People's Bank branch office moved to 410 South Street, it was located in a relatively new building and obviously the bank hoped to compete with the Blitzstein bank and Lipshutz's former employer, Morris Rosenbaum, for the lucrative downtown immigrant banking business. But matters took a different turn. On October 20, 1923, the People's Bank merged with the People's Trust Company to become the People's Bank and Trust Company, and by 1924 the new company opened its main offices at 18-20-22 South 15th

Street. At the same time the branch office here was closed.[111]

Model Theatre: 425-427 South Street. In late 1910 Max Katzman opened a new one-story moving picture theatre here. It seated 621 people and the cost to build it was $16,000. By 1914 the theatre was owned by the Model Amusement Co. This theatre, as well as other theatres in the Jewish quarter, was used for serious endeavors as well as entertainment.

In March 1915, Dr. Charles D. Spivak, by then the secretary of the JCRS in Denver, returned to Philadelphia to give two talks on the need to address a formidable enemy of the Jewish people: tuberculosis. There was a folk-belief that Russian Jews were immune to the disease, but when east European Jews settled in the crowded ghettos of the large cities of the United States, they quickly fell victim to it. On Thursday, March 18, 1915, Spivak addressed the United Hebrew Charities on the ravages of the disease, and on Sunday of that week Spivak presented an illustrated lecture before a crowded audience of over 800 people.[112]

On the stage that Sunday with Spivak, as speakers, were Dr. Lawrence F. Flick, the founder of the Henry Phipps Institute in Philadelphia, an institute devoted to the study, treatment, and prevention of tuberculosis; and Dr. Solomon Solis-Cohen, Philadelphia physician, scholar, and poet who, along with Flick and Spivak, was identified in the press as an expert on tuberculosis. Dr. Reisman of the University of Pennsylvania referred to the three doctors that day as the "super-dreadnoughts of their profession." Reisman also said: "...the tuberculosis campaign...served as an inspiration for similar fights against other diseases such as cancer...." In a short talk, Flick stated that more than a million people die every year from consumption. Spivak illustrated his lecture with lantern slides and told of his work in Denver. He explained that any success achieved was because of the support of the Jewish masses by means of their small donations: "You will not find in the list of donors and contributors to the [Denver] sanatorium names of renowned philanthropists and men of great wealth. The pennies and the dollars of the great masses of Jews throughout America have fought the battle against the dread White Plague [tuberculosis]."

After his talk, many in the audience who had been patients of Spivak years before came forward to shake his hand. The newspaper reporters could not help but take note of the great respect shown Spivak, although it had been almost twenty years since he left the city. The committee that organized the lecture included Spivak's old friends, Bernard Harris and George Goward (Goward founded the Hebrew Literature Society in 1885).

In 1936, ownership of the Model Theatre changed, and it was taken over by the Stanley Co. of America. In the fall of 1941, extensive interior alterations were made at an estimated cost of $25,000. The number of seats was reduced and a new front was added.[113] Most Jewish residents in the area went to the Model, and it was here during the years of World War II that they saw the "News of the Day" and learned about the progress of the war.

In 1955, the building was converted into a retail store.

N. Snellenburg & Co.: 5th, South and Passyunk Ave. The four-story Retail Depot of N. Snellenburg & Co. occupied this triangular property from the early 1880's well into the 20th century. From January 1, 1889, until May 24, 1890, Snellenburg used nearly five million yards of woolen cloth, cotton cloth, linings, canvas, etc. in making men's clothing that it sold at its two retail operations: one store here, and the other on Market Street. During the same short period, Snellenburg used ten million buttons and thirty-three hundred pounds of sewing silk. They used enough basting thread to go around the globe 120 times. A total of 1,600 cutters, sewers, buttonhole makers and operators were employed. Snellenburg proudly advertised that ninety-five percent of the money value of the labor to produce the goods it sold remained in Philadelphia. Even more proudly, a Snellenburg advertisement stated: "The Brand of Cain that some of the Philadelphia Semi-Middlemen would put on Philadelphia-made clothing is reacting like a Boomerang on their 'sing twice' stuff. 'Where are your workshops?' we ask them. No answer; naught but silence. To see ours, take the elevator for the upper floors. It'll repay you. You can truthfully say: 'I've seen the finest and most complete clothing cutting room in the world.'"[114]

Neither Snellenburg, nor any other clothier, advertised the location where clothing was tacked, sewed, basted or pressed, other than to say that it was done in Philadelphia.[115]

South Street, 1930. Looking east from 5th Street. The traffic pattern was one way, east to west. Today, traffic moves in the opposite direction. The Model Theatre marquee can be seen on the north side of the street.

Courtesy of the Archives of the City of Philadelphia and Steven Kujolic

Yiddish Newspaper Stand: Southwest corner of 5th & South Streets. Moses Freeman did not have $5 to rent a newspaper stand, but good friends came to his aid and, on March 8, 1888, Freeman rented a stand here and went into business. He carried English dailies as well as Yiddish newspapers from New York. His stand was the first place in Philadelphia where Yiddish newspapers were sold (Pinchas Thomashevsky did not open his newspaper agency at 519 S. 3rd Street until the following year). The first Yiddish newspaper was not printed in Philadelphia until 1891 and Freeman was also responsible for that effort, see 708 S. 5th Street. Although Freeman owned the stand, a Mr. Kenter ran it. Charles (Judah) Cohen, aged thirteen, worked for Kenter at the stand in 1892. Cohen liked to read the Yiddish serials of that day. Writing in the early 1940's, Cohen remembered one serial entitled "The Mysteries of the Tsars of Russia." Every week a new pamphlet came out and he read them here.

As early as 1888, the corner of 5th & South Streets, according to Freeman, was a place of assembly, for intellectuals and workers alike. Cohen's recollections track those of Freeman:

> Anarchism and Atheism were very popular among the young immigrants. It was very often discussed at 5th & South Streets. Anarchism, I didn't take to it, but Atheism was something else again. It relieved one of doing things that a believer is supposed to do. That suited me fine so I became an atheist. When I became 13 years old, my father wanted to buy me Tefilin. I persuaded him not to. I told him I would never use them and that we needed the money that it would cost for bread. It was 1892 and a depression or, as it was called then, a panic just started. I remember one could have bought two loaves of bread for a nickel. Most people didn't have the nickel. They stood in lines to get bread or soup free....The corner of 5th & South Streets was the gathering place of all working people. It was called the *'chazer mark* [pig or hog market, a place where cheap labor could be hired].' They were talking about unions but there were not any. Whenever a manufacturer or contractor wanted a worker, he would go to the above corner and call out whatever worker he wanted and a dozen would answer his call.[116]

Princess Theatre: 508 South Street. In September 1908, Abraham L. Levis, the restauranteur from around the corner on S. 6th Street, purchased the property at 508 South Street from Nathan Snellenburg as a site to construct a "large moving picture theatre."[117] It was remembered in later years as a place of Yiddish vaudeville. Designed for Levis by Barnet J. Medoff,[118] it was a whitewashed one-story structure set awkwardly on this street so well known for its retail clothing stores. Above an archway, within which was set a recessed pint-sized ticket-booth, foot-high letters spelled out the original name of the theatre, BIOGRAPH. The building had a 20' front along South Street with the entrance on the east side. Ushers wore military style uniforms, with small, peaked caps.

Princess Theatre, 508 South Street, circa 1908.
Courtesy of The Library Company of Philadelphia

Levis owned the soda fountain in the lobby of the Princess Theatre. It was reputedly one of the oldest such counters in the world.[119] By 1913, or perhaps earlier, the name of the theatre was changed to the Princess. Until July 1916, Yiddish vaudeville and *shund* were featured. From this short period only one name has come down to us as a performer, Jennie Atlas (1880-1927). She played here for one season. Atlas, who came to this country when she was four years old, played vaudeville in New York and had her own company. She also played in the legitimate theatre, here in Philadelphia for a year, and in New York where she had the opportunity to perform with Adler and Thomashevsky.[120]

The Jacob Gordin Dramatic Society (formerly the Progressive Dramatic Circle) produced amateur plays here.[121] The Yiddish theater, amateur and professional, was a true cultural institution for the Russian Jews. Among its patrons were young men and women from the so-called Russian intelligentsia. For them the theatre was a necessity, and it was not uncommon to see young men and women come to the theatre with a book under their arm. In these people a desire arose for better Yiddish drama, especially the drama of Jacob Gordin. At the end of a performance, they would discuss which actors understood their roles and which actors merely spoke a chapter of prose. Members of the Jacob Gordin Dramatic Society in Philadelphia included: Aaron Kanievsky; Miss Kortchnoy; Schwartz; Dr. Janoff; Hershman and Abe Cohen. They put on *Yukl, the Thief*, by Zvi Ben Sholom; *Father and Son*, by An-ski, and other plays.

In July 1916, at an estimated cost of $8,500, the building was converted into a store and a 40' x 60' warehouse was added at the back of the property.[122] It is not known when the building was torn down.

BAINBRIDGE STREET

That portion of Bainbridge Street west of 6th Street was renowned for its second-hand clothing stores. In the edition of the *Times-Philadelphia* for Sunday, July 16, 1887, S. S. Skidelsky described the Russian-Jews in Philadelphia. The headlines read: "The Russian Hebrews; A Peculiar People Settled in Philadelphia; How they are getting along in their various trades." In the article Skidelsky wrote: "It is a remarkable fact that of the many Russian Jewish shopkeepers situated all along South, Bainbridge and a number of other down-town streets, very few are able to make themselves understood in English, and how they manage to get along and conduct their businesses is a wonder. Some of them are doing a thriving business without as much as being able to form an English sentence. They seem to prefer to live within their own sphere, to form their own circles, to associate with their own countrymen and to speak their own language - a mixture of German, Hebrew, Russian and Polish."

Washington Market: Between 3rd Street and 5th Street on Bainbridge[123]. At first, the market was called Shippen Market and later the name was changed to Washington Market. It was a shambles (a slaughterhouse), a series of sheds made up of open wooden stands or stalls. Sheep were driven here from the farms to the south, on roads such as Passyunk.

The market's opening in the fall of 1857 was an event long remembered. In those days, before Jews settled in the area, each butcher was permitted to sell but one kind of meat. For example, there were beef butchers, pork butchers, and mutton butchers. One butcher sold the meat from five hundred sheep in one week. Religious services were held in the sheds by itinerant preachers on Sunday mornings and afternoons, and during political campaigns the west end, which fronted the intersection of Bainbridge, 5th, and Passyunk, was a favorite place for holding meetings. Washington's birthday was made a gala day each year by the butchers, who, attired in silk hats and mounted on their most fiery steeds - and headed by the famous butchers'

Washington Market, between 3rd & 5th Streets, on Bainbridge, 1893.

Courtesy of the Archives of the City of Philadelphia

band, paraded all over town.

Although the market did not play a significant role in the Jewish history of the area, some Jews did sell from here since it was located centrally in the Jewish quarter. The market was torn down about 1902 or 1903.

The Open Stand of Louis Moskovitz in the Washington Market: Moskovitz, an anarchist, had a stand opposite the synagogue at 322 Bainbridge Street.[124] An incident that occurred here on Yom Kippur morning of 1888 or 1889 has been preserved, and it gives us a glimpse into anarchistic thinking. Anti-religious fervor in Russian Jewish Philadelphia was at its peak and a confrontation, instigated by Moskovitz to provoke pious Jews, began quietly enough this Yom Kippur morning.

Moskovitz sold beans, grains, and cereal in an open wooden stand in the shambles. Being an anarchist, Moskovitz, of course, did not go to synagogue. On this Yom Kippur Day he opened his stand and proceeded to put on his *kittel*, or white linen robe worn by Jews on solemn occasions, and *taleysim*, or prayer shawl. The act of putting on these religious garments in the market was designed to enrage the pious. He sat down at his stand to read his "worthy prayers" (the latest anarchist or socialist literature, printed especially to be read on Yom Kippur). Although he expected no customers that day, since it was Yom Kippur, he said to himself, "a demonstration against the pious Jews in *shul*, now, that is a good thing!"

While the Torah was being read across the street in the synagogue, worshippers in their *kitlen* and *taleysim* came outside to get a breath of fresh air. When they saw Moskovitz "at his God-blasphemy," they surrounded the heretic and became so distraught by his wearing the white robe and his actions that they began to express themselves by gesticulating. Moskovitz pretended not to notice, and the crowd around him grew more animated. From a distance away, an Irish policeman interpreted the gestures as threatening to Moskovitz. The policeman quickly called the station house and summoned two patrol wagons with reserves. Soon the Orthodox Jews, in *kitlen* and *taleysim*, were thrown into patrol wagons and taken to the station house where they were held the rest of the day. From that day on, Moskovitz became a symbol of all that was wicked to the pious Jews.

But like others who in their youth took radical positions, the leading anarchists in Philadelphia mellowed and in later years directed their energies in more traditional directions. Max Staller, the leader of the cloakmakers' strike in 1890, eventually became a well-known and much respected surgeon. David Apotheker, the radical writer and publisher, also made a living as a notary, real estate broker, and insurance salesman. Isadore Prenner, a leader of the cloakmakers in 1890, became a lawyer and a Zionist, and Moskovitz himself, the apostate, became, as difficult as it is to believe, the *gabbai* of the *chevra kadisha*. Its membership included the most devout and God-fearing in the community.

Ahavas Chesed-Anshe Shavel, 322 Bainbridge Street, 1943.

Courtesy of the Historical Society of Pennsylvania, Philadelphia, Pennsylvania

Ahavath Chesed-Anshe Shavel: 322 Bainbridge Street. Chartered in 1887, Chevra Ahavath Chesed-Anshe Shavel, or Love of Mercy, Men of Shavel (a town in Lithuania), was a signatory congregation that agreed to bring Rabbi Bernard L. Levinthal to Philadelphia. The *shul* was known as the *litvak shul*, because Jews from Lithuania prayed here.

The earliest record we have of a place of prayer for Anshe Shavel is 516 S. 7th Street in 1894. Several years later, the congregation moved here to the former Howard Sunday school Hall.[125] The only description of the interior of the building is contained in the Yiddish writings of David B. Tierkel (when the old hall was used by the HLS): "In 1893, the Hebrew Literature Society was located in a spacious building at 322 Bainbridge Street. At the entrance was an Orthodox shul, which also served as a reading room, and in a room at the back was the library in which Hebrew, Yiddish and Russian books were to be found."[126] The rabbi at Anshe Shavel, Abraham H. Erschler, was the most beloved of all the rabbis in the Jewish immigrant districts of Philadelphia at the turn of the last century.

Rabbi Abraham H. Erschler, circa 1890.
He was the rabbi at Ahavas Chesed-Anshe Shavel
from the middle 1890's to 1910.

Courtesy of Suzanne Grossman

Erschler, who is hardly remembered today, came to Philadelphia in the middle nineties. After serving for a short time as the rabbi at another small Philadelphia *chevra*, Shaare Zedek-Anshe Rezischev, he came to Ahavath Chesed-Anshe Shavel.[127] He was born in 1860 in the border city of Neustadt Shugind, Kovno Province, Russia. His father, Rabbi Abba, was from a family of sages and his mother was from the family of the Vilna Gaon. When Erschler was fourteen, he was sent to the yeshiva at Mir where he studied for two and a half years. From there he went to Volozhin where he learned Torah from the sage, the Netziv (Rabbi Naphtali Zvi Yehuda Berlin) for three years. He married young, and at the age of twenty he was ordained a rabbi by the great Jewish scholars of Lithuania. Eager to continue his education, Erschler went to Heidelberg, Germany, studied for four years, and then came to the United States and settled in Cleveland, Ohio.[128] In the early 1890's, Erschler moved to Elmira, New York and came to Philadelphia from either Elmira or Cleveland.

Anshe Shavel had a *Besmedresh* (Ohavei Zedek) and Erschler was the rabbi at the house of prayer and the house of study. He spoke at dedicatory ceremonies and was involved in the founding of many Jewish organizations and *chevras* in the Russian colony. As a reward for his service to the community, his congregation presented him with a house at 515 S. 9th Street. Active in civic matters, he was named a delegate to the Pennsylvania Arbitration and Peace Conference, held in Philadelphia in 1908. He was rabbi to at least five other congregations, ministering to thousands of devoted followers. Erschler was a staunch defender of Orthodoxy. In response to criticism of Orthodox Jewish practices and belief, he answered the Jewish Reform establishment in the general circulation English-language press, a medium the Orthodox Jewish community in Philadelphia did not use regularly (except Rabbi Levinthal):

The reformers think that they are improving the religion by introducing modern forms of worship. They say that the orthodox Jews are too ancient in their religious ways. Before Abraham Geiger introduced the reform movement there were no orthodox Jews. There were only Israelites, who worshiped God as did their forefathers. Such are the views of the right thinking Jews to-day, and if the doctrines of orthodoxy were foolish or false, Judaism would have ceased long before the birth of Geiger.[129]

Erschler took sick in 1909, suffering from kidney trouble and heart disease, and in the summer of 1910 his condition worsened. While convalescing in Atlantic City, he was called to visit an inmate in Moyamensing Prision in Philadelphia where he acted as chaplain. Returning from the jail on a streetcar, he suffered a stroke. At the age of fifty Rabbi Erschler died on Saturday morning, November 19, 1910. Upon his death, the moderate social-democratic *Jewish Daily Forward* tried to fix Erschler's place in the Jewish community, juxtaposing Erschler's *mentchlikhkayt* (humaneness) with its socialist view of the rabbinate: "Rabbi Erschler was a rabbi one seldom sees in America. He was by nature a very honest, good-hearted and cultured person. Besides knowing Talmud and Hebrew, he also knew Russian, German, English, and was not unfamiliar with other languages. By nature he hated hypocrites and always turned away in disgust from rabbinical politics. Therefore, naturally one heard little from him and as a result he was always lonely and in poverty."[130]

The *Forward* article continued in its simultaneous effort to praise Erschler while not-too-delicately questioning the very underpinnings of the American rabbinate: "To a reporter from the *Forward*, he [Erschler] once said that he would joyously value making a living from something besides the rabbinate. 'To be a rabbi is a beautiful thing,' he said 'but only when you do not have to make a living from it. In America the rabbinate is not to my liking,' and he sighed heavily when he said this."

"He [Erschler] was far from being a fanatic," the *Forward* concluded: "He valued every honest person. It did not make a difference if the person who came into contact with him was a freethinker. 'It makes no difference what a person is - a religious person or a freethinker,' he once told a reporter from the *Forward*, 'as long as he is honest to that which he feels and thinks, he has earned the respect of everyone.'" To print in a socialist newspaper in 1910 that a "religious person" could earn the respect of everyone, took great courage. Here we see Cahan's newspaper at its best, reluctant to sledgehammer religion into oblivion and careful to recognize basic human values - even at the expense of socialistic doctrine. Cahan was at his finest in tragedy and, as this article suggests, struggled to bring the Jewish people together. The funeral took place on Sunday, November 20, 1910:

Never before in the history of the Jewish community of Philadelphia was there so impressive a funeral as that of Rabbi Erschler, last Sunday. More than five thousand persons - men and women, old and young, rich and poor - assembled to pay their tribute to the rabbi whom they loved and honored. From the late residence of the deceased, the funeral procession went to the Ahavath Chesed Synagogue, Third and Bainbridge street. From here the vast throng proceeded to the Kesher Israel Synagogue, Fourth and Lombard streets, and thence to the B'nai Abraham Synagogue, Sixth and Lombard streets. Among those who participated in the services were Rabbis Joseph Grossman, S. Englander, N. H. Brenner, Z. Rivkind, and Mr. H. Yudelson. Rabbi B.L. Levinthal, being a Cohen, was unable to speak in the synagogue in the presence of the deceased, but will deliver a eulogy for the departed rabbi next Sunday afternoon at the B'nai Abraham Synagogue.

Interment was made at the Har Nebo Cemetery, where thousands of Jews assembled to give their rabbi the honor due him. All those who knew the rabbi and spoke of him, expressed the same opinion of the man. There was an indefinable something in Rabbi Erschler's nature that won everybody. Everyone who came in close contact with him was devoted to him. His very appearance suggested gentleness of disposition coupled with strength of mind and character.[131]

Notwithstanding Erschler's death, in 1911 Ahavath Chesed-Anshe Shavel rebuilt the synagogue and the following year it celebrated its 25th anniversary. Members of the synagogue and their friends, as well as a number of representatives from other congregations, assembled at B'nai Abraham and from there marched to the synagogue at 322 Bainbridge Street. At the celebration Rabbi Levinthal emphasized the importance of unity and harmony among Jews and appealed for cooperation. Unfortunately, tragedy was to continue to strike Anshe Shavel. Less than two years after being rebuilt, the building was damaged by fire. When told of the fire, Rabbi Levinthal was shocked.[132]

Many Torah scrolls were destroyed in the fire. Some accounts put the total as high as thirty. Three weeks later the immigrant colony buried the desecrated Torahs as required by Jewish tradition. Orthodox Jews saw the wrath of God in the fire. At the ceremony that accompanied the burial, Rabbi Brenner declared the "recent visitation of fire upon the old Bainbridge street temple as a direct warning from God against the widening gap between orthodoxy and the new thought."[133] But as much as Brenner, Englander, and Levinthal railed at it, the gap widened between those Jews who sought to continue to follow the ways of their mothers and fathers and those who sought to forge a new direction for Judaism in America.

After the fire, the synagogue was rebuilt and *litvaks* continued to pray here. But adversity was to continue to strike the congregation. In the early morning hours of June 6, 1943, fire again ravaged the building. This time firemen did manage to save the Torah scrolls and several Bibles but little else. While the congregation announced plans to rebuild, the synagogue was not rebuilt on the site.[134] In 1951, Anshe Shavel disbanded at a final dinner held at the Colonial Cafe, 514 S. 5th Street. The Torahs were donated to a synagogue in Israel. It is not known if the building standing at this location today is the same building used by Anshe Shavel. In form and silhouette, it is similar.

The Young Women's Union of Philadelphia: 422-428 Bainbridge Street. After wandering for fifteen years, the Young Women's Union of Philadelphia put down permanent roots here.[135] In 1896, the executors of the estate of Simon Muhr, industrialist, Jewelry merchant and devoted friend of the Russian immigrant, offered $5,000 to the YWU for a building or endowment fund on the condition that an equal amount be raised by the community within thirty days, which was done. A building committee purchased a 70' x 80' lot here for $13,000, and a four-story Georgian Revival style edifice was constructed. Built of brick with white trimmings, the chief architectural features were a pedimented entry with sidelights; six-pane, double hung windows; flat arches with pronounced keystones; and three pedimented

Young Women's Union, 422–428 Bainbridge Street, 1910.
Designed by Baker & Dallet in the Georgian Revival style, it was built in 1900 and torn down during Redevelopment. In 1911, it took 124 volunteers to provide the services offered to the immigrants from this building.

dormers. Designed by Baker & Dallett, the building was dedicated on Sunday, February 4, 1900. At first the YWU provided only kindergarten, household services, and a nursery to educate and aid the children of the Russian poor. By 1911, however, the YWU maintained a day nursery, resident nursing services, public baths, a kindergarten, a sewing school, a library, a playground, classes in Hebrew, manual training programs, music (piano and violin), drawing,[136] millinery, cooking, nursing, homemaking, needlework, gymnastics, dancing, clubs (literary, debating, and athletic), and a drum and fife corps. It also sponsored a Vacation Home for working girls at 6041 Kingsessing Avenue.

The organization was supported by a small band of young women from uptown and no better example of German Jews helping Russian immigrants can be found in the Jewish quarter. The older generation of German Jews, especially those in the clothing business, made fortunes on the backs of their less fortunate coreligionists. When Russian Jews acquired capital and invested in clothing manufacturing, they too made fortunes on the backs of their brothers and sisters. Some of these fortunes were returned to the community in the form of charity: Simon Muhr has already been mentioned. The Fels family generously donated money from their soap business, and Samuel S. Fleisher founded the Graphic Sketch Club. But it was the daughters of German Jewish industrialists and merchants, like Fanny (Hoffman) Binswanger and other women, drawn at an early age to the Jewish quarter, who tirelessly devoted their young lives to the betterment of Russian Jewry in Philadelphia. The building of the YWU stood on this spot until the 1970's when it was torn down.[137]

The Intersection of 5th Street, Bainbridge and Passyunk Avenue: "Fifth Street and Bainbridge and Passyunk in crossing made quite an open space which is rendered less bare looking by the old market sheds to the east on Bainbridge [written in 1891]. The sheds are not particularly well kept, but at night when the artificial light softens the squalor of the surroundings, this spot is quite attractive and picturesque. The arc-lights, gasoline lamps, and gas jets, all throw a variety of rays on the buxom women and the plump maidens, many of the latter with color and form that are worth an artist's pencil, but the vividness of the attire suggests that the taste of the wearer is not built on the laws laid down by Oscar Wilde."[138]

MONROE STREET

Hitzelberger Hall: 240 Monroe Street. As early as 1888, the building was called Hitzelberger Hall. B'nai Reuben met here from 1883 until 1889.[139] In May and August 1890, Cloakmakers' Union No.1, of the Jewish Federation of Labor, met here during the eighteen week cloakmakers' strike that year; and on a Friday evening in August, Abraham Cahan came from New York to give a talk on Darwinism.[140] In June 1891, during a one-week strike, the rank and file of the Tailors' Union No.1 of the Jewish Federation of Labor met here.

In the nineties the hall was converted into a bathhouse with a kosher mikvah, and for two years at the turn of the century Nathan Cooperman ran a Russian and Turkish bathhouse here. In 1905, Nathan Preminger was the proprietor. He improved the bathhouse by putting in thirty beds. It is not clear when the building was torn down, but it may have been many years ago.

Kratchmans' Bathhouses - Paradise on Earth: 313-321 Monroe Street. Terra cotta fronts of two former side-by-side bathhouses grace this tranquil tree-shaded block of Monroe Street. A small plaque on the wall of 317 Monroe Street states: "Bath House Court." The history of the bathhouses goes back to 1896 when the first proprietors, Kanevsky and Bershadsky, opened a bathhouse at 315 Monroe Street and advertised that it was a true "earthly paradise."[141] The next year the bathhouse was run by Kanevsky and Hyman Kretchman (Herman Kratchman) and within three years, Kratchman took over the operation of the bathhouse outright. Kratchman soon acquired 313 Monroe Street. In quick succession the properties at 317, 319 and 321 became part of the bathhouse and Herman's son, Abraham, became the proprietor. In 1921, Abraham broke away from the rest of the family and opened "Abe's New Baths" at 317-319-321 Monroe Street, which operated concurrently with the old bathhouse at 313-315 Monroe Street next door.[142]

Russian and Turkish baths were popular with the immigrants, and the Russian Colony in Philadelphia teemed with them. Generally, bathhouses or *shvitz* in Yiddish, had a cook who specialized in preparing such dishes as *kreplach*, roast chicken, black raddish, and chopped liver heavy with chicken fat. On Sunday

Abe's Baths, 317–321 Monroe Street, circa 1930. Abraham Kratchman left his brothers and his father and struck out on his own in 1921. *Courtesy of Ethel Kratchman*

mornings there could be lox, white fish, and homemade *schmaltz* herring. In some bathhouses, there was a Turkish room with benches surrounded by hissing radiators and with boulders heated with wood or coal, and later by gas. Some of the Russian rooms were covered with white tile and lined with a three-tiered wooden grandstand (Kratchmans' had white tile throughout). Cold water pipes ran alongside the benches with spigots that emptied into wooden buckets. A bucket full of ice-cold water was available to cool down the sweating patrons when the temperature reached two hundred degrees.

The immigrants came to the Kratchman bathhouses to relieve their aches and pains, to exchange caustic Yiddish oaths with *landslayt* from the *alte heym*, and to forget their daily struggles. It was located only several blocks from the Emigrant Depot at the foot of Washington Avenue, and some came directly from arriving steamers. Kratchmans' featured Russian baths, swimming pools, kosher mikvahs, and, prior to World War II, *zaltz vanes*, or salt baths. Rabbi Englander supervised the running of the mikvahs and the *zalts vanes*.[143]

Like other bathhouses, Kratchmans' offered a rub down with oak leaves, called a *pleytse*. A *pleytse* in Yiddish means shoulder, but in this context it meant a Russian massage. The *pleytse* began with the gathering of oak leaves, which were collected periodically, sometimes from as far away as Fairmount Park. The leaves were brought back to the bathhouse and hung to dry. When ready for use, the leaves were made into bundles and shaped into large balls, called a "broom." The broom, which had a 5" or 6" handle, was put into wooden buckets full of hot soapy water. The customer laid face down on the top plank of the wooden *shvitz-bank*, or sweating bench, and his head was covered with an old felt hat. The attendant, called in Yiddish, a *patchik*, swished the ball of hot leaves over the customer's back, especially the shoulders. The rubdown lasted about ten minutes. After the *pleytse*, which at Abe's New Baths in 1940 cost $1 and included a wash and an alcohol rub, one had a *bisl schnops* (whiskey or brandy) and on Saturday evenings settled down for an evening of cards, away from the store.[144] The camaraderie of male companionship in cards and drink at Abe's and Kratchman's was much prized. After cards, Abe offered his clients a clean bed to sleep in and many took advantage of the offer.

Just how many slept at Abe's we learn from the story of a robbery that occurred here early in the morning of Sunday, December 16, 1928.[145] At 3:30 A.M., Samuel "Shorty" Feldman, out on bail in connection with the McLoon and O'Leary murders,[146] and four masked accomplices drew up to the curb at Abe's in a sedan. The men piled out, one guarding the front door. Kratchman, the only one up at that time of night, had gone upstairs for a few minutes and left the safe unattended. Just as one of the bandits swung the safe open, two patrons came into the office. The patrons were told to face the wall, and the bandits made off. A few minutes later Kratchman returned to discover what had happened. Because the gang cut the telephone wires,

Kratchman ran outside to call Street Sergeant Kelly. In the ensuing commotion, fifty patrons, who had been sleeping in the dormitory were awakened, but another one hundred and fifty patrons slept through the excitement. Feldman, after a lengthy rooftop chase, was captured. If two hundred men slept here on a Saturday evening - or fifty or sixty - the Kratchmans must have been doing something right. But the bathhouse was doing no more than following through on its promise made to the Yiddish reading public in 1896; in fact, Kratchmans' was as close as most of the immigrants would ever get to Paradise on Earth.

In the late 1970's, the property at 313 Monroe Street was torn down, and in 1981 the properties at 315 to 321 Monroe Street were converted into the Bath House Court condominiums.

FITZWATER STREET

B'nai Israel-Anshe Poland: 324-326 Fitzwater Street. In June 1918, B'nai Israel-Anshe Poland converted an old tenement here into a synagogue at a cost of $8,000. Inside, partitions were removed and galleries were added. Outside, major renovations were made. The architect for the project was Herman H. Kline. The long-time rabbi at Congregation B'nai Israel,[147] Nathan Brenner agreed to become the rabbi at Anshe Poland. Born in Lithuania about 1862, Brenner was educated at a Yeshiva in Kovno and emigrated to this country while still a young man. He was one of three Philadelphia rabbis identified by Charles S. Bernheimer in 1906 as being a recognized authority on Jewish law in the Russian community (the other two were Rabbis Levinthal and Erschler).

The installation of Rabbi Brenner took place here on Sunday, August 17, 1919. Friends of the rabbi went to his home in Port Richmond at 2856 Tulip Street and from there escorted him to Anshe Poland in a flag-bedecked automobile.[148] As Brenner entered the new synagogue, the congregation rose and an orchestra played the national anthem. A banquet and speeches followed. Brenner's son-in-law, Rev. M. H. Kaaplander, the rabbi of Congregation Kesher Israel, Reading, Pennsylvania, acted as master of ceremonies.

Rabbi Brenner did not stay here long. Shortly after being installed, Brenner became the rabbi at Ateres Israel in South Philadelphia where he served for many years. Anshe Poland remained here until at least 1942. It is not known when the building was torn down. The properties are private residences.

CATHARINE STREET

Quiet and serene, Catharine Street saw two of the most popular immigrant organizations settle permanently on this street: the Hebrew Literature Society and the Central Talmud Torah. Both buildings, built on the south side of the 300 hundred block during the immigrant period, stand today as monuments to Jewish education.

The First Yom Kippur Ball: 2nd & Catharine Streets (exact address unknown). Anarchistic and socialistic Russian Jews who scoffed at *Kol Nidre* and the day of Atonement held a ball and a banquet on the upper floor of a house at 2nd & Catharine Streets on Friday, October 4, and Saturday, October 5, 1889, Kol Nidre evening and Yom Kippur day. Tickets were sold for 25¢. Organized by the *Ritter der Freiheit*, or Knights of Liberty, the radicals ate herring sandwiches and washed them down with barrels of beer. While less than one hundred apostates participated, their actions caused religious Jews much pain.

The aim of the Jewish anarchists was to destroy the Jewish religion. If it could not be done in one year, they were prepared for a drawn-out struggle. For Yom Kippur 1890, a parade through the Jewish quarter and a banquet were planned; but, because the leaders were awaiting trial on criminal charges growing out of the riot at Dramatic Hall on Sunday afternoon, August 3, 1890, wiser heads prevailed and the festivities were cancelled. A year later, the same group made plans for a Yom Kippur picnic in Camden, and a parade and banquet in Philadelphia. Because of police persuasion and pressure exerted by pious Jews, however, the festivities were scaled back and only the making of speeches in a hall took place. Although the anarchist movement in Philadelphia remained strong, we learn little of anti-religious activities on the Day of Atonement after 1891.[149]

Hebrew Literature Society: 310-312 Catharine Street. At a meeting in 1899 or 1900, when Dr. David Feldman was president, Adolf Wachs was vice president, and the HLS met at 226 Catharine Street, Feldman told the Society: "Inasmuch as the organization is poor and cannot pay $25 a month rent, therefore, we must buy our own large building which will have enough space for hundreds of visitors." Those present at the meeting burst out in laughter since they did not have money for the current month's rent. But the president was serious. He wanted the Society to have its own building and end its gypsy existence. At once, he undertook a campaign to raise funds. The first large donation, in the amount of $500, was given by the banker Morris Rosenbaum, who is described in the history of the Hebrew Literature Society as "a Hungarian Jew who had a great measure of intelligence and a heart that was open wide for every cultural undertaking." The largest donations were given by Maurice and Samuel Fels, soap manufacturers, who gave $3,000. With these principal gifts, other ones followed quickly and the Society was able to purchase the properties at 310-312 Catharine Street.

"Built originally as a two story house with center hall plan, it had already been extended by 1836 with a nine foot wide kitchen addition on the west side." The building was modified in 1900 by providing for two reading rooms on the ground floor and a lecture hall with a seating capacity of 175 on the second floor. The Society occupied the building until 1904 when it recognized that it was inadequate for the rapidly increasing membership and it was completely rebuilt. Designed by Philadelphia architects Wilson, Harris & Richards, an additional story was added and the interior was totally redesigned. Constructed in brick, the new edifice is topped with a shingled mansard roof and pierced by four, six-over-six double hung sashes. A Greek Revival styled door surround occupies the eastern bay on the ground floor. A close inspection of the entrance reveals a worn marble step, possibly reduced in height by thousands of immigrant's shoes and boots anxious to enter the building years ago. As rebuilt, the first floor was partitioned into two large reading rooms, a president's office and a board of director's room. A lecture hall which could seat five hundred people occupied the second floor, and the third floor was laid out for a gymnasium and dances. In 1905, the library had a total of four thousand books - in English, Russian, Hebrew, Yiddish, and German. The Society had seven hundred members.[150]

New Building of the Hebrew Literature Society
310-312 Catharine Street, Philadelphia

The Hebrew Literature Society was an unusual society. A picture of an American flag with forty-five stars is found on the cover of its 1905 souvenir program. The word "Liberty" is at the top of the cover page and the word "Education" below. Proclaimed throughout the land only blocks from this location, liberty was a living concept for refugees from Russia. But it was the role that the Society played in educating the immigrants that set it apart from other organizations. For the older generation it meant listening to a lecture in Yiddish after long hours in the shop. It meant being exposed to new ideas, argued passionately in a smoke filled auditorium. It meant learning about the American system of labor and capital. For the younger generation, it meant openly studying subjects which in the tradition-oriented *shtetl* might have to be studied in secret: bacteriology, French history, and sociology. Lectures were offered in Yiddish on Friday evenings and in English on Sunday afternoons. Not only did the finest Jewish speakers lecture here, but professors from the University of Pennsylvania, most of whom were not Jewish, were featured on Sundays. Talks given at the Hebrew Literature Society on Sundays in the Spring of 1905 included: March 12, Professor Arthur W. Goodspeed, the X-rays; April 2, Professor G. Clarence Childs, the English Language; April 16, Professor James S. Willard, the Medieval English Town; and April 30, Professor Carl Kelsey, Social Service. Altogether, from 1901 to 1905,

Hebrew Literature Society, 310–312 Catharine Street; 1905 Editorial Board* of the Hebrew Literature Society.

Courtesy of the YIVO Institute of Jewish Research, New York

sixteen different professors spoke to the immigrants at the Hebrew Literature Society.[151]

The relationship between the Hebrew Literature Society and the University of Pennsylvania was one of which both institutions could be proud. Poor Russian-Jewish boys and girls who listened to lectures on bacteriology on Sundays, wanted to attend the University of Pennsylvania upon High School graduation.[152] In 1914, girls were admitted to the University of Pennsylvania as regular undergraduate students. Even though the girls were restricted to the School of Education, they could take classes outside that School. In the early 1920's when conservative views swept the country, other Ivy league schools asked on their admission forms: "Have you or your family ever changed your last name and if you have, what was the name before it was changed?" But the University of Pennsylvania took the opposite view. Instead of bowing to the wishes of narrow-minded alumni as was done at other universities, the University of Pennsylvania gladly received the children of the Russian Jewish immigrants. Given the mood of the country in 1922, this welcome was remarkable.[153]

The Hebrew Literature Society hired a professional librarian. Immigrants directly off the steamers from Liverpool and Hamburg could take out their first book in English. Newspapers were received in many languages. If the religious soul of the Jewish quarter was B'nai Abraham, the intellectual soul was here. The men who worked so hard to make educational opportunities available to the immigrants, George Goward, Adolph Wachs, Samuel S. Fineman, Bernard Pockrass, Dr. David Feldman, Judah Baroway, Sol Meisach, David B. Tierkel, and others truly performed acts of loving kindness towards their fellow Jews.

Not only professors spoke here, the greatest Yiddish dramatists did also. At the end of October 1905, a testimonial evening to honor Abraham Goldfadn, the father of the Yiddish theatre, was given by the Society. Famous performers from New York took part and prominent speakers participated. The guest of the evening, Goldfadn, spoke about the beginnings of the Yiddish theatre. Melodies written many years before were played and sung by the assembled throng. Three years later, on Sunday, September 13, 1908, Jacob Gordin, the father of serious Yiddish drama, spoke here. He was particularly irritated that evening by what he declared was the failure of producers of Yiddish drama to pay royalties. "Here in Philadelphia where Max Thomashevsky is the manager," Gordin said, "my plays are performed at the Columbia Theatre without my knowledge and without my permission." Entitlement to payment of royalties for performances, however, like most claims, had two sides, and Thomashevsky immediately contested Gordin's claim.[154] And as Gordin himself well knew, the enforcement of alleged rights to royalties and the enjoining of claimed unauthorized performances were not easy matters to prove.[155]

The decline of the Hebrew Literature Society began in the early 1920's and quickly accelerated. In his history of immigrant Jewish Philadelphia in 1929, Freeman wrote: "Uncountable intelligentsia, professionals, and successful entrepreneurs of all sorts, as greenhorns or school boys, received their first general education in the

* Left to right: (Standing) David B. Tierkel, Hillel Malachovsky, and Dr. Simon Wendkos. (Seated) Marcus Goldman, the long-time librarian of the Society, and Nathan Grayev.

Hebrew Literature Society, graduation of the Sunday School, June 21, 1920. The third graduate from the right, seated, is Rebecca Davidow, mother of the author. She became a teacher at the Sunday school following graduation.

Hebrew Literature Society. Where are they now? Sadness and disappointment seizes me as we pass this place, which is forsaken and mourned as a living protest against its former children, who, in their private lives, were supplied with a rich background for their professions or for their profitable businesses. They do not seem to care that their former educational institute is at death's door." Although the Society held on for several more years, the vibrancy of its early period could not be maintained without new immigrants. It faltered at the same time the *Yidishe Velt*, the synagogues in the area, and many other beneficial and communal organizations began to decline. And for the same reasons. Although the building stands, the Hebrew Literature Society vanished many years ago. Today, the building is a multi-family dwelling.

Central Talmud Torah: 314-320 Catharine Street. Constructed of buff tapestry brick, terra cotta, limestone, granite and cast stone, the building of the Central Talmud Torah, standing four stories tall, is undoubtedly the most magnificent structure built by the east European Jewish immigrants in Philadelphia. It was certainly the most expensive. Built at a cost approaching $100,000, it stands today, a forgotten legacy to Jewish religious education. "Set amidst a row of two and three story red brick row houses, the light coloration, larger size, and highly ornamented neo-classical facade of the former school house distinguishes it from its neighbors, and asserts a formal, imposing presence on the streetscape."[156] The Central Talmud Torah is an example of the work of the important Philadelphia architectural firm of Magaziner and Potter.

In 1909, the properties at 318-320 Catharine Street were purchased[157] and plans were made to tear down four properties and build a new Talmud Torah.[158] On November 30, 1910, the school vacated the properties and held classes next door at the Hebrew Literature Society and in nearby synagogues. At this time the name of the school was changed to the Central Talmud Torah (previously it had been called the Downtown Talmud Torah), the dedication of which took place on Sunday, October 29, 1911, before 5,000 people. The square of Catharine Street between 3rd and 4th was decorated with American, Jewish, and Philadelphia flags. Electric lights were strung along both sides of the street. The celebration lasted for an entire week. On Tuesday evening, Jacob B. Rosenblum of B'nai Abraham, spoke: "Mr. Rosenblum compared the erection of the new Central Talmud Torah to the building of the Temple of old. When Solomon built the Temple, it was not a matter of boasting for him. His attitude was an apologetic one. He apologized for not having had one until then and expressed hope that the Bamoth -

the undesirable places of worship - would be no more. So, too, with the erection of this Talmud Torah. The Jews of Philadelphia should not boast of this accomplishment but rather apologize for not having had it until now."[159] Rabbi Simon (Sheftel) Fyne, the rabbi at the Montefiore synagogue, was elected principal.[160] Upon opening, two thousand children gathered each day after public school for Jewish religious training.

The Central Talmud Torah offered a six-year program of ten hours a week, which supplemented public school education. There were seventeen classes of eight grades daily for two hours a day. Studies included Hebrew prayers, reading and writing Hebrew, Torah, the commentary of Rashi, the early prophets, Jewish history, customs, and ceremonies. The day-to-day activities of the school were maintained by eight young women: Miss A. Bodek, Gertrude Lichtenstein, Sarah Kates, Sarah Fox, Adelaide Aronson, Dora Bahof, Belle Elfman and Lenora Levy.[161]

It is not quite clear what happened to Rabbi Simon Fyne, but within less than one year after the Talmud Torah opened its new building, Rabbi David Englander, the son of Rabbi Simon J. Englander, was installed as the new principal. The younger Englander, who had studied for thirteen years in Jerusalem and was strict in his approach to Orthodox Jewish practices, was brought from Providence, Rhode Island in October 1912 to carry out the wishes of the more traditional members of the Board of Directors. Shortly before Passover in 1913, the Board announced that the services of seven teachers who supported the *haskala* were no longer desired, and they were asked to leave. The decision split the Jewish community. When the students learned that the teachers were to be dismissed, their young souls - obviously prodded by "Enlightened" (those adhering to the *haskala*) parents at home - rebelled. The matter came to a head when eight hundred students assembled in the school for the purpose of listening to a musical entertainment. As soon as the new principal entered the room, the children arose and began hissing, catcalling, and breaking chairs. The disturbance reached the point where police were called to restore order. In the ensuing weeks there were strikes, marches, meetings, threats, and much division and rancor within the community.[162]

As during the kosher meat disputes, the immigrant Jewish community was again split on the question of how to follow traditional Jewish practices in America. One faction looked back to Russia and one looked forward to a new Judaism. Perhaps today, Hebrew school children do not have the passion to strike and demonstrate in support of one position or the other, but in the early days of the Russian Jewish settlement in Philadelphia, the way one practiced Judaism went to the fiber of one's being even if he or she was a school child of tender years.[163]

In 1925, the Yeshiva Mishkan Yisroel moved here. "About 120 students studied at the Yeshiva at one time, all graduates of either the Central Talmud Torah or one of the newer Talmud Torahs subsequently established in the city." In 1952, the building at 314-320 Catharine Street was sold to Beth Jacob School of Philadelphia, a Jewish parochial school. Beth Jacob was sold in 1963. Today, the building is a condominium.

Rebecca Gratz Club: 700 block of Catharine Street. In 1907, five properties were condemned and new houses were built at a total cost of $17,500 ($3,500 each). Two of the properties were leased by the Rebecca Gratz Club for a home for immigrant Jewish working girls.[164]

Declaring the situation of the shop girl who earned $3 a week to be hopeless, Miss Rose Somerfield, head of the Clara De Hirsch Home for Girls in New York city, presented in *Homes for Working Girls*, a featured paper at the fourth biennial meeting of the National Conference of Jewish Charities, held at the Jewish Foster Home and Orphan Asylum, Church Lane and Chew Street, Philadelphia, on May 7, 1906.[165] In her paper, Somerfield wrote: "The working girl problem is one of the very greatest with which charity workers have to deal. These young girls come to the city from the country, or else immigrate, and if they do not fall into the right surroundings are driven into temptation. It is for the purpose of helping them in their unfortunate condition that 'Homes' are being founded in cities all over the land." Whether this paper spurred the founding of the Rebecca Gratz home is not known, but soon after the reading of the paper, plans were made for using these homes on Catharine Street for working Jewish girls.

The two handsome Philadelphia row homes here had a total of twenty-six rooms. The offices, a library, dining room, living room, kitchen and pantry were located on the first floor. Seventeen of the rooms were bedrooms; each, with the exception of the two third-story front rooms, contained two single beds; rooms on the third stories were fitted up for three persons. The first housemother, or matron, was Miss Chrystal. In June 1913, a successor housemother, Miss Smulyn, questioned why one of the girls, who worked at Quaker City Knitting Mills for $4 a week, could not pay for her board and also afford lunch. The girl had asked the home to provide lunch for her as she said that there was not enough money remaining after she paid board to buy lunch. Miss Smulyn felt confident that she could show the girl how to live on $4 a week and even save a few pennies.

CHRISTIAN STREET

The buildings identified on Christian Street have been torn down.

Independent Chevra Kadisha: 408-412 Christian Street. Founded in September 1892, the Independent Chevra Kadisha (Burial Society) was established to give free burial to the Jewish poor. By 1905, it could afford its own building and contracted to build a "mortuary, stable and privies" here. How long the Chevra Kadisha was located here is not clear.

The College Settlement of Philadelphia: 429-435 Christian Street. Like the Phipps Institute, this was not a Jewish organization, but is included because it was closely connected with the Russian Jewish community. Founded in 1890, the College Settlement of Philadelphia had four locations in Philadelphia, this being the only one in the Jewish quarter.

The College Settlement was run by women from different colleges and focused its attention on the social needs of the community. At 433 Christian Street in 1905 a regular morning kindergarten was maintained. When the children entered the kindergarten they had, as a rule, little knowledge of English. "A tri-lingual (Jewish-Italian-English) Kindergarten, of children from three to six years old, has its own requirements and difficulties." During the vacation months of July and August a summer kindergarten was run and there was "...play hour for the' little mothers,' girls from eight to twelve or thirteen years, whose infant brothers and sisters were ever with them."

At the end of a play yard at 435 Christian Street were three showers. They were partially enclosed and consequently in use during the warm weather only. In the summer of 1905 five babies were brought in, who were never, on the admission of their mothers, bathed before. The babies, brought by their mothers, were usually in the care of older sisters. Many girls borrowed babies as cards of admission so that they could take a shower.[166]

Stained glass windows of Kesher Israel, 1995. *Photograph by Fred Wagner*

SOUTH SECOND STREET

There were many Jewish businesses along S. 2nd Street - clothing stores, bakeries, furniture stores, dry goods, etc. East of 2nd Street, along Pine, Delancey, and Dock Streets, wholesale produce merchants flourished. There were several kosher-style restaurants in the 300 block of S. 2nd Street. On Front Street there were wholesale poultry and fish merchants. The poultry market had a *shoykhet*, a ritual slaughterer.

Goldensky's Photographic Studio: 270 S. 2nd Street. Elias Goldensky, the famous art photographer, rented an equipped photography studio here on the second floor in November 1895. Known as the Captain James Abercrombie House, this four and one-half story building, built in 1759, had been used for photography studios since 1862. Goldensky expanded his studio by taking the entire third floor and a room on the fourth floor. In his early years, he photographed Israel Zangwill, the bright star of the Anglo-American literary scene; Rabbi Levinthal; Naphtali Herz Imber, the author of Hatikvah and a frequent visitor to Philadelphia; Maxim Gorky; and Madame de Hirsch, the wife of Baron de Hirsch. Later, politicians and celebrities such as President Franklin Delano Roosevelt, Al Jolson, and Rabbi Joseph Krauskopf had their portraits taken by him.[1]

Congregation Ahavas Achim-Anshe Nezin: 771 S. 2nd Street. The story is told that a neighborhood tailor lost his wife soon after immigrating to Philadelphia. He was from the town of Nezin (Nezhin) and he wanted to say *kaddish*, the memorial prayer, as he had learned it in Russia. But when he found a synagogue in which to say the prayer, it was not said with the *nusakh* (rite) he had learned. He called together a group of *landslayt* from Nezin, and they founded the Neziner congregation on August 24, 1889, at 217 Pine Street. The official name of the synagogue was Ahavas Achim-Anshe Nezin, Nusach Ha-Ari, or Brotherly Love-People of Nezin, the rite of Ari (Rabbi Isaac Luria). This rite, adopted by Hassidic communities in Russia, was a modified form of the Sephardic rite, where, among other things, the words *ve-yatzmakh purkoney viykorev meshikhey* (and may He cause His redemption to sprout and bring his Messiah near) appear in the *kaddish*, though they are not found in the regular Ashkenazic rite. This modified Sephardic rite is called *Ha-Ari*.

Nezin was a small *shtetl* in southern Russia. While little scholarly attention has been paid to the geographic origin of the Russian Jews who settled in Philadelphia, anecdotal evidence suggests that many immigrants who settled here came from the southern part of Russia. Towns like Nezin, while not as far south as other large towns such as Uman, Smela, Kremenchug, Ekaterinoslav, Zolotonosha, Boguslav, and Odessa, supplied Philadelphia with many immigrants, especially after each series of pogroms that erupted in the south of Russia in the early decades of this century.

After two years, the Neziner congregation moved to 322 Bainbridge Street, and in the middle 1890's it moved to Heartfellow Hall, 754-756 S. 3rd Street, where it remained for about ten years. When Heartfellow Hall became too small, the congregation purchased the old Third Baptist Church meeting house at 771 S. 2nd Street.[2] In August of 1809, twenty-eight members of the First Baptist Church solicited a letter of dismission to form the Third Baptist Church in Southwark. The congregation numbered 128 members. It acquired the property here and work commenced on the construction of a two-story stone meeting house. Built on the east side of S. 2nd Street north of Catharine and set back from the building line, the roughcast building, 50' wide and 60' deep, was located at the rear of a large courtyard. The pews were large and high and were called "square boxes." The pulpit was perched up to a great height and was enclosed by doors. The church was dedicated on February 28, 1811. It is the building standing here today.

A sketch made in 1837 for the purpose of a fire insurance survey shows the arrangement of the interior.[3] The pulpit was placed at the east end of the sturdy little meeting house. There were three aisles running parallel to the north and south side walls. Fourteen pews were located between each of the outside aisles and the side walls, and twenty-seven pews were located in each center block. There were galleries on three sides. Whether the galleries date back to the original construction is not known. In 1854, interior improvements were made to the building at a cost of $5,500, but it is unclear what these improvements were.

During the Civil War, the church, which was located close to the busy rail yards on Washington Avenue, was offered as a temporary hospital for the wounded in transit to their homes. But not all of them made it home: "The pastor's [Rev. Jared H. Peters] strength was much drawn upon in attendance upon funeral of soldiers." On December 8th, 9th, and 10th, 1879, the congregation celebrated its 70th anniversary, but within a few years the "ingress of foreigners in our neighborhood has caused the removal to distant places of many of our active workers and a natural decrease in the attendance." The church voted to sell the building since a new church had been planned at Broad and Ritner Streets. By 1896, members of the Third Baptist Church had been "driven from our old field by foreign population."

At that time, the Southwark area around 2nd & Catharine Streets was heavily Polish and the Third Baptist Church was sold to the First Polish National Society of Philadelphia, a Catholic splinter group not answerable to Catholic church hierarchy. The dissident church, however, did not become popular with the devout Polish Roman Catholics in the neighborhood and, on February 2, 1902, the property, along with a parsonage house - built, according to some sources in 1754 - was sold by the sheriff. Several years later the property was bought by Henry J. Ettelson who, on February 27, 1905, sold it to Ahavas Achim-Anshe Nezin, or as it would be called for many years, the Neziner congregation or *shul*.

Immediately, work was started to convert the building to a synagogue. Neziner was the only congregation in the Jewish quarter to have a courtyard in front. Upon acquisition, graves on the sides and at the rear of the property were opened and the bodies were disinterred and reburied elsewhere. The principal entrance through the western wall was retained, thus permitting the ark to be placed in its traditional eastern location. The eastern wall was torn down, and the *ornkoydesh* was placed upon a new wall. The *ornkoydesh*, which was made of hand-carved wood and painted white, was mounted on a wall of large white squares. Small lighting fixtures were attached over the galleries and a delicately turned brass chandelier was suspended proudly above the main sanctuary. The entire room, including the solid balcony fronts, was painted white in the Colonial style. The pews, doors, floor, and the entire rear portion of the sanctuary were not changed. As a synagogue, the building could seat eight hundred worshipers. The name of the congregation was written in Hebrew letters above the massive front doors.[4]

Inside, the building contained vestry rooms on the ground floor, which were used by the congregants for weekday services and as meeting places. The synagogue was one flight up. Outside, the lot in the back was used as a play yard and the plot of ground on the south side was used for the *sukkah*. "The front garden afforded a touch of botanical splendor, thanks to an abundance of sunflowers in the appropriate season." The dedication occurred on Sunday, July 16, 1905.[5] Services began at Heartfellow Hall where Rabbis Levinthal and Erschler spoke. Afterwards, participants numbering several hundred formed in line for a parade and, headed by the Stars and Stripes and the blue and white emblem of Zion, they marched "about the streets" before going to the new building on S. 2nd Street.

Two thousand Jews from the southern section of the city greeted the marchers who were waiting for them at the new synagogue. Both groups mixed together, and everyone scrambled to get inside to view the festivities first-hand. Jacob Edelman, chairman of the building committee and a muscular man, took a stand halfway up the outside staircase attempting to stay the rush. After holding back the throng for several minutes, he gave up and dashed into the synagogue, the crowd at his feet. The building was decorated in gold and white with purple hangings. A boys' choir under the direction of Rev. Kritshmar opened the exercises with singing. Addresses were made by Rabbis Levinthal, Grossman, and Brenner. The move to these larger quarters on S. 2nd Street also made it possible to engage a permanent hazzan, Cantor Hayyim Harris.

The most interesting personality associated with the Neziner synagogue was David Goldstein, the sexton and conductor of *shiurim* (study sessions).[6] Men came to Goldstein for advice and women would ask him to *opshprekh an eyn-hore* (to ward off the evil eye, if a malady afflicted their children). Born Yehudah Leib David Wallach, in the tiny Lithuanian hamlet of Stayachechik in 1868 (the town had only twenty Jewish households), he was trained in the yeshiva of Lida and received *smicha* (ordination) there. He was a *shoykhet*. Upon his arrival in New York friends convinced him to change his name from Wallach to Goldstein because he was told Goldstein was a better-known Jewish name. He came to Philadelphia and after peddling for a short time, he became the *shames* for the Neziner congregation at Heartfellow Hall.

Goldstein organized the *chevra mishnayes* and the

Neziner building, 771 S. 2nd Street, 1998. This sturdy little meeting house was built in 1811. It was home to the Third Baptist Church from 1811 to 1896, to the First Polish National Society of Philadelphia from 1898 to 1902, and to the Neziner congregation from 1905 to 1983.

Photograph by Gene Michael Brown

chevra shas (the Mishna and Talmud study groups). He ran the daily prayer service and provided *minyans* (quorums) for *Yahrzeit* observances. He enforced the payment of dues and attended to the arrangement of weddings, circumcisions, and funerals. The religious piety and devotion fostered by Goldstein was commingled with a genial community feeling that he transplanted from the *shtetl* in Russia.

During World War I, residents of the Jewish quarter prospered and many took advantage of the opportunity to move to other parts of the city. These were hard times for the old *shuls* in the Jewish quarter. From 1918 to 1920, there was a "ray of prosperity" during the administration of Sol Stamm when the second mortgage was "cleared." But membership thereafter quickly declined. In the late twenties and the Depression, the synagogue had another rebirth under the leadership of Isaac Schreider. It was also at this time that Florence Rosenthal formed a sisterhood and it flourished for many years.[7]

Just prior to World War II, Dr. John Craig Roak, Minister of Gloria Dei Church, popularly called Old Swedes' Church (a national shrine located at Swanson and Christian Streets, slightly to the east and south of the old Jewish quarter), began interfaith services with the Neziner congregation. Roak did much in South Philadelphia to bring about a better understanding among the various religious groups, and services with the Neziner congregation were carried on for years. The interfaith service held at Old Swedes' Church on February 21, 1954, featured an address by the Honorable John S. Fine, Governor of Pennsylvania. But attendance and membership continued to decline at Neziner. In 1983, the congregation merged with Beth Zion-Beth Israel, 18th & Spruce Streets, and the building was sold.

Today, this handsomely restored meeting house (it is a condominium) includes a decorative lunette in the western gable and central doors flanked by majestic rounded windows. The design of the windows goes back to at least 1885 and perhaps to the founding of the church.

Isadore Joseph Cooper: Foot of Washington Avenue at the Delaware River. In 1914, Isadore Joseph Cooper had a steamship ticket office for the American Line. He advertised in the *Yidishe Velt* that he was located at the Foot of Washington Avenue. The lack of an exact address does not appear to have harmed his business, and his name is mentioned favorably by the immigrants in testimony taken before the special boards of inquiry.[8] Cooper provided services that were vital to the immigrant community, especially to those separated from loved ones in Russia. He patiently explained to immigrants already here how they might bring family and friends to these shores.

SOUTH THIRD STREET

Before electronic communication was used, such as the telephone and radio, information was exchanged in person. Nowhere was this more conveniently done than in a hall, and no street in the Jewish quarter had more halls than S. 3rd Street. Fittingly, these halls were located just blocks from two of the most famous halls in the United States, Independence Hall and Carpenter's Hall. (APPENDIX E contains a listing of the halls in the Jewish quarter.)

Initially, they were simply called halls. Later, many were called catering halls. They were used for dances, political and union gatherings, parties, socialist and anarchistic meetings, and gambling, but no activity was more closely associated with these halls than a Jewish wedding.

Powel House: 244 S. 3rd Street: Not surprisingly, the revival of colonial history in the area had its roots in the immigrant Jewish community. In 1904, Wolf Klebansky purchased the old Powel House, the magnificent city house of Samuel Powel, the first mayor of Philadelphia under the Republic (for *Klebansky,* see *246 S. 3rd Street*). In 1907, Klebansky gave some thought to tearing the house down. However, when informed by the Colonial Dames of America of the historic value of the house and that George Washington danced and was entertained here, Klebansky hesitated. He realized the value of the mansion to America and said: "I understand the feeling which loyal Americans bear towards this house and do not wish to seem a vandal. Nevertheless, while this building stands idle, I lose money." But lose money or not, he did not tear the building down. Rather, he agreed to rent the front part of the house to the Colonial Dames. A plan was laid out for various historical societies to rent one room in the mansion thereby securing its survival, but only the Indian Rights Society rented a room. The intervention of the Colonial Dames may have diverted Klebansky temporarily, but two years later he had a new idea for the old house.

In February 1909, Klebansky requested the architectural firm of Watson & Huckel to prepare a plan that provided for a new front, as well as lowering the first floor to the street level.[9] He wanted to convert the Powel House into a financial institution that he was in the process of forming. Again, the Society of Colonial Dames made an ineffectual effort to purchase the property, and Klebansky did not carry through with his plans.

In December 1930, Klebansky proposed to tear down the Powel House and erect a garage. Upon learning of the proposal, a delegation of interested citizens, headed by H. Louis Duhring, an architect, visited the mansion and announced plans to raise funds to purchase both 244 and 246 S. 3rd Street, and to preserve and restore the Powel House. At this point the *Ledgers* picked up the story and for the next two months they covered it extensively. The *Ledgers'* even-handed reporting of the story emphasized that Klebansky had for many years paid taxes and other maintenance costs on the Powel mansion "without any return."[10] Duhring founded the Philadelphia Society for the Preservation of Landmarks, an organization that bought the Powel House in 1931. The following year the restoration process began. Open to the public.

The Home of Wolf Klebansky: 246 S. 3rd Street. Wolf Klebansky purchased this property in May 1899. He was a philanthropist who lived among his people and gave liberally of his time and fortune. Klebansky helped to finance the construction of new buildings for the Central Talmud Torah on Catharine Street and the *Moyshev Zkeynim* on S. 3rd Street. During World War I, he was the treasurer of the Central Relief Committee of Philadelphia. He was the president and treasurer of the Central Talmud Torah and Congregation Kesher Israel. Born in 1859 in the small village of Nemaksciai, Kovno Guberniya, Russia, Klebansky came to the United States about 1884 and quickly became a successful importer and dealer in Russian and Siberian horsehair and bristles. In Philadelphia, he dealt in manes and all kinds of animal hair that he supplied to the curled hair trade. He was also a manufacturer of drawn hair for the supply of brush manufacturers.[11] The business premises of the firm were located on S. Orianna Street at the rear of his home.

Klebansky married Chaya Dobra Braude, a descendant of the illustrious Braude family from Kelm. Childless, the Klebanskys devoted their lives to those in greatest need: orphans, the elderly, and the poor. No one was more attentive to the needs of the children of the Jewish quarter than Wolf and Chaya Klebansky.[12] He called a meeting at his home on the night of May 4, 1913, to hear out both sides of the strike then in progress at the Talmud Torah (see 314-320 Catharine Street). Present were Akiba Fleishman, president of the National Association of Jewish Religious School Teachers, and Dr. Benjamin L. Gordon, chairman of the Education Committee of the Talmud Torah, who attended on behalf of the dismissed teachers. After meeting all night, it was announced that a new corps of teachers would be selected and the dismissed teachers would not be reinstated. From this and other decisions he made, it us clear that Klebansky sided with the more traditional elements of Orthodoxy.

Powel House, 244 S. 3rd Street, 1903.
The Powel House, center, was purchased by Wolf Klebansky in 1904 and sold in 1931.

Courtesy of Historical Society of Pennsylvania, Philadelphia, Pennsylvania

Chaya Dobra died on July 30, 1929 and Wolf died three years later.[13] Wolf Klebansky is remembered today - if for anything - as the owner of the Powel House. Ownership of the Powel House during his lifetime occupied little of his time but brought him negative publicity and little else. His philanthropy and good deeds to the immigrant Jewish community have been virtually forgotten. The property at 246 S. 3rd Street was torn down in 1932, and today the lot is used as the garden for the Powel House.

Tombstones* of Wolf Klebansky and Chaya Dobra Klebansky. Har Nebo Cemetery, Oxford Avenue, Philadelphia.

The Jewish Sheltering Homes: 315-317 S. 3rd Street. Comprised of the *Hakhnosses Orkhim* (Hospitality to Strangers) and the *Moyshev Zkeynim* (Old Age Home), these two organizations were collectively called the Sheltering Homes. They were dedicated here on June 14, 1908. Previously, the homes had been located at 218-220 Lombard Street. At the time of the dedication, Chaya Dobra Klebansky was president. The building, four stories in height, had prominent Hebrew lettering inscribed on the stringcourse between the second and third floors: פרויען פאריין (Woman's Organization). Between the first floor and the second floor the following Hebrew words were inscribed:

הכנסת אורחים ומושב זקנים

* His tombstone reads: "One of the eminent and honorable people of the city. Scholar of Torah and Keeper of the Commandments who holds the rabbis in high esteem and in good faith takes care of the needs of the community." Her tombstone reads: "All of her days she dealt with the needs of the community."

or Hospitality to Strangers and Old Age Home. Each Hebrew letter was over one foot in height.

Small balconies with windows on the second, third, and fourth floors on the western side of the building permitted the late afternoon sun to bathe the rooms in sunlight. Twin lateral steps led to a center door, and windows on the first floor were shuttered in the Federal style. Inside were thirty-eight large rooms and two synagogues. Adjoining the building was a spacious lot planted with trees and various plants. Two thousand people attended the dedication ceremony that began at Kesher Israel. Another six hundred were denied admittance to the building because of lack of room. In the tradition of the Russian Jews, the dedicatory ceremonies lasted throughout the week. During Redevelopment, the building was torn down to make room for a parking lot.

"The Time of Singing is Come": Corner of 3rd & Lombard Streets. In 1913, A. Imber advertised his real estate brokerage services in the Yiddish newspaper, the *Jewish Herald*. At this time real estate offices were on almost every corner. A 1913 advertisement in the *Herald* began

The Moyshev Zkeynim (Old People's Home) and the *Hakhnosses Orkhim* (Hospitality to Strangers), 315-317 S. 3rd Street, circa 1910.

Philadelphia Jewish Archives Center

as follows: עת הזמיר הגיע or the Time of Singing is Come. Russian Jews would have instantly recognized the words from Song of Songs (2:12). In fact, the line would probably not have been used if it weren't so well known. But why had the time of singing come? The advertisement asked: Do you want "fresh air?" and "beautiful country landscape?" and concluded: "Then buy a home near Fairmount Park in Strawberry Mansion." These advertisements were apparently very successful for within a generation, the Russian Jew was again on the move, this time not from Russia to Philadelphia, but from the crowded Jewish quarter to the fresh air and beautiful countryside of Strawberry Mansion. Philadelphia Jews who grew up in the Mansion, as Strawberry Mansion was known by a generation of Jews from the 1920's to the 1950's, believed that they had been raised in one of the most beautiful spots on earth, a land where the time of singing had truly come.

The Southwark Hose Company Firehouse: 512 S. 3rd Street. The Southwark Hose Company Firehouse was constructed in 1856, and The Fire Association of Philadelphia owned it well into the immigrant period. In 1897, Meyer B. (Berko) Sarshik, the owner of a peddler's supply store, acquired the building, and he kept it until 1909. The years Sarshik owned the building, the first floor was used for commercial purposes and the second floor was used as a hall.

Sarshik, whose name in Russia was Beryl Zeitchik, was born in Russian Poland in 1862, and he came to Philadelphia about 1886. As many of the earliest settlers did, Sarshik became a peddler, a pack on his back from early morning. In 1887, he rented a store at 430 S. 7th Street and began to sell to peddlers. The following year he moved to 719 South Street. Although little is known of the details of the business dealings of the early Jews on South Street, we do know that Sarshik carried "a stock of cheap jewelry notions." Established credit bureaus made recommendations to deal with Sarkshik carefully: "Sell him [Sarshik] only for cash & do not recommend him in any other way." It was difficult for the immigrants to establish credit. Surely many feared to wander out of their Yiddish beginnings and found it easy to buy from and sell to other immigrants. An assessment of Sarshik's earlier business (430 S. 7th Street), "[L]ocation poor, can't make over a basic existence...," could have been made of many of the early businesses in the Jewish quarter.[14]

By the time Sarshik moved his store to the first floor of this former firehouse, he had already been in business many years. He carried hosiery, notions, household items – whatever there was a demand for. When a green family came to the Jewish quarter and the man of the house began to peddle, he came to a store like Sarshik's. Some peddlers refreshed their stock every evening. Others, like those with whom Sarshik dealt, usually came once a week.

Like many of the early settlers, Sarshik was very *frum* (pious). He closed his store for *Shabbes*, helped to found B'nai Reuben (he was a charter member), and arranged marriages for four of his five daughters (his youngest daughter chose her own husband).

For a number of years near the end of the 19th century (before Sarshik acquired the property), an amateur theatrical company called the Star Specialty Club produced Yiddish plays in the hall on the second floor. Dr. Max Staller, the former union leader and later a well-known surgeon, was one of the leaders of the group. A play produced here was *Sailor in Distress*, by Rudoph Marks, a favorite piece with the first east European Jewish immigrants. After a time the play lost its com-

Old Firehouse, 512 S. 3rd Street, 1959. Used for the Yiddish theatre in the last years of the 19th century.
Courtesy of the Philadelphia City Archives

mercial box office value, but it continued to draw new arrivals to halls and theatres to witness amateur productions. In addition to being used as a hall, the second floor of this old firehouse was used as a synagogue. Agudas Achim, organized in 1904, met here for over a decade.

Today the building is a commercial establishment

The Rosenbaum Bank: 603-605 S. 3rd Street. Morris Rosenbaum, one of the most colorful and well-known figures in the Jewish quarter, was born on August 11, 1858, in Nagyvarad, Hungary, and immigrated to this country in 1878.

He settled in Buffalo, New York, and several years later came to Philadelphia. He was among the founding members of the Pannonia Society, a fraternal society formed to help fellow Hungarian immigrants. The following story is told within the Rosenbaum family as to how Morris got started as an immigrant banker: "He was employed at Philadelphia in a private bank or steamship agency which was about to fail. The legend is that Young Morris, to placate the irate mob who were storming the place to claim their money, jumped up on the counter and calmed them by stating that if they would trust him to take care of the business, he assured them that they would get back their money with no losses. He won the day and that was how he launched himself into his own steamship and banking business."[15] This exciting legend, however, is beyond the ability of an historian to verify in the last years of the 20th century.

What we do know is that Morris Rosenbaum was identified with the German Jewish community. He was a member of Rodeph Shalom Congregation, which he joined shortly after arriving in Philadelphia. Rosenbaum, however, was also active in Russian Jewish communal life. He financed the first Yiddish newspaper in Philadelphia and was the first contributor to the fund for the new building of the Hebrew Literature Society. And there may have been personal reasons for his affinity for the Russians. Rosenbaum's father, Salamon Itzsak, was born in Russia, drafted into the Russian Army and, as part of an attacking Russian force, Salamon Itzsak entered Hungary. After being wounded, perhaps at the battle of Debreczin, he made his way to Nagyvarad and during the departure of his unit, hid in a barrel. Salamon Itzsak was cared for by the townspeople, and he did not return to Russia. Whether his father's Russian Jewish origins had meaning to Morris Rosenbaum is not known, but, however strict and Victorian his own family remembered him, Morris was a caring person who helped the Russian immigrants in many ways.

Morris Rosenbaum purchased the building here in 1900, and several years later he added a Renaissance Revival limestone front at a cost of $8,000. The architects were Magaziner & Potter.[16] Rosenbaum moved his immigrant bank business here at the height of Russian Jewish immigration in 1907 *(for Rosenbaum's first bank, see 609 S. 3rd Street)*. Symmetrical in plan, today the bank's rich classical detail contrasts sharply with altered nearby storefronts. During the height of east European immigration, a scaled model of the *Nord Deutsche Lloyd SS Kronprinzessin Cecilie*, a typical steamship of the day, stood prominently in the office of the bank. Appointed to the Philadelphia School Board, Morris Rosenbaum also played a role in the education of the youth of the immigrants.

There was a movement within educational circles to have the children of immigrants educated separately. Some saw the immigrant child as different from the other children, a difference caused by two factors: the unusually large number of pupils of foreign birth and the elementary school teacher's inability to cope with the situation. The handling of the immigrant child was described as a problem. The separatist movement was gaining momentum when Rosenbaum was appointed

Rosenbaum Bank, 603-605 S. 3rd Street, early part of 20th century. Morris Rosenbaum, standing on the left. Others unidentified. *Courtesy of Edward W. Rosenbaum*

to the Board of Education. In an address on this subject before district superintendents and supervising principals, given on December 5, 1907, Rosenbaum spoke directly to the question:

> A proposition to establish separate schools, or separate classes for immigrant children is almost provocative of amusement. Where is the necessity for it? Children who are deaf and dumb; children who are mentally defective; children who for such grave reasons are physically unable to acquire learning by the ordinary methods - for these we establish separate schools. But are we to segregate a whole class of children for the sole reason that they lack such a comprehension of the English language as their American-born school-mates?
>
> It is this very contact with those English-speaking companions that has upon them the most important influence. The mere teaching of facts is not the only purpose of our public school system. It is in these schools where all students find themselves on the same level, from which they can rise only by competition, that the first principles of democracy are instilled into the child. It would be criminal to cut off these helpless children, ignorant only of the sounds which we call our language, from those associations which should be theirs upon their first entry into our public school. For purely social reasons, therefore, even though mere pedagogy were not involved, the establishment of separate grades or schools for immigrant children is a mistake in policy and an inconsistency in principle.[17]

Rosenbaum would often walk down to the waterfront to personally greet the newcomers. The bank was on a sound footing and held on for several years after passage of the immigration quota law of 1924.[18] Rosenbaum sold the bank building on February 4, 1931, and he died five days later. In 1974, plans were made to build a multi-story residential complex on this site, but through the intervention of the South Street Renaissance Association (a group of four hundred residents, property owners, and business people representing community interests in the area) and the Queen Village Neighbors Association, pressure was brought to bear on the City Planning Commission and other agencies and individuals not to build the complex. As a result, the plans were discarded.

A plaque has been affixed to the building by a grandson of the founder:

THIS BUILDING WAS
MORRIS ROSENBAUM'S
PRIVATE BANK AND STEAMSHIP TICKET OFFICE
1888-1933
THIS PLAQUE GIVEN BY
COL. EDWARD W. ROSENBAUM
IN RESPECTFUL MEMORY

It is the only plaque affixed to a building in the area by one of the pioneer families.

Rosenbaum's First Bank: 609 S. 3rd Street. Alexander Kopperl and Morris Rosenbaum founded a "transportation" business here in 1887. Beginning the following year, Kopperl's name was dropped from the enterprise and Rosenbaum continued the business here as a passenger agent, ticket agent, and private banker. His was one of the first immigrant banks in the area and although dozens of other steamship and railroad offices opened near his bank during the immigrant period, almost all of them closed within a short time. One of the many reasons for Rosenbaum's success was the keen business judgment of his employee, Charles Lipshutz *(see 410 South Street)*.

Charles Lipshutz, who over a decade later was to become a co-founder of People's Bank, came to Rosenbaum's in 1890 to learn the immigrant banking trade. While Lipshutz was here, he became known throughout the Jewish quarter and South Philadelphia, and he brought Rosenbaum a brisk immigrant business. An example of how the immigrants viewed the services that Rosenbaum and Lipshutz could provide is set forth in the memoirs of Manual F. Lisan, an early Zionist who came to Philadelphia at the turn of the century. Lisan received a post card from his mother in Odessa, advising him that his father died. Lisan, believing it was his responsibility to bring his mother and five small brothers and sisters to the United States, immediately sought help: "I walked as fast as my feet could carry me to reach Rosenbaum Bank at 3rd and South St. where my friend Charles Lipshitz [Lipshutz] was ready to retire for the day. Nevertheless, he had taken my order for transportation for my mother and children to come to Philadelphia. It was all the money I had saved in the Bank, but who could be more satisfied and happier than I was, thinking that my mother and the rest of the family, will be with us within the next few weeks."[19]

In 1907, Rosenbaum moved to 603-605 S. 3rd Street.

New Central Hall and New Arcadia Hall: 610 S. 3rd Street. This property was used as a hall for over twenty years. Proprietors in 1904, "Professor" Rosenthal from New York and Jacob Ben Israel Fleet, sought weddings and other affairs for the hall through frequent advertisements in the *Jewish Daily Forward*. At first it was called Central Hall.

Born in Russia in 1854, Fleet came to Philadelphia in his mid-thirties. By 1893, he was selling "segars [cigars]" here.[20] Fleet acquired the property outright in 1906, added a three-story, 35' extension onto the building, installed a banquet range, and made other alterations. J. Elwin Jackson designed the improvements. The hall was known as New Central Hall from 1906 to 1918, and New Arcadia Hall from 1918 until 1924. During the time it was New Central Hall, or slightly earlier, the Podolier Association, a mutual benefit society, met here. When it was New Arcadia Hall, strike headquarters for Vest Makers' and Children's Clothing Locals 143-249-281 were located here. About the time of World War I, the hall was identified as a dance hall.[21]

Halls in the Jewish quarter were used for "pleasure socials," weddings, and balls or masquerade dances for charity. The pleasure social was one of the most popular forms of entertainment for the younger generation at the turn of the 20th century. According to Charles S. Bernheimer, there were three distinct types of pleasure socials: (1) a group of a dozen or more young men who would band together to hold a social for pleasure, with

New Central Hall, 610 S. 3rd Street, 1993.

the sub-motive of profit: (2) several young men would band together in a business association giving dances for profit alone, and (3) the chartered social, which was a gambling business, masquerading under names such as the Early Rose, the Jolly Fifteen, the Jolly Bunch, or the Ad Libitum (At pleasure).[22]

Window placards called attention to a dance. At the turn of the century the following placard (for another dance hall) could be seen in windows in the neighborhood:

ROUDIOS SOCIAL
Kilgallon, America's White Champion
CAKE WALKER
Last Chance to see him prior to him
going to NEW YORK
PRIZE WALTZ for up-towners and down-towners
GREAT SPORT Ad. 15 cents Pennsylvania Hall

Charlie Johnson and Dora Dean are shown here in an 1897 photograph doing the cakewalk. Their dancing soon started the pair on a career described as "the world's greatest big time vaudeville record from 1897 to 1914."
Courtesy of AP/Wide World Photos

The larger halls, like Washington Hall on S. 4th Street, were rented for $25.00 and an orchestra hired for $12.00. Admission costs were nominal. Those who sponsored the social made their profits from the bar normally stocked with multiple kegs of beer. Although the inducement to drink was always present, noticeable drunkenness was seldom seen.

A favorite in the dance halls of the Jewish quarter was the cakewalk, a strutting dance developed by African Americans in the South where the dancers competed for the prize of a cake. Charles S. Bernheimer described the cakewalk in a "Jewish" hall in Philadelphia around 1900:

> First impressions are indeed dispiriting. The room is cold, half filled, and every sound echoes from its unclean, barren walls. There is a little desultory music which does not affect the young men huddled on one row of benches or the young women opposite on another. Spirits are apparently at a low ebb. Suddenly, the big drum booms, the fiddle squalls horribly with every vocal cord, the clarionet playfully caterwauls, the piano emits fearful jangles, people jump into the air, electrified by this orchestral joke, and the dance begins.

At midnight the cakewalk started. The girls were "fantastically and hideously" dressed and "[p]rize medals won at cakewalks at other socials proudly decorated their little chests. Pair by pair they go down the lines of clapping spectators, through the contortions of the cakewalk." After the customary walk, general dancing continued for an hour or two. Then there was a prize waltz.

In 1924, the hall was sold to George Orlowitz who owned the property for many years. From 1920 until 1926, and perhaps longer, Congregation Kesher Torah, Anshe Lubliner occupied the building. It is used for commercial purposes today.

The Philadelphia Jewish Herald: 626 S. 3rd Street. The Oser brothers, Harris E., Abraham, and Aaron, rented this property for $18 a month beginning in 1896, and for the next twenty years used it as a printing plant. In 1904, Oser Bros. had as many as four Linotype machines in operation here. The best known of the brothers was Harris E. Oser. He was born in Kremenchug in 1876 and came to the United States as a boy. Oser learned the printing trade and helped found a Yiddish weekly, the *Stadt-Zeitung* at 710 S. 3rd Street.[23]

At the end of March 1913, the Oser brothers and Max Gillies founded the *Jewish Herald* here, a weekly Yiddish newspaper dedicated to Philadelphia Jewish interests. Collaborators included David B. Tierkel. A very helpful feature of the *Jewish Herald* was a meeting directory. It listed the kinds of organizations which met in the Jewish quarter, and it gives us our best view of the breadth of immigrant Jewish communal activities and interests at the time.[24]

Harris E. Oser, early 20th century. One of the "best known and beloved persons of the local Jewish Streets," Harris E. Oser came to Philadelphia as a boy. He became a printer and although still very young, Oser was instrumental in the founding of the *Stadt-Zeitung* in 1894; twenty years later he founded the *Jewish Herald.* In the teens and twenties, Oser printed almost all Yiddish theatre notices in Philadelphia.

Courtesy of Seth Oser

On August 4, 1913, President Judge Martin of the Court of Common Pleas No. 5, heard evidence in support of a petition filed by Max Gillies for an injunction to restrain the Oser Brothers from further publishing the newspaper. Gillies claimed that in return for doing editing, soliciting, and advertising for the paper, he was entitled to a portion of the proceeds.[25] The Judge refused to grant the relief requested by Gillies, but the Osers were not in a position to continue the business and the newspaper ceased publication.

As with so many of the Philadelphia Yiddish newspapers, the life of the paper was short. After the turn of the century, the Philadelphia edition of the *Forward,* the moderate newspaper published by Abraham Cahan in New York, displaced the weaker Philadelphia papers. From 1891 to 1928, there were twenty-five Yiddish newspapers and journals founded in Philadelphia, many of them within three or four blocks of Osers' printing shop. Only four or five of them, however, survived for more than a year.[26] The *Jewish Herald* ended in controversy and litigation. Others collapsed when financial backing was withdrawn. By 1942, Philadelphia Yiddish papers stopped publishing. The most popular and most successful, *Di Yidishe Velt,* was published, with short periods of interruption, for twenty-eight years (1914-1942).

It is not known when the Oser Bros. printing operations moved. It may have been in the late 1920's or early 1930's.

Philadelphia Stadt-Zeitung (The Philadelphia City Newspaper): 710 S. 3rd Street. The *Stadt-Zeitung* began here in January 1894. Although it lasted for only eighty-three weeks, Sholom Aleichem, Simeon Frug, Abraham Reisen, and other writers from Russia sent articles.[27] A *Galitzianer* named Warhoftik, whom we know little about, invested $1,000 to start the paper. This was a large sum of money, given that the *Forward,* according to Leon Kobrin, was started with only $800. Printed in a large format on four pages with six columns per page, the *Stadt-Zeitung* sold for 1¢.[28]

The language of American Yiddish newspapers at the time - except for the New York socialist *Arbeiter Zeitung,* Abraham Cahan's paper before he founded the *Forward* - was, according to Kobrin, wooden, difficult, clumsy, and bombastically revolutionary. They were written in *Deitshmerish* (Yiddish, with German words). The *Stadt-*

Zeitung, on the other hand, was written in a modest, clear Yiddish. The paper had two editors. From its founding until August of that year, the editor was Chaim Malitz (1861-1924). Under Malitz, the paper was known for its radical tendencies. Malitz was born in Tarashcha, Kiev Guberniya, and while still in Russia he wrote articles for *Hamelitz* and *Hatsefira*. When in Russia, Malitz signed his pieces: "*Chumetz* from Tarashcha." Writing for the Hebrew press in Eastern Europe before he came to America gave Malitz an entrée to leading Russian writers and when he came to the *Stadt-Zeitung*, he was instrumental in getting his old friends to send pieces from Russia. The second editor was Rabbi Chaim Shraga Brodsky, the rabbi at B'nai Jacob, who, unlike Malitz, was not a radical. Brodsky was a *maskil*, an enlightened one, and a follower of the *Haskole* or *Haskala*. He wrote a weekly *droshe*, often a scholarly interpretation of the weekly Torah *parshe*.

The first issues of the *Stadt-Zeitung* included pieces by Kobrin (who had unsuccessfully tried writing for the *Freie Arbeiter Stimme*) and other writers about whom we know little. The paper carried news items, articles, stories, novels and a series of critical essays by Kobrin entitled "Letters to Russia about Yiddish Literature in America."

The building was torn down, but it is not clear when this occurred.

New Auditorium Hall: 747-753 S. 3rd Street. On April 1, 1905, Simon Borowsky, a local businessman, and others, took out a permit to build an "Amusement Hall & Dining Room." Immediately, three properties that stood here were torn down and work was started to construct New Auditorium Hall, which opened in the later part of 1905. The architects were Charles W. Bolton and John D. Dull, the same architects who designed B'nai Reuben the previous year. Estimated to cost $20,700, this hall was one of the most expensive commercial structures built by the immigrants in the Jewish quarter. Sometimes called the Great Hall, in truth it was a great hall. The exterior was magnificent. With three bays on either side of a monumental, enriched, compound arch, the hall was set off from the neighborhood row houses by its size and striking terra cotta finish. It was taller than the surrounding buildings, and for a few years it was the nucleus of the social life in the Jewish quarter at the height of immigration.[29]

Surprisingly, with all its opulence, the *poshete* (ordinary Jews) used New Auditorium Hall, apparently on a regular basis. Formal balls were held here, the proceeds of which financed beneficial and charitable undertakings.[30] Not only balls and dances were given, weddings, the most popular hall event, also took place here. In the *shtetl*, weddings were held in the courtyard of the synagogue. In the Jewish quarter of Philadelphia, the synagogues did not have courtyards (except the Neziner synagogue). Had courtyards existed, it is still doubtful that wedding ceremonies would have been held in them because the youth of the Jewish quarter wanted to be married in an American hall.

An invitation in Yiddish, using a generous measure of German words printed in Hebrew lettering, announced the wedding. In addition to invited guests, the poor tailor returning to his boarding house after work was welcomed. The uninvited, but hungry passer-by was sometimes asked to check his hat for 25¢. Once inside the hall, however, the "hat check" guest was treated the same as everyone else, and he could consume great quantities of home-prepared food just as the invited guests did. If the invitation called for the wedding to take place at six o'clock, carriages called for the groom and the nearest friends of the couple at seven o'clock. The carriage train proceeded to the home of the bride to escort her to the hall. In front of a stage at the hall, upon a raised platform painted with a *Mogen Dovid*, and punctuated with red, white, and blue electric lights, the pair received their friends. When the last stragglers arrived at the hall between ten and eleven o'clock, the *khupa* was pushed to the center of the room, and the wedding began - according to Jewish time. "The orchestra plays the latest two-step and the groom, followed by ten friends holding candles aloft, slowly goes to meet his bride. Half solemn, half laughing, the bridal party marches under the canopy. The rabbi lifts his voice in the strange wail of the ritual."[31] The onlookers laughed and whispered, and an old man beside the groom flashed his somber eyes on the young offenders. The old man lifted his candle and peered at them. !שא שטיל Be quiet there! he cried. After the glass was broken and *mazel tov!* or Congratulations! was shouted, the music of the *sher*, a Bulgarian quadrille, was played. Food and bottled beer were consumed in great quantities and telegrams of congratulations were read. Guests danced until four o'clock in the morning.

This hall was also used for political rallies and meetings. The police, especially after 1908, closely watched socialist meetings here. The close police scrutiny came about as a result of the Broad Street Riot, as it became known in Philadelphia. There are many versions of the riot and how it started, but some facts are common to all the versions. Jews, Italians, and African Americans rallied at New Auditorium Hall on February 20, 1908. After hearing various speakers - what they said and whether they urged the rioters to action is disputed - the unemployed marched on City Hall and, in a skirmish between the marchers and the police, the police came out victorious. Within hours after the rioters were dispersed or arrested, the police identified New Auditorium Hall as the hall at which the riot began. Headed by Lt. Woods, a contingent of police rushed to the hall and took the manager to City Hall where Assistant Superintendent O'Leary questioned him. Woods complained to O'Leary that the hall was used for socialist meetings and that the manager of the hall failed to notify police in advance of the content of the speeches.[32]

In 1911, Frank E. Hahn of the architectural firm of Sauer & Hahn prepared plans to convert the hall into a motion picture house. The modifications were completed the following year at an estimated cost of $12,000, and the building was renamed the Franklin Theatre. In addition to presenting silent movies, professional Yiddish shows were produced here by Max Thomashevsky.[33]

In 1923, general interior alterations of the Franklin Theatre were completed at a cost of $14,500. Silent movies were shown until the beginning of the Depression. Warner Bros. acquired ownership of the building and took out a permit to tear it down in 1944.

קול ששון וקול שמחה קול חתן וקול כלה

CEREMONY

A. A.

מר. אונד מרס. א. שטערן

מרס. ב. אלשער

לאדען זיא אונד איהרע ווערטהע פאמילי העפליכסט איין

צור האכצייט פון זייערע קינדער

מיסס עני שטערן

צו

מר. איימין אלשער

וועלכע ווירד שטאטפינדען דינסטאג דען 1 טען סעפטעמבער 1908

אום 6 אוהר אבענדס

אין ניו אדיטאריום האלל, 747-53 ס. 3 טע סטריט

פילאדעלפיע

כלה'ס וואהנונג 409 נארד 5 טע סטריט

Wedding Invitation, New Auditorium Hall, 747-753 S. 3rd Street. The invitation to the wedding of Miss Annie Stern and Mr. Hyman Alsher stated that the ceremony was called for "six o'clock in the evening" on Tuesday, September 1, 1908.

Courtesy of Mark Alsher

Congregation Ahavas Achim-Anshe Nezin: 754-756 S. 3rd Street Known as Heartfellow Hall, the three-story building here was used as a union hall and for a synagogue for many years. The Neziner synagogue moved here in 1895. That year the congregation hired David Goldstein to be its *shames* (sexton). "Our synagogue, on Third and Fitzwater, was a three-story building that had been converted from a former Polish church. The actual house of worship was one flight up, and above it were two floors with meeting rooms that were rented out to societies." David Goldstein married Fannie Silver and brought her to his home in the basement of this building, and this was where their first son, Israel, was born the following year. Goldstein combined the post of sexton with *shekhitah* (ritual slaughtering) which he did in the back yard of the synagogue. Young Israel Goldstein, years later the leader of the Zionist Organization of America, remembered his synagogal duties here as a young boy. He circulated among the male worshippers on Sabbaths and festivals and offered them a *shmek tabak* (a pinch of snuff) from the communal snuffbox "to add to their enjoyment of the prayer service."[34]

at left: Franklin Theatre, 747-753 S. 3rd Street. Poster for silent movie "Kosher Kitty Kelly" at the Franklin Theatre on February 16 and 17, 1927. Kosher Kitty Kelly, a popular play both on Broadway and in Philadelphia (it played at the Forrest in 1926, and was quickly made into a movie), was an attempt by Hollywood to close the huge gap that existed between the Jews and the Irish. Hollywood accomplished what the church and the synagogue could not do. Here the gulf was bridged with humor.

Courtesy of the Philadelphia Jewish Archives Center

below:
Heartfellow Hall, 754-756 S. 3rd Street, 1993.

When the Neziners moved to S. 2nd Street in the summer of 1905, Heartfellow Hall was sold to a Romanian congregation, Porath Joseph. This congregation enlarged and remodeled the hall and Rabbi Abraham H. Erschler, assisted by Rabbis Blenden, Kahana (a Romanian rabbi), Englander, and Brenner helped to dedicate the building on Sunday, September 24, 1905. As enlarged, the synagogue could seat four hundred worshippers. A small women's gallery was later added. Porath Joseph used the building until 1936, when the congregation either changed its name or a congregation by the name of Kahal Adath Jeshurun occupied the building. For the past twenty-six years, it has been an African American church. The gallery is still in use.

SOUTH FOURTH STREET (DER FERDER)

The immigrants shopped at the S. 4th Street fish markets, especially on Jewish holidays. For Rosh Hashana, Jews came from all sections of the city. Pike, carp and other freshwater fish were sold to make *gefilte* (stuffed) fish. The fish would be brought home live on the trolley car, to be released into the bath tub until the *Yontif* (holiday) meal was ready to be prepared.

Washington Hall: 521-525 S. 4th Street. This four-story structure was one of the largest buildings in the area during the immigrant period, and it still is today. Opened as Washington Hall in 1896, it was a hall that could be rented by radicals and socialists. From 1907 until 1917, it was called New Academy Hall, and from 1917 until 1919, it was known as Majestic Hall.

There was great competition in the lucrative, but small, Philadelphia Yiddish newspaper market, and papers fought among themselves for readers. Many of the New York Yiddish papers had Philadelphia editions, and they also entered the fray. For example, there was the *Philadelphia Jewish Day*, the *Jewish Daily Forward* (see 131 S. 5th Street), and the *New York Jewish Daily News & Gazette*, which had offices here at Washington Hall and across the street at 528-530 S. 4th Street. These New York papers quarreled not only with the Philadelphia papers, they fought among themselves.

A typical joust between New York papers ended here. It began at Pennsylvania Hall, 926-928 S. 6th Street, on Sunday, February 3, 1901. The *Jewish Daily Forward* had invited Joseph Barondess, a popular East Side orator and labor leader, to Philadelphia to explain the actions of the *Jewish Daily News & Gazette*, which, according to the *Forward*, had "...sided with the strikers in the recent bakers' trouble in New York and afterward went over with the employers." Barondess was to tell the crowd about the actions of the *News* and frame resolutions to boycott the paper. The Philadelphia representative of the *News* got wind of this and induced the "bluecoats" (police), in the person of Acting Lieutenant Wood of the Second Police District, to stop the gathering. The hall was closed, as requested. Undaunted by this action, the "gathering adjourned to Washington Hall, at Fourth and South streets, right over the office of the *News*." The same representative of the *News* who had successfully closed Pennsylvania Hall then went to the 4th & Delancey Street police station. "After hearing his story, Lieutenant O'Brien, seeing it was impossible to stop the meeting at that time, detailed Sergeant Wood and a squad of men to see that nothing serious happened. When the police arrived on the scene, the meeting was in full blast and all assembled visibly excited, but seeing the bluecoats quieted down and they finally adjourned without any definite action."[35] The story concluded that everything in the "colony" was quiet that evening.

In the Spring of 1907, when the building was being remodeled and New Academy Hall was being readied to open, the main stairway was changed and the floor was raised. The Yiddish reading public was advised of the changes by the new owner, Jacob Rosenfield, 335 Gaskill Street. Readers of *Der Shtern* (or the *Star*, a Zionist journal in Philadelphia) were advised that for a short time "anyone could use the hall for a wedding free of charge." Rosenfield also touted his hall as the best for "balls and entertainment."

During a Kosher butcher's strike on July 22, 1907, retail butchers met here. Not only did Jewish women strike at that time, refusing to pay the penny increase in the price for meat, but four hundred retail butchers of the Hebrew Butchers' Association refused to sell kosher meat to the Jewish community of Philadelphia. Exactly why the butchers would not sell meat during the strike is not clear. The strike was called off several weeks later, however, when many who had observed *Tisha B'Av*, or the fast of the 9th of *Av*, clamored for meat after the fast. (During the nine days, from *Rosh Hodesh Av* until *Tisha B'Av*, meat is not eaten except on *Shabbes*.) The butchers capitulated to the demands of the observant.

The hall was also used for *landsmanshaftn* and other organization meetings. On Sunday and Monday, August 25 and 26, 1907, the third annual convention of the Sons of Jacob was held here. There were 114 delegates to the convention, many coming from out-of-town.

Since 1919 the building has been used for commercial purposes.

Push Cart Market: It is not clear when push carts first appeared on S. 4th Street. They may have already been here in the early 1890's when immigration increased so dramatically. By 1912, push carts lined S. 4th Street from Lombard to Carpenter. Fruits, vegetables, shouting, oaths, hub-bub - it was the closest that the Jews came to reviving the *yarid (yarmarka)*.[36]

Push cart operators took their stands early in the

700 block of S. 4th Street, 1926. Looking northward from the east side of 4th Street above Fitzwater.

Courtesy of Philadelphia City Archives

morning. They lined up against the curb stones on S. 4th Street and attempted to persuade "demanding *balebustes*" to buy their goods, which consisted of produce, notions, and other small articles. About five hundred Jewish men in the city earned their livelihood in this manner in 1912. Most were either recent immigrants or tubercular (making indoor work dangerous for them). Push cart or curb markets more closely resembled the method of food distribution in Russia where little capital was needed to enter business.

In Philadelphia, licenses were required from city hall to sell from a push cart. Licenses for all the push carts, which during the 1920's cost $5 each, were bought up by three or four individuals who happily re-sold them to the immigrant push cart owners for 25¢ a day.[37] But for some, these little carts were profitable and men were able to educate large families from the earnings. Children who grew up in Strawberry Mansion would shout hello to an uncle or other relative at his push cart as they passed on the No. 9 trolley on their way to weekly music lessons at Settlement Music School.

Standard Hall: 622-624 S. 4th Street. This hall was used by the immigrants as early as 1897 and remained a hall until 1909.

On Sunday, May 10, 1897, Ephraim Deinard, the agent of the Jewish Colonization Society - having for its object the colonization of a number of Philadelphia Russian Jewish families in California - addressed a meeting here. The hall was packed with between 300 to 400 listeners who were in sympathy with the purpose of the meeting. Letters were read from two boys who had been sent to the Agricultural College at Berkley, California. Later that year thirty-seven colonists were sent to be settled in California, but twenty-three of them returned before the year was out.[38]

SOUTH FIFTH STREET

Yiddish newspapers and the Jewish Cafe District dominated South 5th Street.

Jewish Daily Forward: 131 S. 5th Street, between Walnut and Library Streets. A two-story building here, the Philadelphia office of the *Jewish Daily Forward*, was located across the street from Independence Hall. Three semicircular fanlights, placed above a portico in the Doric order and above two flanking first-story windows, highlighted the 5th Street facade. The most popular of all Yiddish newspapers, the *Forward*, was read by three generations of east European immigrants as a guide to enter American life. Built of brick and marble, the building was the home of the local edition of the paper from 1928 until the early 1950's.[39] It housed a news room and advertising offices. During the time it was headquartered here, the manager was Harry Berger

(1887-1972), an influential leader in the Jewish labor movement.[40] The *Forward* was published and printed on the lower East Side of New York.

Abraham Cahan, the newspaper's co-founder and long-time editor, brought the paper name recognition within the immigrant community that no Philadelphia Yiddish newspaper could match. By 1924, the *Forward* reached a world-wide daily circulation of 224,000 copies. The paper was very popular in Philadelphia, even more so after 1942 when the *Yidishe Velt* stopped publishing. During and after World War II, the *Forward* was read by an aging generation of east European Jewish immigrants, and by Holocaust survivors, the last large group of immigrants to enter the city who spoke Yiddish as their native language.

Jewish Daily Forward, 131 S. 5th Street, 1951.

Courtesy of Independence National Historical Park, Philadelphia, Pennsylvania

The paper had a Sunday rotogravure section. Material was gathered in Philadelphia for the Sunday edition, and on Saturday mornings the Philadelphia manager would send a messenger by train to the newspaper's main office in New York with items that were to appear on Sunday. Normally, one of the girls in the office would make the trip to New York. She would be furnished with train fare and money for lunch. Her final instructions were to take the rest of the day off and to enjoy herself. For a poor working girl from Philadelphia, this was heaven. The Philadelphia edition of the paper was sold at center city news stands, located on Market Street from 4th Street to 15th. The paper, which moved from this 5th Street location about 1953, also had carriers with established routes.

The building was acquired by the federal government and torn down for Independence Park in 1959.

Di Yidishe Velt (The Jewish World): 233 S. 5th Street. ***Di Yidishe Velt***, the most popular Yiddish newspaper printed in Philadelphia, was published here daily and Sunday with some slight disruptions during periods of financial setbacks for twenty-eight years.[41] Over 44,000 copies of the first issue of the *Yidishe Velt* were distributed throughout Philadelphia on Sunday, February 1, 1914. Jacob Ginsburg was the president and William B. Leaf was the secretary and treasurer. They were also the publishers. Under its respected editor, Moshe Katz, the newspaper had a rich staff of writers. Initially, over forty-four men worked in its various departments.[42] Hillel Vichnin, was the city editor from 1914 until 1942. Vichnin, who knew twelve languages, was the music critic for the paper and during the time he was at the *Yidishe Velt*, he translated 150 operas into Yiddish. Vichnin also did much to advance young musical talent.[43]

Moshe Katz, a playwright, translator, lecturer, and novelist, and in his earlier years an active anarchist, was the long-time editor of the *Yidishe Velt* (1914-1940). He was born into a Hassidic family in Mohilev, Ukraine, in 1864 and immigrated to the United States in the late eighties. Katz worked on several Yiddish language newspapers in New York, including the *Jewish Daily Forward*, the *Jewish Herald*, and the *Warheit*, and came to Philadelphia for the first time in 1906.[44] After a few years here, he moved back to New York, but returned to help found the *Yidishe Velt*. He wrote more than twenty Yiddish novels and a number of

Di Yidishe Velt (The Jewish World), 233 S. 5th Street.

Courtesy of the Philadelphia Jewish Archives Center

Yiddish plays.[45] Shortly after the newspaper was founded, World War I broke out, and immediately the immigrants looked to Moshe Katz:

> America was drawn into the war, and the Bolshevist overthrow in Russia added more confusion to the mind. More than a few Jewish newspapers and more than a few Jewish speakers made many errors in the course of those years - errors that even to this day [1925] cannot be corrected. It was a difficult time, a difficult experience for a Jewish newspaper. The *Yidishe Velt* did everything possible to hold high her task, to serve the best interests of the Jewish people and at the same time to remain faithful and devoted to our land, to America. And if the *Yidishe Velt* avoided regrettable errors, if it often went against the grain and did not allow itself to be misled by deceptions and empty delusions, it has most to thank Moshe Katz's deep and far-sighted vision and his courage as a spiritual leader.[46]

Because of ill health Katz retired from the paper in 1940, and he died on June 14, 1941. Upon his death the paper carried many tributes to him. One of these by Joseph Gross (1880-1951), an attorney and leader of the immigrant Jewish community, captured the essence of not only Katz, but of many in the immigrant generation who abandoned the Jewish religion but not *Yiddishkayt*. He wrote that Katz was an "unbeliever" but one who nevertheless loved Yiddish; he was a "free thinker without bitterness." Gross, however, was puzzled by Katz's frequent use of quotations from the bible, called it to Katz's attention, and did not forget his response: "The writings are also holy to me. But there is one small difference. The believers say that God produced the Torah. Well, that is no wonder. But I believe that the Jewish people - my nation - with its genius produced the writings. This is perhaps a greater miracle. And this makes the old pages - my pages - even holier to me than to the pious."

Jacob Ginsburg, one of the publishers, was born in Russia in 1870 and came to the United States in his teens. An authority on the Talmud, he was a dedicated Zionist from his youth. Later he was a member of Philadelphia City Council and the School Board.[47] During the 1920's, Ginsburg's popularity in Philadelphia rivaled that of Rabbi Levinthal. When fire struck B'nai Abraham, the leadership of the synagogue turned to Ginsburg for advice as to whether it should be rebuilt.[48] Ginsburg summarized the role the *Yidishe Velt* played in the Jewish community:

> From the first day, the *Yidishe Velt* took on the task to serve the interests of the Jewish people generally, and the best interests of the inhabitants of the local Jewish population in particular - without discrimination as to party or direction. This, its chief task, it has tried to fulfill during its eleven-year existence [1925]. The paper has served as an information means to create more than a few new and useful Jewish institutions while helping to develop and strengthen old ones. In quarrels and disputes between factions, between capital and labor, and other opposing elements, the paper always searches and often succeeds in finding a middle ground, which leads to joy and unity. In the development of the national feeling among local Jews in the growth of the Zionist movement, in the able and serious work which was done in Philadelphia by the American Jewish Congress, and in the growing interest for a National Jewish home in Palestine, the *Yidishe Velt* without any doubt, is a great and important factor.[49]

In January 1932, the newspaper went into receivership, but continued to publish pending reorga-

Moshe Katz, 1925, editor of the *Jewish World* from 1914 to 1940.

M. Katz, Zamelbukh, 1925.

nization. Two years later, Ginsburg relinquished ownership, and the following year the paper went into receivership. After a month's suspension of operations, publication was resumed as a cooperative, called the Jewish World Employes Association, Inc. As an Association, the employees ran the paper and printed eight pages in the daily issue and twelve on Sunday. One page was in English. In 1935, equity receivers were appointed to operate the paper for a short time, and in July 1940, the newspaper stopped publishing. Circulation dropped to 21,000 copies daily. In September of that year, however, the paper was given a new life with an enlarged editorial staff and added features. Just before it finally ceased publication in 1942, Jacob Ginsburg again purchased the *Yidishe Velt.*[50]

The scene so familiar to a generation of Jews living today, that of their grandparents reading the torn and folded pages of the Yiddish paper, long ago disappeared. The sight of an old man in a beard and a tie, or a women in a worn house dress, is etched in memory. They sat in a favorite upholstered chair in a small living room in South Philadelphia or Strawberry Mansion and read the paper from cover to cover. Intently, they poured over every detail. Wrapped up in that tiny bit of Yiddish newsprint was their world, and they grasped hold of it with all their remaining strength.

The building suffered major fire damage in May 1950. It is not known when it was torn down.

The Yiddish Theatre (Never Built): 5th Street, below Locust Street. In July 1906, at the height of Russian Jewish immigration into the city, architects Andrew J. Sauer and Frank E. Hahn completed plans and specifications for a Yiddish theatre to be erected on a portion of the old Quaker burial ground on 5th Street, below Locust. As drawn by Sauer & Hahn, the theatre was to be built of brick and terra cotta in the Byzantine style of architecture. It was to measure 68' x 152' and to seat 1800 people, which would have made it one of the largest buildings in the Jewish quarter of Philadelphia.[51] It is not known who the principals were behind the plan or why it was never built.

Der Volks-Vechter (The People's Watchman): 310 S. 5th Street. This newspaper, whose motto was "For Justice, Literature and the General Interest of the People," was published from August 18, 1893, to August 3, 1894. The publishers and editors were Bernard Harris[52] and Johan Paley.[53] Collaborators included Alexander Harkavy, the famous author of the Yiddish-English-Hebrew dictionary; the poet Morris Rosenfeld; David Apotheker, a contributor to a number of Yiddish newspapers in Philadelphia at that time and the following year editor and publisher of *Die Gegenwart*; and Dr. Charles D. Spivak.

There were three periods of Yiddish journalism. During the first, the language used was *Deitshmerish*, a Yiddish heavily laden with German words. Most examples of this style were published in the late 1880's in New York. *Der Volks-Vechter*, although published later, was a Philadelphia example of this style. The second period involved the use of a "purer" Yiddish. This style was freer of German words and marked a period of transition in the life of the newcomers from insecure alien-immigrant to confident naturalized-American citizen. The third period, which began about World War I, involved writing Yiddish with many English words. During this last period sentences were even constructed using English syntax. In the third period, English words written in Hebrew lettering appeared extensively in articles and advertisements.

טליתים און מחזורים
האָלסייל און ריטייל
מאלערמאן'ס בוך סטאר
404 ס. 5טע סטריט
דאָס איז דער בעסטער פּלאַץ און
גרעסטער אויסוואהל פון
וואָלענע און סילקענע טליתים,
מחזורים מיט פערשיעדענע איבער-
זעצונגען, ווי אויך ספרי תורות,
תפילין ומזוזות מארץ ישראל, כלי
קודש זילבער, פּרוכת'ן און
מענטעלאך
די פולע ווערטה פאר אייער געלד
בעסטע, נייעסטע, אידישע, העברע-
אישע, רוסישע און ענגלישע ביכער.

S. MALERMAN'S
LITERARY PUBLISHING CO.
404 S. 5th St. **Bell, Lombard 4293**

Malerman's Hebrew Bookstore, 404 S. 5th Street. Samuel Malerman was born in Tomashvo, Poland in 1869, studied in a yeshiva, and came to the United States when he was forty-two years old.

Courtesy of YIVO Institute for Jewish Research, New York

Costumer: 417 S. 5th Street. In 1905, Louis Forman ran a costume store here. He rented Prince Albert suits and gowns for the many balls that took place in the Jewish quarter. Balls were very popular, especially after 1905 when New Auditorium Hall was opened. Obviously, purchase of a gown for a ball was out of the question, but rental of a gown made sense. Forman advertised extensively in the *Forward:* "You need be embarrassed no more when you go to a wedding or a ball. Be dressed as nice as everyone if you go to L. Forman."

Lettering surrounded the bulk windows of his store. Printed in English on the sides and above the window were the words, "Wedding and Ball Dresses; Tuxedo Suits for Hire; Prince Albert Suits for Hire; Ladies Hair Dressing - Manicuring Parlor." Printed in Yiddish below the window were the words *"khupe un bal kleyder* [next word, unclear] *bargains"* (bargain wedding dresses and gowns) and *"sheytln in tsep"* (wigs with braids).

Louis Forman, costumer, 417 S. 5th Street, circa, 1905.
Courtesy of the Historical Society of Pennsylvania, Philadelphia, Pennsylvania

Himmelstein's Restaurant: 500-502 S. 5th Street. Himmelstein's, which in 1928 was a hotel and restaurant, remained here until Redevelopment.[54]

The 500 block of S. 5th Street was the heart of the Jewish cafe district. Many of the original buildings still stand on the west side of the 500 block of S. 5th Street (one carries the date 1896 in the gable). Some say you can still hear the Yiddish of the street and the music from an old phonograph through the open windows of the long-since-closed Colonial Cafe. If you listen closely, you may even hear the sweet clarinet of a young Bobby Block, the present popular band leader in Philadelphia, who played this street so many years ago. Although the world of the immigrant has disappeared, Block's special music reminds us of this earlier time.

Himmelstein's was one of three banquet restaurants where marriages were performed after the older halls closed. Himmelstein's, Uhr's Roumanian Restaurant, and the Colonial Cafe, all located on the 500 block of S. 5th Street, had kosher restaurants on the first floor and banquet rooms on the second. As soon as the glass was broken to signal the end of a Jewish wedding ceremony and the beginning of the festivities, musicians *shlepped* their instruments downstairs for the cocktail hour while the upstairs was converted from a wedding hall to a banquet room. The musicians then *shlepped* their instruments back upstairs to entertain the guests during dinner and dancing.

Bogoslovsky's Bakery: 505 S. 5th Street. This was a site of one of the most well-known Jewish bakeries in Philadelphia. In 1914, the building that stood here was torn down and at a cost of $4,500, Samuel Bogoslovsky built his bakery in this three-story, three-bay building. Bogoslovsky, having some sense for history, inscribed the date of construction and his initials in the tin parapet at the top of the building. The bakery shop was busy until the middle 1960's.

The Jewish Daily Forward: 508 S. 5th Street. Although the *Forward* has not been located here for over eighty years (it was here in 1912), the name of the newspaper can still be seen in the mosaic white-tiled step.

Uhr's Roumanian Restaurant: 507-509 S. 5th Street. In 1876, William Adams ran a four-story hotel at 509 S. 5th Street named Literary Hall. He advertised that accommodations were available for the Centennial celebrations held in Philadelphia that year. Oysters, served in every style, were the main feature of the hotel's restaurant. During that year the Wheatley Dramatic Association met here. The first floor of the hotel was a saloon. When the Thomashevskys played next door at Dramatic Hall in 1890, the family enlisted the help of little Emma Thomashevsky to bring paying customers into the theatre. On the night of a performance, Emma circulated among the patrons in the saloon. She sold tickets for 25¢, and with every ticket she handed out a bottle of soda *vasser* (soda water). The gift or her smile-worked magic as she brought throngs into the theatre, much to the delight of her starving brothers and sisters.[55]

Stern's Hotel, 509 S. 5th Street.

The *Gegenwart*, January 24, 1896.

By 1896, the name of the hotel was changed to Stern's Hotel. It had a restaurant and a coffee house. The name was changed again in 1905, this time to the Cosmopolitan Hotel, and it was here on the evening of February 23, 1905, that forty-four men gathered to found the Independent Order of Brith Sholom, the most successful benevolent association founded in the Jewish quarter of Philadelphia during the immigrant period.[56]

Uhr's Roumanian Restaurant,
509 S. 5th Street, 1967.

Courtesy of the National Museum of American Jewish History, Philadelphia, Pennsylvania

After World War I, Jack Uhr, acquired a proprietary interest in a busy restaurant and hotel located here owned by Maurice Leblang. In October 1930, Uhr tore the building down and built Uhr's Roumanian Restaurant, a site that was to become the most popular Jewish catering hall in the city.[57] Businessmen met monthly and families gathered for festive celebrations, but it was the weddings that are still remembered in family circle meetings to this day. In the late 1930's and the early 1940's, the inside of the hall was finished in the Art Deco style. The floor had geometric patterns and the modern wall trim featured simple vertical lighting, both hanging and wall-mounted. A painting on one wall featured two jitter-buggers, swinging atop a 78 rpm record. In the years immediately following the end of World War II, Jewish soldiers and sailors streamed back into South Philadelphia and Strawberry Mansion, renewed old love affairs, met new loves, and found their way to the *khupa* at Uhr's.

For thirty-seven years, until it was torn down during the week of September 11, 1967, Uhr's was the heart of the Jewish cafe district, even after the district itself had disappeared.[58]

Sylvia Cohen and Aaron Levin dancing at their wedding at Uhr's Roumanian Restaurant on March 23, 1947. Aaron enlisted in the Coast Guard before the war and was in Bombay, India with his ship on Pearl Harbor day. He participated in seven invasions and his ship survived several torpedo attacks during four years of sea duty. Sylvia spent much of her spare time during the war as a hostess at the USO canteen at the YMHA at Broad and Pine Streets. They met after the war.

Courtesy of Sylvia and Aaron Levin

Judelsohn's Banking & Passage Exchange Office: 510 S. 5th Street. The three-story property here has two bays, brick facing, corbelled pilasters and a tin parapet.

Beth Elohim congregation, formed by twenty-one men from Cracow, Austria, rented a room here in 1876 and worshipped on the Sabbath. Before the Russian immigrants came into the area, however, the congregation moved to 417 Pine Street. In 1884, Bernstein & Judelsohn opened a branch office of their banking business here (the main office was in New York). In 1885, after Judelsohn left Bernstein, Judelsohn moved his passage order business to the St. Charles Hotel, 56-58 N. 3rd Street.

Office of the Independent Order of Brith Sholom: 510-512 S. 5th Street. This three-story building has brick facing, stone lintels, and a French Gothic peaked parapet with molded tin eave.

The offices of the Independent Order of Brith Sholom were located here for a short time. During its seventh annual convention, celebrations were held here. On Saturday evening, May 27, 1911, the entire block of 5th Street between Lombard and South Streets "...was beautifully decorated with arches and electric lights and committees were busily engaged in receiving the out of town delegates. The reception here lasted until midnight."[59]

Wheatley Dramatic Hall/Hungarian Synagogue 511 S. 5th Street. Prior to 1802 there was a one-story carpenter's shop here. On March 30, 1802, the property was acquired in trust for the use of the 4th Presbyterian Church. The shop was torn down and on July 4, 1802, the cornerstone for the church was laid. When completed, the 4th Presbyterian Church had a plain, roughcast exterior, which, after a lapse of years, was whitewashed. The entrance to the church was through a central doorway on Delaware 5th Street, which had a wooden frame and pillars. The windows were square. The proportions gave the building greater breadth than height. Mr. George Potts was minister, and the 4th Presbyterian congregation worshiped here for nearly forty years. Thereafter, the building was sold to an African American Methodist congregation, prophetically named "Israel Congregational."[60]

In 1867, possession of the property was transferred to the Wheatley Dramatic Association, and for thirteen years it met next door at 509 S. 5th Street and regularly produced classic drama here at Wheatley Dramatic Hall, then called Literature Hall. At least one of the plays produced by the Wheatley Dramatic Society had a Jewish theme.[61] (For Wheatley Dramatic Hall when it was used for the Yiddish theatre, *see Yiddish Theatre.*) When the hall was used by the east European Jews, many leaders spoke here. To appreciate the rich variety of speakers and actors who came here, we have to look back to just one year, 1890. Boris Thomashevsky, Eliakum Zunser, Jacob P. Adler, Abraham Cahan,[62] Max Staller,[63] and Isadore Prenner appeared that year on the little stage of Dramatic Hall.

For most of its existence, however, this building was used as a synagogue. Chevra Emunas Israel, or Faith of Israel, known throughout its history as the Hungarian shul, or the Hungarian synagogue, was founded by twenty-five young men from Hungary at the corner of 7th & South Streets in July 1880. Although the Hungarian Jews were on South Street before the Russians, the beginning of the immigrant period is traditionally measured from the Russian arrival rather than from the establishment of the earlier, but smaller, Hungarian outpost. (Hungarian Jews do not appear to have settled in Philadelphia in great numbers, but like many aspects of east European Jewish immigration to Philadelphia, few empirical studies have been done.) The congregation received its charter on September 1, 1884 and soon moved to Clifton Street, below South Street.[64]

The congregation grew quickly and it purchased Wheatley Dramatic Hall in May 1888. However, it would take the congregation more than three years to raise enough money to convert the hall into a synagogue. It was during this interim period that the building was used for synagogal worship and Yiddish theatre, concurrent uses that stirred a rare emotional outburst from the normally unruffled *Jewish Exponent* : "The use of the same hall for a Jewish worship during the day and for theatrical or similar performances at night is beyond doubt highly improper and here again a certain class of our brethren are in want of vast improvement. Let them learn what a deep impression is conveyed by a dignified and elevating worship, which their system does not even remotely resemble."[65]

In early 1891, Chevra Emunas Israel merged with Oheb Sholem, or Lovers of Peace, a small *chevra* which was established in 1884 at the corner of 4th & Gaskill Streets. Now 250 strong, the new congregation, named

Chevra Emunas Israel-Oheb Sholem, began work to convert the old hall into a synagogue. Between June and September 1891, carpenters and masons completely remodeled the building, converting it into a Moorish style synagogue. Onion-shaped domes were placed above the stair towers.[66] Just as striking was the placement of horseshoe arches and keyhole windows in the S. 5th Street and Gaskill Street facades.[67] The building was finished in plaster made to resemble stone. The entrance on the west side on S. 5th Street was reached through a modest portal. Inside, the lower floor was fitted for a school, and the synagogue was placed on the second floor. The *bimah* was set in the center of the room in the Orthodox manner. The women's gallery was reached by staircases from the vestibule, and the Holy Ark, placed on the eastern wall, was ornamented with a white curtain with Hebrew lettering.

left: Hungarian shul, 511 S. 5th Street (5th & Gaskill Streets), 1959. Synagogue on the right and Uhr's Roumanian restaurant on the left. Keyhole windows added in the summer of 1891. Onion domes taken down after 1920. *Courtesy of Philadelphia City Archives*

right: Hungarian shul, along Gaskill Street, 1959. *Courtesy of Philadelphia City Archives*

The building was consecrated as a synagogue on Sunday, September 13, 1891. Hungarian and American flags greeted the throng who came to witness the festivities. Participants assembled on the first floor and bearing Torah scrolls, thirteen in all, they proceeded upstairs where the Torahs were carried around the synagogue seven times. At each circuit *(hakofe)* a different person carried the Torah. The *Ner Tomid* (perpetual lamp) was lit by Sabato Morais, who also spoke with what the *Jewish Exponent* described as even more than his usual earnestness and fervor: "Like one of the ancient prophets, he [Morais] proclaimed the true purposes for which a house of God should be devoted, and with great ardor he warned against the false hopes that the possession of a synagogue might arouse. The synagogue should be open to all; no Israelite should be prevented from entering the inner sanctuary. Not only in the house of God, but in their stores, their workshops, their homes, in their daily intercourse with men, they should carry out the precepts of their faith."[68]

The first rabbi of Emunas Israel-Oheb Sholem, Rev. Elias Fried, remained at the synagogue only a short time. The second rabbi, Moses Weinberger, born in Sborow, Hungary, in 1855, studied in Europe and came to the United States in 1880. After spending ten years in New York and two years in Scranton, Pennsylvania, he was installed as the rabbi at Emunas Israel-Oheb Sholem on September 18, 1892. He came to the synagogue directly from Scranton, being received at the train station by a committee in carriages and driven straightway to the synagogue. At the installation ceremony, the Cantor, Rev. Nathan Goldsmith, together with a choir, intoned a psalm, after which twenty-four boys entered carrying lighted candles. Charles Hoffman and Sabato Morais delivered addresses in English, and Rabbi Weinberger spoke in German.[69]

As with B'nai Abraham, it was the third rabbi at Emunas Israel-Oheb Sholem who is remembered today. The saintly Rabbi Simon J. Englander came to the congregation about 1895 and remained the rabbi until his death in 1942. A quiet and learned man - humility was an integral part of his personality - Englander liked to be known by his Hebrew name, Shimshon Juda ben Rachel. Born on August 1, 1850, in Szeben, Hungary, one of five children of Emanuel Zvi Engelhardt and Rachel Schantzer, Englander was married in 1871, probably in Kamenitz, Hungary. He was educated in a yeshiva across the border in Nowy-Sacz (Zanz), Galicia, where he studied under the Sanzer Rav, Chaim ben Leibush Halberstam (1793-1876), head of a Hassidic

The Englander family in Cleveland, circa 1893. Left to right: Anna, Fany (Mrs. Simon J. Englander), Elias, Nina, Rabbi Simon J. Englander, and David.

Courtesy of the Piltch family

dynasty. Englander immigrated to Cleveland in the early 1890's and stayed for about three years before coming to Philadelphia. "Rabbi Englander served the synagogue faithfully and devotedly for over 50 years. Every day, between *Mincha* and *Maariv* (the afternoon and evening services), he conducted a class in *Mishna* and *Chumesh* with Rashi. His salary during the entire period was the colossal sum of $5.00 a week. The Rabbi was too modest and self-effacing to ask for more money. It is also doubtful if he would have gotten any more even if he had asked, as the Hungarian Jews were very economical."[70] Rabbi Englander, whatever he was paid, made an instant and positive impression on the Jewish quarter, and therefore, he was asked to speak and participate on many public occasions.

Like Erschler and Levinthal, Englander endeared himself to his congregation and in response, the congregation expressed its affection in a practical way. On Sunday, May 29, 1904, friends and members of the congregation gave Englander a home at 841 S. 3rd Street. The ceremonial presentation of the home was made by Rabbi Levinthal. As we have already seen, the Hungarian congregants were poor, and the greater part of the money to buy the home was contributed by friends who did not belong to the congregation.

It is difficult not to compare Englander to Levinthal. Both were ardent Zionists, beloved in their Orthodox congregations. Unlike Levinthal, however, Englander did not seek a wider role in the larger Jewish community. The following story, told by a great-grandson, is illustrative of Rabbi Englander's humility. Walking home down S. 3rd Street on *Shabbes* after services, if Englander saw a congregant smoking a cigar or cigarette (forbidden on *Shabbes*), Englander would cross the street so as not to meet the man face-to-face, sparing the man the embarrassment of meeting his rabbi on the Sabbath while smoking.

Other stories are told of Englander's humility. Before Passover, he would go to the country and make arrangements with a farmer for milk for his family for the holidays. Believing claims could be made that the milk might not be ritually pure, Englander would not certify the milk fit for others, concerned that they might not agree with his *halachic* rulings (scriptural ordinances). He would, therefore, only use the milk for his own family. In 1921, Englander wrote an ethical will in which he gave his children careful instruction: "Separate yourselves; not only from atheists but also from reformers, not only to the point of agreement with them but even to the extent of association with them, especially as concerns a reformer who attempts to exhibit a degree of *frumigheit* [devoutness]. It is they who have caused the destruction of the religion of Judaism and have caused the Torah to be almost forgotten by the Jewish people, may God have mercy." Englander, like Brenner, struggled to address the "new thought" he observed daily in America.

When Englander died in 1942, his son, Rabbi David Englander, succeeded him. The younger Englander was installed in the synagogue on Sunday evening, June 20, 1943. Guest speakers for the occasion included Rabbi Levinthal, Rabbi Klein, and Rabbi Shapiro from Atlantic City. Rabbi David Englander stayed a short time and eventually returned to the new State of Israel.

The synagogue was a busy place during the immigrant period and no one was busier than the *shames* (beadle). Beitchman states in his essay:

> The Shul also had a number of *Shammeshim*. The last one was Mr. August. The *Shammes* lived in rooms within the Synagogue. Very often the *Shammes* had to purchase the position from the retiring *Shammes*. The price was perhaps two or three thousand dollars. In years back, the *Shammes* made a wonderful living - what with selling liquor for *Yahrzeit*, wine for *Pesach*, taking care of *Kaddish* and *Yiskor*. The Shul in bygone days was a beehive of activity. There used to be three *minyanim* in the morning - at 6, 7, and 8. In the evening, between *Mincha* and *Maariv*, you could find three tables of men studying. With the advent of the 1950's and 1960's, conditions started to be very bad. It became very difficult to get a *minyan* together. Mr. Jacoby, the *Shammes*, would stay outside and beg people to come in to make a *minyan*. Nathan Leidner would go into Uhr's Restaurant and ask people to come help make a *minyan*.

Prior to World War II, the delicately shapes domes were removed from atop the stair towers. In 1959, when Nathan Leidner was president of the congregation, Emunas Israel-Oheb Sholem voted to change its name to the Society Hill Free Synagogue to emphasize that the synagogue did not charge dues, either for affiliation or any service, thereby hoping to attract unaffiliated Jews moving into Society Hill. In May of 1960, negotiations began in an attempt to merge Emunas Israel-Oheb Sholem with the Roumanian American Congregation, but nothing came of these talks and several years later it was decided to close the old shul. At the time the congregation numbered twenty-three members.

During the week of September 11, 1967, a wrecking crew showed up at the site of the Hungarian synagogue and Uhr's Roumanian Restaurant and both buildings were torn down.

The Colonial Cafe: 514 S. 5th Street. This cafe was the third and oldest of the great cafes or banquet halls on the 500 block of S. 5th Street. In the early years of this century, it was the most popular late-night meeting place for east European immigrants in the Jewish quarter. Although not identified by name in a *Record* article in 1911, the Colonial Cafe was surely the place described: "One of the most widely known of the Fifth street cafes is the rendezvous for any Jewish players who happen to be in the city. Several years ago when Jacob Adler was here he went every evening after the play to this restaurant and sat and feasted at a long table with his actor folk around him."[71]

The Colonial Cafe was located in what was called the Jewish cafe district. "Much space would be needed to give in detail a pen picture of the Jewish cafe district. It is only a few short squares from the Italian restaurants, and is situated on Fourth and Fifth streets in the vicinity of Lombard and South streets."[72] It is not known when the Colonial Cafe opened, but it was probably in the early years of the 20th century.[73] The Sunday evening following the Broad Street Riot on February 20, 1908, anarchists came here to plan their next move and to hire a lawyer to represent those arrested. In July 1908, significant changes were made to the building. The old front wall was torn down and a stairway was removed. A new front was added which featured revealed windows, stone lintels with keystones, a stone belt course between the second and third stories, and a Palladian window.

In 1909, Boris Thomashevsky's theatre newspaper, *Di Yiddische Bihne*, reported that Philadelphia had a cafe which was frequented by the Yiddish theatre crowd. Although the identity of the cafe was not given, there is little doubt that the Colonial Cafe was intended: "We [Philadelphians] also have a coffee house, a la Marcus, where actors, actresses, choristers, musicians, bill-posters, ushers, *patriotn, kibitzers,* and just plain *leydik-geyers* [loafers], gather for discussion, critique and intrigue. The *patriotn* are divided into two hostile armies, from which the greater half belongs for the time being to [Max] Thomashevsky's Arch Street Theater. A well-known merchant in 5th Street, who was awarded a medal as the 'Chief Kibitzer,' actually threatened not to play pinochle with those who go to Adler's Theatre."[74] Tickets to the Arch Street Theater and Adler's Theatre were sold at the Colonial Cafe.

After the performance of the *Merchant of Venice* at Adler's Theatre on Saturday evening, November 20, 1909,[75] a banquet was tendered to Adler by several prominent downtown merchants. Although the location of the banquet was again not given, it was surely tendered at the Colonial Cafe. J. Bernstine, identified as the lessee of the Thalia Theatre (presumably, the Adler Theatre) was the toastmaster. Speeches were made by J. A. Seidman, Joseph R. Friedberg, M. Luber, S. Abrahamson and Sara Adler.[76]

At this time, a phonograph furnished music in the Jewish cafes on S. 5th Street. "In the selection of tunes there was much unconscious humor. First, 'I love a Lassie,' one of Harry Lauder's famous songs, then follows a Jewish chant, and after that a popular song is again heard."[77] Readers of the Yiddish press at the turn of the century were told that the "best class" of people dined at the Colonial Cafe; moreover, these same readers learned that special prices were offered to lodges and societies for banquets.[78] In addition, Philadelphia Jews were told that the Cafe was open both "day and night."

During most of its existence, the Colonial Cafe was run by Frank Lippenholtz, an immigrant from Russia. Lippenholtz was born in Glubake, Vilna Guberniya, in 1890, and he emigrated via Liverpool and the port of Philadelphia aboard the *S. S. Haverford* on December 26, 1906. Like Jack Uhr, Lippenholtz worked as a waiter when he first came to America. He bought the Colonial Cafe in 1915. It was used for rallies, banquets, and campaigns by various Jewish immigrant organizations, and tickets for the Arch Street Theater were sold here as late as 1917. Between the wars, improvements continued to be made and it remained open until the late 1950's. Unlike the buildings for Uhr's and Himmelstein's, however, the building which housed the Colonial Cafe still stands.

Die Gegenwart (The Present): 522 S. 5th Street. The Gegenwart, a Yiddish literary newspaper published by David Apotheker, was issued every Friday for almost three and a half years, from the first week of August, 1895 to the end of 1898. A weekly with the motto "Let Thine Eyes Look Right Forward [Proverbs 4:25]," the *Gegenwart* had eight pages, five columns and sold for 2¢. For the first two years, it was published at 824 S. 5th Street, and for the last year and a half it was published here. Apotheker, in addition to being the editor and publisher, was a writer, typesetter, real estate agent, notary public, and an insurance broker.

Born on August 28, 1855, in Ponievezh, Kovno Guberniya, Russia, Apotheker studied at Wilkomir under M. L. Lilienblum. Later, he was arrested in Kiev for Nihilist agitation, escaped to Czernowitz, Bukovina, and ran a bookstore there for a number of years. He immigrated to the United States in 1888 and worked as a printer in Brooklyn until he came to Philadelphia. Writers for the *Gegenwart* included Tierkel; A. Tannenbaum, later connected with the *Forward;* Menachem M. Dolitzky, a well-known Hebrew poet; and Morris Rosenfeld, the famous Yiddish poet.

A participant in the anarchistic movement in Philadelphia in his early years, Apotheker eventually went into business, but fellow anarchists continued to use his office for meetings, both formal and informal. He was a fluent writer with an old-time enlightened humor that charmed and pleased his readers. His short stories were signed with the nom de plume the "limping wretch," as he believed he had no *mazel.* Apotheker was an intelligent man who was much respected. However, he dressed over-elegantly, usually in a new suit of clothes with a high stove-pipe hat, thus making an unconventional appearance. Small in stature and eccentric in manner, he was one of the more colorful personalities of the Jewish quarter.[79]

Tierkel remembered that when Apotheker, a sentimental man, described Jewish life in Russia in a speech at a rally, most likely one of the mass rallies following the Kishinev riots, "tears poured forth from his eyes."[80] The following story about Apotheker was told by his wife:

> Late at night, I [Tzilko Apotheker] went down from my bedroom and found my husband at his writing table. Tears covered his eyes and earnestness was spread over his face. I knew that he was writing a serious article or poem. Probably, about the sorrow of a worker, or about the misery of an unlucky family. If, however, he gave me a smile, then I knew he was working on a humorous article or a feuilleton.[81]

In 1909, Boris Thomashevsky asked Apotheker to come to New York to write for *Die Yiddische Bihne,* the theatrical weekly founded by Thomashevsky that year. Apotheker again picked up his family and moved. More than most immigrants who came to Philadelphia, Apotheker symbolized the wandering Jew. Nowhere and everywhere was home. He had no profession and many jobs. He was considered an old-timer in Philadelphia, yet he lived here just fourteen years. He spoke many languages but there was always a new language to learn. During his wanderings he wrote

Intersection of 5th, Passyunk and Bainbridge Streets, 1920. In the center, Snellenberg's Clothing Depot.
To the left of Snellenberg's (in the background) the onion domes of the Hungarian shul. On the left (partially hidden by the telephone pole) "Magil's Printing", 716 S. 5th."

Courtesy of Philadelphia City Archives

over ten full-length Yiddish plays. Although highly admired by a small band of friends and Yiddish-speaking intellectuals, in the wider world he was hardly known. After his death, his friends arranged a benefit for his family at the Thalia Theatre in New York.

South of South Street: 600 block S. 5th Street. In ultra-conservative Colonial Philadelphia, Cedar Street (South Street) separated Philadelphia from the neighboring "wicked" districts to the south. Philadelphia Quaker mores were strict. What could not be enjoyed north of Cedar Street, however, could be enjoyed to the south in the district of Southwark. For example, the first theatre nearby William Penn's old city was built on the south side of Cedar Street, which in Quaker times left it just outside the range of Penn's puritanical scythe. Surprisingly, differences in life styles north and south of South Street persisted into the immigrant era. The *Record*, in its 1911 article about the Jewish cafe district, commented upon this continuing difference:

> We find an entirely different class of patrons at another cafe on Fifth street, below South. There the Jewish newspaper men, the radicals and the tireless talkers, come. Politics are discussed and there are arguments pro and con concerning different forms of government, the Jewish 'drayma' [drama], and the advance of science. Early in the evening the arguments start and toward midnight the crowd becomes larger and nosier. Usually it does not disperse until early in the morning.

The Jewish cafes on 5th Street below South have disappeared, but not the flamboyance of the young. Till today, laughter from students can be enjoyed, and now the tireless talkers are found along both sides of South Street. Those thirsting for conversation, ideas, and dreams still come to gather, drawn by a force that has not waned in all the intervening years.

Max Pomerantz - Photographer: 700 S. 5th Street (Southwest corner of 5th & Bainbridge Streets). Photography was a meaningful part of the life of the immigrant. A photographer could be found on almost every business street in the Jewish quarter. As soon as an immigrant got off the boat, he bought (new, if he could manage it, used, if he could not), or more likely, borrowed a suit and went directly to a photographer to have his picture taken. The popularity of portrait photography was at its height. A *carte-de-visit*, a small, palm-sized image on a card, could be acquired at a professional photography studio and mailed back to the *shtetl* in Russia with endearing Yiddish terms written on the reverse side. The *carte-de-visit* was the immigrant's proof that he had arrived. His mother and father could show everyone in the *shtetl* that their son was doing "very nicely in America." We can assume that there were hundreds of thousands of these cherished remembrances in the hands of elderly parents in the towns and villages of Poland and Russia when Hitler's armies invaded Eastern Europe, violated the sanctity of the Jewish home, killed the occupants, and burned their possessions.

In January 1907, Max Pomerantz made significant changes, including building a third story addition at a total cost of $3,100. In 1913, Pomerantz sold a dozen copies of a portrait (in Yiddish – קאבינעט בילדער) for $2.99.[82]

Dos Telegraph (The Telegraph): 702 S. 5th Street. Yiddish newspaper publishing and printing began in Philadelphia on the 700 block of S. 5th Street in 1891. Printing, book publishing, and wholesale and retail selling of Jewish religious books remained a dominant trade here for almost a generation.

One of the early newspapers was *The Telegraph*. The editors and publishers were Joshua Wagman and Yakov S. Sherbow. First published in March 1898, it was a weekly paper, whose motto was: "Truth and Peace." Four pages and published in a large format, it sold for 1¢. The paper had an aggressive format, with screaming front-page headlines in large print. It was the first "yellow" newspaper for Russian Jewry in Philadelphia, but only lasted until March 24, 1899, or perhaps slightly later. There is some evidence that it may have changed its name to *The Philadelphia Post* (see *708 S. 5th Street*).[83]

Home of David Apotheker: 706 S. 5th Street. Many Jewish intellectuals lived on this block. Abraham Magil, a lifelong Yiddishist, grew up next door to David Apotheker, and as a young boy believed Apotheker to be very "indolent."[84] Magil's belief was based on the fact that he often heard Apotheker's wife shout up to him from the backyard in the late morning or early afternoon to wake him up. While the tireless talkers enjoyed staying up half the night, others, such as Magil, certainly had a difficult time as youngsters understanding such conduct. Later in life Abraham Magil befriended the Apotheker children and admired them very much.

Moses Freeman and Joseph Magil: 708 S. 5th Street. Yiddish newspapers were printed at this location for almost a decade. *Dos Licht*, or the *Light*, the first Yiddish newspaper printed in Philadelphia, was published here by Moses Freeman in October 1891. The motto of the paper was "To Spread Light, Religion and Knowledge." Backed financially by Morris Rosenbaum, the immigrant banker who opened his steamship and railroad ticket office four years earlier, *Dos Licht* was published weekly in a large format, with eight pages and sold for 3¢. The editor was the Rev. Nehimiah Mosessohn. For reasons that are not clear, Rosenbaum withdrew his financial backing in July 1892, and the newspaper immediately ceased publishing.[85]

Freeman had a strong desire to see Philadelphia join other American cities which had one or more Yiddish newspapers. Toward that end, on August 26, 1892, less than two months after *Dos Licht* failed, Freeman again began publishing, this time, *Di Yidishe Prese*, or the Jewish Press. In this effort, Freeman collaborated with Professor Selikovitsch, Dr. Charles D. Spivak, and others. The newspaper lasted eighty-four weeks and closed on March 23, 1894.[86]

Freeman abandoned his dream to print a Yiddish newspaper in Philadelphia but kept his hand in the newspaper business and, acting as an agent for New York newspapers sold in Philadelphia, moved his offices to 424 S. 4th Street. However, Freeman may have left his printing presses at the S. 5th Street address because eight months after *Di Yidishe Prese* stopped publishing, the Magilnitzky brothers opened a print shop here and began publishing another Yiddish newspaper, *Di Yidishe Volks-Blatt*, or the People's Paper.[87] Issued every Sunday, it contained political, religious, scientific, and literary matter as well as news concerning the Jewish people. The paper was published by one of the brothers, Joseph Magilnitzky, who later shortened his last name to Magil.

Joseph Magil, a pedagogue, writer, teacher, printer, and leader of the B'nai Zion school in Philadelphia, was the only Philadelphian noted in Eisenstadt's 1903 classic work on east European Jewish scholars who was not a rabbi.[88] Born in Rassein, Kovno Guberniya, Russia on Purim in 1870, Magil had a typical *kheyde*r and yeshiva education. At age sixteen, he secretly began studying Russian and modern Hebrew while continuing his religious studies. He wrote for *Hamelitz*, published in St. Petersburg. In 1892, Magil came to Philadelphia and began to publish *Di Yidishe Volks-Blatt*. When he wrote for the Jewish press he used the pen name, Channah Magilnitzky, which was his sister's name.

Magil raised his family here, at 716 and at 722 S. 5th Street. At each property, he also had a print shop. At some point, he purchased a Linotype machine. He also conducted a Hebrew school and ran a store. In the store he sold prayer shawls, religious books which he printed on the premises, books in Yiddish, and Hebrew calendars. Magil and his wife Rachel (nee Lessem, who traced her descent from Rabbi Abraham, the brother of the Vilna Gaon) were pioneer Zionists in Philadelphia.[89]

Abraham, the only son of Rachel and Joseph Magil (they had three daughters), was born in the United States, grew up here, but his first language was Yiddish, not English. At play in the streets around 5th &

Bainbridge Streets, the children spoke Yiddish. Abraham was very proud of his father because he spoke English with very little accent and was able to pronounce the "th" sound correctly.[90] The Magils, not unlike other families in the area, had no bathroom in their home. They used an outdoor privy in the backyard and bathed in a large tin washtub in the summer. Abraham and the rest of the family were elated when they moved to 716 S. 5th Street where there was a flush toilet and a bathtub with running water. The Magils lived on the western border of the Jewish quarter. Abraham Magil described this border territory: "[T]here were many Italians who lived in that area. In fact, our backyard opened on a narrow street populated almost entirely by Italians. There was no friendly contact between the two communities."[91]

Joseph Magil is best known, even today, as the publisher of a linear translation of the *Five Books of Moses*, the *Book of Joshua* and one or two other books of the Hebrew Bible translated from Hebrew into Yiddish. Magil published at least twenty-four different linear translations of Hebrew books for adults and children. Books came with a שטודיר קארטע, a study card written in Yiddish. It was a small card physically attached to the binding of the book by a six-inch string. Instructions for its use were printed on the card:

> *Study Card:* Cover the translation until the line which you have to learn. Read the line of *Khumush* (Pentateuch) and the translation for it very slowly and carefully until you are able to say the translation by heart. Then move the card aside in order to cover the translation and read the line of *Khumush* one time and translate it by heart. Then move the card down and read the translation inside to prove to yourself that you have translated it correctly. When you have, repeat it several times in order to remember. When you have learned a verse this way, repeat it again. This time you must first translate each line by heart but you must not omit any line until you have moved the card down and convinced yourself from what is written that you have translated it correctly.[92]

Magil's books were sold both in the United States and in Europe. His selling agent in Russia was his brother-in-law, Shachno Lessem, who lived in Vilna. Magil composed *Pentateuch for Schools; Guides for Teachers and Students; the Scroll of Esther for Schools and Home; a Haggadah for Children; Collections of Songs of Zion; a Pentateuch for Beginners*; a work entitled, *Teacher of Torah and Language; Hebrew for Every Man;* and other books.

Magilnitzky's Folk Shul: 716 S. 5th Street. Joseph Magil moved his folk shul here. Magil's printing shop and store were also at this address in 1920. He sold *taleysim* and religious Hebrew books, wholesale and retail.

The Home of Three Yiddish Newspapers: 718 S. 5th Street. In the first decade of the 20th century, three Yiddish newspapers were published here:

From 1900 to 1913, Jacob Ginsburg, later the publisher of the *Yidishe Velt,* was the manager and publisher of the *Philadelphia Jewish Evening Post*. It was the only Yiddish daily newspaper then printed in the city. The Post may have been printed here as early as 1902.

The second paper was the *Philadelphia Jewish Morning Journal*. The *Morning Journal*, unlike the *Post*, was not printed in Philadelphia. It was printed in New York. From 1908 to 1914, the editor and publisher of the *Morning Journal* was Jacob Ginsburg.[93]

The third paper published or printed here was the *Filadelfia Morgen Zeitung*. Harris E. Oser and his brothers began to publish the *Morgen Zeitung* from this address on January 18, 1907.[94] The Osers could only manage to publish fifty-nine daily issues before publication was stopped.

In 1914, Ginsburg left here to start the *Yidishe Velt* and at the same time the *Philadelphia Jewish Morning Journal* moved to the southwest corner of 5th & Pine streets. It is not known what happened to the *Philadelphia Jewish Evening Post*.

Joseph Magil Company: 722 S. 5th Street. Joseph Magil bought this property in 1923. He had his business and lived here until his death in 1945.[95] He sold *taleysim* and Hebrew books retail and wholesale from a store located here and was known throughout the country for his Hebrew wall and pocket calendars. Magil founded and served as first chairman of the central relief committee which raised funds for Jewish war refugees during World War I.

The Magils, the Osers, Samuel Malerman, and Moses Freeman were the backbone of early Yiddish publishing in Philadelphia when Yiddish was read by the man on the street.

B'nai Israel: 5th above Catharine Street. In 1839, the Episcopal Church of the Evangelists dedicated an old church building on the east side of 5th Street, one house north of the northeast corner of 5th and Catharine Streets. Long before the east European Jews came to this area, Jews from Holland settled around South Street. In the 1850's, these Hollanders formed B'nai Israel. Three years later they leased a place of worship at 3rd and Catharine Streets. Leaders of the congregation, Abraham Solomons, president, and Messrs. Munchweiler and Blitz, lived on South Street. In 1856, B'nai Israel purchased the old church building here and converted it into a synagogue. Like the Third Baptist Church building on 2nd Street and Wheatley Dramatic Hall on 5th Street, the church was built on the east side of the street. When converted to a synagogue, the ark could easily be placed on the eastern wall. The ark was opened at the dedication of B'nai Israel.[96] The 1856 plans to modify the church building included providing seats for 250 people in the main room and about seventy-five to one hundred in the gallery. Thirty-five-year-old Moses Dropsie delivered the main address at the dedication.[97]

The congregation disbanded in 1879, two years before the east European Jewish settlement began. By 1889, the synagogue building was torn down and homes were built on the lot.

PASSYUNK AVENUE

Unlike the other streets in the area, Passyunk does not run north-south or east-west, but runs diagonally northeast-southwest. In its early period it was a country road, the scene of considerable travel between the South and New York. At one time, Passyunk Avenue was the dividing line between the District of Moyamensing and the District of Southwark.

On a fall evening in 1891, a reporter for the *Press* described the intersection at Passyunk and South Streets, just east of 5th Street:

> "In the glare of the electric lights which fairly bedazzle one, proving that Chestnut Street and its stores do not enjoy a monopoly of brilliant illumination, can be seen the peasants of Italy, who, perhaps, a few months ago knew nothing above the light of a candle, walking along in gorgeous purple skirts, green bodices with yellow scarves as a head covering. These women carry themselves well and jostle freely with the Russian Hebrews and the Poles and the Hungarians, Scandinavians from the land of the midnight sun, and Turks from the land of the burning noons, and in fact a most motley and conglomerate lot."[98]

The Philadelphia Jewish American: 703 Passyunk Avenue. The offices of the Yiddish newspaper, *The Philadelphia Jewish American*, were located on the east side of Passyunk Avenue, forty-one feet south of the intersection of Bainbridge Street. The office was a little over 18' wide and extended back approximately 60'. The paper was printed in New York at the offices of the *Morgen Zhurnal*.

Published by David B. Tierkel from March 6, 1908, to 1910, *The Philadelphia Jewish American* was a literary newspaper. It was issued in a half-page format and sold for 3¢. Contributors included Joseph Gross, A. L Wolfson, Dr. Benjamin L. Gordon, and other Philadelphians. Besides his newspaper work, Tierkel was active in immigrant benevolent societies. He was an officer of the Hebrew Literature Society, the Jewish Consumptive Institute, the Talmud Torah, the Yeshiva Mishkan Yisroel, the Jewish National Fund, and other organizations.[99]

The building was torn down in 1914, and the State Bank of Philadelphia[100] was built in 1915 on both this property and the corner property at 701 Passyunk Avenue.

Paperhangers Union, Local 306: 755 Passyunk Avenue. The first paperhangers' union in Philadelphia, the Paperhangers' Protective Association, was organized in 1893. At the beginning of World War I, Jewish immigrants began to earn a little extra money, and many began to decorate their homes with wallpaper. It was a sign that they had "arrived" in America. At this time Jewish paperhangers formed their own Local, No. 306.

When Local 306 met here, notes of the meetings were recorded in Yiddish. A typical meeting was held on Saturday, November 1, 1919. An arbitration clause was addressed and sick-fund benefits were discussed; requests were made for ladders and wider trestles and scaffolds; a recommendation for the local to join as a member of the Women's Trade Union League was approved; ticket sales to a ball for the benefit of the local were explained; and money was approved to sustain two sick members. Business was good and the local prospered for many years.

On June 17, 1939, however, Local 306 received formal notice that its charter had been revoked because it called for a Jewish local where only members of the Jewish faith were accepted. When the local was organized, the majority of Jewish paperhangers could not speak or understand the English language, and therefore they sought and were granted authority to found their own union. Although the local did hire a lawyer in 1939 and instituted litigation to contest the charter revocation, the suit was withdrawn. The Jewish paperhangers recognized that the United States of the late 1930's was not the United States of 1916. Americanization was expected. Separatism, although forced upon the Jews of Russia, was viewed as a curse by a majority of Americans, Jews and non-Jews alike. Older members found the change to a new local difficult. They had to learn English. Most entered another local (No. 587), and they continued their union association in the broader-based local.[101]

SOUTH SIXTH STREET

Levis Hot Dogs: 507 S. 6th Street. It is impossible for a Jewish Philadelphian - and for many Italian American, African American, Polish American and Irish American Philadelphians - born before World War II to say the words "Levis Hot Dogs" without smiling. The smile comes from memories of years ago. These three words not only bring to mind tastes and smells of another time, they bring back the clang of the bell of the trolley car on 6th Street which frequently stopped to let passengers off to order a hot dog and a glass of Champ Cherry Soda, without regard to the traffic back-up and blowing horns.[102]

Levis Hot Dogs, 507 S. 6th Street, 1982.

Courtesy of Urban Archives, Temple University Philadelphia, Pennsylvania

Abraham L. Levis was the only son of a Lithuanian miller. At age fourteen, he immigrated to Philadelphia (in 1885), found work in a clothing factory, and began his schooling at night. Soon, he married Anna Solo, a good cook, and together they opened a lunchroom in the basement of a house on 6th Street, probably 513 S. 6th Street. Anna and Abe sold fishcakes and hot dogs from Anna's own recipe. Levis acquired the property at 507 S. 6th Street in 1910. The architect and the contractor for a new building here were Nathan and Morris Yacknitz. On the parapet above the cornice are the words: "A. L. Levis, Est. 1896, Soda Water Ice Cream & Light Lunch." Above the front window are the words: "EST LEVIS 1895 THAT'S ALL." Why the dates are different is not clear. Did Levis invent the hot dog as we know it? Did he or Anna invent the hot dog roll? Did they have the first soda fountain in the United States? Different authorities on these matters have addressed these questions over the years. One authority wrote: "Abe's twin specialties were fish-cakes and sausages. Mrs. Levis, being of practical nature, soon resolved the dish-washing problem by serving the sausages in rolls. Abe quickly picked up the cue and began baking his own rolls, shaping them long to conform with the 'forward look' of the sausages. And just like that, the Hot Dog was born!" Concerning the origination of the soda fountain, we are told: "Abe Levis was not content to be remembered simply as the 'wizard of the wiener,' however. He went on to develop another specialty of the house 'Champ Cherry Soda.' To glorify it, he installed an ornate little dispensing cabinet, complete with dark carved wood, mirrors and marble. He called it 'the soda-fountain.'"[103]

Levis developed an early interest in the movies and acquired several nickelodeons (as has already been shown, he built the first theatre on South Street). In addition, anticipating outdoor movies by several decades, Levis erected a giant screen on the roof at 507 S. 6th Street, and he showed free movies that could be seen from the playground across the street. The crowds, when they got hungry and thirsty, naturally came to Levis' to satisfy their appetites. Abraham Levis, more than any other personality in the Jewish quarter, is still remembered today. And although the Levis family no longer operates the business at 507 S. 6th Street (the family left in 1992), the Levis mystique does not die easily. On July 1, 1994, as hundreds of people gathered on the corner of 27th & Poplar Streets in the Fairmount section of Philadelphia, the neon sign "Levis," which had previously been at 507 S. 6th Street was put on the roof and lit again, this time by the mayor of Philadelphia, Edward G. Rendell.[104]

Tickets courtesy of Robert Helms

Congregation Chevra B'nai Reuben, Anshe Sfard: 615-621 S. 6th Street, southeast corner of 6th & Kater Streets. Congregation Chevra B'nai Reuben, Anshe Sfard was the first congregation to build a synagogue in the Jewish quarter. This was not done until 1905, twenty-four years after the Jewish quarter was founded.

Throughout its history B'nai Reuben, the city's first Hassidic congregation, welcomed rabbis from Russia and cared for them while they stayed in the city. The beginnings of the congregation go back to 1883 when Rabbi Reuben, the son of Fishel Cohen Kanefsky, founded the congregation at 730 Passyunk Avenue.

> A respected Jew from the old country, from the town of Shvarts-Tume [i.e., Belaya Tserkov], Kiev Guberniya, Russia, Rabbi Reuben brought with him the Jewish way of mercy and charity with the full hand. Every Thursday and Friday, summer and winter, in hot and cold weather, one could see old Rabbi Reuben with a sack on his shoulders going to *'landslayt'* and friends, gathering bread and food for the poor and the needy for Shabbes.[105]

Rabbi Reuben, the founder and first president of B'nai Reuben, also brought with him from the old country a prized possession, a Torah, which he kept as a treasure his entire life. On December 31, 1888, B'nai Reuben obtained its charter from the Court of Common Pleas to "...maintain a synagogue for the worship of God, according to the customs, usages and ritual of the orthodox Jewish church." B'nai Reuben-Anshe Sfard first met at the home of Reuben Kanefsky. Until a congregation was organized, not only were prayer services held at 730 Passyunk Avenue, but Kanefsky also maintained a mikvah here, the first built in the Jewish quarter.[106]

At the turn of the last century, B'nai Reuben acquired the rectangular lot on the south side of Kater Street, between S. 6th & Fairhill Streets. As soon as an application was made for a building permit on April 8, 1904, five brick houses and a stable that stood on the property were taken down.[107] The lot measured 96' along Kater Street and 67' along the two north-south streets. The building, which measures 92' x 54', was completed in January 1905, at a cost of $60,000, a huge sum of money for the immigrants. Described as Roman Baroque in style,

> [the building] is arranged with flanking towers that rise above the roof line and are formed by onion domes faced with pedimented dormers that carry ocular windows. The third story facade is pierced in its center portion with a seven window arcade, five of which have been infilled. At this level

the tower windows have keystoned terra cotta surrounds, similar to those found at the second story level. The principal architectural feature is the elaborate two story entrance way - formed with a great arch opening topped with an elaborately-consoled window, that is covered with a broken, curved pediment. Within the pediment is a cartouche set on a bed of leaves which carries the menorah.[108]

The inscription stones which flank the elaborate two-story 6th-Street entranceway state the year the synagogue was built. Within two stone wreaths in the haunch are words from the Hallel: "This is the gate of the Lord; the righteous shall enter into it [Psalms 118:20]." The architects were Charles W. Bolton (the architect of B'nai Abraham five years later) and John J. Dull.[109]

The building of B'nai Reuben has survived. Today, it is used for commercial purposes, and only recently have its secrets been explored. A 13' wide passageway or alley between the southern wall of B'nai Reuben and the adjoining property make this synagogue a free-standing structure, certainly an unusual feature in a neighborhood of densely packed attached buildings. One reason for the unusual passageway is apparent. It permits afternoon sunlight to penetrate the high windows of the southern wall. The sun was apparently the main source of light, as a modest centered chandelier (which still hangs high above the main hall) could have hardly provided a significant amount of artificial light for the worshippers.

Another reason for the placement of the passageway, however, is also possible: Recently, what is thought to have been a doorway leading to the women's gallery stairs has been located off this 13' passageway. It is found near the front of the building.[110] The doorway most likely permitted access for women to enter the gallery stairs direct from the passageway. If this theory is correct, men entered through the main entrance on S. 6th Street and women entered through this secluded, off-street doorway. At some time, however, probably prior to the 1940's, the western entrance to the passageway was sealed by the erection of a wall along S. 6th Street. While it was still physically possible for women to enter the passageway from the east by using Fairhill Street, it would seem unlikely they did so. More likely, women probably used the main entrance on S. 6th Street, the same entrance used by the men. Once inside the building, however, the women would have used the stairs to reach the *ezras noshim.*

On the first floor there was a large assembly hall seating three hundred persons and upstairs in the main room, including the galleries, the seating capacity was sixteen hundred. The *ezras noshim* ran around the northern, western and southern walls. Today, the galleries, the *orenkoydesh*, the *ner tomid*, the *bimah* and the benches have all been removed. Twelve murals of ancient Israel, however, adorn ceiling panels above where the northern and southern galleries were hung. There are six murals on each side.[111]

The corner-laying of the synagogue was held on Sunday, May 22, 1904. The cornerstones carry the date in Hebrew and English. After preliminary services at New Pennsylvania Hall, members formed a procession and paraded up 6th Street to the new site. Short talks were given by Rabbis Levinthal, Erschler and Englander. Placed inside one cornerstone was the history of the congregation, the names of the members and their - families, newspaper clippings, and other articles. Rabbi Levinthal was chosen to be the rabbi of the synagogue.[112] Preceding the dedication of the new building on Sunday afternoon, January 8, 1905, officers and members of the synagogue assembled at B'nai Abraham where a procession through the local streets began.

Torah scrolls were carried by members of a special committee that formed the head of the long procession. After stopping at several of the older synagogues, the committee reached the new building at 2:30 P. M. There the crowd had grown to such proportions that traffic was impeded, and it required the efforts of a large force of police to clear the way to go to the synagogue.[113]

The *Press* and the *Record* carried similar reports, but only in the *North American* do we get a glimpse of the true excitement that day. The article in the *North American* was accompanied by a photograph taken outside the synagogue on 6th Street looking south. It was one of the first photographs of the Jewish streets of Philadelphia to appear in the press. People blanket the street. Men in bowler hats stand shoulder-to-shoulder as far as the eye can see. The crowd was estimated to be more than two thousand. American flags fly from the synagogue and men and boys can be seen atop store-front awnings. A cordon of police is visible in front of the main entrance to B'nai Reuben.

When the carriages arrived, the police opened a passageway for the rabbis and the committee to enter. Scarcely had the crowd started to follow when a mad rush began. Rioters trampled each other and surged

B'nai Reuben building, 615-621 S. 6th Street, 1998. Detail of northern flanking tower. Today, the domes on the building of B'nai Reuben are the only domes remaining on a synagogue building in the Jewish quarter.

Photograph by Gene Michael Brown

forward in a wild effort to gain entrance to the building to witness the dedicatory exercises. "Those in the rear mounted to the shoulders of others and endeavored to walk over the heads of the struggling human mass." Attempts were made to quiet the huge throng: "From the upper windows of the building the members of the Dedicatory Committee leaned forth and implored the crowd to preserve order. They might as well have attempted to whistle down the wind." After a one-hour battle between seventy police officers and the crowd, sixteen hundred were seated. The aisles and the rear of the building were filled, and several hundred were turned away. On the *bimah*, American and "Zionist" flags were displayed. The president of Mount Sinai Hospital, Jacob Lit - introduced to the throng as a representative of the uptown Jews - praised Rabbis Levinthal and Erschler for the work they had accomplished in connection with building the first synagogue downtown.[114]

During the 1920's and 1930's, B'nai Reuben, because of its large size and seating capacity, was often the site of cantorial concerts. These were given by the most popular cantors of that time. However, even B'nai Reuben could not be used when cantors like Zavl Kwartin came to town. For his concerts only the Arch Street Theater was large enough to hold the crowds. Cantorial concerts at B'nai Reuben were very popular. The visiting cantor, dressed in a slouch fur coat and carrying a gilded cane, commanded the attention of everyone even before he entered the synagogue. Most programs included a local choir of ten voices. The synagogue was always packed for these concerts.[115]

B'nai Reuben was a great center of Orthodox ideas in the Jewish quarter. "The friendly and intimate life which the members of the synagogue family led was heartfelt and without bounds, where all were brothers and sisters of one father and one mother." On the evening of March 20, 1942, the congregation celebrated its founding. B'nai Reuben abandoned the structure at 615-621 S. 6th Street as a house of prayer in 1956.

CONCLUSION

A MENTSH TRAKHT UN GOT LAKHT [1]

Many in the Jewish quarter tried to preserve the sweetness of the Jewish life they knew as children in the *shtetl*. For each, the decision was individual. Joseph Gross, the popular lawyer and free-thinker, poured out his spiritual homesickness to Moshe Katz, the editor of the *Yidishe Velt*. Katz comforted Gross with these words: "Even I, an ardent heretic, have moments of God-praising. No sensitive person can be free of them." Moskovitz, the anarchist, came back to the other side and became an officer of the Chevra Kadisha. And Abraham Cahan, the peripatetic socialist visitor to Philadelphia, stood next to Orthodox Rabbi Levinthal in tragedy. The middle of the spiritual Jewish quarter was wide and many sought the solace they found there.

Within this wide spectrum of immigrant life, the short stay of the immigrant generation was played out on the colonial streets of Quaker Philadelphia. One culture was artificially grafted upon another, but there is little indication that the American soul penetrated deeply into the world of the immigrant. The Irish, the African Americans, the Poles, the Quakers, the Italians - not one of them had a great influence on daily actions of the Russian-born newcomers in the Jewish quarter. Although the immigrant Jewish drama was played out in front of these diverse groups, they were but the audience, far from the actors upon their tiny stage. What influenced the older east European Jewish immigrants was their beloved Yiddish language and *sprikhverter* (proverbs) learned at a place they called - *di alte heym* (the old home). Physically, the immigrants had crossed a wide ocean and immigrated to a country where liberty was proclaimed throughout the land. But spiritually, many in the immigrant generation never left the *shtetl*. It would take the children of the immigrants to find the University of Pennsylvania and the larger world beyond.

The immigrants had grand plans. They sought safety and something to eat. And freedom from fear and murder. The idea of escaping from Russia was a dream. And yet, they did the impossible. They did escape, and they did it with their children.

How grand were their plans! Not only were they able to breathe free in America, they arrived in the Jewish quarter at the same time the great idea of the Jewish people surfaced: Zionism. Everyone was a Zionist. When the residents of the Jewish quarter were instructed to purchase the *shekel*, the self-imposed tax levied upon every living Jew, they purchased it in great numbers. The idea of Zionism spread like a New Jersey brush fire throughout the Jewish quarter of Philadelphia. It was the one unifying ideal that each immigrant understood.

The immigrants came and expended their life's strength in shops and stores that fronted cobblestone streets. Today, we walk these streets and feel the soft air pass through the trees around us. The immigrants, huddled in the stuffy sweatshops, feared that tuberculosis rode on these same breezes. Today, urban pioneers, Americans who in the 1950's and 1960's moved back into Society Hill and Queen Village, live in magnificently restored colonial city houses. The immigrants, who lived in these same houses, hung their work clothes on nails. Today, the grandeur of the area overwhelms the visitor and transports us back in time to an idyllic past. The immigrants, however, had little time to dream. But they did plan, and we wonder whether God is not smiling at their plans, knowing that what they started others have continued in ways they could have never imagined.

---

[1] *A person plans and God laughs.*

Notes and Acknowledgments to the History of the Jewish Quarter

1. *Russkii Yevrei* (Russian Jew), Friday, April 24, 1881. *Russkii Yevrei*, published in St. Petersburg, Russia, from August 1879 to December 1884, was a weekly journal that supported modern assimilation for the Jews of Russia. In English the name of the town was also spelled Elisavetgrad; the Jews of the town pronounced it *Yelizavetgrad*, with the accent on the first syllable.
2. Bibliographic sources to the 1881 pogroms: (1) *Sistematicheskii Ukazatel' Literatury o Evreiakh* (Systematic Index of Literature about Jews), St. Petersburg, Russia, 1892, a comprehensive index containing references to over three hundred newspaper articles and essays; and (2) *Materialy dlya Istorii Antievreiskikh Pogromov v Rossi* (Materials for the History of the Anti-Jewish Pogroms in Russia), vol. II, the 1880's (April 15, 1881, to February 29, 1882), ed. G. Y. Krasnovo-Admoni, Gosudarstvennoe Izdatel'noi (Petrograd, Moskva, 1923), for a town-by-town description of the pogroms.
3. *New York Times*, June 12, 1882. The description here is for early 1882. The conditions in Brody in 1881 are given by Zosa Szajkowski in "The European Attitude to East European Jewish Immigration (1881-1893)," *PAJHS*, vol. XLI, no. 2 (December, 1951), pp. 127-162. A recent description of the major ports of embarkation (Bremen, Bremerhaven, Hamburg, and Liverpool) during the height of Jewish emigration to the United States can be found in Karin Schulz's, *Hoffnung AmerikA Europäische Auswanderung in die Neue Welt* (America the Hope - Emigration from Europe to the New World), (Bremerhaven: NWD Verlag, 1994).
4. *Razvet* (Dawn), No. 41 (cols. 1583-1584), September 13, 1882, St. Petersburg, Russia. *Razvet*, a weekly journal, supported assimilation until the 1881 pogroms. Afterwards it supported emigration from Russia. In Philadelphia the role played by German Jews in securing employment for the Russians was viewed much differently by them. The 13th Annual Report of the Society of the United Hebrew Charities of Philadelphia, a society made up of German Jewish manufacturers, not Russian Jewish laborers, found that 116 immigrants were sent to Philadelphia from New York in October 1881 and were provided with temporary homes, and that "every male among them obtained employment through the arduous efforts of a special committee appointed for the purpose." APS I owe much thanks to Roy E. Goodman, Curator of Printed Materials at the American Philosophical Society, for offering me help in many areas.
5. "Iron Ship Building: The Yards on the Delaware River," *New York Times,* March 15, 1873. For an excellent study of Cramp's shipyards, see Gail E. Farr and Brett F. Bostwick with the assistance of Merville Willis, *Shipbuilding at Cramp & Sons: A History and Guide to Collections of the William Cramp & Sons Ship and Engine Building Company (1830-1927) and the Cramp Ship Building Company (1941-46) of Philadelphia* (Philadelphia: Philadelphia Maritime Museum, 1991). From time to time, during the early years, other vessels were chartered by the American Line to run to Philadelphia, such as the *British Prince*, the *British Crown*, the *British Queen*, the *Lord Gough* and the *Lord Clive*. Competition for the immigrant trade was fierce. In 1882, there were twelve first-rate lines of steam-packets plying between New York and Europe, besides the lines running to Boston, Baltimore, Philadelphia, and New Orleans. S. G. W. Benjamin, "Ocean Steam-Ships," in *The Century Magazine* (September 1882), pp. 666-678. For helping me with the intricacies of the Liverpool waterfront, I want to thank Mrs. Eileen Edwards and J. Gordon Read, Merseyside Maritime Museum, Liverpool, England.
6. *Hamagid*, vol. XVII, no. 19 (May 14, 1873), quoted in Lloyd P. Gartner, "Rumania and America, 1873: Leon Horowitz' Rumanian Tour and its background," *PAJHS*, vol. XLV, no. 2 (December, 1955), p. 75.
7. *Inquirer*, February 24, 1882. The word "Philadelphia" has been omitted from the title of most Philadelphia newspapers. For the full titles of Philadelphia newspapers, see *A Checklist of Pennsylvania Newspapers, Volume I, Philadelphia County*, prepared by The Pennsylvania Historical Survey, Division of Community Programs, Works Progress Administration (Harrisburg: Pennsylvania Historical Commission, 1944). Manifests for the early sailings contain little meaningful data. The manifest for the February 1882 sailing of the *Illinois* contains the name, age, sex, and occupation of the emigrant. It also identified to which country the emigrant "belonged," and which country the emigrant intended to inhabit, but it did not include the names of towns - in the old country or in the United States. Manifest for the *Illinois,* February 23, 1882, NAP. Later manifests include town names. The general background concerning the arrival of the steamer *Illinois* on February 23, 1882, is found in David Sulzberger's, "The Beginnings of Russo-Jewish Immigration to Philadelphia," *PAJHS*, vol. XIX (1910), pp. 125-150.
8. While no statistics are available to prove through what port most east European Jewish emigrants who settled in Philadelphia came, overwhelming anecdotal evidence suggests that most came through Castle Garden, the first emigrant aid station in New York, and after 1892 through Ellis Island. Between 1886 and 1898 a total of 34,781 Jewish emigrants came through the port of Philadelphia; many, however, left within a day or two after arrival, destined for other east-coast cities or the west. For example, within two days after the arrival of the steamship *Pennsylvania* at the port of Philadelphia on July 13, 1882, nearly three hundred Jewish refugees from Odessa and Kiev left for the West. *New York Times*, July 15, 1882. On October 13, 1885, a total of forty-four Jewish emigrants arrived on the *British King*, of whom only three remained in Philadelphia. During the year 1885, a total of 2,310 Jewish emigrants arrived at the port; of these arrivals, 26 percent remained in Philadelphia.
9. *Jewish Record*, September 12, 1884. On August 18, 1884, the United Hebrew Charities of New York sent a letter to Jewish relief organizations in Europe, which stated in part: "It is hard that overcrowded European cities should be burdened with these refugees, consumers not producers, but it is certainly harder to forward them to a strange country, thousands of miles away, only to be immediately returned as paupers upon their arrival in this country." Quoted by Zosa Szajkowski, "The Attitude of American Jews to East European Jewish Immigration (1881-1893)," *PAJHS*, vol. XL, no. 3

(March, 1951), pp. 226, 227. The incident involving the pauper immigrants from Romania aboard the *Westphalia* was also covered in the Hebrew press of Eastern Europe. *Hamagid*, Vol. XXVIII (October 2, 1884), p. 330, 331. I would like to thank Dr. Neil Rosenstein of Elizabeth, New Jersey, for bringing the articles in *Hamagid* to my attention. An almost identical anti-pauper position was still being actively pursued by the Society of the United Hebrew Charities in Philadelphia six years later. The *Record* for July 25, 1890, quoted from a letter written by the United Hebrew Charities of Philadelphia: "We believe that the Government officials at the immigration office in New York are lax in the enforcement of the laws relating to paupers. At the meeting of our Board last Monday we wrote to the United Charities in New York, asking if something could not be done to stir up the immigration officials to a severer scrutiny in regard to paupers."

10. *Inquirer*, September 9, 1884. For a history of the HEAS, see Gilbert Osofsky, "The Hebrew Emigrant Aid Society of the United States (1881-1883)," *PAJHS*, vol. XLIX, no. 3 (March 1960), pp. 173-187. Judelsohn's move to Philadelphia is found in the *Jewish Record*, April 25, 1884.
11. *Inquirer*, September 9, 1884. The early immigration process at the port of Philadelphia involved the examination of the immigrants' baggage; later the immigrants themselves were subjected to examination; and finally Boards of Special Inquiry were established to review decisions of the inspectors concerning the admission of immigrants. New arrivals were examined on the ship, on the wharf, and at the immigrant stations. In the 1880's, the Emigrant Passenger Depot of the Pennsylvania Railroad, which was connected by planking to the decks of the steamships of the American Line, housed a telegraph office, an exchange office, a baggage express office, and a ticket office.
12. J. Judelsohn to Rev. Sabato Morais, September 19, 1884, Sabato Morais papers, CJS. The Russian immigrants quickly learned Morais was their greatest friend. Born in Leghorn, Italy and educated in the English language in London, Morais not only understood the plight of the poor but also sought to better the lives of the newcomers. On Morais generally, Max Samuel Nussenbaum, *Champion of Orthodox Judaism: A Biography of the Reverend Sabato Morais, LL.D.*, diss., Yeshiva University, June 1964; Rabbi Alex J. Goldman, "Sabato Morais, Pillar of Strength and Determination," in *Giants of Faith* (New York: The Citadel Press, 1964), and Robert E. Fierstien, "Sabato Morais and the Founding of the Jewish Theological Seminary," in *When Philadelphia Was the Capital of Jewish America,* ed. Murray Friedman (Philadelphia: The Balch Institute Press, 1993). Morais' extensive correspondence is located at CJS.
13. Philip Cowen to Henry Morais, September 24, 1884, Henry Morais papers, YUA.
14. J. Judelsohn to Rev. Sabato Morais, September 25, 1884, Sabato Morais papers, CJS.
15. *Public Ledger*, September 25, 1884. A history of the *Public Ledger* was published in a supplement to the *Inquirer*, September 16, 1962.
16. Philip Cowen to Henry Morais, October 8, 1884, Henry Morais papers, YUA. The founding of the Association of Jewish Immigrants of Philadelphia was reported in Eastern Europe in *Hamagid,* Vol. XXVIII (October 30, 1884), pp. 354, 355. When Cowen attacked Judelsohn publicly, the *Jewish Record* in Philadelphia defended Judelsohn and his plans to help the emigrants. *Jewish Record*, October 10, 17, 1884.
17. Dr. A. E. Hartogensis to Sabato Morais, December 30, 1891, Sabato Morais papers, CJS. Hartogensis was Judelsohn's father-in-law. Fifteen days after Judelsohn's death, his son - also Jacob Judelsohn - was born. Forty-eight years after the Association of Jewish Immigrants of Philadelphia was founded, Cowen, in his autobiography, recognized "J. Judelson" as one of the outstanding men among the newcomers in the 1880's. Although Cowen used no first name and spelled Judelsohn without an *"h,"* it is clear that Cowen was referring to Judelsohn, since there was no other leader in the immigrant community at that time with an identical or similar name. Cowen posthumously gave Judelsohn the *koved* (honor) denied Judelsohn during his lifetime. Philip Cowen, *Memoirs of an American Jew* (New York: The International Press, 1932), p. 295.
18. *Public Ledger*, January 26, 1886.
19. Alfred T. Jones to the president of the Alliance Israélite Universelle, Paris, December 11, 1884, BEA. The swindling of immigrants by unauthorized ticket speculators was publicly denounced by Morris Rosenbaum, a prominent immigrant banker in Philadelphia: "The [steamship] companies have tried in vain to rout these illegitimate speculators, but it is impossible. There is practically no law to prohibit them from carrying on their business. To-day I received a letter which shows how these men operate. The writer who lives in this city patronized one of these so-called agencies and in return for his money received a printed blank addressed to some person in Bremen, with instructions to furnish the bearer with passage to Philadelphia. The writer sent the blank to a relative in Bremen and before the passage was secured the relative was hustled from one port to another and finally landed in New York after he had spent more than his passage in railroad fare. In many cases these blanks are found to be utterly worthless and their bearers are stranded in Hamburg or some of the other ports." *Inquirer*, July 29, 1890. An investigative reporter in Hamburg found conditions greatly changed in 1891. Because of the passage of the Hamburg "Auswanderungegesetz of 1887," a law that compelled steamship companies to take better care of steerage passengers, the selling of tickets was closely regulated and hotelkeepers who charged amounts above fixed prices were punished. Because of these measures, the lot of the poor Russian emigrant in Hamburg improved. *American Hebrew*, May 1, 1891. Conditions, however, worsened again after the turn of the century when immigration was at its height.
20. The true state of affairs, however, remains basically unstudied. In their histories, (i.e, W.E.B. DuBois, *The Philadelphia Negro* (Philadelphia, 1899) and Richard N. Juliani, *The Social Organization of Immigration: The Italians in Philadelphia* (Philadelphia, 1971)), DuBois and Juliani ignored the Jews, just as Moses Freeman, when writing the history of the Jews, ignored the African American and Italian experience. Each camp huddled under its own banner.
21. *Annual Report 1888, Association of Jewish Immigrants of Philadelphia.* APS. The 1888 Annual Report was issued in early November, only weeks after Jones' death. Soon Louis E. Levy took over the Association, but he did not exert his leadership immediately. The meeting of the Association on November 4, 1888, is described in the *American Hebrew* for November 9, 1888 (the date of the meeting is erroneously given as October 4, 1888).
22. *American Hebrew*, November 23, 1888. The Philadelphians, however, naively oversimplified a most complex situation. For example, Gabriel Zoltowski, a Jewish tailor, left Russia and, with his wife and five children, settled in Prussia. On September 12, 1885, the Prussian Government issued an edict, ordering Zoltowski and his family to leave Prussia

before October 1, 1885. With no possibility of returning to Russia, he made his way to Liverpool, where he boarded the *British King*. Zoltowski and his family were admitted at the port of Philadelphia, identified as exiles from Prussia. *Jewish Record*, October 16, 1885. How many others like Gabriel Zoltowski were there?

23. Section 2 of the Act of August 3, 1882, provided that "it shall be the duty of such State commission, board, or officers so designated to examine into the condition of passengers arriving at the ports within such state in any ship or vessel, and for that purpose all or any of such commissioners or officers, or such other person or persons as they shall appoint, shall be authorized to go on board of and through any such ship or vessel; and if on such examination there shall be found among such passengers any convict, lunatic, idiot, or any person unable to take care of himself or herself without becoming a public charge, they shall report the same in writing to the collector of such port, and such persons shall not be permitted to land." 22 Stat. 214.

24. The *Jewish Exponent* for August 10, 1888, contained an appeal from the Board of Directors of the Association of Jewish Immigrants. The English-reading Jewish community was advised that the "large Jewish immigration during the present year has caused an increase in expenditures, and has nearly exhausted the treasury of the Association. It fears that, unless contributions are speedily made, the good work of the Association will be seriously impaired." An appeal by Mayer Sulzberger before the Young Men's Hebrew Association is found in the *American Hebrew*, October 26, 1888: "Is he cultured and civilized who says, 'We have nothing to do with these dirty Poles and Russians [east European Jews]; they had no business to come here; we do not need them or want them; they are none of our concern?' or is he the noble one and the cultured one who says, 'Is he poor and untutored? - so much more does he need our help; let us lift him to that purer air which we are breathing; let us teach and instruct him and his children,' that is true refinement and culture." Under the leadership of Louis E. Levy, which spanned three decades, the Association of Jewish Immigrants grew, changing its name to the Association for the Protection of Jewish Immigrants, and finally in 1913 to the Hebrew Immigrant Aid Society, or as we know it today, HIAS.

25. *Memoirs*, by Charles Judah Cohen, 1947. I would like to thank Ruth M. Cohen, Charles Cohen's daughter, for giving me permission to quote from the typescript.

26. In some instances, possession of an address of a relative was indispensable to landing in this country. A woman and two children who arrived at the port of Philadelphia aboard the *Ohio* on August 12, 1888, were not permitted to land. They were found to be threats to become public charges. The Association of Jewish Immigrants provided free tickets for their return trip from Liverpool to their home in Galicia (the American Line was obligated to return them to Liverpool). The only reason given for believing that they would become public charges was that "[s]he was without the address of relatives." The 1888 Report of the Association of Jewish Immigrants of Philadelphia, p. 21, APS.

27. Years later Charles Judah Cohen still remembered that night. He stated that they walked to 9th Street and got another streetcar. When the Cohens showed the address to where they were going to the conductor, he let them off, directing them to 7th Street. They took another car. That kept up until dawn. Finally, they reached 7th & South Streets. There was a shoe store and they saw a man sitting on a chair, as the morning was hot and humid. When the Cohens showed the man the address, he spoke to them in Yiddish and directed them to their final destination. But not all immigrants had as much trouble with the carefully laid out streets of William Penn's planned town as did the Cohens. Zvi Hirsh Masliansky, the famous Zionist orator who came to Philadelphia in 1896, wrote: "Philadelphia is rightly the opposite of Boston. The streets are laid out straight like a chessboard, squares in her length and breadth. Whereas in Boston it is difficult for a stranger to find its streets and alleys, the round and the winding, so it is in Philadelphia impossible for a stranger even on his first day to get lost. As soon as one knows the number of a house, he is certain that he will find it and need not ask anyone." Zvi Hirsh Masliansky, *Masliansky's Memoirs: Forty Years of Life and Struggle* (New York: The Turberg Press, 1924), p. 255.

28. Samuel Joseph, *History of the Baron de Hirsch Fund* (Baron de Hirsch Fund, 1935), p. 37, and Zosa Szajkowski, "Emigration to America or Reconstruction in Europe," *PAJHS*, vol. XLII, no. 2 (December 1952), pp. 180-186. See also *Record*, July 25, 1890.

29. *Hamagid*, vol. XXXIV, page 230 (1890). Counterforces were at work in the *shtetl*, however, to encourage emigration. Subagents of the steamship lines - men who made good money from the sale of *shifskartes* (steamship tickets) – were forced out of port cities like Hamburg in 1887. Shortly thereafter, subagents of these lines appeared in the *shtetlyekh* of Russia. For each steerage ticket sold, a subagent in the *shtetl* received a commission of ten marks. The idea planted in the emigrant's head that in the United States the streets were paved with gold, the trees were lined with loaves of bread, and "milk and honey [were] conducted to every house by underground pipes" had a serious profit motive behind it. *American Hebrew*, May 1, 1891.

30. The Constitution of the Jewish Alliance of America was printed in the *Jewish Exponent* for February 20, 1891. The Baron de Hirsch Trust did not give its full support to Russian immigration until September 1891. Joseph, *History of the Baron de Hirsch Fund*, pp. 37, 38.

31. *Di Yidishe Velt*, January 14, 1931. Sulzberger was interested in Harris' connection to the *Vilna Gaon*. I would like to thank Chaim Freedman for advising me of the name that Harris was given at birth. For Harris generally, see the *Press*, August 17, 1891; Ellis Paxson Oberholtzer, *Philadelphia: A History of the City and its People*, 4 vols (Philadelphia: S. J. Clarke Publishing Co., 1908), IV: 620-622, and David B. Tierkel, typescript of the history of the Yiddish theatre in Philadelphia (1934), p. 48 (footnote), YIVO. For Harris' role in the founding of the *Volks-Vechter*, see 310 S. 5th Street, in the guide portion of this book.

32. Soon after being admitted to the bar, Harris agreed to represent Leo Alexandroff, a deserter from the Russian Navy. The litigation attracted much local interest and won wide recognition for Harris. Harris argued the case before the lower federal courts and the Supreme Court of the United States, *William R. Tucker v. Leo Alexandroff*, 183 U.S. 424 (1902). The case involved what was said to have been an affair of the heart, a question of international law, and diplomatic relations between the United States and Russia. *Public Ledger*, July 13, 1900, and January 7, 1902. Alexandroff came to Philadelphia in October 1899 in the company of fifty-three men and an officer of the Russian Navy. They were sent here to form part of a crew for the cruiser *Variag*, which was then on the stocks at Cramp's shipyard in the course of construction for the Russian Government. Alexandroff became infatuated with an American girl and deserted. Harris argued

successfully in the lower courts that a ship still on the stocks was not a "ship of war" or a "merchant vessel," and being neither, he argued the Russian government could not invoke an 1832 treaty to force deportation. The District Court agreed with Harris and released Alexandroff, but the litigation proceeded. Vladimir Behr, Master of the cruiser *Variag*, told a reporter for the *Public Ledger* that if the American courts would not sanction the deportation of deserters while waiting for the completion of their ships, the Russian government would no longer build ships in the United States. The Supreme Court, in a 5-4 decision, reversed and ruled against Harris, but Oberholtzer tells us that the Supreme Court decision was "widely criticized in legal circles." Alexandroff eventually went free.

33. Jeanne Lichtman Abrams, *Chasing the Cure: A History of the Jewish Consumptives' Relief Society of Denver*, Ph.D. dissertation, University of Colorado (Colorado, 1983), and Marjorie Hornbein, "Dr. Charles Spivak of Denver: Physician, Social Worker, Yiddish Author," in *WSJHQ*, vol. XI (April, 1979), pp. 195-211. Jeanne Abrams has supported my efforts from the very beginning and I owe her many thanks.

34. *Jewish Daily Forward*, December 21, 1921.

35. Moses Freeman, *Fuftzig Yohr Geshikhte fun Yidishn Leben in Filadelfia*, 2 vols. (Philadelphia: Posy-Shoulson Press, 1929), I: 204, and Dr. Spivak Memorial Issue, *The Sanatorium*, ed. Dr. A. Levinson, XXII, 4 (Oct., Nov., Dec., 1927), p. 18. Spivak described his experiences to the Jews of Russia, see *Na Amerikanskie Fabrike, Nedel'nia Khronika Voskhoda, 1884, 22.* He was a prolific writer. A compilation of his writings is found in the Memorial Issue of *The Sanatorium*. Although repeatedly requested to do so, Spivak adamantly refused to write an autobiography. He was unyielding on this point.

36. *Press*, August 17, 1891. We find Spivak in Philadelphia as early as October 1886 when he advertised he was a "practicing teacher learned in the English, German and Hebrew languages." *Di New Yorker Yudishe Volkszeitung*, October 8, 1886.

37. Spivak did not write about his days at Jefferson, but we do have the poignant memoir of Benjamin Lee Gordon, who entered Jefferson two years after Spivak graduated. A recently arrived Russian Jewish immigrant and a librarian at the YMHA after Spivak, Gordon has left us a narrative picture of his first day at Jefferson: "Let us retrace our path to the twenty-fifth of September, 1892 - a day that I shall always remember. It was on this day that the dream of my life started to mature into reality. I dressed myself in my finest. My suit was freshly pressed; my shoes were shined to perfection; I was wearing a new shirt and tie; my hair was carefully parted in the middle. It was thus that I became a medical student and went to the amphitheater of the college to listen to the introductory lecture which was delivered by Professor Hare. I took a seat in the last row and observed with great interest the decorated operating platform below. The band began to play as the trustees and faculty members marched in in full regalia. The exercises began with the National Anthem and an invocation by a Presbyterian minister. I was dazed and happy that I now belonged to this gathering." Benjamin L. Gordon, M.D., *Between Two Worlds: Memoirs of a Physician* (New York, 1952), pp. 160, 161.

38. Letter from Spivak to Morais, May 21, 1888, CJS. For Spivak's election to the Hebrew Education Society as a teacher, see *American Hebrew*, February 24, 1888, and for his role in the Society, see *Our Philadelphia Letter*, in *American Hebrew*, June 29, 1888. Notwithstanding his many other activities during his medical school days, Spivak also found time to organize young Russian intellectual organizations. Identified as the "Organizer, R. A. O. [Russian American Organization]," on Saturday evening, September 28, 1889, Spivak gave notice that Nikolai Aleinikoff would speak at 203 Pine Street. The title of his talk: "The Socialist Position of the Russians and its Impact on America." *Di New Yorker Yudishe Volkszeitung*, September 27, 1889. Aleinikoff, the leading light of the Kiev *Am Olam* group, was then one of the chief spokesmen for the Jewish immigrant community in New York. Ronald Sanders, *The Downtown Jews* (New York: Harper & Row, 1969), pp. 68, 69. At this time Abraham Cahan had doubts about anarchism; he turned to Spivak: "A few years earlier in a letter to Dr. Chaim D. Spivak of Philadelphia, I had opened my heart and confessed my confusion." Abraham Cahan, *The Education of Abraham Cahan*, translated by Leon Stein, Abraham P. Conan, and Lynn Davison (Philadelphia: JPS, 1969), p. 330.

39. *Jewish Exponent*, August 24, 1888. Morais spoke many languages, as did Spivak, but Morais did not speak Russian or Yiddish.

40. Having studied Talmud in Russia, Spivak was well grounded in Jewish law: "It was characteristic of the former *Yeshiva bokher* and *Talmudist* [Spivak] that for the subject of his dissertation to receive his diploma, he chose 'menstruation,' the Jewish laws of impurity and cleanness, from the laws of the Priests [Leviticus]." Moses Freeman, *Fuftzig Yohr Geshikhte fun Yidishn Leben in Filadelfia*, 2 vols. (Philadelphia: Posy-Shoulson Press, 1929), I:206.

41. *The Public Ledger* for August 4, 1890, reported rabbis in Russia mentioned September as the period for enforcement of the regulations to expel the Jews: "The dread of wholesale transportation to Siberia for failure to observe the edicts will impel the flight westward of many thousands of Jews." Earlier, the Association of Jewish Immigrants of Philadelphia had dispersed immigrants throughout the United States, but its goals did not include settling the immigrants on the land: "Special attention has been given by the Society [Association of Jewish Immigrants of Philadelphia] through its agent [Moses Klein] to divert the current of immigration westward and southward into the interior and away from the seaboard. Our efforts in this direction have resulted in forwarding upwards of 200 people [of a total of 1,761 Jewish immigrants who had entered the port of Philadelphia during the year 1886] who had intended to settle themselves here or in New York City, westward to where friends or acquaintances had been found by us for them." Fifth Annual Report, 1888, p. 10, APS. The primary goal of the Jewish Alliance of America, however, was agriculture pursuits. In August 1890, Spivak said: "It is the duty of the intelligent portion of the Russian Jews to impress upon the emigrants the idea that agricultural is the most lucrative profession if conducted properly."

42. *Press*, August 17, 1891.

43. A. B. Cohn or Cohen was also a founder of the Alliance, but little information is known about him.

44. *Jewish Exponent*, August 15, and September 26, 1890. The founding of the Jewish Alliance of America was front-page news in the Yiddish press, *Folks-Advokat*, August 22 and 29, 1890.

45. The founding of the Jewish Alliance of America was the cover story in the *Jewish Exponent*, February 20, 1891. Delegates came from: Baltimore; Washington; Chicago; Portland, Oregon; Wilkes-Barre; Boston; Albany; Newark; Atlanta, and other cities. Leaders from the American, German, Hungarian, Galician, and Russian Jewish communities attended.

46. Some of the speeches were most unusual, none more so than the one made by the Honorable Simon Wolf of Washington, D.C. "He [Simon Wolf] said the battle we are fighting was not of the Jews alone, but of the Christians as well. It was unnecessary further to propitiate the Russian authorities. Let the Russian Jews come to this country, and if they must be converted, let them be converted to American Christians and not Russian Catholics. If the Jews would look into their own hearts, they would see where the rishus [evil] comes from. 'Congress is with us,' Mr. Wolf said. 'The sympathy of the people is with us.'" Ibid.

47. Letter from Samuel B. Woods to Dr. C. D. Spivak, dated August 9, 1890, quoted in the *Jewish Exponent*, August 15, 1890.

48. *Jewish Exponent*, April 3, and June 19, 1891.

49. *Jewish Exponent*, August 21, 1891. The total number of Jewish immigrants who landed at the port of Philadelphia in July 1891 was exactly five hundred, the largest number of Jewish immigrants to land in Philadelphia in one month since the founding of the Association of Jewish Immigrants. Of the five hundred, 478 came from Russia and Poland; 127 of these were under ten years of age; and only five were over fifty. Of those that came, 278 remained in Philadelphia, eighty-two went to Baltimore, fifty-five to New York and the balance were scattered throughout the country.

50. Zosa Szajkowski, "Emigration to America or Reconstruction in Europe," *PAJHS*, vol. XLII, no. 2 (December 1952), p. 180. Szajkowski continued: "We have seen how the Alliance constantly held to the principle not to improve the condition of the Jews in any country through immigration. Even in 1881 and 1882, when the mass immigration of Russian Jews began, we have already indicated how the Alliance was compelled to help the immigrants and at the same time always guarded itself from establishing any precedent which might create the impression that it sought to solve the Jewish problem in Russia through emigration. All efforts to find new centers of immigration were directed solely to locate places of refuge for Jewish emigrants who had already left their homes. Some place had to be found for them. The mission that Baron de Hirsch sent to Argentina and the founding of the JCA were of an entirely different complexion for it implied that Russian Jews were being invited to migrate, - to recognize that emigration was the best means to solve the Russian-Jewish problem." Ibid.

51. Joseph, *History of the Baron de Hirsch Fund*, p. 37. The conference was held on September 21, 1891, at the Hebrew Institute in New York City.

52. In Berlin, Spivak studied with "Baar and Werchow," presumably well known doctors. The Jewish Alliance of America survived long enough to plan to celebrate its first anniversary in February 1892. There were thirty-four branches in different cities in the United States; membership was counted in the thousands, but only 151 immigrants had been settled throughout the country. The total income was $2,886.43 and the expenditures - $2,605.49, *Public Ledger*, January 12, 1892.

53. In a speech in Philadelphia favoring restrictive immigration, Samuel P. Gompers, head of the recently formed American Federation of Labor, claimed that shiploads of immigrants with "typhus and cholera" had been brought to our shores to the total disregard of the material welfare and general health of the people, *Public Ledger*, December 13, 1892. Gompers inflammatory language was not justified because measures had been taken to seal off emigration from Hamburg so as to control the spread of typhus and cholera. For months during the fall of 1892 no emigrants were permitted to sail. Joseph Medoff, *My Journey to America* (Manuscript, May 10, 1904), CJS.

54. *Inquirer*, May 11, 1903.

55. The dates for the pogroms of 1905 are given in the old style; that is, they accord with the calendar used in Russia in 1905. This calendar was twelve days behind ours in the 19th century and thirteen days behind between 1900 and 1917. All other dates are given in accordance with the new style. For an inside account of the issuance of the October Manifesto, see *The Memoirs of Count Witte*, translated and edited by Sidney Harcave (New York: M. E. Sharpe, Inc., 1990).

56. At his coronation Nicholas swore to rule the empire and preserve autocracy as Emperor and Autocrat of all the Russias. His complete title was: Emperor and Autocrat of all the Russias, Czar of Moscow, Kiev, Vladimir, Novgorod, Kazan, Astrakhan, of Poland, of Siberia, of Tauric Chersonese, of Georgia, Lord of Pskov, Grand Duke of Smolensk, of Lithuania, Volhynia, Podolia and Finland, Prince of Estonia, Livonia, Courland and Semigalia, Samogotia, Bialostock, Karelia, Tver, Yougouris, Perm, Viatka, Bulgaria, and other countries; Lord and Grand Duke of Lower Novgorod, of Tchernigov, Riazan, Polotsk, Rostov, Yaroslav, Belozero, Oudoria, Obdoria, Condia, Vitebsk, Mstislav and all the region to the North, Lord and Sovereign of the countries of Iveria, Cartalinia, Kabardinia and the provinces of Armenia, Sovereign of the Circassian Princes and the Mountain Princes, Lord of Turkestan, Heir of Norway, Duke of Schleswig Holstein, of Storman, of the Ditmars, and of Oldenbourg, etc.

57. For a survey of the 1905 pogroms, see Shlomo Lambroza, *The Pogrom Movement in Tsarist Russia, 1903-1906*, A thesis submitted to the Graduate School of Rutgers, The State University of New Jersey in partial fulfillment of the requirements for the degree of Doctor of Philosophy (New Brunswick, 1981). For individual pogroms, see *Die Judenpogrome in Russland* (The Jewish Pogroms in Russia), *I Allgemeiner Teil and II Einseldarstellungen* (Köln and Leipzig, *Jüdischer Verlag G.M.B.H.*, 1910) 2 vols. Reaction in the United States is described by Zosa Szajkowski, "The Impact of the Russian Revolution of 1905 on American Jewish Life," *YIVO Annual of Jewish Social Science*, vol. XVII (1978), pp. 54-118. Most traditional accounts of this period attribute the heavy Jewish immigration of 1906-1907 to the pogroms. A recent new look at the role pogroms played in emigration from Russia is given by John D. Klier, in "Emigration Mania in Late-Imperial Russia: Legend and Reality," in *Patterns of Migration, 1850-1914*, ed. Aubrey Newman and Stephen W. Massil (London: Jewish Historical Society of England, 1996), pp. 21-29.

58. Although no statistical analysis demonstrates where the Russian Jews who settled in Philadelphia lived in Russia, several avenues of investigation are open. A preliminary review of approximately 750 charters - issued to Jewish *chevras, landmanschaftn* and *fareyns* in Philadelphia by the Courts of Common Pleas - indicates that an overwhelming number of these charters were issued to organizations that included in the name of the organization the name of a town, area or political sub-division in the south of Russia. I would like to thank Elaine Kolinsky of Philadelphia for bringing these charters to my attention. A second avenue of investigation would include the examination of manifests or ship arrival records of the period. The later manifests indicate the name of the immigrant's town or village in Russia and the immigrant's local destination in the United States. For a recent statistical analysis of two 1910

manifests, see I. A. Glazier and Robert J. Kleiner, "Comparative Analysis of Emigrants from Southern and Eastern Europe from U. S. Ship Passenger Lists: 1910," in Patterns of Migration, 1850-1914, pp. 255-265.

59. *Press*, November 30, 1905. The article in the *Press* is illustrated with photographs showing the massive demonstration on the narrow streets of the Jewish quarter. One of these photographs shows the magnificent terra cotta front of New Auditorium Hall, 747-753 S. 3rd Street.

60. Ibid. See also *Inquirer*, November 30, 1905.

61. To accommodate the floodtide of immigrants from Russia and from other European countries where the ambitious and the energetic wanted to leave, in October 1910 the Hamburg-American Line announced that it intended to establish a new steamship service between Hamburg and the port of Philadelphia, assigning three of its best ships to the new route. The announcement led directly to decisions by three other steamship lines to start bringing passengers to the Philadelphia area. These were the Allan Line, which would bring passengers from Glasgow and Liverpool to Gloucester, New Jersey; the Philadelphia Transatlantic Line - from London to Philadelphia, and the North German Lloyd Steamship Company - from Bremen to Philadelphia. The new epoch began on November 10, 1910, when the 13,000-ton steamship *Graf-Waldersee* arrived at pier 53 at the Washington Avenue wharf with 590 passengers. Arrivals for the year 1910 at the port of Philadelphia, as of the date of the arrival of the *Graf-Waldersee*, totaled 49,600 passengers, or 10,000 more than had landed before at the port. By 1913, the large Immigrant Station of the American Line, the Red Star Line and the Hamburg-American Line, loomed over pier 53 at the foot of Washington Avenue at the Delaware River. *North American*, October 13, 1910, and *Inquirer*, November 11, 1910.

62. Leon Boonin, *Memoirs* (Typescript, 1944), PJAC. Leon (1887-1949) was an uncle of the author.

63. During the early years of emigration, winter seas played with the smaller ships. The *British Prince* of the American Line left Liverpool for Philadelphia on January 19, 1887. Four days out, a violent gale was encountered. The following day "...she shipped a heavy sea over the saloon deck, destroying life-boat No. 7 and carrying away the galley skylights. During the pitching of the vessel the stern was constantly thrown out of the water, and the chief officer stated yesterday [February 6] that two of the blades of the propeller were lost and a third one was broken." *Public Ledger*, February 7, 1887. It is difficult to believe that the scrutiny given to all emigrants was uniform throughout all the ports of arrival, but whether examinations at New York were more strict than at Philadelphia is unknown. A scholarly treatment of the myths surrounding the examination of emigrants at Ellis Island is given in Thomas M. Pitkin's, *Keepers of the Gate: A History of Ellis Island* (New York: New York University Press, 1975).

64. *Public Ledger*, February 10, 1919. The article, written in Warsaw, was sent by Special Cable Dispatch to the editor of the *London Times-Public Ledger Service* in London, who transmitted it to Philadelphia. The *Times* in London prefaced the copyrighted story with an editorial regret: "London. Feb. 9. - *The Times*, in printing the following dispatch on the pogroms in Poland, editorially regrets to be compelled to declare its belief that the article is substantially true." Ibid.

65. *Public Ledger*, February 10, 1919.

66. Typical of the horrors facing Jews choosing to leave at that time was the situation at Lapy Station, on the Polish-Lithuanian border. Jews coming to Poland from the Soviet Union were accused of being Bolsheviks and Jews leaving Poland were charged with being spies. Hardly any Jew traveling by this frontier station was able to escape persecutions by the soldiers. At Rzeszow, Jews who applied for traveling permits were stripped, robbed, stretched on benches, tied, and flogged. Ibid.

67. *Evening Bulletin*, June 2, 1919.

68. *Public Ledger* and *Inquirer*, June 3, 1919.

69. *Public Ledger*, June 3, 1919. During the summer of 1919, the Jewish delegation at the Peace Conference in Paris learned that 120,000 Jews had been killed in the Ukrainian pogroms, *Public Ledger*, August 1, 1919. See Elias Heifetz, *The Slaughter of the Jews in the Ukraine in 1919* (New York: 1921).

70. Christopher Morley, *Travels in Philadelphia* (Philadelphia: David McKay Co., 1920), pp. 39-45, and *Evening Bulletin*, March 22 and August 1, 1919.

71. Quickly, the pre-war scramble to leave the Old World resumed. On the crossing of December 9, 1920, a total of 212 cabin and 1,224 steerage passengers were on board the *Haverford*. In early January 1921 the passenger business of the American Line was taken over by the White Star Company, and the *Haverford* was transferred to the British line. The first sailing of the *Haverford* under the White Star flag was on January 24, 1921. On that crossing the ship carried 110 cabin passengers and 425 émigrés in steerage. By March 3, 1921, with the arrival of the Italian liner *America*, nearly 9,000 passengers had arrived at the port of Philadelphia since the beginning of the year, a record. *Evening Bulletin*, March 3, 1921.

72. The 1921 legislation, with President Harding's approval, became a law on May 19, 1921. The number of aliens of any nationality who were to be admitted was not to exceed 3 percent of the number of persons of such nationality who were resident in the United States according to the census of 1910. The Act, however, excluded few of the unwanted, the formula being obviously flawed (from the point of view of the Administration and Congress) because it used a late (1910) base period. Therefore, draconian measures were adopted. The Immigration Act of 1924, enacted May 26, 1924, provided that the number of aliens of any nationality admissible to the United States in any fiscal year would be limited to 2 percent of the number of such persons of such nationality who were resident in the United States according to the census of 1890. As computed in accordance with the 1924 legislative formula, the total quota for 1924-1925 for Russia (European and Asiatic) was 2,248 immigrants.

73. *Evening Bulletin*, September 29, 1924. The *Haverford* made its last trip up river from Liverpool on September 10, 1924; it carried only 136 third-class passengers (capacity in third class was 1,700 passengers). During the war the *Haverford* was used as a British troop transport. It was attacked three times by German submarines: on June 12, 1917, it was attacked off the coast of southern Ireland and escaped unharmed; on June 26, 1917, it was torpedoed off the west coast of Scotland with the loss of eight lives; and on June 17, 1918, it escaped unharmed. Upon the passage of the Immigration Act of 1924, it was sold and scrapped in Italy in 1925. Immigrants coming to Philadelphia after September 1924 were able to enter the country through Ellis Island, which remained open until 1954. Irregular sailings continued into Philadelphia, however, from 1924 to 1945.

74. The dramatic effect of the quota system established by the 1924 legislation can best be seen statistically. In 1907, the peak year of immigration into the United States for all

immigrants, 1,258,349 entered the country. In 1933, a total of 7,793 immigrants entered the United States. *Evening Bulletin*, March 19, 1934. The best study of Jewish immigration statistics during this period is Samuel Joseph, *Jewish Immigration to the United States from 1881 to 1910*, (New York, 1914).

75. *Di Yidishe Velt*, December 24, 1930.
76. Report of the United States Immigration Commission, 1910, p. 203.
77. According to George H. Orth, chief of the division of private banks of the Department of Banking in 1930, the Blitzstein bank was operated under exemption six of the private banking act of 1911. *Evening Bulletin*, December 24, 1930. The sixth exemption to "An Act to provide for licensing and regulating private banking in the Commonwealth of Pennsylvania; and providing penalties for the violation thereof, Approved June 19, 1911," stated that the act did not apply to any entity which conducted "the business of private banking for a period of seven (7) years prior to the approval of this act, and such banking institution is not engaged in the sale, as agent or otherwise, of railroad or steamship tickets." Anna easily met the first requirement (she could prove that she had been in business since 1891). However, the bank continued to sell steamship tickets until the day it closed. How the bank met this second requirement for an exemption is not known.
78. On August 8, 1919, three properties were torn down and cleared for the new Blitzstein bank. The architect was J. Horace Frank (1873-1956). He was born in Philadelphia and graduated from the University of Pennsylvania in 1895.
79. Anna Blitzstein died June 13, 1929. *Di Yidishe Velt*, June 15, 1929. She had retired from the day-to-day operations of the bank several years before her death. My thanks go out to the Blitzsteins for their help: Frimma Seidman; Laura Goldsmith, and Kit Davis.
80. J. Horace Frank designed the 27′ extension on the west side of S. 4th Street, the same architect retained eleven years earlier to design the bank.
81. *Public Ledger*, December 23, 1930. Albert M. Greenfield controlled Bankers Trust Company, and questions persisted for years concerning his role in its closure. Greenfield, a Russian Jew, immigrated to Philadelphia at the age of six. While still a young man, he left the Jewish quarter, married well and amassed a real estate empire. He bought a small bank in West Philadelphia in 1925, moved it to center city and named it Bankers Trust Company. Under Greenfield's guidance Bankers Trust Company grew, and by the summer of 1930 it had acquired nine banks (at the time there were 128 banks in Philadelphia). When it added the Bank of Philadelphia and Trust Co. in July of that year, a bank that showed signs of "going under," a slow drain on the assets of Bankers Trust Company began which ultimately lead to the December collapse. Whether Greenfield was overly optimistic in his acquisition strategy or whether promised help from others did not materialize was never determined. "Philadelphia," *Fortune Magazine* June 1936. As a result of the closure of Bankers Trust Co., *Fortune* found that Greenfield "went more or less broke," but that within six years he was back on top. The road back for his fellow immigrants, however, was *shver* (difficult).
82. That same day (December 22, 1930) the run started at the Franklin Trust Company, it received $5 million from the Federal Reserve Bank, and the sudden infusion of cash permitted it to weather the onslaught (the run on Franklin Trust continued that day until midnight). A week later there was a run on the Aldine Trust Company, which had assets in excess of $9 million, and it closed on December 29, 1930. Thereafter, fifty banks in Philadelphia and its immediate suburbs failed until the moratorium of March 1933 "put an end to the agony." The run on the Blitzstein bank is traceable to the panic created by the closure of the Bankers Trust Company the day before and - if, to anything else - the general condition of the economy at that time.
83. Letter from Anna Blitzstein's granddaughter, Laura Goldsmith, March 14, 1994.
84. *Di Yidishe Velt*, December 24, 1930. Extensive coverage was devoted to the bank's closure by the Yiddish press. *Di Yidishe Velt*, December 24, 25, 27, 28, 1930; February 1, 2, and March 27, 1931. The closure was also widely covered by the English-language press in Philadelphia. When the bankruptcy action started, the bank had nineteen regular employees, all with east European Jewish surnames. Even the guards and the janitors had Jewish surnames. The bi-weekly payroll was $1,187.50. The highest paid employee (bi-weekly) was the Assistant Cashier, J. J. Galanter, $175 (Galanter was Anna Blitzstein's maiden name). Some of the other employees, and their bi-weekly salaries, were: C. B. Voynow, Jr., Cashier ($125); George Voynow, Chief Clerk ($112.50); A. L. Danenberg, Mgr., Foreign Dept. ($87.50); and Vera Taxin, Stenographer - Foreign ($50). Many of the employees were family members.
85. Within days of the bank's closing, bankruptcy proceedings were begun. Upon questioning, Samuel Blitzstein testified that on the day the bank closed, five minutes before the doors were shut, he withdrew almost half of a small account, frankly admitting: "I was very panicky that day like the other depositors." Deposits at the Blitzstein bank totaled $1,250,000. Of the 6,000 depositors, 3,500 filed claims. In the summer of 1931 the liquidating trustees paid claimants a total of $451,551.10, which was 35 percent of claimed deposits. During the next six years, an additional 17 percent of claimed deposits was paid to depositors, the last payment being made on April 21, 1937. In the matter of *M. L. Blitzstein & Company, Bankrupts, Cause No. 13,802, Involuntary Petition in Bankruptcy filed December 26, 1930*, NAP. In view of the fact that over 50 percent of claimed deposits was repaid, a strong guiding hand might have saved the bank. In addition, substantial Administrative claims were paid out in the bankruptcy action, payments that would not have been necessary had bankruptcy been avoided.
86. George M. Price, "Russian Jews in America," *PAJHS*, vol. XLVIII, no. 1 (September, 1958), p. 48. A peddler in America was similar to a haberdasher in Russia.
87. Lucien Moss to Sabato Morais, March 18, 1884, CJS. Arrests of unlicensed peddlers made headlines in Philadelphia in early 1887. By November of that year, the United States Commissioners required that all persons arriving on European steamers at the port of Philadelphia who gave peddling as their previous vocation in eastern Europe were to be specifically reported to them before landing. Reluctantly, the leaders of the Association of Jewish Immigrants had to comply with this edict, but despite hardships and difficulties, peddling remained a favorite occupation of the immigrants for years. Peddler's merchandise "consisted, where possible, of light materials that could be carried in a pack, bag, box or suitcase. The merchandise was usually envelopes, writing paper, matches, hair pins, needles and thread, handkerchiefs, shoe laces, lead pencils, and other such portable articles. As the peddler became more prosperous, he carried heavier loads, and could be seen trudging through snow, or perspiring under his bur-

den in summer, on his way to and from the jobing stores which were usually on South Street or north Second Street." Albert Mordell, "The Refugee Settlers of Philadelphia," *Brooklyn Jewish Center Review*, April 1952, p. 13.

88. *The Peddler* was the most popular of Zunser's American songs. It stressed the benefits of agrarian life, which was one of the main objectives of the Jewish Alliance of America. "The Yiddish writer Joel Entin reported that, when he arrived in New York in the spring of 1891, he heard the melody of *The Peddler* wherever he went. Even the Chinese laundryman played it on the harmonica." Sol Liptzin, *Eliakum Zunser: Poet of his People* (New York: Behrman House, 1950), p. 222.

89. The history of the garment industry on Bank Street began before the Civil War. In 1857, Edwin A. Kelley, located at 16 Bank Street, employed several hundred hands throughout the year. Kelley kept forty sewing machines constantly busy, manufacturing shirts from $5 to $40 a dozen. This was one of the first shirt factories in Philadelphia. Edwin T. Freedley, *Philadelphia and its Manufacturers: A Hand-Book Exhibiting the Development, Variety, and Statistics of the Manufacturing Industry in Philadelphia* (Philadelphia: Edward Young, 1859), p. 222. Moses Sternberger owned the first Jewish shirt manufacturer on Bank Street, M&S Sternberger. Born in Germany in 1815, Sternberger opened a shop at 14 Bank Street in 1859. The business was still active during the early years of Russian Jewish immigration.

90. Report on Sweating System, Under House of Representatives Resolution, February 13, 1892, 52nd Congress, 2nd Session, Report No. 2309, FLP. For a detailed description of the structure and organization of Jewish sweatshops, see Rosara Lucy Passero, "Ethnicity in the Men's Ready-Made Clothing Industry, 1880-1950: The Italian Experience in Philadelphia," presented to the Graduate Faculty of the University of Pennsylvania in Partial Fulfillment of the Requirements for the Degree of Doctor of Philosophy (Philadelphia, 1978); chapter entitled "Eastern European Jews."

91. Lorin Blodget, *Census of Manufacturers of Philadelphia*, (Philadelphia, 1883), p. 20.

92. J. Thomas Scharf and Thompson Westcott, *History of Philadelphia, 1609-1884* (Philadelphia: L. H. Evarts and Co., 1884), III: 2354.

93. *Public Ledger,* February 4, 1887.

94. *The Immigrant Jew in America,* Ed., Edmund J. James (New York: B. F. Buck & Company, 1907), p. 124.

95. Freeman, *Fuftzig Yohr Geshikhte fun Yidishn Leben in Filadelfia*, II: 282, 283. In the 1880's there was no institution in the Jewish quarter founded exclusively for the treatment of tuberculosis. By 1896, the House of Mercy for Consumptive Men was located in the 400 block of Spruce Street, but there is no indication that Jewish men took advantage of what may have been a component of the Protestant Episcopal City Mission. From 1903 to 1905 Jews, along with patients of other religions and races, were treated at the Phipps Institute, 238 Pine Street, a pioneering non-sectarian facility founded for the treatment of tuberculosis. The majority of patients admitted to Phipps were suffering from the disease in an advanced stage, some of them living only a short time after their admission and a few, only days or even hours. Russian Jews of the city formed the Denver Consumptive Aid Association of Philadelphia, an organization that changed its name to the Jewish Consumptive Institute. During the week of September 7, 1910, it dedicated a building on Wharton Street, South Philadelphia, for the treatment of tuberculosis. The Institute sorted the cases coming to it: patients in advanced stages were sent to the Eagleville Sanatorium (outside of Philadelphia) or to Denver, Colorado; milder cases were attended to at the Wharton Street facility.

96. Although the *Jewish Record* was published during the early 1880's, it did not cover union activities, and scholarly research focused on New York adds little to our understanding of this early period in Philadelphia. See the late Professor Nora Levin's, "Socialist Intellectuals Encounter Jewish Workers in America, 1881-84," in *Gratz College Annual of Jewish Studies*, eds. Isidore David Passow and Samuel Tobais Lachs (Philadelphia: Gratz College, 1973), vol II, pp. 75-91. Jewish "shirt operators," an assembly of the Knights of Labor (identified as the S.O.M.A.), met at "203 Pine Street, 3rd Floor, over the Bank," every Wednesday evening in the fall of 1886, *Di New Yorker Yudishe Volkszeitung*, September 24, 1886. This is one of the first Yiddish press notices of a union meeting in the Jewish quarter.

97. *Public Ledger,* February 1, 1887. See also January 24, 27, 31, 1887. The Knights of Labor, which dominated the labor movement in the United States from 1877 to 1887, was founded in Philadelphia by garment cutters. The beginnings of the Knights is steeped in controversy, *Public Ledger*, January 7, 8, 1889, and *Inquirer*, August 30, 1890. Although membership excluded lawyers, bankers, and stockbrokers, it did not restrict membership, at least after 1881, on the basis of race, sex or religion. The Knights, however, did not support a separate branch for women, *Public Ledger,* February 4, 1887, and denied that the Catholic Church exercised undue influence over the affairs of the organization, *Public Ledger*, January 31, 1889.

98. Editorial, *Jewish Exponent*, April 6, 1888, and *American Hebrew*, October 26, 1888.

99. Sanders, *The Downtown Jews*, p. 94; *Times-Philadelphia*, May 17, 1890, and Freeman, *Fuftzig Yohr Geshikhte fun Yidishn Leben in Filadelfia*, I: 63. The late Maxwell Whiteman, the great historian of Jewish Philadelphia, wrote untiringly of the Cloakmakers' Strike of 1890. See Maxwell Whiteman, "The Cloakmakers' Strike of 1890," *Jewish Exponent*, October 16, 23, 1964. At the beginning of the strike Alfred H. Love, president of the Universal Peace Union reminded Morais that he (Morais) and Dr. Jastrow were vice presidents of the Universal Peace Union and, as such, Love stated they had an obligation to "guarantee to adjust the matter." Alfred H. Love to Sabato Morais, May 22, 1890, CJS.

100. *Arbeiter Zeitung*, September 12, 1890 (an article written by Louis Miller which contains interviews with the principals of the strike), and *Jewish Exponent*, August 1, 1890. For the interesting life of Garside, see Ronald Sanders, *The Downtown Jews* (New *York*: Harper & Row, Publishers, 1969), pp. 116-119, 121, 122.

101. The press covered no event in the Russian Jewish quarter during the immigrant years as completely as the 1890 cloakmakers' strike. It drew the attention of Louis Edward Levy, president of the Association of Jewish Immigrants, who was also publisher of a Philadelphia newspaper, the *Sunday Mercury.* A detailed story of the strike appeared in the *Sunday Mercury* of August 10, 1890, see *American Jewish Archives*, vol. IX, April 1957, no. 1, pp. 34-42. See also *Belligerent Strikers*, in the *Bulletin,* August 9, 1890; *Radical Change, in the Inquirer*, August 16, 1890, and at least ten other stories published that summer in the general-circulation press of Philadelphia. The strike was also covered extensively in the Yiddish-language press, see *Freie Arbeiter Stimme*, July 25, 1890, and the article by Louis Miller

already noted.

102. Letter from Randorf to Morais, August 4, 1890, CJS.

103. Letter from Randorf to Morais, August 7, 1890, CJS. For the history of the United Hebrew Charities, see Henry S. Morais, *The Jews of Philadelphia* (Philadelphia: The Levytype Company: 1894), pp. 112-114. German Jews, who comprised the UHC, gave generously of their time and money. In the Russian enclave, however, there was much bitterness and resentment: "At that time [circa 1890] there was a wall which divided the German *Yahudi* from the newly arrived Jewish immigrant from Russia, Poland, Romania, and Galacia. It was a thick, hardened wall, full of contempt and humiliation from one class of Jews to another. In the eyes of our elder and greater brethren, we had no other name than Russian *schnorers* [beggars] and 'Yom Kippur Ball Dancers,' and the treatment of every needy person who had to receive aid from them was humiliating." Freeman, *Fuftzig Yohr Geshikhte fun Yidishn Leben in Filadelfia*, I: 206. The Germans recognized that a "helping hand" was not sufficient: "Centuries of oppression and repression have resulted in greatly reducing their [the Russian Jews'] cultural level and they come to us not ignorant, but unenlightened; not thriftless, but impoverished, demanding even more our charitable consideration than a helping hand." Annual Report 1888, Association of Jewish Immigrants of Philadelphia, APS.

104. Letter from Randorf to Morais, September 19, 1890, CJS. Randorf left the Association of Jewish Immigrants on September 20, 1890.

105. On the day the working tailors struck, boss tailors met, formed the Tailors' Employers Protective Association and elected as President, Abraham Simon; Vice President, Lewis Cohen; Secretary, Bernard Weintraub; Treasurer, Jacob Kay; Executive Committee, W.B. Goldstein; Abraham Pressman; David Frank; Barney Blaskey; Harry Levin; Gustave Cooper and Charles Levi. There were approximately one hundred boss tailors at this time, seventy-three of whom belonged to the new Association. One of the demands of the workers, identified in the newspapers as anarchists, was an eight-hour workday. *Public Ledger,* June 15, 16, 19, 24, 25, 1891.

106. The Jewish population of Philadelphia in 1890 was 28,000. By June 1892, the number of Russian Jews in Philadelphia was approximately 15,000. Immigration from Russia to the port of Philadelphia in 1890 was 1,424; in 1891 - 2,447; and in 1892 - 3,929. Total Russian Jewish immigration at the ports of New York, Philadelphia and Baltimore for the same years was: 1890 - 20,981; 1891 - 43,457, and 1892 - 64,253. Samuel Joseph, *Jewish Immigration to the United States*, pp. 160, 161.

107. *Fifth Annual Report of the Factory Inspector of the Commonwealth of Pennsylvania* (for the year 1894), Clarence M. Busch, State Printer of Pennsylvania, 1895, p. 358, PSA. The Fifth Annual Report includes two special reports on the sweatshop investigation (one by O'Reilly and one by O'Keefe), in which they identify over one hundred sweatshops in the Jewish quarter and just outside the Jewish quarter (they also identify sweatshops in the Italian quarter). Ibid, pp. 357-417. For each sweatshop, identified in the special reports as a "contractor or sub-contractor," the special investigators provide the name, address, kind of goods made, for whom the goods were made, i.e., the name of the wholesale clothier or clothing house, the address of the wholesale clothier or clothing house, the number of men, women and children at work, the average wage earned per week and general notes, including conditions found and other observations.

108. *Evening Bulletin* and *Public Ledger,* May 3, 1895. The strikers met at Caledonian Hall, 214-216 Pine Street, where Max Freedman, chairman of the Executive Committee, Samuel Hyneman, and Abram Meirowitz presided. The strikers demanded that fifty-seven hours should constitute a week's work instead of the longer hours then enforced; no day, piece or task work was to be accepted; payday was to be Saturday instead of at any time, as was then the practice; and no work was to be done in private houses, as under the sweating system.

109. Four years earlier, in September 1891, Jewish tailors had left the Jewish Federation of Labor. In an article in the *Inquirer* on October 25, 1891, we learn that two hundred members of the "Tailors' Union" (not further identified) met in Philopatrian Hall the evening before in connection with a strike. The article continued: "The Hebrews, who formerly had a society of their own, have left that organization and entered the union." Apparently, in the fall of 1891 the "Hebrews" had re-entered the Knights of Labor (i.e., the "union.") The Knights continued until 1917, but little was heard from the organization in its last years.

110. *Public Ledger,* May 4, 6, 1895. In May 1895, headquarters of Local Assembly No. 1109 of the Knights of Labor, which met at Heartfellow Hall, 754 S. 3rd Street, was crowded with over five hundred children's jacket makers; the number of strikers swelled to four thousand. The union, being anxious to abolish the small sweatshop, refused to recognize any contractor who could not run more than five sewing machines. Pantaloon makers belonging to Local Assembly No. 1117 of the Knights of Labor (at that time not on strike) met at 754 S. 3rd Street to express their support for the striking garment workers. Also urging support for the strikers were the German Trades Unions uptown and about five hundred Lithuanians.

111. *Public Ledger,* May 11, 1895, and *Stadt-Zeitung* (Philadelphia), May 12, 1895.

112. The differences between the clothing factory and the wholesale clothier were marked. Garments were cut, tacked or basted, sewn, and finished at a clothing factory. A many-floored plant, the clothing factory grew in size and importance, especially after 1895. By 1903, two plants just north of the Jewish quarter employed huge numbers of immigrants: one employed 681 workers in the making of men's clothing and the other employed six hundred workers in the manufacture of men's and boys' shirts. In 1909, over nine hundred workers, many young Jewish girls, were engaged in the manufacture of shirtwaists in a plant at the corner of 5th & Locust Streets. These factories, and other smaller ones, provided work for the masses that arrived during the years of heaviest immigration.

113. The beginnings of the women's ready made clothing industry in the Jewish quarter are less well documented than the early years in the men's clothing industry. Little has come down to us prior to 1909. John J. Macfarlane, A.M., in *Manufacturing in Philadelphia* 1683-1912 (Philadelphia, 1912), stated at page 39: "Fifty years ago the manufacture of women's clothing was so small as not to be noticed even in the census reports, and was then a handmade industry. To-day ingenious machinery has replaced nimble fingers, and suits are now turned out by the thousands where one was turned out then. The growth of this industry in Philadelphia has been phenomenal. In 1899 there were one hundred and ninety-one establishments, with an output valued at $9,452,000. In 1909 there were three hundred and fifty-one establishments, with an output valued at $30,133,000, or more than three times as much as ten years

before. This rapid growth has placed Philadelphia second only to New York in the value of the output of women's clothing. There were 12,215 wage earners employed in the manufacture of men's clothing and 13,500 in women's clothing in 1909." For post-1909 data concerning the women's clothing industry, see Third Annual Historical Edition, Waist, Silk Suit and Children's Dress Makers Union Local 15, I.L.G.W.U. of A., 1918, PJAC.

114. *Press*, December 5, 1909.

115. December 21, 1909. In addition, *Press*, December 22, 26, 27, 1909, and *Record*, December 20, 21, 1909. Abraham Rosenberg, the international president of the ILGWU, came to Philadelphia from New York.

116. *Press*, December 26, 1909. Mary Charsky may have been May Charsky, later known as May Arno. Arno, a younger sister of Jennie Charsky, was a well-known feminist and actress. For Jennie Charsky, see *guide*, 511 Spruce Street.

117. While separately denominated Jewish unions in the men's clothing industry were only formed during a short period of time, most Jewish tailors believed they belonged to Jewish unions, however they were titled. At work they spoke Yiddish. On Yom Kippur, almost no one was at work. To support Jewish parades and demonstrations, clothing factories and other plants closed. The older generation read *the Forward* and the *Yidishe Velt.* For major battles fought in the 1920's in the men's clothing industry, see Elden LaMar, The *Clothing Workers in Philadelphia: History of Their Struggles for Union and Security*, ed. J.B.S. Hardman (Philadelphia, 1940).

118. The lone exception found is the attendance by Russian-Jewish immigrants at Rosh Hashana services at Reform Congregation Keneseth Israel, 6th & Brown Streets, where they attended the first day (the second day they returned to work), listened to a choir composed of men and women, prayed without a skull cap and after a half-hour sermon in German by Rabbi Hirsch *(Love Thy Brother as Thyself)*, dispersed. Letter from an "Immigrant" dated September 25, 1882, *Razvet*, No. 41.

119. *Jewish Record*, October 2, 1885. Despite these words, Morais' actions tell of nothing but his wholehearted support for the Russian *chevras*. Morais may have changed his mind on the subject Russian Jewish Orthodox practices or have been drawn into them.

120. James B. Thompson in the *Old Pine Street Church News*, February, 1896, quoted by Hughes Oliphant Gibbons, *A History of Old Pine Street* (Philadelphia: Winston, 1905), pp. 259, 260. The "Presbyterian Church" (i.e., the 4th Presbyterian Congregation) occupied the property at 5th and Gaskill Streets (1802-1841); it was taken over by the Hungarian Synagogue in 1891. The "Universalist Church" edifice became Kesher Israel in 1894. The "African Methodist," may have been one of two churches: (1) the small Colored Methodist Church building, 620 Minster (now Addison) Street, which became B'nai Reuben in the early 1890's; or (2) the Wesley Methodist Church, 521-527 Lombard Street, which became B'nai Abraham in 1885.

121. Albert Mordell, "The Refugee Settlers of Philadelphia," in *Brooklyn Jewish Center Review*, April 1952, p. 15, and "Life Among the Philadelphia Russian Jews in the Nineties," *Jewish Exponent*, June 8, 1962, pp. 34, 36.

122. The history of the Yiddish theatre in the Jewish quarter of Philadelphia can be found in (1) David B. Tierkel, *History of the Yiddish Theatre in Philadelphia*, Yiddish typescript, 1934, *YIVO*; (2) Boris Thomashevsky, *Mayn Lebens-Geshikhte* (New York, Trio Press, Inc., 1937); (3) Bessie Thomashevsky, *Mayn Lebens Geshikhte* (New York: Warheit Publishing Company, 1916); (4) Boris Thomashevsky, *Die Yiddische Bihne*, December 10, 17, 1909, and (5) Moses Freeman, *Fuftzig Yohr Geshikte fun Yidishn Leben in Filadelfia*, II:189-198. See also Zalmen Zylbercweig's *Leksikon fun Yidishn Teater*, 5 vols. (New York and Mexico City, 1931 through 1937). Maxwell Scarf translated the Chapter on the Yiddish Theatre in Freeman's book into English. I would like to thank Lily G. Schwartz, Archivist, Philadelphia Jewish Archives Center, for giving me permission to use the Scarf translation.

123. *American Hebrew*, May 11, 1888.

124. The District of Northern Liberties was located immediately north of Market Street and east of N. 6th Street. In 1854, it became part of the City of Philadelphia. For a recent popular history of Northern Liberties, see Mary L. Dankanis et al, *Guide to Northern Liberties* (Philadelphia: Northern Liberties Neighbors Association, 1982). For the early use of the hall, *Evening Bulletin*, July 13, 1937.

125. See Von C. F. Huch, "Das deutsche Theatre in Philadelphia seit dem Bürgekriege," in *Mitteilungen des Deutschen Pionier-Vereins von Philadelphia* (Philadelphia: Achtes Heft, 1908), pp. 26, 27. I would like to thank the German Historical Society of Philadelphia for helping with the German research.

126. In his memoirs Boris Thomashevsky does not state the year the first performance took place in Philadelphia, but based on information that Thomashevsky furnished to David B. Tierkel and Moses Freeman, the performance likely occurred sometime between 1883 and 1885. Tierkel and Freeman, historians of immigrant Russian Jewish Philadelphia, describe the first Yiddish show in Philadelphia, but Tierkel did not immigrate to the United States until 1893 and Freeman was in Lisbon Falls, Maine. Neither had first-hand knowledge of the performance. Both wrote in the early 1930's and quote Thomashevsky. Freeman and Thomashevsky tell us that the first performance took place at *peysekh* (Passover), but it is not clear what year. From Von C. F. Huch we learn that Kost was the manager of the Germania from September 1882 to 1885, making a Passover 1883, 1884 or 1885 performance possible (1882 may be eliminated as a possibility since Kost assumed management of the theatre after *peysekh*). Tierkel, on the other hand, quotes Thomashevsky as stating that the first performance took place in the "fall of 1883." I was unable to resolve these conflicts. The Thomashevskys produced the first Yiddish show in New York, Philadelphia and Chicago. For New York, see Thomashevsky's autobiography. For Chicago, see, James K. Popkin, "Taking Chicago by Storm," A Thesis Presented to the Faculty of the American Culture Department, Northwestern University, In Partial Fulfillment of the Requirements for the Bachelor of Arts Degree (Chicago, 1983).

127. Thomashevsky took on great responsibility at a young age, but just how young is difficult to determine because his date of birth is hard to pin down. Obituary notices in two editions of the *New York Times* for July 10, 1939, for Thomashevsky (he died the previous day) contain different birth dates: one states that he was born April 21, 1864; the other, that he was born, May 12, 1868. Obviously, after one edition was published, an error was discovered and corrected. Which birth date is correct, however, is not known. I have chosen the later date as correct because it appears to be consistent with the sense of the Thomashevsky memoir and other accounts. However, I recognize that the earlier date may be the correct one.

128. A word must be included about the memoirs of Boris Thomashevsky. As an actor Boris Thomashevsky was big-

ger than life, but as an historian he has been received with lesser applause. The most significant criticism: (1) he exaggerates; (2) his chronology is not accurate; (3) he borrows from other incidents and rearranges the facts, and (4) he magnifies his own position. Aaron B. Seidman, "The First Performance of Yiddish Theatre in America," in *Jewish Social Studies*, vol. X, no. 1 (January 1948), pp. 67-70. The use of uncorroborated memoirs to prove what happened in the past makes historians nervous. A healthy dose of skepticism is the normal treatment recommended for this malady; and when dealing with the memoirs of Boris Thomashevsky, a double dose is sometimes recommended. That done, however, we may move forward. Thomashevsky's memoirs have been used repeatedly by the greatest writers of the Yiddish stage. And rightly so. I believe that enough contemporaneous materials exist to clear up most questions, and the few which remain should not interfere with our enjoyment of the basic story. Thomashevsky's writings are a joy to read and they give us an insight into the beginnings of the Yiddish theatre in Philadelphia that could have come from the pen of no other person.

129. The only Jewish paper printed in Philadelphia at this time was the *Jewish Record* (1875-1886), the English-language weekly published by Alfred T. Jones. But it does not contain an article or advertisement about the performance. The first Yiddish newspaper was not published in Philadelphia until 1891. Although a daily German-language newspaper was issued in the early 1880's (Tageblatt, 613 Callowhill Street), Thomashevsky does not state that notices were included in the German press. Upon a cursory review, no notice of the performance could be found in the *Tageblatt*. Handbills - small printed notices passed out by hand - were used to advertise performances. The abuses associated with handbills were well known in Philadelphia long before the Thomashevskys arrived: "Hand-bills, flaming in every color of paper and type, and proclaiming the name of the star in display letters a foot or a yard long, epithets of every kind - 'distinguished,' 'popular,' 'unrivalled,' 'unparalleled,' 'immensely successful,' 'the great American,' 'the great English,' 'the wonder of two hemispheres,' - are set forth with profuse and lying ostentation." William B. Wood, *Personal Recollections of the Stage* (Philadelphia: Henry Carey Baird, 1855), p. 452.

130. Moses Freeman, *Fuftzig Yohr Geshikhte fun Yidishn Leben in Filadelfia*, II: 193.

131. In 1901, the Germania became the Globe. In the summer of 1902, the theatre again changed hands, this time it became the Columbia Theatre, a stock company under the management of Carrie Radcliffe. Not only did management change, the theatre underwent significant improvements. "The house, the surroundings and the company were all a genuine surprise. Even Miss Radcliffe's most sanguine friends failed to realize until they had 'looked twice' just what a gem of a theatre Miss Radcliffe and Manager Martinetti had evolved from all but a barren waste. The rich carpeting, the soft and pretty blending of tints in the decorations, the comfortable ladies' room, the neatly uniformed ushers, the new curtain, everything was pleasing to the eye and refreshing to the mental senses. There wasn't a detail omitted." *Inquirer*, August 31, 1902. See also *New York Dramatic Mirrow*, September 6, 1902. The grand promise of the Columbia Theatre, however, never materialized. Quickly, the theatre fell into obscurity and languished for several years.

132. Max Thomashvsky was born near Kiev (Kamenke) in 1873 and came to America with the rest of his family in the early 1880's. (Boris was born in the nearby *mesteschko* (village) of Asitniacka.) Like the rest of the family, Max was drawn to the Yiddish theatre, but not as an actor. He preferred to remain behind the scenes. Paraphrasing an old Yiddish folk saying, Max Thomashevsky summed up his career this way: "It is better to be a good manager than a bad actor." *Di Yidishe Velt*, July 25, 1932. In Philadelphia, Max Thomashevsky managed the Arch Street Theater, the Garden Theatre, 8th & Race Streets; the Franklin Theatre; the National; the American; the Metropolitan Opera House; and the Roumanian Opera House. Just when Max Thomashevsky first brought Yiddish theatre to 532 N. 3rd Street is unknown, but it was probably in 1904.

133. *Public Ledger*, September 11, 1854, and *Bulletin*, September 12, 1854. A detailed history of the building at 417-427 Callowhill Street is given by Andrew Craig Morrison in "The City Museum - Remnant of a Bygone Era," *Marquee: The Journal of the Theatre Historical Society* (Fourth Quarter, 1971), vol. 3, no. 4, p. 1. Mrs. Geraldine Duclow, Head, Theatre Collection, Free Library of Philadelphia, offered much valuable advice on the theatre in Philadelphia.

134. Kost worked for Conceid and Hermann for three years and it is not difficult to imagine that Kost heard the name Thalia often during these years, and it stayed with Kost when he left the Germania and went over to the Concordia. Von C. F. Huch, "Das deutsche Theater in Philadelphia seit dem Bürgerkriege," in *Mitteilungen des Deutschen Pionier-Vereins von Philadelphia* (Philadelphia: Achtes Heft, 1908), p. 27.

135. I was not been able to identify any play by name produced here during the 1886-1887 season. The first documented performances of Yiddish theatre in Philadelphia did not occur at the Thalia. They were *Sulamita* (Shulamis) and Immigration to America and were produced at McCaull's Opera House, 261 S. Broad Street. *Di New Yorker Yudishe Volkszeitung*, June 24, 1887, and *Jewish Exponent*, July 1, 8, 1887. The Oriental Theatre Company from New York produced these summer performances. In the early years of Yiddish theatre, a troupe was both a stock company and a traveling company. Early troupes, with perhaps the exception of the Thomashevskys, played New York during the season *(fin sikes biz peysekh)* and the provinces after *peysekh* (the provinces in this context were mainly the cities and towns of the northeastern United States). In the Yiddish theatre world there was even a word, *gastrolarin*, used to describe touring the provinces. In its review, *the Exponent* reminded its readers just how difficult it was to attend the theatre on a sweltering Philadelphia summer evening: "The audience at the opening night, when *'Sulamita'* was presented, was also of special interest, and considering it must have been 150 degrees in the gaslight of the galleries it was remarkably well behaved."

136. Bessie's talent was recognized early: "No one would have believed several months ago that [Bessie] possesses such a great dramatic talent. The wealth of her talent in the fullest sense of the word shows itself in the moments when a woman's heart suffers pain and degradation from her beloved or from the world that surrounds her." The paper continued in this vein, stating she acted "truthfully and meant each word she spoke; every sigh went out deeply from her heart, every look told histories of suffering, pain. True tears poured forth from her eyes. She lives these moments with the life of that unfortunate woman whom she portrays. And this is the sign of the rich, extraordinary talent which she possesses and which she reveals each time, more and more, on the stage." *Di New Yorker Yudishe Volkszeitung*, May 6, 1887. Bessie was fourteen years old at

this time. For a recent description of the first meeting and courtship of the Thomashevskys, see Samuel Wolf, "Bessie Meets Boris Thomashevsky in Baltimore," *Generations, The Magazine of the Jewish Historical Society of Maryland*, summer 1991, pp. 4-8.

137. For Gartenstein, see Zylbercweig, *Lexicon of the Yiddish Theatre*, I: 462. Zylbercweig wrote that Gartenstein had a troupe in Philadelphia in 1880, but this early date is obviously mistaken (the zero may be nothing more than a typographical error; he may have intended 1886). Gartenstein acted with Goldfadn in Russia and for several years was a director in Berdichev. At the Thalia Theatre in Philadelphia in November and early December 1887 Gartenstein produced: *Di Tsvey Kuni Lemels; Two Orphans; Der Dibuk; Der Judische Puritz;* and *Der Protsentnik*, *Di New Yorker Yudishe Volkszeitung*, November 11, and December 2, 1887. Gartenstein's company included Joseph Wachtel, as rægisseur; Elias Dorf, business manager; Varnowitzky, orchestra leader and violinist, and the following actors and actresses: Mr. & Mrs. Abromowitz, Madame Holder, and Mr. Friedman.

138. *Jewish Exponent*, November 11, 1887 (Gartenstein "showed his dramatic talent in a very difficult role.") *Jewish Exponent*, December 14, 1888 (Gartenstein played his role with "marked talent.") *Di New Yorker Yudishe Volkszeitung*, December 23, 1887 (Gartenstein played the role of Dr. Almasada as a "talented artist."). Gartenstein would have gone further in the Yiddish theatre except he could not sing; this weakness was exposed early. He retired from the stage while still young and in 1900 ran a beer saloon on Broad Street at Ridge Avenue in Philadelphia.

139. Thomashevsky had been in Boston earlier that winter. *Di New Yorker Yudishe Volkszeitung*, December 2, and 23, 1887.

140. Theatre notices for the Thalia Theatre, *Jewish Exponent*, March 9, 16, 30, 1888. These are the first contemporary notices for Thomashevsky ("Thomashefski") productions in Philadelphia.

141. *Jewish Exponent*, September 26, 1888. This is the earliest critical review in the Anglo-Jewish press of Philadelphia concerning a Thomashevsky production. Unfortunately, the article does not identify which Thomashevsky was intended, Boris or Pinchas. During 1888, of seven advertisements that appeared in the *Jewish Exponent* for Thomashevsky productions that year, three specifically identified the manager as B. Thomashevsky or Boris Thomashevsky. None identified P. or Pinchas Thomashevsky as the manager. Based on this skimpy proof, I have concluded that although Boris was only twenty years old, the review of September 26th refers to Boris and not Pinchas.

142. *Jewish Exponent*, February 15, 1889. In New York in the early 1880's, Randorf used the name William Dickens when he was the rægisseur of a Yiddish theatre there.

143. The performances by Mogulesko at this time at the Thalia are described in Our Philadelphia Letter: "During the last few weeks we had here [in Philadelphia] all the companies from New York, and there was a hard struggle going on for supremacy. Having ruined one another, two companies left for other cities, and that of Magaleski [Mogulesko] has come to stay here, and gives its performances three times a week at the Thalia Theatre." *American Hebrew*, May 11, 1888.

144. Boris Thomashevsky, *Mayn Lebens-Geshikhte*, p. 197.

145. Thomashevsky and Gartenstein had their *patriotn* and, when performing at different theatres, the two troupes were in competition with one another. George Randorf - the former New York rægisseur, and in 1890, the Agent for the Association of Jewish Immigrants of Philadelphia - questioned the need for two Yiddish theatres in Philadelphia: "...here Mr. Thomashevsky plays at the Dramatic Hall, while Mr. Gartenstein rents Thalia Theatre. Both of the latter have some good material to enter into a strong company, but divided they are crippled and cripple each other. True competition has benefitted [*sic*] the public to an extent, by compelling the theatrical managers to pay more attention to scenery, costumes, and the acting itself, but there is not a very large number of theatre goers, and immigrants are not so well up as to justify the existence of two companies on any rational grounds whatever." *Jewish Exponent*, February 15, 1889. At other times, however, Gartenstein performed in Thomashevsky's company.

146. The Yiddish stage had a number of fathers. To honor a guest performance by Boris Thomashevsky years later in Philadelphia, Zalmen Zylbercweig wrote: "The Yiddish theatre has only one father and he is Abraham Goldfadn and the Yiddish stage in America has only one father and he is our present guest in Philadelphia, Boris Thomashevsky, *Di Yidishe Velt*, May 1, 1931. A generation earlier, however, Pinchas [Philip] Thomashevsky was identified as the "Father of the Jewish Stage." *New York Times*, December 21, 1913.

147. *Daily Evening Telegraph*, April 18, 1867. A sketch of the theatre and photographs of the principal actors, including William Wheatley, can be found in the Sunday *North American*, May 1, 1904. The Historical Society of Pennsylvania has an excellent collection of playbills from the Wheatley Dramatic Association.

148. Jacob Spivakovsky was born on December 25, 1852, in Bucharest, Romania, and spent a good part of his youth in Odessa, Russia. In 1887, Spivakovsky came to the United States with Abraham Goldfadn, and he leased Dramatic Hall. A newspaper review of Spivakovsky's first performances at Dramatic Hall sparkles with tidbits of immigrant gossip: Miss Linton and Professor (Goetzel) Selikovitsch were "noticed" in the left proscenium box; there was a large number of strikingly beautiful women in the audience; and "Professor" Selikovitsch recited several couplets that were warmly received by the audience. *Di New Yorker Yudishe Volkszeitung*, October 7, 1887. A monograph, *Geklibene Shriftn fun Prof. G. Selikovitsch*, Prof. Joseph Kahn, Chairman, Selikovitsch Jubilee Committee, New York, 1913, contains biographical information, *YIVO*.

149. Boris Thomashevsky, *Mayn Lebens-Geshikhte*, p. 195. Thomashevsky makes a distinction between the "heart" of the Jewish quarter (Market House Hall, 735 Christian Street, which Thomashevsky called Christie Street), and "downtown" in the Jewish quarter, the area around S. 5th & South Streets. It was a problem for Thomashevsky that Market House Hall was not located downtown, even though the two halls were not that far apart. He had another problem with Market House Hall. "One had to creep up thirty wooden steps. In addition, the street where the theatre was found [Christian Street] was dark and out of the way....The whole day there was a market [the front of the building was used as a market during the day; in the rear molasses was stored in barrels]. One can imagine how much dirt you had to pass through before you arrived at the hall." Ibid, 205.

150. Freeman states that Dramatic Hall was home to Yiddish theatre for four years, from 1887 until 1890, *Fuftzig Yohr Geshikhte fun Yidishn Leben in Filadelfia*, II: 197. Thomashevsky and Tierkel made similar statements. Freeman's conclusion appears to be correct, but I was only

able to identify specific performances here during a small segment of this four-year period. Dramatic Hall was closed during the week of February 26, 1889, because the hall had no fire escapes, and it is doubtful that Yiddish theatre was performed here during the rest of 1889. This condition, however, was corrected by July 1890 because several meetings were held here that month. *Arbeiter Zeitung*, July 11, 1890 (notice concerning a meeting of the Socialist Workers' Party, where the hall is identified as the Oriental Theatre). The photograph of Dramatic Hall in this book, which was taken in 1890, shows a fire escape on the south wall. No handbills or posters have survived for Dramatic Hall.

151. *Times-Philadelphia*, January 20, 1889. While the reporter remains unidentified, two names are offered for possible further research: (1) Mary (Molly) Moss (1864-1914), the Philadelphia-born and Chestnut Hill-bred daughter of Civil War doctor, William Moss, was an author of some renown who wrote in the Philadelphia press about the Yiddish theatre (none of her articles about the Yiddish theatre have been identified); and (2) Simon S. Skidelsky, a Russian Jew who wrote for the *Times-Philadelphia* in 1887. It is likely that the writer of the article was American born since use of the phrase "the opera was apparently very funny," points to a non-Yiddish speaker. If true, this would disqualify Skidelsky as the author. With respect to the *Times-Philadelphia* article itself, Randorf, in his letter of February 3, 1889, to the *Exponent*, stated that it was published to cause a sensation, but he did not state why he thought the publication would cause a sensation and leaves us to guess at the reasons. Randorf denied authorship of the article.

152. *Die Yiddische Bihne*, December 10, 1909. Published in New York in 1909 and 1910 by Boris Thomashevsky, *Die Yiddische Bihne* was a weekly theatrical newspaper about the Yiddish stage. Bessie wrote a weekly column for her fans. David Apotheker, a peripatetic poet, publisher, and dramatist, left the Jewish quarter in 1909 to join the staff of the newspaper (for *Apotheker*, see 522 S. 5th Street in the guide).

153. *Times-Philadelphia*, January 20, 1889. For the tragic life of Emma Thomashevsky, see Lulla Adler Rosenfeld, *The Yiddish Theatre and Jacob P. Adler* (New York: Shapolsky Publishers, Inc, 1988), pp. 293-303.

154. Boris Thomashevsky, *Mayn Lebens-Geshikhte*, p. 205.

155. Bessie Thomashevksy, *Mayn Lebens Geshikhte*, pp. 81, 82.

156. *Jewish Exponent*, November 16, 30, and December 7, 1888. In at least one of these plays Boris Thomashevsky is identified as the manager. Whether he also acted in these performances is not stated, but it is assumed that he did.

157. A play produced at Dramatic Hall by the Thomashevskys at this time, *Mysteries of Philadelphia*, has, unfortunately, not been preserved.

158. Bessie Thomashevsky, *Mayn Lebens Geshikhte*, pp. 86-89. It is not known how the Thomashevskys got the horse to the tiny stage. There was a rear door onto Gaskill Street and perhaps stairs from this doorway led to the stage on the second floor.

159. Among the immigrants there was a strange young man named Schitalnikoff. He was full of imagination and "sporadic enthusiasm." According to Randorf, it was Schitalnikoff who wrote *The Spanish Inquisition*: "That gifted youth it was who, having read a Hebrew work on the same subject *[The Spanish Inquisition]*, attempted to carry out the difficult scheme of presenting to the people a piece which had at once an historical and dramatic interest." Randorf wrote that after Schitalnikoff died in Philadelphia in 1888, Pinchas Thomashevsky labored to rewrite the play. Randorf's February 3, 1889, letter in the *Jewish Exponent*, February 15, 1889.

160. Boris Thomashevsky told the story of Adler's first performance in Philadelphia at least three times. He told the story in 1909 in *Die Yiddische Bihne*, December 10, 17, 1909. In the early 1930's, Thomashevsky came to Philadelphia to put on benefit performances. It must have been during one of these visits that he related the story to David B. Tierkel; see *History of the Yiddish Theatre in Philadelphia*, pp. 12-18. The story was told a third time in *Mayn Lebens-Geshikhte*, Chapter 13, published in 1937.

161. Boris Thomashevsky, *Mayn Lebens-Geshikhte*, p. 210.

162. Lulla Adler Rosenfeld has called *Uriel Acosta*, the Yiddish *Hamlet*. For a review of Adler in *Uriel Acosta*, see *Folks Advokat*, September 27, 1889. In this New York performance, Keni Liptzin played Judith, the female lead. Sonia Heine played Judith in New York, with Adler as Acosta, on Friday, April 25, 1890. This April performance appears to have been the last New York performance for 1890 by Adler and Sonia Heine.

163. Seidman properly criticized Thomashevsky's claim that the first Yiddish performance in New York was sold out in advance. Thomashevsky was not well known in 1882 and Seidman doubted that tickets would have been sold out in advance to see an actor whose name was not on the lips of the immigrants. I have no similar criticism, however. There is no reason why tickets to see Jacob P. Adler perform in the Jewish quarter of Philadelphia in 1890 would not have sold out in advance. We know from a contemporaneous article in the *Jewish Exponent* that over a thousand spectators witnessed an historical drama on the weekend of November 30, and December 1, 1888, at Dramatic Hall. How much more excitement would there have been to see the Great Eagle? Adler was well known in 1890. In addition, a dramatic image of Adler appeared in the New York Yiddish press the previous summer when he came from London, *Di New Yorker Yudishe Volkszeitung*, July 26, and August 2, 1889. Surely, Yiddish-reading Jews in Philadelphia saw this image! If the tickets were sold in a few days, this may explain why Thomashevsky found no need to place advertisements in the New York Yiddish press. Everyone already knew "Mr. Adler" was coming.

164. Thomashevsky wrote that in Philadelphia players from his troupe went to the train station to greet Adler and that they were accompanied by an entourage of Jews who had known Adler in Russia and London (Adler played London immediately before coming to New York in July 1889). English-language newspapers in Philadelphia, as well as the New York Yiddish press, according to Thomashevsky, sent reporters and photographers to the station. But despite the publicity and notoriety, I was not able to locate a newspaper account of Adler's 1890 arrival in Philadelphia. In her autobiography, Bessie Thomashevsky (p. 133) states that Adler came in August, but she does not give a year. I have eliminated August 1889, since Adler had just arrived from London, and it is not clear if he knew Sonia Heine at that time. I have also eliminated August 1891, since Dramatic Hall was then in the last stages of being fitted to be the Hungarian *shul*, and busy workmen were adding onion-shaped domes and keyhole windows. And if Bessie is correct, Adler's first performance took place in August 1890. I was not able to establish a day or month when Adler gave his first performance in Philadelphia.

165. The Thomashevskys both identify Nadler's Hotel in their autobiographies (Boris spells the name Nagler). Bessie placed it on Pine Street. Simon Nadler's "Kosher Restaurant

and Hotel," located at 429 S. 4th Street according to *Gopsill's* Philadelphia directory for 1890, served, "the finest and freshest food in the city." The restaurant was one of the earliest in the Jewish cafe district. *Yudishe Herold*, April and May 1890. I could not reconcile the Pine Street location for Nadler's Hotel with the S. 4th Street address for the hotel in *Gopsill's*. The 429 S. 4th Street location, however, was less than one city block from Pine Street. Perhaps the restaurant was at 429 S. 4th Street, and the hotel was on Pine Street.

166. Adler and Thomashevsky also visited a brothel on 8th Street (it was here that Adler taught the young "women and girls of Philadelphia" the dances of the Odessa playboys). B. Gorin, the historian of the Yiddish stage, puts such conduct in its historical setting. Discussing patrons of the Yiddish theatre, who included the very dross of the town - people from the underworld, Gorin wrote: "In the company of these folks, [actors] start to live a fast life. As soon as one wipes the makeup off one's face after a performance, one puts oneself entirely in the hands of these folks, and wanders taverns and restaurants where one eats and gets drunk without limit, and from there moves on to the brothels (*freylekhe hayzlekh*) and parties as long as one can stand on one's feet." Bernard Gorin, *Di Geshikhte fun Yidishn Teater*, 2 vols. (New York: 1918), I: 218. For the citation to and translation of the quote from Gorin, I owe much thanks to Professor Michael C. Steinlauf.

167. Dina came to Philadelphia, perhaps seeking reconciliation. She arrived with her infant daughter Celia and attempted to seclude herself after Adler fled. With respect to Adler's sudden flight from the city, Thomashevsky told the public that Jacob P. Adler had *"gekatch a kold"* and could not perform. But because Thomashevsky had no more guest stars (Sonia had moved from Nadler's Hotel and took a furnished apartment), Dina agreed to put on several performances for Thomashevsky (*Deborah* and *Di Meshig'ne ois Libe*). Dina Adler was introduced to the immigrants of Philadelphia as a "guest from London." In later years, Celia Adler fondly related that she appeared on the Yiddish stage for the first time in her mother's arms when she was six months old. These first appearances may have been at Dramatic Hall.

168. Christian Street Hall was also used by the Hebrew Sunday school Society. It was a large hall. For on Sunday morning of Chanukah, 1888, a total of 1,500 children from the northern and southern Hebrew Sunday School Societies assembled here for an entertainment. *American Hebrew*, December 7, 1888.

169. For the performances at the Standard at the end of June, see *Yudishe Herold*, June 27, 1890. In the *Herold* article, Tanzman was identified as the "most famous Jewish primadonna in America." Born in Riga in 1856, Bertha Tanzman performed in Warsaw, where she met her husband, the comic actor Jacob Tanzman. She was described as "intelligent, beautiful and saucy with a good deal of charm." In Lemberg, where she played for an extended time, she was carried through the streets on the arms of her admirers. Tanzman made her debut in New York in February 1890. A notice for the July performances at the Standard can be found in the *Jewish Exponent*, July 25, 1890. Benefit performances, very popular with the first immigrants, were staged for worthy causes. Two performances at the Standard on June 14, 16, 1893, by the United Opera Company from New York, managed by Rudolph Marks, made a profit of $400 for the HLS (*Shulamis* and *Shomer Yisroel* were produced).

170. On July 26, 1909, nominees for Adler purchased the building, and by the fall legal title to the Standard was transferred to the Great Eagle. *The Moving Picture World*, Vol. 4, No. 12, March 20, 1909, and the *Press*, July 27, 1909. Title to the Standard was transferred to Max Heine (a son of Sara Adler's by her first marriage) on November 20, 1909, and he transferred it to Jacob P. Adler on November 22, 1909. Sara and Jacob P. Adler conveyed the property to their daughter Frances on September 19, 1913, and she transferred the property to Max Heine on April 20, 1914. In addition to the Deeds, see *Press*, November 21, 1909, *Inquirer*, December 3, 1909, and *New York Clipper*, December 4, 1909. More than ten years earlier, Adler and Maurice Finkel rented the Arch Street Theater in Philadelphia. This earlier foray into Philadelphia by Adler as a lessee was apparently short-lived, see *Yiddishes Tageblatt,* November 22, 1897.

171. *Jewish American,* November 12, 1909.

172. Selig Itzik Lemisch died on November 24, 1891, several months after Jacob Gordin, the legendary Yiddish playwright, came to the United States. If Gordin did write the play about Lemisch, he probably did it based upon stories that grew up around Lemisch after his death.

173. Adler's November 1909 Yiddish production of *The Merchant of Venice* was not covered in the English-language press in Philadelphia. Six years earlier, however, on Saturday evening, May 9, 1903, Adler, speaking in Yiddish, gave his first performance of Shylock with an English speaking cast, an event that took place in Philadelphia at the Academy of Music. The 1903 performance was covered by all the major Philadelphia papers. Not only was the performance heralded the previous week in unprecedented coverage, opening night was attended by Mayor and Mrs. Weaver, Congressman George D. McCreary, Judge Mayer Sulzberger, and other dignitaries. Singular praise was showered on Adler: "With memories of Booth undimmed by time and with the conceptions of Irving and other of our foremost tragedians fresh in mind, it would be perhaps considered an exaggeration to say that the Shylock of Jacob P. Adler is the greatest ever seen on the American stage. But there were veteran theatre-goers and Shakespearean students who saw the Jewish tragedian at the Academy of Music last night who unhesitatingly expressed that view." *Inquirer*, May 10, 1903. See also *Public Ledger* and *Record*, May 10, 1903, and *Bulletin*, May 11, 1903. For sharing her insights and love of the Yiddish theatre with me, I am especially grateful to Lulla Adler Rosenfeld, biographer and devoted granddaughter of Jacob P. Adler.

174. *Die Yiddische Bihne*, December 3, 1909.

175. *American Hebrew*, November 2, 1888. *The Marriage*, a classic farce by Nikolai Gogol, was first performed in St. Petersburg, Russia in 1842. So enamored were the immigrants with anything Russian, that men of high character and principles, like Spivak and Goldensky, closed their eyes to Gogol's rabid anti-Semitism.

176. Six years later, the Russian Dramatic Circle, on Wednesday evening, April 25, 1894, again produced *The Marriage*. The cast included Dr. & Mrs. Charles D. Spivak and Elias Goldensky. This performance was put on at Kelly's Hall. An earlier Russian effort at Kelly's Hall, on October 6, 1892, was *Zhena Na Proka*t (Wife for Rent), a comedy translated into Russian from the German. Goldensky and "Madame Spivak" acted in this play.

177. Gary D. Saretzky, Elias Goldensky: *Wizard of Photography* (Typescript, Copyright 1994). Many thanks to Gary Saretzky for giving me permission to quote from his essay. Elias Goldensky became a world famous art photographer, starting his career at the studio of Frederick Gutekunst (1831-1917). Gutekunst employed Goldensky in his studio

in the latter part of 1892, and it is more than possible that the wedding photograph of Charles D. Spivak and Jennie Charsky, taken in March 1893 at the studio of Gutekunst and included in this book, was taken by Goldensky. For more background on Goldensky, see Elizabeth Holland, "Reflections of the Community: Through the Eyes of Jewish Photographers," *Traditions in Transition*, ed. Gail F. Stern (Philadelphia: Balch Institute for Ethnic Studies, 1989), pp. 74, 75 (Exhibition Catalogue). For Goldensky's studio, see 270 S. 2nd Street in the guide.

178. David B. Tierkel states in *The Juvenile Stage: A History of the Yiddish-Hebrew Dramatic Societies* (Philadelphia: The Federal Press, 1940), p. 15, that Elias Goldensky founded the first dramatic society composed of east European Jews in Philadelphia in 1891. But the Russian Dramatic Circle was founded as early as 1888. *Jewish Exponent,* October 26, 1888, and the *American Hebrew*, November 2, 1888.
179. John F. Watson, *Annuals of Philadelphia and Pennsylvania, in the olden time*, 3 vols. (Philadelphia: Elijah Thomas, 1857), I: 484; J. Thomas Scharf and Thompson Westcott, *History of Philadelphia*, 1609-1884, 3 vols. (Philadelphia: L. H. Evarts Co., 1884), I: 89, 202, and Horace Mather Lippincott, *Early Philadelphia Its People, Life and Progress* (Philadelphia: Lippincott, 1917), p. 28.
180. *Evening Bulletin*, July 3, 1957.
181. *Evening Bulletin*, June 27, 1950.
182. *Evening Bulletin*, October 30, 1957. For an excellent treatment of the redevelopment of Society Hill, including the roles played by the Philadelphia Redevelopment Authority, the City Planning Commission, the National Park Service, the Philadelphia Historical Commission and by Mayors Joseph S. Clark and Richardson Dilworth, see Valerie Sue Halverson Pace, "Society Hill, Philadelphia: Historic Preservation and Urban Renewal in Washington Square East," a thesis submitted to the faculty of the Graduate School of the University of Minnesota in partial fulfillment of the requirements for the degree of Doctor of Philosophy (June 1976).

Notes and Acknowledgments to the East / West Streets of the Jewish Quarter

---

1. *Jewish Exponent*, August 15, 1890. Articles in the Philadelphia press concerning the threats made against the Jews of Russia at this time can be found in the *Inquirer*, August 1, 2, 1890, *Press*, August 2, 1890, and *Public Ledger*, August 4, 1890. A detailed synopsis of the meeting at Dr. Spivak's office can be found in the *Inquirer*, August 8, 1890. Other newspapers sent reporters to investigate the threats. For example, the *American Hebrew* sent a reporter to Hamburg, but this was not done until the following spring, see "The Emigrant in Hamburg," *American Hebrew*, April 17, 1891.
2. Letter from Spivak to Morais, August 14, 1890, CJS. At a meeting on Sunday, August 10, 1890, Spivak was elected temporary president and Bernard Harris, secretary. "A call was placed on the minutes asking for a mass-meeting during the present week to arouse the interest and attention in the great scheme of the entire Jewish population of this city." *Inquirer*, August 11, 1890.
3. Leon Kobrin, *Mayne Fuftzig Yohr in Amerike* (Buenos Aires: Farlag, 1955), p. 116. Kobrin and Spivak spoke to one another in Russian.
4. R. A. Smith, *Philadelphia as it is, in 1852* (Philadelphia: Lindsay and Blakiston, 1852), pp. 310, 311. For the early history of the church, see *Public Ledger* May 9, 1896. A short biography of Thomas U. Walter can be found in the *Public Ledger*, October 31, 1887. See also *Restoration of Society Hill Synagogue (Spruce Street Baptist Church, built 1829 & 1851): Historic Structures Report, Architectural Research and Documentation, Paint and Color Analysis,* by Abraham Levy, Architect, March 1, 1978 (research and documentation by Herbert W. Levy). I would like to thank Rabbi Ivan Caine and Evelyn Segal - and many others at the synagogue - for their encouragement and support.
5. *Jewish Exponent*, June 2, 1911. Rivkind lived at 319 S. 5th Street, and his house was open at all hours to members of his congregation.
6. *Jewish Exponent*, July 28, 1911.
7. See Abraham J. Karp, "New York Chooses a Chief Rabbi," *PAJHS*, vol. XLIV, no. 3 (March, 1955), pp. 162-167 (Chapter XII *Kashrut: Problems and Pitfalls*); Simon M. Dubnow, *History of the Jews in Russia and Poland,* 3 vols. (Philadelphia, 1916), II: 61, and Levitats, pp. 26-28.
8. *Jewish Exponent*, July 28, 1911, and also July 7, 14, 1911. Not only was a second *Vaad* set up by Rivkind, a third was started by the Philadelphia Butchers' Association. Rabbis Ben Zion Hoffman and Isaac Lubarsky administered this Vaad. When asked why there was a multiplicity of *Vaads,* Rabbi Hoffman responded: "We are not forming this *Vaad*

Hakashruth willingly, but are practically forced to do so. This question has almost nothing to do with Kashruth [ritual lawfulness]. Indeed, some responsa claim that it is wrong to cause disturbance in a city on account of outside meat. The whole question of placing a ban on outside meat originated in Russia and has no force in America."

9. *Press*, September 4, 1911.
10. The trouble at Beth Hamedresh Hagodol was covered in great detail by the press: *Evening Bulletin*, July 12, 17, 25, and September 20, 1912; *Inquirer*, July 20, 1912; *Public Ledger*, July 20, 1912, and *Exponent*, July 26, and September 13, 1912.
11. *Legal Intelligencer,* August 8, 1913. The building was sold at sheriff's sale several years later. Title was transferred to the Roumanian American Congregation on August 31, 1916.
12. In 1878, Romanian Jews were guaranteed religious freedom by Article 44 of the Treaty of Berlin, which formalized the end of the Russo-Turkish War. By the terms of that article, Romanian Jews native to the soil were to be citizens of Romania. But the Treaty was meaningless within Romania. Not only were the Jews not made citizens, they were not even considered subjects. They were classified as aliens in their own country. While Jews had previously been persecuted in Romania, persecutions - upon the signing of the Treaty of Berlin - reached new depths, especially after each series of pogroms in Russia. Regressive measures in Russia kindled flight in Romania. Emigration from Romania increased dramatically in the spring of 1900 when thousands left the country, bound for the United States. Emigration reached its high-water mark in 1903 following the Kishinev pogroms. In the spring of 1907, many Moldavian towns were devastated and for a short time emigration to the United States increased. In an article of July 7, 1916, the *Jewish Exponent* noted that Rabbi Levinthal would be connected to the new congregation.
13. The records from Porath Joseph have not been located. The records of Roumanian Congregation Or Chodosh- Agudas Achim are located at YIVO, RG1101. The Romanians began to organize in 1907. That year they formed a permanent relief committee, the Roumanian Hebrew Aid Association. The first annual convention of the Philadelphia Federation of Roumanian Jews was held in 1910. The annual conventions the next two years were held at New Lyric Hall, 928-934 S. 6th Street. The sixth convention, held here on Spruce Street, drew representatives from seventy-five local organizations. In 1917, the first national convention of Roumanian Jews was held in Philadelphia.
14. *Jewish Times*, October 4, 1940. I would like to thank the Society Hill Synagogue for making the Golden Jubilee booklet available. A golden jubilee in 1945 points to an 1895 founding, but neither the *Times* article nor the booklet shed light on the beginnings of either *chevra.*
15. *Press*, April 19, 1893. Association Hall was located at 101 S. 15th Street. Revolutionaries not only studied the Constitution in Russia; the immigrants in Philadelphia studied it. During the fall of 1889, the Russian-American League sponsored a lecture series at 203 Pine Street. Spivak gave the first lecture on September 27, 1889; his topic was, The Constitution of the United States.
16. Letter of March 29, 1997, from Adele Karsh, a granddaughter of Jennie Charsky Spivak. According to the records at Cornell, Charsky registered as Evgenya Lazarevna Charsky. She took and passed contracts, agency, crimes and torts, domestic relations, and real property.
17. *Jewish Exponent*, August 29, 1890. As soon as the Jennie Charsky Spivak settled in Denver, she began to write for the *Jewish Exponent* in Philadelphia. Her front-page article, "The Greatest Effort in His Life," appeared on April 16, 1897.
18. *Jewish Exponent*, June 12, 1914.
19. "Helping Women," a speech delivered by Henry S. Morais to celebrate the twenty-fifth anniversary of the organization, January 4, 1899. *Twenty-fifth Annual Report of The Jewish Maternity Association of Philadelphia*, 1898, pp. 21, 22, YIVO.
20. *Public Ledger*, January 13, 1892. Built in the Federal style, the city houses at 530, 532, and 534 Spruce Street were outwardly identical and while 532 and 534 were torn down in 1913, the National Landmark at 530 (which was never part of the hospital) remains today, a masterpiece of 19th century grandeur. In 1828 and 1829, Thomas Sully, unquestionably the best portrait painter of his generation, lived at 530 Spruce Street. Sully's famous paintings of Rebecca Gratz, the city's most beloved Jewess, were done in 1830 and 1831.
21. *Jewish Exponent*, January 15, 1892.
22. *Twenty-fifth Annual Report of the Jewish Maternity Association of Philadelphia,* YIVO.
23. Report of the president, dated May 3, 1915, *Forty-first Annual Report of the Jewish Maternity Hospital of Philadelphia*, YIVO. The hospital had a 44' 8" front; it was 140' deep and had a solarium on the roof. It was capable of accommodating forty maternity cases at one time. Administrative offices were on the first floor, along with the kitchen and a dining room for the nurses and physicians. Patients' rooms were on the second and third floors.
24. Rebecca Gratz spent most of her life just blocks from this location. Born in Philadelphia on March 4, 1781, she grew up at 107 Sassafras Street, but at the turn of the century moved with the family to 258 Market Street - on the south side of Market near the corner of 8th Street (these are the old colonial addresses). At about the time of her father's death in 1811, the family's fortunes improved and a stately mansion was acquired on the north side of Chestnut Street between Delaware 7th & Delaware 8th (the property, then identified as 219 Chestnut Street, was next to the Grand Lodge). After financial reversals in the late 1820's, the family moved further west on Chestnut Street to 2 Boston Row (later identified as 1209 Chestnut Street). In her last years Rebecca Gratz was lovingly cared for by her nephew, Horace Moses, whom Rebecca raised from childhood after her sister Rachel's early death. Moses lived at 920 Spruce Street. Rebecca Gratz died on August 27, 1869, and is buried in the Jewish cemetery on Spruce Street between 8th and 9th Streets.
25. *Public Ledger*, July 15, 1867. A plaque mounted on the south wall tells us that the building is modeled after the Loggia Consiglio of Padua, Italy. A description and a photograph of the Loggia in Padua have been preserved: "Less famous, the Loggia del Consiglio at Padua - the Veronese building is also assigned to the Council - in the Piazza della Signoria is nevertheless a satisfactory ensemble which was erected in the 15th century by Biagio Rossetti, a Ferranese artist." Some Italian Loggias, in the *American Architect & Building News,* October 28, 1905, p. 141 (the photograph of the Loggia del Consiglio at Padua follows the article).
26. *Exponent,* March 9, 1888. Anecdotal history teaches that anarchism dominated the lecture circuit at this time, but talks on Washington and Jefferson also drew large audiences. For background on anarchism in Philadelphia, see Joseph Cohen's *Di Yidish-Anarkhistishe Bavegung in Amerika* (Philadelphia: Radical Library Branch 273, Workman's Circle, 1945), pp. 142-153, 258-267, and 374-387.

27. *Jewish Exponent*, December 21, 1888. At this meeting the *Exponent* reporter noted: "Only a few young ladies were present. And while on this point, we may suggest that the smoke-ridden atmosphere probably derives [*sic*] the gentler members out of the rooms. It is certainly an objectionable practice to indulge in smoking during the debates, or at any time at all."
28. See 310-312 Catharine Street.
29. *Public Ledger*, April 28, 1886, and Horace Mather Lippincott's, *Early Philadelphia Its People, Life and Progress* (Philadelphia and London: Lippincott, 1917), p. 39.
30. Little has come down to us concerning the history of the garment cutters. In 1886, non-Jewish cutters in the men's clothing industry earned from $18 to $25 a week, a handsome salary. A strike by cutters in May of that year for even more money convinced the leadership of the Philadelphia Clothing Exchange that they needed to teach the newly arriving Russians the cutting trade. They intended to do this at the Hebrew Education Society, thereby hoping to make inroads into the monopoly of the non-Jewish garment cutters. *American Hebrew*, May 28, and September 3, 1886 (see also *Public Ledger*, February 3, 4, 7, 8, 9, 18, and 25, 1887). Whatever the motives of the Exchange, the cutting school at the Hebrew Education Society in Port Richmond was established and sessions were held throughout the summer of 1886. From that time on Jewish cutters entered the tailor trade. In February 1904, Clothing Cutters' Union No. 110, a component of the ineffective United Garment Workers' of America, sought to benefit itself by threatening to throw the entire men's clothing industry into turmoil by calling a general strike. It took five more years before Jewish cutters were strong enough (in the women's clothing industry) to call its meeting here.
31. *Evening Bulletin*, April 26, 1922. Many of the buildings that played a significant role in the Jewish history of the area, as we have already seen, have been torn down. I have used the term "torn down," as that is the term used in city records.
32. *American Hebrew*, May 13, 1892.
33. *Jewish Exponent*, July 26, 1907.
34. *The History of The Young Women's Union of Philadelphia*, ed. Mrs. Morris Jastrow and others (Philadelphia: YWU, 1910), p. 3. A description of the hall can be found in the *Public Ledger*, February 23, 1881.
35. The House of Zion was used for more than Zionist causes. It was used by the Jewish community as a meeting place to discuss ways to combat physical violence against the Jews of the neighborhood. *Jewish Exponent*, May 17, 1907 (the *Exponent* euphemistically called these assaults and beatings "Down-town rowdyism."). The need for vigilance was championed by Dr. Benjamin L. Gordon, an immigrant and a fearless doctor. Five years after Gordon called the 1907 meeting, Gordon himself was the subject of an attack. He was beaten severely on the head (diagnosed by Dr. Max Staller as a possible fractured skull). Five teeth were loosened when three "ward workers" knocked him unconscious. See *Inquirer* and *Public Ledger*, August 3, 1912, and all the Philadelphia papers for weeks following the attack.
36. Elizabeth Pennell, *Our Philadelphia* (Philadelphia: J. B. Lippincott Company, 1914), pp. 460, 463. Pennell's fears with respect to St. Peter's were not well founded. St. Peter's is as stately today as it was in colonial times and its graveyard has survived to inspire a new generation of Americans. Among the many heros of the nation who lie buried here is Stephen Decatur, the famous American naval hero of the early years of the 19th century. An Ionic marble pillar on which an eagle stands triumphant marks Decatur's grave.
37. Hughes Oliphant Gibbons, *A History of Old Pine Street* (Philadelphia: John C. Winston Company, 1905), pp. 258, 259.
38. *Evening Bulletin*, July 31, 1922. Among the individual defendants were Sidney Hillman, general president of the garment workers; Joseph Schlosberg, general secretary; Lazarus Marcovitz, member of the general executive board; N. Koslovsky, chairman of the Philadelphia Joint Board; Aristodene Cavalieri, resident organizing agent, and Filippo De Lucca, business manager of the Philadelphia Joint Board. Hillman (1887-1946), an advisor to President Roosevelt and a frequent visitor to the White House, did not favor strikes and generally sought to resolve disputes through arbitration.
39. *Inquirer*, December 31, 1928. Samuel Blasenstein, the third Deputy Grandmaster, was in charge of the dedicatory ceremonies. Speakers at the dedication included Mayor Mackey, Congressman Nathan Pearlman from New York, and Rabbi Levinthal (who was identified by the *Public Ledger* as "the chief orthodox rabbi of the United States and Canada, Rabbi at B'nai Reuben."). In the basement of the building was a restaurant. Club and lodge rooms were on the second floor.
40. Letter from Cyrus Adler to Martin O. Levy, Grand Secretary, Brith Sholom, dated March 18, 1935, JTA.
41. *Inquirer*, February 23, 1925. For a number of years the Jewish Court of Arbitration tried cases at the Brith Sholom building. The first case, tried on June 12, 1934, involved a young man and his grandfather. Decisions of the Court had the same legal status as decisions of the Courts of Common Pleas. Established under the Pennsylvania Uniform Arbitration Act of 1927, decrees were to be filed in City Hall and unwilling witnesses could be summoned through the sheriff's office. The purpose of the Court was to provide a forum where cases involving only Jews could be settled in a less formal setting. Cases on the docket included a claim of non-support by elderly parents, a dispute over the internal management of a synagogue, controversies involving business partners, marital disputes, and matters otherwise within the jurisdiction of the Orphan's Court. Judges on the Jewish Court of Arbitration included Judge Charles Klein of the Orphan's Court; Rabbi Levinthal; Jacob Ginsburg, publisher of the *Yidishe Velt;* Judge William M. Lewis, Grand Master of Brith Sholom and Judge of the Municipal Court and Albert H. Lieberman, a prominent realtor. *Record*, June 12, 1934, and *Evening Bulletin*, November 22, 1935.
42. The Brith Sholom building was not only used for its own purposes, others used it. When B'nai Abraham suffered fire damage, the Brith Sholom building was made available to the synagogue for worship in 1926. When the Blitzstein bank needed a meeting place in late December 1930, the building was made available to 1,500 frightened depositors. In recent years Brith Sholom moved from the Jewish quarter. Today, it is located at 3939 Conshohocken Avenue in Philadelphia. The credo of Brith Sholom includes providing a common ground for American Jewry of all backgrounds to meet in fellowship; presenting a united and strong voice on public issues affecting the Jewish people; and for providing a means for organized participation in many charitable and communal events.
43. See the *Silver Jubilee booklet for The Vilna Shul*, January 19, 1941. My thanks are extended to David and Fannie Robbins of Philadelphia for a copy of the booklet. The name of the *shul* is carved in Hebrew upon the stone stringcourse

between the first and second floors of the former row house at 509 Pine Street. Two charters were approved and recorded: the first was issued to Beis Hakneseth Deanshei Vilna (Synagogue of the Congregation of the Men of Vilna) in 1912; the second was issued to the Sons of Abraham Aba Shapiro Congregation of Vilna in 1922 (the second charter is an amendment to the first). Both charters have been framed and are on display at the synagogue. The dedication of the synagogue can be found in the *Jewish Exponent,* September 15, 1922.

44. *Jewish Record*, January 11, 1884.
45. Four-stories in height, the building overwhelmed this block of Pine Street. B'nai Abraham moved from here to Lombard Street in 1885 and the building was converted into a cigar factory. Large letters written boldly across the stringcourse between the second and third floors advertised: CUBAN HAND MADE CIGARS. Across the stringcourse between the first and second floors were the words: GRAY, MORALES & CO. Gray, Morales & Co. employed 150 to 200 hands in the manufacture of cigars in 1890. It is not known when the cigar factory closed.
46. I owe many thanks to the loving and friendly Spivak family: Adele Karsh, Eugene Spivak, and especially Charlesa Feinstein, a granddaughter beautifully named for her grandfather. The details of the happenings of the evening of February 28, 1896, are taken from notes written on the flyleaves of a book presented to the Spivaks (the poems of James Russell Lowell). The book is inscribed with the names of 42 friends who attended that evening. Dr. Rachel Skidelsky (1855-1909) was born in Russia and came to the United States in 1879. She was graduated from Women's Medical College in 1894, was a well-known physician in Philadelphia, and for years worked among the poor. "The opening of several piers along the Delaware River, as breathing spaces during the summer for those confined otherwise to tenement houses, the courts and alleys of a great city, [was] entirely her [Dr. Skidelsky's] own work." She was the president of the Hebrew Ladies' Emergency Society, an active member of the Council of Jewish Women, and a member of Reform Congregation Keneseth Israel. At that time, she was one of the few Russian immigrants to be active in Keneseth Israel. Her husband, Simon Skidelsky (1862-1927), wrote for the *Times-Philadelphia.* His story, *The Russian-Hebrews: A Particular People who are settled in Philadelphia*, for July 16, 1887, was one of the earliest pieces to appear in the Philadelphia English-language press about the Russian Jews.
47. Gillis Alley (Gillis Street) runs parallel to S. 5th Street from Lombard to South, just west of S. 5th. As late as the 1870's, three stables, a blacksmith shop, and wooden hovels lined the little thoroughfare. In 1897, it acquired its current name, Reese Street.
48. A biographical essay about Spivak published in Vilna can be found in Zalman Reisen's, *Leksikon fun der Idisher literatur Prese un Filologie*, 2 vols. (Vilna: B. Kletzkin, 1927), II, cols. 687-690.
49. The details of Spivak's trip to Poland and the Soviet Union in 1920 are described in Dr. Boris D. Bogen's article, "Dr. Spivak, as a Social Worker," in *The Sanatorium*, vol XXII, October-December 1927, pp. 5-7.
50. Freeman, I: 207. If anyone ever chose not to rest in peace for eternity, it was Spivak. He had too much still to accomplish. His unsatisfied desire to help mankind did not end with his death. Concerned that Jewish medical students in the United States were given Christian cadavers to learn from in medical school, but that the opposite was not true, Spivak donated his body to science, directing his executor: "The body should be embalmed and shipped to the nearest medical college for an equal number of non-Jewish and Jewish students to carefully dissect. After my body has been dissected the bones should be articulated by an expert and the skeleton shipped to the University in Jerusalem with a request that the same be used for demonstration purposes in the department of anatomy." *Denver Post*, October 18, 1927. This was the testament of a man of action. Only in Spivak's Will can we understand why he would not write his memoirs. He did not want to talk. He wanted to act, to help, to heal - the mark of a physician down through the ages.
51. *Boslover Ahavas Achim Belzer Association, Appellant v. Philadelphia Redevelopment Authority,* 425 Pa. 535 (1967). Background information is found in the *Evening Bulletin*, April 25, 1966, May 4, 1967, and May 2, 1968. Older residents in the neighborhood today defend the actions of the Redevelopment Authority. They state that when the hall was rented to others (organizations other than Boslover), raucous activities accompanied parties and celebrations, activities that residents believed were out of place in a residential neighborhood.
52. *Journal of the Thirty-Fifth Anniversary of the Elisavetgrad Beneficial Association of Philadelphia,* Monday, December 31, 1928, YIVO. The most famous son of Elizabetgrad, Moses Gomberg (1866-1947), was - true to the town's assimilationist character - not a rabbinical scholar, but one of the world's truly great organic chemists. Gomberg attended school in Elizabetgrad. In 1884, when his father was accused of political conspiracy, both father and son fled to America. Gomberg settled in Ann Arbor where he became the chairman of the Department of Chemistry at the University of Michigan.
53. Lazar Levinthal, "Grandpa," in the *Brooklyn Jewish Center Review*, October 1952, p. 9. Levinthal added a one-story 10' X 14' brick kitchen at the rear of the property. So many guests ate at the rabbi's home, it was necessary to expand the cooking facilities with this separate building. Building Permit No. 3465, May 15, 1906.
54. Rabbi Louis Feinberg, "Rabbi Levinthal, the Educator," *Jewish Exponent*, October 6, 1916.
55. *Memoirs of Manuel F. Lisan* (1867-1975), pp. 61, 62, PJAC.
56. Dr. Israel H. Levinthal, "Memoirs of My Childhood," in the *Brooklyn Jewish Center Review.* Between 1945 and 1952 many articles about Levinthal were published in the *Brooklyn Jewish Center Review.* These were written by Albert Mordell, Rabbi C. David Matt, and Rabbi Levinthal's son, Dr. Israel H. Levinthal, who was also a rabbi. When young Israel Levinthal was installed as a rabbi in Brooklyn, his father was told by one of the members of the Brooklyn congregation: "Your son has made a very fine impression - but he is so youthful." Glancing around the congregation, Rabbi Bernard L. Levinthal responded: "Never mind, I think he will age very soon here."
57. *Jewish Exponent*, September 5, 1902. When it was founded in 1891, the membership totaled 400 women. The house at 430 Lombard Street had twelve rooms, sixteen beds, baths, etc. From April 24 to June 24, 1891, a total of 348 persons were sheltered at 430 Lombard Street. Of these, 246 were men, forty-nine were women, and fifty-three were children. An average of twelve meals was served to each person during their stay. Shelter was afforded from one to ten days. The women who ran the home were soon overwhelmed by the huge number of immigrants passing through the city and within only a few months, the home moved to 218 Lombard Street.

58. On June 25, 1793, a subscription paper was prepared to raise money for the ground and a meeting house. The plot had a frontage along the south side of Lombard Street of ninety feet and extended seventy-eight feet in depth. It was purchased for the sum of five hundred pounds ($1,333.33). Abel C. Thomas, *A Century of Universalism in Philadelphia and New York* (Philadelphia: 1872), pp. 62-65. The Vestry Books of the First Universalist Church (1810-1888) are located at the Historical Society of Pennsylvania. I would like to thank the officers of the HSP for extending many courtesies during the writing of this book. I would also like to thank the Philadelphia Historical Commission for furnishing a copy of the Nomination form for Kesher Israel and Ira Kauderer for sharing his research with me. During the Revolutionary War, Israel Israel served on the Committee of Safety and worked to help finance the war. Israel died on March 17, 1822, Poulson's *The American Daily Advertiser,* March 19, 1822, and he was buried with full Masonic regalia (brethren were "dressed in black, with white gloves, and appropriate aprons and hangings") in the graveyard here. Additional information on Israel Israel may be found in Hannah R. London, *Portraits of Jews* (New York: William Edwin Rudge, 1927), pp. 26-30; Henry S. Morais, *The Jews of Philadelphia,* pp. 31-34; Edwin Wolf 2nd and Maxwell Whiteman, *The History of the Jews of Philadelphia* (Philadelphia: JPS, 1975), pp. 31, 32, and 209; and Wayne A. Huss, *The Master Builders: A History of the Grand Lodge of Free and Accepted Masons of Pennsylvania,* 3 vols. (Philadelphia: Grand Lodge F. & A.M. of Philadelphia), III: 57-59 (the Huss essay has a detailed bibliography).

59. For background on the founding of the Universalist church, see the twin essays by Georgene E. Bowen, *Rescued from Obscurity* (Typescript, 1977), and Thomas McConkey, *The Church at Four Twelve Lombard Street: A Monument to Liberal Religion* (Typescript, 1977). I would like to thank Thomas McConkey for giving me permission to quote from the essays. For the first years the church was merely a voluntary association, without any legal existence. It was incorporated in 1801 as the First Independent Church of Christ, commonly called Universalists.

60. *Gazette of the United States*, February 16, 1796; *Independent Gazetteer*, February 17, 1796, and *Memoirs of Dr. Priestley,* ed. John Towill Rutt (London: 1832), vol. II, p. 333. Priestley, born in England in 1733, is best remembered today as the discoverer of oxygen, but it is interesting to note that as a boy of twelve, he studied Hebrew "on the holidays" and when still a young man he gave instructions in Hebrew. In a letter in October 1794, Priestley wrote: "Philadelphia is unpleasant, unhealthy, and intolerably expensive. I have never read so much Hebrew as I have since I left England." Edgar F. Smith, *Priestley in America: 1794-1804* (Philadelphia: P. Blakiston's & Co., 1920), p. 53.

61. Rutt, *Memoirs of Dr. Priestley*, pp. 333-336. On April 8, 1796, Priestley wrote to a friend: "A considerable proportion of the members of Congress, and all the principal officers of state, are my constant hearers. As Mr. Adams, the Vice-President, is most punctual in his attendance, and an old acquaintance and correspondent, I shall dedicate the discourses I am delivering to him." (Priestly and Adams met ten years earlier in April 1786 when Adams was in London). Adams accepted the dedication philosophically and on March 13, 1796, wrote to his wife: "I am going to hear Dr. Priestly. His discources are learned, ingenious, and useful. They will be printed, and, he says, dedicated to me. Don't tell this secret, though, for no other being knows it. It will get me the character of a heretic, I fear. I presume, however, that dedicating a book to a man will not imply that he approves everything in it." Charles Francis Adams, *The Works of John Adams,* 10 vols. (Boston: Little, Brown and Company, 1856), I: 487-488. Priestly did publish the discourses and did dedicate them to Adams: Joseph Priestly, *Discourses relating to the Evidences of Revealed Religion delivered in the Church of the Universalists at Philadelphia, 1796* (Philadelphia: John Thompson, 1796).

62. Edgar F. Smith, *Priestley in America,* p. 80. The Records of the Unitarian Society 1796-1823, concerning Priestley's sermon on February 14, 1796, tell us that the "principal inhabitants of the city attended" and Congress was then in session, AUC. As a consequence of a series of lectures given by Priestley that spring (all of the lectures were presumably given at 412 Lombard Street), on June 12, 1796, fourteen persons "professing those views commonly entitled 'Unitarian,' assembled for the first time for the purpose of social worship in a room of the University of Pennsylvania." *Laying of the Corner Stone of the Third Church Edifice of the First Unitarian Society of Philadelphia, on Tuesday, March 25, 1885* (Philadelphia: Grant & Faires, Printers, 1885), p. 25, FLP. The first church in the United States to bear the name Unitarian was organized in Philadelphia as a result of the June 12, 1796, meeting. For further background on the founding of the Unitarian church, see "Agreement of Several Gentlemen to form an Association for Unitarian Worship - 1796," dated June 12, 1796, AUC.

63. *Philadelphia Minerva,* Saturday, January 14, 1797. Years later, in 1813 the Unitarians built their own church at 10th & Locust Streets. In 1825, Reverend William H. Furness became the minister of the First Unitarian Society and remained so for many years. One of Furness' most ardent admirers, Rebecca Gratz, came to hear him often.

64. By the 1830's, a number of changes had taken place. Entrance to the building was now on the east side. From a layout of the individual pews contained in the Vestry Book for 1836, we can see that the pulpit was on the west side of the building and the vestibule on the east (this orientation was retained by J. Franklin Stuckert in 1896). Recently, this building has been described as the site of the December 1839 speech by Joseph Smith (1805-1844). "Site of Joseph Smith's 1839 Philadelphia Sermon Identified," in *The Ensign*/May 1993, pp. 101, 102 (within the Mormon Church, this speech is considered a "landmark" sermon). The article in *The Ensign* quotes a source that stated about "three thousand people assembled to hear him." It is doubtful that the building could hold 3,000 people - then or now. Surely, many remained outside the building. A balcony could have held scores of persons, but in 1836 there was no balcony, and it does not appear that one was built between 1836 and 1839. The change of name of the Universalist church was authorized by an Act of the General Assembly. Minutes, in the Vestry Book, April 18, 1842, HSP.

65. In June 1868, the building was closed so that improvements could be made. Iron railings and gas fixtures were installed and wallpaper was hung. On December 16, 1868, these improvements were completed and the building was again opened for pubic worship. Church attendance began to decline in the 1870's. By 1879 the building was already vacant but not wholly abandoned. For the next eight years, it continued to be used periodically by local Methodist ministers for mission work. The description of the 1868 improvements can be found in the *Evening Bulletin*, December 12, 1868, and a general history of the church - in the *Sunday Republic*, January 28, 1872. Both articles are included in the Vestry Book minutes, HSP.

66. The B'nai Jacob charter application is described in the

American Hebrew, February 26, 1886. Pursuant to a provision of the 1887 agreement of sale with B'nai Jacob, the First Universalist Church opened sixty-one graves in the small burial ground behind the church building and reburials were effected on the outskirts of the city. Interments in the small graveyard at 412-418 Lombard Street had taken place from 1794 to 1833, but not thereafter (Israel Israel was buried here in 1822). A copy of the Petition for Leave to Abandon the Burial Ground, filed in Court of Common Pleas No. 2, December Term, 1887, and the Order entered thereon approving the Petition on March 12, 1888, are found in the Vestry Books. The story of removing the dead from the small burial ground was published under the heading: "Selling a Graveyard," *Press*, Monday, January 23, 1888.

67. *American Hebrew*, June 12, 1889.

68. Ben-zion Eisenstadt, *Chokhmei Israel B'Amerika* (Israel's Scholars in America) (New York: A. H. Rosenberg, 1903), pp. 22, 23.

69. Brodsky published two books (in Hebrew): *The Work of C(haim) S(hraga) B(rodsky), Ten sermons*, New York, 1907, 56 pages. The book contains 21 approbations. As late as 1907, the book included only one approbation from an American rabbi (Levinthal). The other 20 were written by east European rabbis, including one from Volozhin, and several by famous religious Zionists. The other book was *Divre Hoshev*.

70. *Inquirer* and *Press*, January 25, 1897. The building's western orientation did not permit the traditional eastern placement of the *orenkoydesh*.

71. *Press*, January 25, 1897. The raised platform that was surrounded by an iron fence railing is the centered *bimah*. The words "back of the altar" mean behind the altar and separate from it. The "cabinet" is the Ark of the Law (*ornkoydesh)*. Today, the platform in front of the Ark and the *bimah* have balustraded wooden railings and square newel posts. Brass lights with hanging crystals adorn the corners of the *bimah*.

72. *Press* and *Public Ledger*, January 25, 1897. At the rededication, the cantor entered through the north aisle, chanting as he advanced and proceeded to the *bimah*, which was decorated with palms and lilies. "The scrolls containing the Ten Commandments were carried in procession through the synagogue, the people touching them reverently with the tips of their fingers and then touching their fingers to their lips." A Sunday School was started in the fall, and Dr. Benjamin L. Gordon was chosen as the superintendent. On the last Sunday of his life, Rev. Dr. Sabato Morais spent the morning talking to the children of the Sunday School here.

73. Zvi Hirsch Masliansky, *Masliansky's Memoirs* (New York: The Turberg Press, Inc., 1924), pp. 255, 256. Afterwards Masliansky was introduced to the judge and together they went to Sulzberger's study to spend a few hours in "Torah and wisdom." Masliansky went to see Morais, then seventy-three years old: "We visited the Spanish and Portuguese rabbi of that time, the famous Rabbi Sabato Morais. I saw in him an old-time honest righteous man, a *tsadik*, innocent, who gave his entire soul to traditional Jewry in the pure Sephardic and Portuguese character." Ibid.,, p. 255. Masliansky does not mention it in his memoirs, but the city directories indicate that Masliansky was the rabbi at Kesher Israel from 1897 to 1899. It is doubtful, however, that he was at Kesher Israel daily. More likely, he spoke at Kesher Israel periodically, the congregation considering these appearances qualifying him as its rabbi. Such a scenario would have allowed Masliansky the opportunity to travel to different cities to spread the word of Zionism.

74. *Jewish Exponent*, October 22, 1897. Ohavei Zion was founded in Philadelphia on June 25, 1897, at the home of Dr. Benjamin L. Gordon, 419 Christian Street. The founders elected a delegate to attend a national convention called for July in New York. The convention in turn elected a delegate to the first Zionist Congress in Basle. Benjamin L. Gordon, *Between Two Worlds: The Memoirs of a Physician* (New York: Bookman Associates, Inc., 1952), p. 185.

75. *Jewish Exponent*, May 8, 1903.

76. *Evening Bulletin*, February 14, 1912. Wolf Klebansky (see 246 S. 3rd Street) was the president of Kesher Israel at this time. Klebansky, a *frumer Yid* (a devout Jew), who was president of the *Vaad Hakashruth* and the Central Talmud Torah, faithfully executed Levinthal's directions. It is difficult to imagine that a close friendship did not exist between these men of similar views. After Klebansky's death in 1932, Levinthal had no hand in the running of the synagogue. The Ladies Auxiliary of Kesher Israel was responsible for a "complete renovation of the Synagogue building" in 1932 and during the years of the Depression kept it "attractive and in repair."

77. Kesher Israel's decision to join the conservative movement is described in the *Jewish Times*, March 17, 1939. I am indebted to Moishe Snapir, the son of Rabbi Snapir, for biographical information and photographs. See also *Inquirer,* August 31, 1971. Coincident with the publication of this book, a groundbreaking exhibition opened at the National Museum of American Jewish History in Philadelphia. An artifact in the exhibition is a sign, upon which is printed in bold lettering: "Rabbi J[ospeh Hillel] Snapir WEDDING - SALON - One Flight Up." Although the sign was used by Rabbi Snapir in Brooklyn, the story behind the sign was a universal one. Moishe Snapir writes that in the late 1930's his father was "...the spiritual leader of Cong. Beth Yehuda in Brooklyn, N. Y. To augment his income, he [Rabbi Snapir] used the largest room (actually three adjoining rooms) at his residence for 'small weddings' i.e., there being the Great Depression - couples could not necessarily afford a large wedding; so there was the 'Wedding Salon.' At such weddings there were usually the Bride, Groom, immediate family and a few friends. On the bureau was a large punch bowl. Maybe a few snacks. My sister was the pianist - she played the Mendelsohn Wedding March as the groom strode toward the canopy. Then she played the Wagner wedding march as the Bride came up the aisle. At a signal a boy sang Reginald De Koven's 'Oh Promise Me' (Popular for weddings at that time) (I was the not very talented boy singer). The groom smashed the glass - and the pianist (not quite as good as Myra Hess) played something merry. People called out 'Mazel Tov' and the Rabbi made sure that two witnesses signed the marriage license (and that the Bride received the *Ketubah*). And the Rabbi - I guess - received his small 'augmentation.'"

78. All the buildings on the north side of the 400 block of Lombard Street were torn down in 1965. See letter to the Chairman of the PHC, dated January 15, 1964, PHC, and the *Evening Bulletin*, July 9, 1965. The reasons given in the letter (only one house older than 1810 and the presence of "mediocre houses") hardly support the action taken. Ironically, the north side of the 400 block, which was torn down, was subject to redevelopment legislation, whereas the south side of the block, which was not subject to the legislation, was not disturbed and flourishes today.

79. Simon M. Dubnow (1860-1941), the great historian of Russian Jewry, was born one year after Freeman. Both lived amongst the Russian Jews they wrote about, Dubnow in

Russia and Freeman in Philadelphia. Freeman, symbolizing the east European Jewish immigrant experience in the United States, reached his twilight years in freedom. Dubnow was brutally murdered by the Nazis in the Riga ghetto at age eighty-one.

80. This was true in Russia and in the United States. "The inhabitants of Zvenigorodka [Russia] complained that the condition of the ritual bath was terrible, despite the fact that 1,600 rubles were spent on it annually." Levitats, p. 175.

81. *Souvenir: Dedication Exercises of the Synagogue of the Congregation B'nai Abraham*, 521-27 Lombard Street, ed. Simon Borowsky and others, April 3, 1927, PJAC. I would like to thank Mark Alsher for translating the booklet from Yiddish and Hebrew, and Lily G. Schwartz, Archivist, PJAC, for her help over a number of years. The Souvenir booklet contains large photographs of Rabbi B. L. Levinthal; Simon Borowsky, president for several terms; Nathan Silberman, vice president; Nathan Perilstein, treasurer; Jos. M. Frank, secretary; Louis Eilberg, first gabbai for several terms; Jacob Wapner, second gabbai for several terms; and B. C. Friedman, former president. Many have shown me kindnesses during the writing of this book, but none more so than Rabbi Shraga Sherman, the current rabbi at B'nai Abraham. The recent article in the *Jewish Exponent*, entitled: "Reaching Out: Helping others is a way of life for consummate Lubavitcher," is a heartfelt tribute to Rabbi Sherman. *Exponent,* April 16, 1998.

82. The early prayer houses of B'nai Abraham were located on South Street, between 7th & 8th Streets; on 7th Street, between Lombard & South Streets; on the southwest corner of 5th & South Streets above a saloon, and on the 500 block of Pine Street. The litigation that led to the purchase of the church was reported in the *Public Ledger*, September 23, 1885, and *Jewish Record*, October 2, 1885. On September 28, 1885, the church approved the sale and ownership was acquired two months later. *Jewish Record*, December 11, 1885.

83. The church was called the Wesley Church in 1820. It was also known by other names: the First Wesley Methodist Church, the First Colored Wesley Methodist Church, and Wesley AME Zion Church. During the early years, ministers were supplied to the church by the Methodist Church and the Zion Connection. For a history, see Harry C. Brown, *The History of the AME Zion Church*, 1500 Lombard Street, Philadelphia, Pennsylvania. Brown, a trustee and officer of the church, wrote his thoughtful history in the 1960's. The church was located at 521-527 Lombard Street from 1820 to 1885. In 1885, it moved to 1500 Lombard Street and in 1936 split into two churches: (1) Wesley AME Zion, 1500 Lombard Street, and (2) First Colored Wesley Methodist Church, 17th & Fitzwater Streets. I would like to thank both churches (and especially Rev. Joseph L. Walton) for helping me in my research. A description of the leading role the Wesley Church played in the 19th century African American community when it was located at 521-527 Lombard Street can be found in John J. Moore's, *History of the AME Zion Church in America* (York, Pennsylvania: Teachers Journal Office, 1884).

84. On May 15, 1820, Alphonso C. Ireland conveyed to church trustees two contiguous lots of ground "on the north side of Lombard Street, 162' 6", east of Delaware Sixth" The lot, forty eight feet fronting on Lombard Street, extended 141' in depth to what would be called Alford Street (today, Addison Street). When two factions contested rightful ownership, the birth pains of the new church reached the Supreme Court of Pennsylvania, *The Commonwealth against Murray*, 11 Pa. 72 (1824). A companion civil case may have also reached the Supreme Court of Pennsylvania. The life of one of the lawyers in the criminal case, Samson Levy, is detailed in Morais, *The Jews of Philadelphia,* pp. 38-41. An early description of the building can be found in the Appendix to Rev. William T. Catto's *A Semi-Centenary Discourse* (Philadelphia: Joseph M. Wilson, 1857).

85. *Regulations of Congregation B'nai Abraham Anshe Russia,* enacted on August 18, 1886, and printed by S. Rubin, 808 S. 6th Street, forty-four pages; Rules revised March 1903, under a committee chaired by Simon Borowsky, PJAC. I would like to thank Gary Unger of Philadelphia for translating the regulations from German (written in Hebrew letters) into English and the staff of the American Jewish Archives Center in Cincinnati for typing the rules.

86. A ballot box of the period is pictured in Stern, *Traditions in Transition*, p. 90.

87. In Russia "the synagogue served as the only place of assembly, where the political parties fought their verbal battles, where the illegal groups held their meetings and where they even hid some of their weapons." Levitats, p. 117. In the Jewish quarter of Philadelphia, however, the synagogue was not the only place of assembly. Halls and society rooms were used extensively almost from the very beginning of the settlement, none more so than Wheatley Dramatic Hall. After 1882 a number of private residential properties were converted to public use. In addition, many new halls were opened. About the time the motion picture parlor made its appearance in the area in 1908, the halls began to disappear. And when radio broadcasting began in the early 1920's, only a few halls remained. But places to meet and discuss the news of the day remained important to the immigrant. When Uhr's Roumanian Restaurant was built, it was intended as a place for "Public Assembly" and restaurant. (Building Permit No. 5837, October 3, 1930). The various halls are identified, in the guide by address, in the Index by name, or in APPENDIX E.

88. To see how the self-defense forces operated during a pogrom in Russia, we turn to the town of Elizabetgrad some years later. In early October 1905, the Elizabetgrad self-defense force had 380 Zionists; 160 Social Democrats and 25 Bundists. The defenders had about 450 pistols (mostly small caliber) and a large number of daggers, iron pipes and clubs. During the pogrom of October 20-22, 1905 (O.S.), the force met with many difficulties: "(1) On Theaterstrasse [Theatre Street] a self-defense team of twenty-six came upon a mob of about two hundred rioters without Cossack escort. It chased them onto Moskovskaya [street] and from there along Mirgorodskaya to Nizhni-Donskaya. The rioters dispersed in flight and the self-defenders returned to their station on Theaterstrasse. There thirty Cossacks with one officer pounced on them and arrested twelve who had not yet reached their station. (2) At the corner of Michailovskaya a self-defense group of thirty confronted about one hundred rioters and chased them onto Uspenskaya. There again the Cossacks rushed in and, with their *nargeikes* [a bludgeon with a wooden handle, steel spring and pointed lead ball] dispersed the self-defenders....(3) On Alexandrovskaya, both a team of the general self-defense and one of the family self-defense operated. When a mob of about three hundred looters came storming on, the looters were easily driven back to Uspensakaya. At that moment the Cossacks came and dispersed the self-defenders. (4) When about one hundred rioters from the suburb of Kutschevka tried to penetrate into the inner town, a defense team of forty-five confronted them, whereupon the pogromists scattered in panicky flight." The self-defense

had considerable losses, six dead, fifty wounded and, in addition, there were three other murder victims. *Die Judenpogrome in Russland, Zionistischen Hilsfonds in London,* Köln and Leipzig, Jüdischer Verlag G.M.B.H., 1910, I: 395.

89. Assaults on Jews, especially the religious, were common. Leon Kobrin, after arriving in Philadelphia in 1892, learned about these matters immediately: "Abraham-Ber told me about the troubles which Jews with beards suffer in America from *skutzim* [pejorative for young male gentile] and even from adult gentiles. They catch a Jew with a beard, but not in the Jewish area [in Philadelphia at this time most Jews were 'caught' south of Washington Avenue; later they were caught elsewhere]. They attack him with stones, pull his beard and cry: *'zshzsh'* and *'sheeny'*." Leon Kobrin, *Mayne Fuftzig Yohr in Amerike* (Buenos Aires, 1955), p. 45. Illustrative is an attack on Rabbi Lazar Tittlebaum on Monday evening, October 3, 1904. Tittlebaum, who lived on S. 4th Street, below Fitzwater, left his home with several friends in an open express wagon to go to the Broad Street Station. Once beyond the confines of the Jewish quarter, twenty-five boys attacked the group. Despite the efforts of the rabbi and his friends, the boys - who had sticks - boarded the wagon. They struck the rabbi, pulled his whiskers and cut the rabbi's friends on the head. This attack took place in front of the Academy of Music. *Jewish Exponent,* October 7, 1904.

90. Rabbi C. David Matt, "A great Rabbi Attains Four-Score," in Brooklyn Jewish Center Review (May 1945), p. 9. See also Philip Rosen "Orthodox Institution Builder: Rabbi Bernard Lewis Levinthal," in *When Philadelphia Was the Capital of Jewish America,* ed. Murray Friedman (Philadelphia, 1993), pp. 126-144, and Rabbi Alex J. Goldman, "Bernard L. Levinthal: Nestor of the American Orthodox Rabbinate" in *Giants of Faith; Great American Rabbis* (New York, 1964), pp. 160-176. The first rabbi at B'nai Abraham, Israel Moses Sachs, was born in Neustadt, Russia, in 1837. He became a rabbi in his hometown where he conducted a school to prepare young men for the rabbinate. About two hundred students attended the school. He later became chief rabbi of Sagarn, Hungary. Sachs emigrated to the United States in 1885 and after a few months became the rabbi at B'nai Abraham. He gave sermons in Yiddish and Hebrew (it does not appear that he spoke English). He was a consumptive and was greatly weakened by the disease. In the early summer of 1889 he went to Saratoga Springs, New York, to improve his health. His condition, however, worsened, and he died on August 26, 1889, at the age of fifty-two.

91. Many tributes were paid to Levinthal, none more remarkable than the tribute paid to him upon his 25th anniversary as rabbi and chief Orthodox leader of the Jewish community of Philadelphia. The ceremony was held at the Metropolitan Opera House on October 29, 1916. Over four thousand people came to honor Levinthal. The dias was crowded with the most famous Jews of that day. Louis D. Brandeis, Justice of the Supreme Court of the United States and Zionist leader, was called away by President Wilson or else he would have attended and spoken. The most striking address was delivered by Rabbi Stephen S. Wise: "I am going to say something which is sure to be misunderstood, the vicious circle of which will probable [*sic*] be perfected next Friday morning; I am going to say that I rejoice, I glory in this exhibition of good will and power on behalf of your orthodox leader - I, a teacher of reformed Judaism. Little do you understand these liberal Jews if you imagine we regret the strength, the power, the loyalty of the orthodoxy of American Judaism. Far from regretting it, I regret that it is not ten times more powerful than it is. We need an orthodoxy, self-conscious, rugged, fundamentally sincere. We have a right to ask this of the orthodox Jew, just as they have the right to ask of us that we be Jews both before and after we have been liberals. We must be Jews first, last and all the time; Jews absolutely uncompromising in the essentials of Jewish life and faith." *Evening Bulletin,* October 30, 1916.

92. Dr. Israel Levinthal, "Memories of My Childhood," in *Brooklyn Center Jewish Review.*

93. *The Philadelphia Real Estate Record and Builder's Guide,* vol. XXIII - No. 49, December 2, 1908, Architect Notes. During the twenty-four years that B'nai Abraham used the church building it does not appear that significant changes were made, although unidentified improvements were made just prior to Levinthal's arrival. *Jewish Exponent,* October 2, 1891. Some thought was given to tearing down the old building in 1900 because architect J. Elvin Jackson prepared plans for a new building, but nothing came of these plans. *The Philadelphia Real Estate Record and Builder's Guide,* vol. XV. - No. 43, October 24, 1900, Architects Notes.

94. *Jewish Exponent,* July 23, 1909. The cantor at the synagogue was Abraham Solotist, known as the "King of the Cantors." When Solotist performed in concert, a choir and orchestra of seventy-five persons "assisted" him.

95. *Jewish Exponent,* July 23, 1909, where Bolton is identified as the architect. Further proof is found in the 3rd Survey District office; Survey Request signed by Bolton, dated February 23, 1909, for 521-525 Lombard Street, "Situate on the N. side of Lombard Street, 162 ft. 3 + or - ins. from the E. side of 6th street. Having a frontage on Lombard Street of 48 ft. 0 ins. and a depth of 141 ft. 0 ins.," addressed to W. C. Cranmer, Surveyor 3rd Survey District. I would like to thank Barry Slepion of Philadelphia for his many valuable suggestions concerning survey records. Charles W. Bolton (1855-1942), a Presbyterian, was born in Zellenpole, Pennsylvania and was graduated from Lafayette College in 1880. During a long career as an architect, Bolton designed over five hundred churches, most for the working classes. Bolton's plans for the synagogue have not been located (scholarly sources mistakenly state that his papers are at Lafayette College). The Athenæum in Philadelphia does have plans for proposed modifications to B'nai Abraham in 1936.

96. *Souvenir Booklet,* p. 13. A photograph of the exterior of the Kalvarier shul is found in Jo Renee Fine (photographs) and Gerard R. Wolf (text), *The Synagogues of New York's Lower East Side* (New York: Washington Mews Books, 1978), p. 89. Fine also photographed the interior of the synagogue, pp. 90-94.

97. The gallery can be reached from twin-tower stairs. The bi-level stairs can be accessed from the street or from the portico. Entrance is gained at the street level through a single door, and the stairs can be ascended from inside the building. Alternatively, and when the outside lateral stair gates are open, gallery access may be gained by ascending exterior lateral stairs to the portico; at that level the gallery stairs may be accessed. This design allowed for both men and women to use the same stairs to reach the main synagogue floor. From there, the women used the next flight of the tower stairs as gallery stairs. Of note are the stone voussiors in the arch of the portico. Synagogues in Russia often included in the design alternating parallel rows of dark and light stone. Bolton apparently tried to introduce this Russian motif by using alternating dark and light colored voussiors in the interior of the portico arches. Today, the street-side of the voussiors are painted white, but the alternating design can still be seen from the building side of the portico.

98. Little in the interior of the main sanctuary has changed in the last three generations. A close inspection of the walls, the bare cement casings holding the rose windows, the modest columns, the wooden benches, the woodwork, and the chandeliers, reveals the use of inexpensive building materials. Built for the working classes for prayer and assembly, few would have predicted in 1910 that the synagogue would outlive the immigrants.

99. *Jewish Exponent,* April 8, 1910. Although Levinthal was proficient in English, in public he spoke Yiddish.

100. *Jewish Record,* August 28, 1885.

101. *Public Ledger,* September 12, 1891, and *Inquirer,* January 23, 1893.

102. "A New Public Bath and Wash House," in *The Philadelphia Medical Journal,* vol. I, no. 17, April 23, 1898. The article includes detailed floor plans for the bathhouse at 410-412 Gaskill Street. The ground cost $5,750, and the building - $22,000. See also *Public Ledger,* April 21, 1898. Provisions for men's and women's concurrent usage did not prove practical. Soon, the women requested a more private arrangement and their request was honored by the bathhouse managers by the erection of a separate building across the street. A city inspector, Burton D. Blair, surveyed the properties at 413-415 Gaskill and made the following report, dated May 17, 1904: "I have surveyed the above premises [413-415] used as a public bath house and laundry for women, and find it built according to plan dated March 4, 1903 and revised March 20, 1903, which is on file at this [Survey] office. Building is heated by direct radiation from plant across the street and light - from the same place."

103. *Philadelphia Manufacturer,* June 11, 1898. For later information, see *Record,* January 12, 1913.

104. *Evening Telegraph,* December 2, 1898.

105. Clarence Andrew Young, A.M., "The Down-town Church," A Thesis presented to the faculty of the Graduate School of the University of Pennsylvania, in partial fulfillment of the requirements for the degree of Doctor of Philosophy (Lancaster: Intelligencer Printing Company, 1912), p. 32.

106. Moses Freeman, *Fuftzig Yohr Geshikhte fun Yidishn Leben in Filadelfia,* II: 19.

107. Charles Judah Cohen, *Memoirs,* p. 13. It is unclear when horse-drawn wagons disappeared and push cart peddlers arrived. Looking back to this early period in 1930, a writer for the *Evening Bulletin* stated: "To the east end [of South Street] years ago came the push cart peddlers, now trading on other highways nearby, but who filled South Street so tightly at times with their carts and got into so many squabbles with the police that about twenty years ago the South Street Curb Market was legislated out of existence." *Evening Bulletin,* July 8, 1930.

108. *Inquirer,* January 28, 1915. Not only was it claimed that the permanent awnings were unsightly, but the city contended "they interfered with traffic, shut off the light, and in many instances the dark shadows cast by the awnings aided in the commission of crimes, as thieves could operate with less danger of being detected." Moveable awnings, which could be raised or lowered and which did not extend more than seven feet beyond the building line, were not prohibited by the ordinance of June 11, 1914. The storekeepers had unsuccessfully contended that the ordinance discriminated against them since it applied only to permanent awnings on South Street.

109. *Evening Bulletin,* April 28, 1928, and June 20, 1936.

110. Joseph Snellenburg died on August 23, 1868. His oldest son, Isaac, was killed during the Civil War at Seven Days Battle, on July 1, 1862. Isaac was 19 years of age.

111. *Financing an Empire: History of Banking in Pennsylvania, Banks and Bankers,* 4 vols. (Chicago-Philadelphia: The J. S.. Clarke Publishing Company, 1928), IV:154,155.

112. Although it is difficult to believe, the press could not agree on the location of the talk. The Friday before the *Exponent* advised its readers that the talk would be given at the Model. In its story the following week, however, the *Exponent* stated that it was given at Touro Hall, 10th & Carpenter Streets. *Jewish Exponent,* March 19, 26, 1915. *The Yidishe Velt* agreed (see paper for March 22, 1915). *The Record,* however, stated that the Sunday talk was given at the Model Theatre, March 22, 1915. I have set the talk at the Model, but I recognize that it could have taken place at Touro Hall.

113. Building Permit, No. 6382, October 31, 1941.

114. *Times-Philadelphia,* May 24, 1890.

115. In the early 1890's, reformers believed that disease could be spread via garments sewn in sweatshops. A Bill was proposed in the Pennsylvania Senate to prevent the manufacture of clothing in unhealthy places, and to require that clothing be identified by tag or label "showing the street and number of any house or building where such clothing was made." Philadelphia clothing manufacturers formed organizations to defeat the bill. The first meeting was held in the offices of the actuary of the Philadelphia Clothing Exchange. *Jewish Exponent,* April 22, 1892. One argument advanced against the bill by the German Jewish clothing manufacturers was that if it passed, it might be "prejudicial to co-religionists [Russian Jews] who are largely employed in this industry." The thrust of this clever argument was that if the bill passed and if the sweatshops had to be identified, many of them would not pass a health inspection. They would be closed by the authorities and the immigrants would have no work.

116. Charles Judah Cohen, *Memoirs,* pp. 17,18.

117. *The Moving Picture World,* September 12, 1908. Located at 508 South Street, the building was 120' deep. The width of the deepest 50' was extended in April 1909 from 20' to 40'. This added width was located to the rear of 506 South Street, to the east. According to the *Moving Picture World,* December 5, 1908, Messrs. Isaac and Louis Solomon purchased a moving picture theatre at 506 South Street from S. F. & J. Goodman for $13,000. There was not another theatre next door to the Biograph. Rather, 506 South Street was purchased by the Solomons as a place to expand the rear width of the theatre at 508. While a building permit for 508 South Street (Permit No. 8531) states that as of December 12, 1908, the Motion Picture Parlor was still owned by A. Levis & Co., 513 S. 6th Street, by April 19, 1909 (Permit No. 2718), ownership of the Biograph had been transferred to the Solomon Bros. Permit 2718 confirms that the Solomon Bros. intended to expand the width of the theatre to include the rear of 506 South Street. By 1911, ownership of the theatre had been acquired by Segal & Sternberg.

118. Medoff (1859-1917) was born in a little town outside of Kiev, married when he was very young, had his first son before he was fifteen, and came to the United States in 1892. He taught in Rabbi Levinthal's Hebrew High School. In 1900, at the age of forty, he enrolled in the course of architecture at the University of Pennsylvania and graduated in 1904. One of his first jobs was to design galvanized iron covers for two towers at B'nai Halberstam Synagogue, 610-618 N. 6th Street. He also designed residences for immigrants of the

Jewish quarter: (1) for Dora Levin, on the northeast corner of 3rd & Monroe Streets, for $4,250 in 1908; and (2) for Jacob Litz at 809 Passyunk Avenue, for $4,000 in 1909. Later, Medoff designed theatres, Russian and Turkish bathhouses, and other public buildings.

119. Many years later the soda fountain was boldly claimed to be the "oldest" in the world. *Evening Public Ledger,* December 17, 1934. It was then forty-one years old. In 1932, Levis refused numerous offers to exhibit the old counter at the Century of Progress Show in Chicago, declaring that the stand belonged to Philadelphia. At that time, the theatre on South Street had been closed for many years and the soda fountain was located around the corner at 507 S. 6th Street.

120. Zylbercweig, *Leksikon fun Yidishn Teater,* I: 47.

121. Tierkel, *Di Yungtlekhe Bihne,* p. 41.

122. Building Permit No. 5165, July 27, 1916.

123. In 1857, two parallel streets, Oak Street to the north and Shippen Street to the south, separated by a small strip of land, ran between 3rd & 5th Streets, one block south of South Street. It was on the strip of land that the market was built. Today, there are two parallel streets at this location, one used for east-bound traffic and the other used for west-bound; collectively they are called Bainbridge Street.

124. Cohen, *Di Yidish-Anarkhistishe Baveygung in Amerike,* pp. 71-73.

125. Many Jewish organizations used the Howard Sunday School Hall before Anshe Shavel moved here. The Hebrew Literature Society was located here from 1891 to 1896. In the early 1890's, the Neziner congregation, the Hebrew Free School, Hebrew Education Society, and the Talmud Torah met here. Ownership of the building was transferred by the trustees of the Howard Sunday School to Isaac Schwarz on January 16, 1896, and he transferred it to Anshe Shavel in October 1897. The congregation was poor, and early improvements were of the most basic kind. A 7' x 27' privy was built "for the convenience of the members of the congregation" to the rear of the synagogue (Building Permit No. 3555, August 21, 1908).

126. Tierkel, *Di Yungtlekhe Bihne,* p. 23. This description is of the building three years before Anshe Shavel moved here. The synagogue may have been the Neziner congregation.

127. Eisenstadt, pp. 109, 110, and *Jewish Exponent*, November 25, 1910. I would like to thank Sidney A. Jaffe and Suzanne Grossman, grandchildren of Rabbi Erschler, and Arlene Blank Rich, for their help.

128. Within a year or two of his arrival in Cleveland, Erschler became the principal of the Moses Montefiore Hebrew School, the forerunner of the Cleveland Hebrew Schools. But tragedy struck quickly thereafter. Erschler's wife died on December 24, 1886, and his only daughter died on September 29, 1891. For reasons that are not clear, Erschler left his three sons with his father-in-law (who legally adopted them, changing their name to Peskind).

129. *Press,* November 21, 1909. Abraham Geiger (1810-1874) was one of the pioneers of Reform Judaism. While studying at Heildelberg, Erschler may have come into contact with Geiger's disciples. Erschler, like all the rabbis in the Jewish quarter at this time, was a Zionist and was a delegate to the second FAZ conference held Baltimore in June 1899.

130. *Jewish Daily Forward,* November 20, 1910. As a socialist, Abraham Cahan said that it was "impossible for me to write in a friendly manner about a religious subject." Nevertheless, Cahan wrote sympathetically and with much understanding about the rabbinate: "Progressive persons among us were convinced that in America a rabbi could not escape hypocrisy. Often I said, publicly as well as privately, that there were genuinely admirable and honest rabbis in the old country. But the new world was hostile to the orthodox spirit that flourished in the old-world Jewish centers." Abraham Cahan, *The Education of Abraham Cahan,* translated by Leon Stein, Abraham P. Conan, and Lynn Davison from the Yiddish autobiography (Philadelphia: JPS, 1969), p. 395. On Erschler's illness, *Evening Bulletin,* July 25, and October 31, 1910. On his death, *Evening Bulletin,* November 19, 1910, and *Public Ledger,* November 20, 1910.

131. *Jewish Exponent,* November 25, 1910. Erschler's funeral was also reported in the *Forward:* "Philadelphia. Yesterday afternoon the funeral of Rabbi Erschler took place and it was one of the largest funerals ever seen in Philadelphia. Thousands of people paid their last respects to the worthy rabbi, accompanying him a long distance. The deceased's body was brought into three synagogues and funeral eulogies were said. He was buried at Har Nebo Cemetery." *Forward,* November 21, 1910. Another large funeral was that of Sabato Morais, November 15, 1897. See Arthur Kiron, *Dust and Ashes: The Funeral and Forgetting of Sabato Morais,* PAJHS, vol. 84 (September 1996), pp. 155-188. Kiron examines not only the phenomenon of mass Jewish funerals in Russian Jewish areas during the immigrant period, he explores possible reasons why Morais has been so completely forgotten.

132. Within less than a year after Rabbi Erschler's death, the congregation built a 36' x 15' rear two-story addition with a passageway to the gallery. The improvement, costing $4,800, was presumably made in contemplation of the synagogue's 25th anniversary. After the 1914 fire, $3,000 was spent to rebuild the synagogue; Frederick Griesler was the architect for this effort. In 1928, the synagogue installed indoor plumbing and Herman H. Kline was the architect. In the late 1930's, daily services were held in a small room at the front of the building; the main room was used on Shabbes. At this time the women did not sit in the gallery; they sat on the same floor as the men, separated by a *mekhitza.* It is not known if the gallery was destroyed in the 1914 fire.

133. *Record,* February 23, 1914. On Sunday, February 22, 1914, thousands of Jews accompanied the bier bearing the fire-damaged Torah scrolls to five downtown synagogues (estimates of the number of mourners ranged from 3,000 to 10,000). The Philadelphia general-circulation newspapers were in awe of the reverence shown by the Jews for the Torah: "As ancient Israel bore its holy dead to the sepulchre, as a beloved monarch might be laid in his tomb amid the universal mourning of his people - the 'torah' or sacred scrolls of Ahaveth Chesed Synagogue were taken from the temple ruins at No. 322 Bainbridge street yesterday, and after ceremonies, the like of which have never before been witnessed in America, were buried in a sealed casket in Har Nebo Cemetery, Frankford." *Record,* February 23, 1914 (the long article, which was carried on the front page, was accompanied by three photographs, one showing a small part of the huge throng massed in front of B'nai Reuben synagogue). The *North American* also carried a front-page story. The *Public Ledger* advised its readership that at Har Nebo the scrolls were placed in clay urns and the urns were buried beside the grave of Rabbi Erschler.

134. *Philadelphia Inquirer*, June 6, 1943. Rather than rebuild on the site, Ahavas Chesed-Anshe Shavel purchased the old Rosenbaum bank building, 603-605 S. 3rd Street and used it for a synagogue for seven years. While Anshe Shavel was at Rosenbaum's, Morris Balk painted scenes from ancient

Israel on the walls of the second floor.

135. *The History of The Young Women's Union of Philadelphia: 1885-1910,* editorial committee, Mrs. Morris Jastrow and others (Philadelphia: YWU, 1910). For the dedication of the building, *Public Ledger,* January 26, 1900.

136. The art class, opened by Samuel S. Fleisher, formed the nucleus of what would become the Graphic Sketch Club. Finding the space too confining, the Graphic Sketch Club moved, first to a row house on the 700 block of Catharine Street in 1911, and to its permanent home at 715-719 Catharine Street in 1924. See *History of the Samuel S. Fleisher Art Memorial 1886-1963,* by Irene N. Zieget (Philadelphia: 1963); and Harvey M. Watts, "The Graphic Sketch Club," in *Philadelphia Forum Magazine,* March 1924, pp. 9-11, 31-33.

137. See Robert A. Woods and Albert J. Kennedy, *Handbook of Settlements* (New York: Russell Sage Foundation, 1911), pp. 280, 281. See also *Jewish Exponent,* May 2, and 17, 1904, and February 11, 1910. A total of 124 volunteers (110 women and 14 men) ran the YWU in 1911. The organization was reincorporated and named the Neighborhood Centre in 1918. Its records, which includes 38 boxes of case studies, 1904-1950, are housed at the PJAC and are available for research. See *PJAC News*, September 1978, No. 8.

138. *Press,* October 25, 1891.

139. The hall was described as "beautiful and splendid" (*Volkszeitung,* August 5, 1887). For Rosh Hashana and Yom Kippur, 1887, B'nai Reuben intended to hire the "magnificent cantor, Itzok Isaac Silberberg who would *daven* with four fine singers." Readers of the *Volkszeitung* were urged to "run quickly" to buy tickets from Reuben Kanevsky, the president, and other named officers.

140. *Die Arbeiter Zeitung,* August 1, 1890. In the same notice we learn Cahan also intended to speak at Dramatic Hall two nights later. The speech at Dramatic Hall was to be sponsored by the Jewish section of the SLP *(Socialist Arbeiter Parti)* in Philadelphia. Cahan and an unidentified German speaker planned to address the socialists, but because of the police raid on Dramatic Hall earlier that day to break up a cloakmakers' meeting, it is not known if Cahan spoke as scheduled. See 511 S. 5th Street.

141. *Gegenwart,* January 24, 1896. The year it opened, the bathhouse featured Russian and Turkish baths, a kosher *mikvah,* and *zalts vanes* (salt baths). I would like to thank Ethel Kratchman for allowing me to use the photograph of Abe's New Baths, and Ed Snader, who worked at Abe's in the late 1930's, for sharing his memories of the Kratchman bathhouses. Generally, see Barry Newman, "If its a Russian Rub You Want, Have We Got a Place!" in *The Wall Street Journal,* May 3, 1974. For an excellent essay concerning the benefits of the *mikvah* and *t'vila* (dunking in the ritual bath), see "By the waters...The *mitzvah* of mikveh, from a purely personal perspective," *Jewish Exponent*, March 3, 1995. For weekly gatherings at the *shvitz* (the biggest items were "herring, Litvaks, and tea") see, Sara Colton, "Ladies' Night in a Turkish Bath," *Brith Sholom News,* February 1929.

142. During the early years, improvements and repairs were constantly being made. Between 1907 and 1924, a total of twenty-one building permits were issued to the Kratchmans. Most significant among the improvements were the 1907 conversion of 313 Monroe Street; a 1914 installation of new floors, stairs, a brick wall, a ceiling, and a one-story addition at 313-315 Monroe at a cost of $7,800; general improvements made to greet the returning doughboys from the battle fields of World War I (*Di Yidishe Velt,* March 2, 1919); and the 1921 addition of the terra cotta fronts. Firebrick ovens were constantly being repaired and modified. The last significant improvement was in 1924 when Abe Kratchman built a 15,000 gallon tank for his new baths. The only building permit issued to the Kratchmans during the next twenty years was in 1944 when repairs were made to a water tank at 315 Monroe Street. During the Depression of the 1930's, no repairs, modifications or improvements were made to the bathhouses. The architect used for the most significant improvements and alterations was Herman H. Kline.

143. *Di Yidishe Velt,* October 13, 1914. There were three *shvitz* at the bathhouses, one at the old bathhouse (20' long, 12' wide and 8' high, with wooden benches along one side and both ends) and two at Abe's (12' x 12' by 8' high), one upstairs and one downstairs. The bathhouses had two mikvahs, both approximately 4' square and about 4' deep. White tiled steps ran down to the bottom of the mikvahs. Little is known of the *zalts vanes* at Kratchmans'. Most salt baths in the Philadelphia metropolitan area are remembered today as being in Atlantic City. Generally, at Abe's the *mikvah* was used by men on Friday afternoons and by women before marriage. The Russian bath was also used by gentiles in the neighborhood. Both Abe's and Kratchman's had swimming pools. Kratchman's restaurant was really a little stand. The water was heated by oil at Abe's. Wood was used at the older bathhouse; it was delivered daily.

144. Another service, available only at the old bathhouse, was cupping, in Yiddish, called *shteln bankes.* It was a remedy for back, arm, leg, and shoulder aches and pains. *Bankes,* or cupping glasses, were shaped like tumblers about 2" in diameter and 2" high (almost like the old 4 oz. sour cream glasses). The *bankes* was usually applied to the customer by one of the *patchiks.* It was put on the skin in order to draw blood to the surface. To make the glass adhere to the surface of the skin, rubbing alcohol was applied to the inside of the glass and the fumes were ignited. The process consumed oxygen and created a vacuum that caused the glass to adhere to the skin. The cups were put around the affected areas and left rings when removed. The closer these so-called rings (caused by the sticking cups) came to the pain, the darker the color of the rings. Right over the ache or pain the color was dark or black. Why this was so was part of the mystery of the *bankes.* Some found *bankes* an effective remedy; others found it useless.

145. *Evening Ledger* and *Record,* December 17, 1928. As remembered by Ed Snader in the early 1940's, there were about 50 to 60 beds. Whether the dormitory was larger in 1928 is not known.

146. A recent analysis of the McLoon and O'Leary murders can be found in "Bootlegging in the 1920's," *Urban Archives Notes,* Urban Archives, Paley Library, Temple University, no. 43, Spring 1995. I owe much thanks to the entire staff at the Urban Archives: Margaret Jerrido, Archivist & Head; George Brightbill, Associate; Brenda Galloway-Wright, Assistant Archivist, and Cheryl Johnson, Secretary.

147. In 1876, B'nai Israel was located in Port Richmond at Tulip and Wayne Streets, *Jewish Record,* May 14, 1886. Its next location was at Tulip and William Streets, *Press,* February 20, 1905. The last building of B'nai Israel in Port Richmond is located at Tulip and Auburn Streets.

148. *Evening Bulletin,* August 18, 1919, and *Jewish Exponent,* August 22, 1919. To escort a rabbi to his new congregation was a long-standing tradition among Russian Jews. In the old country it was customary for residents from a new community to take the rabbi away in a decorated vehicle with a double span of horses.

149. The loss to the Jewish religion caused by the anarchists can

never be calculated. These idealists (Randorf called them "cranks") caused the worse kind of destruction - the tearing out of the heart. No one put this better than Moses Freeman. Speaking about the moral defeat the anarchists brought about, Freeman wrote: "The evil which these Jewish anti-Semites [anarchists] perpetrated was far-reaching. A whole generation was poisoned with hatred against their own fathers and mothers. They implanted hatred, not only against their religion but to the Jewish people as a whole."

150. The history of the Hebrew Literature Society is found in a 1905 Souvenir and History (located at CJS) and in the nomination form for the property, PHC. The dedication of the building at 310-312 Catharine Street on April 21, 1901, is described in the *Jewish Exponent,* April 26, 1901. Morris Rosenbaum was the chairman of the building committee, and for his much-appreciated efforts, an evening was tendered to him by the Society on June 12, 1902. Rabbi Joseph Krauskopf, from Reform Congregation Keneseth Israel, and Rabbi Levinthal spoke. At the dinner, Bernard Harris was one of the main speakers. Articles concerning the laying of the cornerstone for the new building in 1904 are found in the *Inquirer* and *Public Ledger,* August 1, 1904. The dedication of the new building occurred on December 25, 1904, *Jewish Exponent,* December 30, 1904, and *New Yorker Morgen Blatt,* December 30, 1904. The 20th-anniversary celebrations of the HLS are described in the 1905 Souvenir booklet. For the description of the outside of the building, see *The Philadelphia Register of Historic Places: Hebrew Literature Society Building,* May 12, 1982.

151. The Rev. Dr. Marcus Jastrow, rabbi at Rodeph Shalom Congregation (1866-1892), delivered the first lecture before the Hebrew Literature Society, but it was his son Morris who brought the immigrants and the professors together. Born on August 13, 1861, in Warsaw, Poland, Morris Jastrow graduated from the University of Pennsylvania in 1881 and for the next four years studied abroad at universities in Breslau, Leipzig, Strasburg, and Paris. He returned to Penn in 1885 and in 1886 was appointed Professor of Arabic and Rabbinical Literature. In 1901, Samuel M. Israeli, Chairman of the English Literary Committee, HLS, and Judah Baroway approached Professor Jastrow, explained to him the aims of the HLS, and quickly secured his full and hearty cooperation. "And it was through his [Professor Jastrow's] help, often his initiative, that very many of the gentlemen lectured before our Society [HLS] during that year." At the dedication of the building of the Hebrew Literature Society on April 21, 1901, Jastrow gave the dedicatory address, and at the dedication of the new building three years later Jastrow gave one of the principal addresses.

152. First-generation American Jews, those who were born in the Jewish quarter or who came to this country as very small children, went on to the University of Pennsylvania and include, among others: Louis Levinthal, judge and president of the Zionist Organization of America; Israel Goldstein, rabbi and president of the Zionist Organization of America; Marc Blitzstein, composer, Abraham Magil, writer, Dr. Katharine (Rosenbaum) Boucot Sturgis, the first woman president of the Philadelphia County Medical Society; and many others.

153. For the policy concerning the admission of women to the University at this time, see William W. Brickman, *Pedagogy, Professionalism, and Policy, History of the Graduate School of Education at the University of Pennsylvania,* (University of Pennsylvania, 1986), pp. 81 and 86.

154. *Philadelphia Jewish American,* September 18, 1908.

155. Tierkel, *Di Yungtlikhe Bihne,* pp. 33, 34. Only recently has the subject of protecting intellectual property rights in Yiddish plays been addressed in historical writings. In the early years (prior to 1909), few Yiddish authors filed for the copyright protection provided for in the Constitution. Rather than taking advantage of this federal right, these authors sought protection through informal verbal agreements or assignments, procedures that led to bickering and disputes, and which also made the enforcement of claimed proprietary rights difficult. With regard to Gordin's claim that Max Thomashevsky was not authorized to use his (Gordin's) works, Thomashevsky advertised his productions widely and was open in his use of printed materials. Whether Gordin tried to restrain Thomashevsky's productions in Philadelphia is not known. Gordin did, however, try to restrain New York performances. For a splendid article concerning Gordin's unsuccessful efforts in New York, based primarily on New York Supreme Court Common Orders, see Leo Hershkowitz's, "A Bagel for Lazarus," in *Patterns of Migration, 1850-1914,* pp. 129-140. Zachary Baker's scholarly essay "The Lawrence Marwick Collection of Copyrighted Yiddish Plays at the Library of Congress: Introduction to the Annotated Bibliography," (1997), adds much to our knowledge in this area. I would like to thank Peggy K. Pearlstein, Area Specialist, Hebraic Section, Library of Congress; and Zachary Baker, Librarian, YIVO, for their help and encouragement.

156. *The Philadelphia Register of Historic Places: The Central Talmud Torah & Yeshivah Yisroel* (February 15, 1991), PHC. This registration form, which was prepared by Ira Kauderer, includes a detailed history of the Central Talmud Torah and Yeshiva Mishkan Yisroel, a survey of the building, and biographical sketches of the architects.

157. Founded by Rabbis Levinthal and Brodsky at 622 S. 9th Street shortly after Levinthal came to Philadelphia, the school was originally called the Downtown Talmud Torah. It moved several times in its early years, first to Howard Hall, 322 Bainbridge Street, next to Liberty Hall on Lombard Street, and then for a short time to 617 Pine Street. In the middle 1890's, the Talmud Torah purchased two homes at 314-316 Catharine Street and set down permanent roots. The school president, Rabbi Werner, hired Dov Aryeh Freedman to be the principal. Freedman altered the curriculum according to the tenets of the *haskala* (enlightenment).

158. See *Public Ledger,* January 23, 1893; *American Hebrew,* January 27, 1893, and *North American,* November 9, 1909. In 1909, the quarters of the Downtown Talmud Torah were found to be inadequate (at that time 500 children were waiting to be admitted to the school) and the new building was constructed on Catharine Street. So many attended the cornerstone laying ceremony in March 1911 that the scaffold built for the occasion was deemed unsafe and could not be used. The throng jammed Catharine Street from 3rd to 4th and from curb to curb. The opening prayer was delivered by Rabbi Englander. Local speakers included Judge Mayer Sulzberger, Joseph L. Kun and Bernard Harris. The privilege of laying the cornerstone was purchased by Mr. and Mrs. Wolf Klebansky for $1,250. Among the new directors were Morris Haber, Benjamin Finberg, Wolf Klebansky, Benjamin Davidson, Misheal Moldower, Henry Wessle, Harry Daroff, Simon Katz, Rabbi B. L. Levinthal, Benjamin H. Lyon, Harry Uditsky and other prominent professional men and merchants.

159. *Jewish Exponent,* November 3, 1911.

160. Rabbi Simon Fyne was born in Kovno, Russia. He was trained by his father and went to England where he was ordained a rabbi by Dr. Herman Adler in 1880. Fyne came to Philadelphia in 1907 and became the superintendent of the Hebrew Orphan's Home. Fyne's appointment as principal of the Central Talmud Torah , however, was not uncontested. Rabbi Levinthal recommended to Cyrus Adler that David Englander, the son of Rabbi Simon J. Englander, be engaged. Letter from Levinthal to Adler, June 8, 1911, CJS.

161. *North American,* March 23, 1913: "The school is entirely maintained through the efforts of the eight young women who are devoting their leisure time to raising money for its perpetuation."

162. A supporter of the dissident teachers stated that the "new principal [Englander] attempted to put into practice certain observances that might have been all very well in Jerusalem in the middle ages, but which have no place in the present day schools in America." Further background may be found in the *Record,* April 29, 30, 1913. On Sunday, May 4, 1913, instead of reporting to their classrooms for registration, hundreds of Jewish children, gathered at the headquarters of the striking teachers at 722 S. 5th Street, and formed a parade. With banners unfurled, the youngsters marched through the downtown streets singing and cheering "We want Hebrew" and "We want our teachers." When they reached the Talmud Torah on Catharine Street, they cheered, especially for the school. *Record,* May 5, 6 and 7, 1913.

163. The yeshiva was begun in Rabbi Levinthal's home as the Hebrew High School. The first class had forty students. One of the first teachers was Barnet J. Medoff who taught while he was attending the University of Pennsylvania. The Hebrew High School was organized by Baruch Anapotsky. See C. David Matt, "Rabbi Bernard Louis Levinthal: A Biography and an Appraisal," in the *Exponent*, May 31, 1935. From Rabbi Levinthal's home, the yeshiva was moved to 323 Catharine Street, then to 922 S. 4th Street, and in 1908, to 526 Wharton Street.

164. *Bulletin*, April 8, 1907, and *Jewish Exponent,* April 12, May 17, 1907. The Rebecca Gratz Club leased the houses on Catharine Street until permanent arrangements were made on N. 6th Street. *Record,* June 27, 1915. In 1928, the Rebecca Gratz Club moved from 719-721 N. 6th Street to 532-536 Spruce Street.

165. *Press,* May 8, 1906.

166. *The Fourteenth Annual Report of the College Settlement of Philadelphia,* 1905, pp. 15, 18, 19, LOC.

Notes and Acknowledgments to the North / South Streets of the Jewish Quarter

1. Gary D. Saretzky, "Elias Goldensky: Wizard of Photography," *Pennsylvania History,* 64:2 (Spring 1997), pp. 206-272.

2. *History of the Third Baptist Church, Second Street, above Catharine, Philadelphia* by Rev. William H. Shermer, Pastor (1884), ABHS. The lot has a 63' frontage on S. 2nd Street and a depth of 200' that widens to 84' at the back of the lot. I would like to thank Janet Reedy of the Philadelphia Baptist Association for her help.

3. Survey by Franklin Fire Insurance Company of Philadelphia, dated February 22, 1837, PHC.

4. Essay by David A. Kraftsow, *History of the Neziner Synagogue,* based, in part, on research done by Alvin H. Plumer (circa 1983). I would like to thank Alvin H. Plumer for sharing his research and the Kraftsow essay. A history of the early years of Southwark and the small streets east of this building is found in Margaret B. Tinkcom's, "Southwark, A River Community: Its Shape and Substance," *Proceedings of the American Philosophical Society,* vol. 114, no. 4, August 1970, pp. 327-342.

5. *Jewish Exponent,* July 21, 1905; *Press* and *North American,* July 17, 1905.

6. Rabbi Israel Goldstein, *My World As A Jew: The Memoirs of Israel Goldstein,* 2 vols. (New York: Herzl Press, Cornwall Books, 1984), I: 28. Goldstein was the oldest child of David and Fannie (Silver) Goldstein. Born on June 18, 1896, in the basement of the synagogue when it was located at 754-756 S. 3rd Street, Rabbi Israel Goldstein said: "I can literally claim that I was born into the synagogue." Rabbi Goldstein served Congregation B'nai Jeshurun in New York City for forty-two years (1918-1960) and during this time headed, among other organizations, the American Jewish Congress (1951-1958); the Zionist Organization of America (1943-1945); the Jewish National Fund (1933-1943); the Synagogue Council of America (1942-1944); the Jewish Conciliation Board of America (1929-1960), and the World Jewish Congress Western Hemisphere Executive (1949-1958). He initiated the establishment of Brandeis University in 1946 and was one of the founders of the National Conference of Christians and Jews. He served as treasurer of the Jewish Agency during the first year of Israel's statehood (1948-1949). *See New York Herald Tribune, May 27, 1956; New York Times, September 14, 1968, and Inquirer, April 13, 1986.* But it was Goldstein's father, David, who played the leading role in the life of the Neziner congregation. The Kraftsow history of the synagogue identifies David Goldstein as the rabbi and, while Israel Goldstein does not identify his father as the rabbi, David Goldstein was certainly the leader of the congregation

whatever his formal title was.

7. *Diamond 75th Anniversary, Neziner Synagogue,* December 1964, PJAC, and Mary B. Plumer, "Neziner Congregation Celebrates 50th Anniversary," *Jewish Times,* November 24, 1939. In November 1939, the congregation honored its ex-presidents and founders: Nathan Feldman, Abraham L. Poland, Harry Daroff, Henry J. Ettelson, Samuel Kaplan, David Greenetz, Morris Latinsky, and Sol Stamm. The cantor for many years was William Caesar.

8. Hearings before the special boards of inquiry of the Immigration and Naturalization Service's District No. 4 office (Philadelphia), date from 1893 to 1909. Records of these hearings have been preserved on eighteen reels of microfilm and are part of Record Group 85, Records of the Immigration and Naturalization Service, National Archives - Philadelphia Branch, NAP. The National Archives in Philadelphia has a nine page Introduction to these records, prepared by Shawn P. Aubitz.

9. *Record* and *Public Ledger,* February 26, 1909. See also *Evening Bulletin,* January 23, 1907.

10. Between December 17, 1930, and August 2, 1931, the Evening Public Ledger and the *Public Ledger* ran a total of 13 articles concerning efforts to save the Powel House.

11. Curled hair was a manufactured product, principally from horsehair imported from Russia. Curled hair was used in the manufacture of matresses. The total value of the curled hair and haircloth output in the United States in 1900 was $7,500,000, and of this Philadelphia produced from 65 to 75 percent, *Record,* July 1, 1906. At least one Philadelphia manufacturer engaged in the curled hair trade (not Klebansky) visited Russia and the fair at Nizhni Novgorod. The holders of goods at that fair, conducted on the banks of the Volga River, included merchants from Siberia, Turkey, Bulgaria, Armenia, Persia, Italy, Austria, and China. *Public Ledger,* October 26, 1891.

12. For example, the Klebanskys were the master and mistress of ceremonies at the first annual ball of the Central and Northeastern Talmud Torahs held at Mercantile Hall, *Jewish Exponent,* January 17, 1913. At that time in Philadelphia there were approximately forty thousand Jewish children, of whom ten thousand were receiving a Jewish education. For the background on the Northeastern Talmud Torah, see letter from Joseph Medoff, principal, to Dr. Cyrus Adler, dated December 10, 1912, CJS.

13. *Di Yidishe Velt,* July 31, 1929. As one of the most prominent woman in the Jewish quarter, Chaya Dobra Klebansky was given an elaborate funeral. Her coffin was brought to Congregation Kesher Israel, and then to the synagogue at the *Moyshev Zkeynim* 315-317 S. 3rd Street where a eulogy was delivered. Wolf Klebansky died on June 2, 1932, at the age of seventy-three. His obituary traced his many charitable endeavors and also noted that he had recently sold the Powel House, which the *Yidshe Velt* mistakenly - but with much pride - told its readers was the "first White House in the History of America." *Di Yidishe Velt,* June 3, 1932. For an exquisite book on the Powel House, see George B. Tatum, *Philadelphia Georgian: The City House of Samuel Powel and Some of its Eighteenth Century Neighbors* (Middletown, Connecticut: Wesleyan University Press, 1976).

14. Registry Unit 004S-07-0075, for 512 S. 3rd Street. The property was acquired by the Southwark Hose Company on April 5, 1856. For the Fire Association, see *The Fire Association of Philadelphia: A Short Account of the Origin and Development of Fire Insurance in Philadelphia* (Philadelphia: privately printed, 1917). I would like to thank David R. Brill, a great grandson of Berko Sarshik, for his letter of June 6, 1995, furnishing additional information. For credit reports on Sarshik, see PA vol. 168, p. 66, R.G. Dun & Co. Collection, Baker Library, Harvard University Graduate School of Business. Tierkel tells us that amateur performances were produced at a hall at 510 S. 3rd Street, but it is assumed that he was referring to 512, as the property at 510 (next door) was never a hall. The records from Agudas Achim have been preserved. YIVO, RG 1101.

15. Edward W. Rosenbaum, *Rosenbaum Family Perspectives* (Philadelphia: Rosenbaum, 1992). I would like to thank Edward W. Rosenbaum for granting me permission to use materials from his delightful family history.

16. *Real Estate Record and Builders' Guide, Philadelphia,* March 15, 1905, Architects' Notes: and Building Permit No. 1618, April 1, 1905. The architects, Louis Magaziner and W. Woodburn Potter, had recently entered into a partnership. Others have identified the style of architecture as Georgian. The seminal article on the Jewish immigrant banking families of Philadelphia is Robert Leiter's "Opening the Door to the New World," *Jewish Exponent,* July 13, 1984.

17. *Jewish Exponent*, December 6, 1907. It is not known how Rosenbaum's speech was received, but after he spoke the Jewish press does not note a continuing separatist movement. Concerning his own children's education, Rosenbaum was very attentive. His daughter Katharine (there were five boys and three girls in the family) - the first woman president of the Philadelphia County Medical Society - remembered that she and her brothers and sisters had to put their lessons on their father's bureau every night: "He looked them over, and if there was a word mispelled or something wrong, he would send for us in the morning - first thing - and have us correct it."

18. Rosenbaum and Blitzstein continued to operate successfully despite the catastrophic affect the legislation had on the sale of steamship tickets. Both banks must have intensified their mainstream banking practices when immigration was reduced to a trickle.

19. *Memoir* by Manuel F. Lisan, typescript, p. 64, PJAC. Manuel F. Lisan, born in Russia in 1883, came to Philadelphia at the turn of the century and helped organize the Friends of Zion. Later he served as the president of the Jewish National Fund. Lisan died in 1975. The Rosenbaum passage order books are at the PJAC.

20. Maynard and Gertrude Abrams, *The Ancestors of Our Children* (Jacksonville: 1984). I would like to thank Gertrude Abrams for allowing me to use her book.

21. *Evening Bulletin,* February 22, 1916.

22. Charles S. Bernheimer, "Philadelphia," in *The Immigrant Jew in America,* ed., Edmund J. James (New York: B. F. Buck & Company, 1907) pp. 233-248. The data for this chapter on Philadelphia was gathered by Bernheimer chiefly in 1900.

23. *Di Yidishe Velt,* July 16, 1933. Harris E. Oser spent almost forty years in the printing business in Philadelphia. During his later years, he printed posters for the Yiddish theatre. Of twenty-two posters for Philadelphia Yiddish theatre performances listed in the *Catalog of the Abram & Frances Pascher Kanof Collection of Yiddish Theatre and Motion Picture Posters* (Waltham, MA: AJHS, 1972), eighteen were printed by the Oser Bros. Harris E. Oser died in 1933. I would like to thank Alan S. and Seth Oser for sharing family photographs.

24. In the *Jewish Herald* for October 31, 1913, notices were printed concerning 196 forthcoming meetings. A breakdown of the total reveals meetings for (1) ninety-eight lodges of Brith Sholom; (2) thirteen lodges of Brith Abraham; (3) twenty *fareyns;* (4) twenty-seven branches of the *arbeiter ring;* (5) twenty-eight unions; and (6) ten socialist organizations.

Most of the meetings, as late as 1913, were still held in the Jewish quarter and not in the heart of South Philadelphia. Meetings were scheduled in twenty separate halls. The relatively few number of socialist meetings belies the oft repeated claim that socialism dominated Jewish immigrant life. Based on the bare statistics above, the promotion of the Jewish religion and education - two aims of Brith Sholom - were at the forefront of communal efforts supported by the immigrants at this time.

25. *Inquirer,* August 12, 1913.
26. David B. Tierkel prepared a chronological list of twenty-five Yiddish newspapers that were published in Philadelphia. See "Bibliography of the Yiddish Press in Philadelphia (1891-1928)" in *Pinkas, a Jewish Journal Quarterly,* edited by Dr. Max Weinreich and others, vol. I, 1927-1928, pp. 260-262, published by the American Section of YIVO.
27. Kobrin, *Mayne Fuftzig Yohr in Amerike,* pp. 394-403. Apparently, Sholom Aleichem did not contribute his own articles. Rather, he forwarded articles written by others, especially young writers.
28. Some sources claim that the *Stadt-Zeitung* was a Sunday paper. Others state it was a daily. In the one issue of the paper that has been preserved, for May 12, 1895 (issue No. 71), the paper is identified as a weekly.
29. Building Permit No. 1690, dated April 3, 1905. The building had a 60' front and was 120' deep. It was built with stone, brick, and terra cotta and had cast iron columns. The Building Permit indicates that the contractor was Jos. W. McCloskey. But see *Real Estate Record and Builders' Guide, Philadelphia,* March 8, 1905, Building and Real Estate Notes, where the builder is listed as Edward Fay. This building should not be confused with another hall with the identical name located at 713 Snyder Avenue. A note on Bolton is included with the information describing B'nai Abraham. A sketch of the life of John J. Dull can be found with the entry for B'nai Reuben, 615-621 S. 6th Street.
30. For example, on February 22, 1907, the Aids of Zion sponsored a dance here; in early February 1908, a ball, given by the Jewish Sheltering Homes, was attended by more than 1,200 persons; on Sunday, February 15, 1908, the friends of Mount Sinai Hospital sponsored a ball; and on April 8, 1908, the United Relief Association sponsored its annual concert and ball, attended by over 800 people.
31. Charles S. Bernheimer, in James, *The Immigrant Jew in America,* pp. 244, 245.
32. *Public Ledger,* February 21, 1908.
33. Zylbercweig, and *Di Yidishe Velt,* July 25, 1932. "Max Thomashevsky was drawn to Philadelphia and in a year when he did not have a theatre, he went around like a lost soul."
34. Goldstein, *My World As A Jew,* I: 19, 20.
35. *Inquirer,* February 4, 1901. David B. Tierkel was the manager and city editor of the *Philadelphia Jewish Day* from 1914 until his death in 1948. Other New York papers had offices in the area: *Warheit,* or *The Truth,* was located at 328 and 332 S. 5th Street from 1917 to the twenties; and *Freiheit,* or *Freedom,* was located at 339 S. 5th Street in 1924, at 340 S. 5th in 1925, and at 426 Pine Street in 1926.
36. The smell of singed chicken feathers, the Yiddish of the streets, the *"dingen zikh"* (haggling), were poignantly recaptured by Robert Lasson in his article, "It's Fourth St. - of another time," *Jewish Exponent,* February 24, 1984.
37. "Trouble Among Down Town Vendors," *Jewish Exponent,* July 26, 1912.
38. *Jewish Exponent,* May 14, 1897, and October 29, 1897; editorials in the *Exponent* May 7, 1897, and November 5, 1897; and Kobrin, pp. 401, 402. A book dealer and adventurer, Deinard bought books for Mayer Sulzberger. Another reason for coming to Philadelphia may have been his dealings with Sulzberger. For a recent excellent essay on Deinard, see Grace Cohen Grossman with Richard Eighme Ahlborn, "The Ephraim Deinard Collection: A New Factor," in *Judaica at the Smithsonian: Cultural Politics as Cultural Model* (Washington, D.C.: Smithsonian Institution Press, 1997), pp 69-79. One of Deinard's most valuable collections forms the basis of the Hebraica Collection at the Library of Congress.
39. In 1904, the Philadelphia office of the *Forward* was located at 341 S. 4th Street. Between 1907 and 1910, the office was located at 511 S. 4th Street. The newspaper was located at 508 S. 5th Street in 1912; after two years here, the paper moved to the northeast corner of 5th & Pine Streets where it remained until 1928. I would like to thank Selma Rabinowitz for her help with the *Forward.*
40. The building of the *Jewish Daily Forward,* 131 S. 5th Street, was dedicated in February, 1928. Abraham Cahan attended the celebration. *Fun Fryant zu a Fryant: a Matune Harry Bergern zu zyan 50tn Gebortstog,* ed., L. Kesner (Philadelphia: Jewish Workers' Movement, Philadelphia, 1936).
41. Newspaper distribution was not made in Philadelphia by newsboys. It was done from news stands, or by carriers for the paper, by those who had established routes. Cohen, *Di Idishe Anarkhistishe Baveygung in Amerike,* p. 166. An Inventory and Appraisal filed in federal court in 1932 lists agents, presumably store owners who carried the newspaper, and carriers of *Di Yidishe Velt* then indebted to the newspaper. Altough the listings are apparently not complete in that they do not list all agents and carriers, these listings do give us some idea of the scope of the paper's distribution system. A total of 157 agents and 49 carriers are listed. Names and addresses are included. In addition to the addresses for agents throughout Philadelphia, agents are listed in Norfolk, Virginia; Camden, Trenton, Audubon, Vineland, and Atlantic City, New Jersey; and Pottstown, Shenandoah, and other towns in Pennsylvania. See *William Kamens and Louis M. Friedman vs. Jewish World Publishing Company,* December Term, No. 6901, 1931, In Equity, Inventory and Appraisement, in the District Court of the United States for the Eastern District of Pennsylvania, NAP.
42. In 1932, when an inventory was taken of the assets of the Jewish World Publishing Company, the firm that published *Di Yidishe Velt* until the middle 1930's, a total of sixteen Mergenthaler Linotype machines were counted. These were the machines used to print the paper. *William Kamens and Louis M. Friedman vs. Jewish World Publishing Company,* NAP. An excellent essay on the Mergenthaler Linotype machine when it was used for Yiddish typesetting can be found in Aaron Lansky's "The Soul of an Old Machine," in *The Book Peddler,* Summer 1991/5751, no. 15, pp. 4-12.
43. Hillel Vichnin was born near Vilna on October 17, 1879. He studied in *kheyder* and at the Rezhitze Yeshiva and immigrated to New York in 1904. After writing for the *Jewish Daily Forward,* Vichnin settled in Philadelphia and helped start the *Yidishe Velt.* He remained at the paper until the day it closed. *Inquirer and Record,* September 14, 1942, and Malamut, pp. 330, 331.
44. *M. Katz, Zamelbukh,* ed. *A. Frumkin and Chaim Fineman* (Philadelphia: March 1925), pp. 140-142, and the *Jewish Times,* June 20, 1941.
45. On Tuesday evening, Novemberr 10, 1914, Katz's *The Eternal Tragedy* opened at the National Theatre, 10th & Callowhill

Streets, a playhouse which had recently been converted into a Yiddish theatre. We are told that the play brought "crowds to the house." The *Jewish Exponent* stated that an unnamed drama critic for the English-language *Public Ledger* said: "A visit to the Yiddish theatre is well worth while, even though the language be strange. But if you do go, leave behind your American prejudices. Go with an open mind, prepared to be interested, fascinated - touched by the pathos of The Eternal Tragedy." *Jewish Exponent,* November 13, 1914.

46. *M. Katz, Zamelbukh,* ed. *A. Frumkin and Chaim Fineman* (Philadelphia: March 1925), p. 133.

47. Y. L. Malamut, a writer for the *Yidishe Velt* in its later years, wrote about Ginsburg's long-time association with Zionism with much pride: "He [Ginsburg] was one of the first members of Hovevei Zion, and it was said about him that he was a Zionist before Dr. Theodore Herzl, z"l [*zichrono livrakha,* of blessed memory], came to Zionism." Malamut, p. 325.

48. Malamut, pp. 324, 325. Ginsburg was a life-long Republican but after Roosevelt came to office, he left the Republican party to support John B. Kelly in his run for mayor. *Inquirer,* July 11, 1944.

49. *M. Katz, Zamelbukh,* p. 133.

50. *Public Ledger,* April 12, 1934; *Record,* March 28, 1940; *Bulletin,* July 26, 1940, and *Bulletin,* August 31, 1940. *The Yidishe Velt* was not the only Yiddish daily newspaper published in the building at 233 S. 5th Street. The Philadelphia Office of the *Jewish Morning Journal* was headquartered here after 1922 (for the history of the *Jewish Morning Journal* from 1900 to 1922, see 718 S. 5th Street). The editor of the *Morning Journal* in 1928 and 1929 was B. Brown. In 1930, the paper again changed its name, this time to the Philadelphia *Jewish Morning Journal* and the *Jewish Daily News,* and continued to publish until 1941. The editors after 1930 were B. Brown and Charles Jaffe. The paper may have moved here to take advantage of the presses and talent of the *Yidishe Velt. A Checklist of Pennsylvania Newspapers,* vol. I, Philadelphia County (Harrisburg: Pennsylvania Historical Commission, 1944), pp. 229, 230.

51. *The Philadelphia Real Estate Record and Builder's Guide,* vol. XXI.-no. 27, July 4, 1906, p. 422, and *New York Dramatic Mirrow,* July 21, 1906. The plans were given to a builder, Henderson & Co., but it is not known if Henderson submitted a bid. *Record,* July 10, 1906. Had this theatre been built, Max Thomashevsky would surely have used it instead of the uptown Arch Street Theater. Stories about the theatre continued to appear, the Philadelphia correspondent for the *Mirrow* claiming as late as August that the theatre would open. See *New York Dramatic Mirrow,* August 18, 1906. The next year Boris and Max Thomashevsky made plans to establish a series of theatres to be leased in Chicago, Baltimore, Cleveland, and St. Louis. Only Yiddish plays were to be presented in these theatres. *New York Times,* November 8, 1907. The Thomashevsky plan did not include Philadelphia because it already had the New Columbia Theatre which had "been handling Yiddish plays for some time."

52. Harris published *Der Volks-Vechter* and then studied law at the University of Pennsylvania. He continued to teach at the Hebrew Education Society while he studied law. During the time he taught, a favorite book he presented to the immigrants who made progress in their English studies was Lucien Wolf's *Sir Moses Montefiore: A Centennial Biography* (New York: Harper & Brothers, 1885).

53. Kobrin admired Paley as an able writer and as the ablest of editors, but smiled upon Paley's use of flowery language. Kobrin, *Mayne Fuftzig Yohr in Amerike,* p. 399,

54. In August 1905, Joseph Klein, the owner of the property, added a new stairway and converted the property to a hall. Klein was the grand secretary of the Independent Order Sons of Jacob, a local Jewish fraternal organization which paid death benefits to its members. Formed three years earlier, by 1907 the Independent Order Sons of Jacob had four thousand members and forty-two lodges. The Order, operating in seven states, was under the supervision of the Insurance Departments in those states. Death benefits could be purchased for $3.62 a year. Samuel Himmelstein took out a party wall to open his restaurant in 1925.

55. In 1864, there was a *messuage* (a dwelling-house) situated at 509 S. 5th. It was torn down and the hotel was erected before 1876. Oysters were such big business in Philadelphia at this time that three wharves on the Delaware River (wharves no. 15, 17 & 18) were identified as "Oyster wharves." For the story of Emma Thomashevsky, see Tierkel, *History of the Yiddish Theatre in Philadelphia,* pp. 10, 11.

56. *Gegenwart,* January 24, 1896, and Freeman, vol. II, pp. 111-121 (Freeman names the forty-four founders.) Kurlander's restaurant occupied 507 S. 5th Street several years later. In 1914, Maurice Leblang, the next restauranteur, engaged architect Frederick Griesler to cut openings in the party wall between 507 and 509 and put in new windows. After 1914, one business was located at 507 and 509 although the properties were owned by different people until the early 1940's. In 1915, Leblang changed the door from where it had been since the days of Stern's Hotel (on the diagonal at the southern corner of 509) and designed a centered doorway between the two properties. As late as 1928 a hotel still operated here.

57. Uhr was born in Nebelitz, Austria, in 1893 and emigrated to Philadelphia aboard the S. S. Hanover in 1911. He worked at Leblang's as a waiter. Uhr built his famous restaurant at an estimated cost of $25,580.

58. *Inquirer,* September 10, 1967.

59. *Jewish Exponent,* June 2, 1911.

60. For the founding of the 4th Presbyterian Church, see Rev. Alfred Nevin, D.D., LL.D., *History of the Presbytery of Philadelphia* (Philadelphia: W. S. Fortescue & Co., 1888), pp. 306, 307. "In the spring of 1841 the Congregation [the 4th Presbyterian Church] resolved to change the location of their house of worship. They sold the house and church on Fifth Street..." *Session Book, Fourth Presbyterian Church, June 6, 1841 to March 19, 1871,* vol. 2, PHS. Neither city nor Presbyterian records indicate to whom the property was sold in 1841, but presumably it was sold to "Israel Congregational," an African American church located here in the 1850's. An unrecorded purchase-money mortgage may have secured the transaction, see abstract of title, Plan 4s7 Lot 120, PHC. During the Civil War, the German Roman Catholic Literary Institute of Philadelphia acquired the proprety. When Israel Congregational was located here in 1857, the building measured 41' along S. 5th Street and 72' along Gaskill Street. A survey in 1907, however, indicated the length of the building along Gaskill Street was 104', meaning that the building had been extended 32' in the intervening years. The extension may have been added in 1867 at the time the building was converted to a theatre, or in 1891 when it was converted to a synagogue.

61. Among the plays put on here by the Wheatley Dramatic Association was *Leah, the Forsaken,* which tells the story of Leah, a 17th century Jewess in Germany who falls in love with a Chirstian farmer. Written by Augustin Daly, *Leah,* or *Leah the Jewish Maiden,* was produced here on Wednesday evening, November 19, 1873. *Leah,* first seen at the Chestnut Street Theatre in 1863, involved betrayal, expulsion, deser-

tion, and loyalty. It was well received and was performed in Philadelphia most years until 1906.

62. *Die Arbeiter Zeitung,* July 11, and August 1, 1890.

63. *Times-Philadelphia,* August 4, 1890. *Die Arbeiter Zeitung,* July 11, 1890. *Public Ledger,* August 8, 1890. Staller spoke at a meeting in Dramatic Hall on August 2, 1890, conducted under the "auspices" of the Knights of Liberty, which was described in the press as a "genuine" anarchist meeting. The police raided the hall while Staller spoke, and he was arrested as he tried to crawl out one of the windows. Staller was charged with making "an incendiary speech and inciting to roit," charges which he steadfastly denied. Staller became one of the most respected surgeons in Philadelphia. He was a founder and the first president of Mount Sinai Hospital and medical director of the Jewish Consumptive Institute.

64. The name of the synagogue on the corporate seal is Chewra Emunas Israel-Oheb Sholem. In this book the word chewra is written with a "v." It is unclear where Chevra Emunas Israel met on Clifton below South Street before it moved to 511 S. 5th Street and merged with Oheb Sholem. It may have met in a row house, or in the Shiloh Baptist Church building located just south of the corner of Clifton and South Streets, an African American church organized in 1842. "The building is of brick, 54 by 40 feet in demension; it has a basement with lecture room and minister's studio. The audience room is of plain, neat finish, and will seat comfortably about 600 persons." Rev. William T. Catto, *A Semi- Centenary Discourse, delivered in The First African Presbyterian Church, Philadelphia* (Philadelphia: Joseph M. Wilson, 1857), Appendix, p. 109.

65. *Jewish Exponent,* February 22, 1889. Since the *Exponent* article referred to the building as a hall, and not a synagogue, synagogal use apparently did not become dominant until 1891. The newspaper in editorials at this time acted as a self-appointed approval authority for immigrant conduct. And like all such authorities, at times it could not resist the temptation to be paternalistic. But the *Exponent* wrote with a great sense of fidelity and loyalty toward the east European Jews. The editors took great interest in the undertakings of the Russian community and reveled in its accomplishments. The sale of the hall to Cherva Emunas Israel-Oheb Sholem included the hotel next door at 509 S. 5th Street. It is not known when the synagogue sold the hotel. For the purchase of 509 and 511 S. 5th Street, see Land Title and Trust Company Settlement Certificate, No. 4580, dated May 7, 1888, and Policy of Insurance, dated May 15, 1888.

66. *Public Ledger,* September 12, 14, 1891.

67. The architect responsible for the changes has not been identified. Concerning Moorish style synagogue architecture in general (and not with reference to the Hungarian *shul*), Philadelphia architect Andrew J. Sauer questioned its use by those whom he saw as insensitive to what he perceived as its basic requirements: "Many synagogues today have have been built of Moorish style, and it seems to have been a very unfortunate move. The greatest delicacy of feeling for both form and color is needed to preserve the beauty of Moorish architecture. The curiously shaped domes, towers and misapplied horse-shoe arches, turrets and pinnacles have often resulted, presenting in many cases a grotesque appearance, rather than the dignity and simplicity that should be retained." *Jewish Exponent,* March 29, 1907. See also *Jewish Exponent,* October 30, 1896. The horse-shoe arches and lovely onion-shaped domes of the Hungarian *shul,* however, were of delicate shape and form. The domes can be seen in a photograph in *The Jewish Encyclopedia,* 12 vols. (New York, Funk & Wagnalls Company, 1905), vol. IX, p. 674; photograph misidentified as the B'nai Abraham synagogue.

68. *Jewish Exponent,* September 18, 1891. See also *Public Ledger,* September 14, 1891. For the sale of Wheatley Dramatic Hall to the Hungarian synagogue, see *Jewish Exponent,* April 13, 1888. I am indebted to Rhoda Piltch, a granddaughter of Rabbi Simon J. Englander, to Marty Piltch, and to the entire Piltch family for many kindnesses.

69. *American Hebrew,* September 23, 1892. Charles Hoffman, one of the speakers, was a rabbi, a lawyer and a founder of the *Jewish Exponent.* Upon graduation from the University of Pennsylvania Law School, where he was selected as student orator at commencement in 1884, Hoffman immediately offered to help the immigrants, serving as the secretary of the Association of Jewish Immigrants for many years. He was deeply interested in the Zionist movement and covered the early World Zionist Congresses for the *Exponent,* where he met Herzl, Nordau and other Zionist leaders. Unlike almost all of the other leaders in the immigrant community, Hoffman was born in the United States. For a tribute to Hoffman, see *Jewish Exponent,* June 8, 1962.

70. Typescript, Harry Beitchman, April 23, 1975, PJAC. Englander's family, while not expressly refuting Beitchman's statement that Englander was paid a regular salary, remembers that Englander was compensated by individual congregants and others for officiating at leading life-cycle events, such as birth, marriage or death. I would like to thank Cantor Gordon Piltch, a great-grandson of Rabbi Englander, for sharing papers and family recollections.

71. *Record,* January 1, 1911.

72. Ibid.

73. Although a Jewish restaurant was located here as early as 1891, nothing is known of it. *Freie Arbeiter Stimme,* December 4, 1891.

74. *Di Yiddische Bihne,* December 3, 1909.

75. This was the performance that was preceded by a riot on South Street when Adler decided to increase the price of a gallery ticket at the last minute *(see Standard Theatre).*

76. *Di Yiddische Bihne,* December 3, 1909.

77. *Record,* January 1, 1911.

78. On January 31, 1915, the management of the *Yidishe Velt* gave a first anniversary banquet at the Colonial Cafe, which was attended by seventy-five writers and workers for the paper. *Jewish Exponent,* February 5, 1915.

79. Apotheker met David B. Tierkel shortly after he arrived in Philadelphia, and the two struck up a friendship. In his typescript on the history of the Yiddish theatre, Tierkel states that it was Apotheker who helped him start to write about the Yiddish theatre in Philadelphia. Apotheker left Philadelphia in 1909 and died in 1911. Most probably, Tierkel put the typescript away, not to pick it up again until the early 1930's. For Apotheker's life, see Zalman Reisen, *Lexicon* (Warsaw: Shriftgiser, 1914), cols. 68-70; Zalman Reisin, *Lexicon,* 2 vols. (Vilna: B. Kletzkin, 1926), I: cols. 151-155; and Tierkel, *The History of the Yiddish Theatre in Philadelphia,* typescript, 1934, pp. 82-92.

80. Ibid, p. 86.

81. Ibid.

82. See also Stern, *Traditions in Transition,* p. 73.

83. David B. Tierkel, "Bibliografie fun der Yidisher Prese in Filadelfia (1891-1928)," *Pinkas, A Quarterly Journal for Jewish Literature, Language, Folklore and Bibliography,* vol. I (New York: YIVO - American Section, 1927-1928), I: 260-262.

The Telegraph moved from 339 S. 5th Street to 702 S. 5th Street in 1898.

84. Letter from Abraham Magil, dated July 2, 1994.
85. Freeman, vol. I, Chapter 19. No more than thirty-five issues were published.
86. Tierkel, Pinkas, I: 262. Issues of the *Yidishe Prese* (1892-1894) have not been preserved, but articles about the Yiddish stage were culled out by David B. Tierkel, and he quoted from them extensively in his typescript on the Yiddish stage in Philadelphia. Tierkel, typescript, pp. 19-53.
87. Tierkel, Pinkas, vol. I: 262. *The Volks-Blatt* was founded in Novmeber 1894.
88. Ben-zion Eisenstadt, *Chokhmei Israel B'Amerika* (Israel's Scholars in America) (New York: A. H. Rosenberg, 1903), pp. 68, 69, and Malamut, pp. 290, 291.
89. Rose I. (Magil) Bender, the oldest daughter, was born about 1895. Rose organized the first Young Judea Club in America when she was eleven years old. In October 1945, Rose Bender became the Executive Director of the Philadelphia Zionist Organization, the only woman in the country to hold such a high post at the time.
90. When Abraham was ten or eleven years old, he came across novels by Dickens and Sir Walter Scott in an old bookcase. Abraham's father, Joseph, used these books to teach himself English. Abraham found writings on the page margins in his father's hand, noting definitions of words in English. Letter from Abraham Magil, dated June 25, 1994.
91. Letter from Abraham Magil, dated July 24, 1994.
92. Joseph Ben Judah Magilnitzky, *Linear School Chumush* (Philadelphia: Joseph Magilnitzky, 1899), Study Card. Magil did not shorten his Russian surname at first. As a printer, however, he was able to set the suffix of his surname in smaller size type before deciding to drop it altogether.
93. The bare genealogy of the paper can be traced in *A Checklist of Pennsylvania Newspapers,* Volume I, Philadelphia County, prepared by The Pennsylvania Historical Survey, Division of Community Service Programs, Works Progress Administration (Harrisburg, 1944), pp. 229, 230. The *Jewish Morning Journal* was published at 718 S. 5th Street from 1900 to 1913, and it was located at the southwest corner of 5th & Pine Streets from 1914 to 1922 (there were three Yiddish newspaper offices on corners at 5th & Pine at this time). It then moved to the building of the *Yidishe Velt*. The *Jewish Morning Journal* may not have been printed in Philadelphia after 1922. Ginsburg was the editor of the paper from 1908 to 1914; the publisher from 1914 to 1929 was the Jewish Journal Publishing Co.
94. Presumably, the Oser Brothers continued their printing business at 626 S. 3rd Street while printing the *Filadelfia Morgen Zeitung*.
95. Joseph Magil died February 10, 1945. *Jewish Exponent,* February 16, 1945, and the *New York Times,* February 12, 1945. Magil was, in addition to being a translator and a publisher, a typesetter. To secure a badly needed loan of $5,000 in 1926, Magil was forced to transfer possession of his book plates to a publishing company in New York as security for a loan. When asked whether he purchased the book plates, Magil answered tersely: "I produced them during 25 years; it is my life's work." Today, we do not picture a Jewish publisher being covered with printer's ink, but Moses Freeman, the Oser Brothers, and Joseph Magil (who also had two brothers in the business, Morris and Meyer) all set type. They did this in addition to writing, editing, translating, publishing, and marketing.
96. *Public Ledger,* January 9, 1857. Newspaper coverage of synagogue dedications before the Civil War is spotty. Some are bland, like the one for this synagogue. Others, however, sparkle with details, none more so than the articles in the *United States Gazette* for April 14, and 15, 1843, which cover the dedication of Rodeph Shalom Congregation when it was located "upon the third story of a building on the west side of Fourth Street, between Vine and Wood Streets." The synagogue was opened for consecration at five o'clock in the afternoon and "crowds of ladies and gentlemen" continued to arrive until the commencement, which was about six o'clock. "The ladies of the choir were all attired in white, presenting generally a very beautiful appearance in face and form as well as in dress. The people of Israel have a large share of female beauty." The audience was very large; the space between the Holy Ark and the bimah (termed the "reading desk") was completely filled by ladies, the writer of the articles pointing out that the area was normally left vacant. The service began with a trumpet "sounded from the choir." The second article includes one of the most beautiful passages written in the English language of a consecration service in a synagogue in Philadelphia. A part is reproduced here: "The procession which entered bearing the books of the law attracted general and undivided attention. The bearers held them nearly upright, inclining upon the shoulders. The scrolls upon which the laws are written are of parchment, bound at the edges with satin, and they are disposed around mahogany rollers, the whole clothed in crimson damask satin. Beneath the drapery appears one end of the roller, which is arranged and serves for a handle, and above, the upper end, is highly decorated with pure silver ornaments and bells, 'sweetly tinkling' as they move." *Niles National Register,* May 6, 1843.
97. The leader of the synagogue, Rev. Samuel B. Breidenbach, was born in Darmstadt, Germany, in 1815. He was well versed in Hebrew and the Torah, and had a good knowledge of Latin. He came to the United States in 1853 and became the first minister of Adath Jeshurun Congregation when it had approximately twenty members and met at Horn's Hall at the southeast corner of 3rd & Brown Streets in Northern Liberties. Breidenbach was at B'nai Israel from 1862 to 1873. After leaving the synagogue, he went into business, but continued as a *shoykhet*. He died on December 25, 1889. A recent detailed history of the synagogue is found in Robert P. Swierenga's, *The Forerunners: Dutch Jewry in the North American Diaspora* (Detroit: Wayne State University Press, 1994), pp. 129-135.
98. *Press,* October 25, 1891.
99. For example, in 1912 when efforts were made by storekeepers on S. 4th Street to close down the peddlers who operated push carts in front of their stores (between Lombard and Carpenter Streets), Tierkel, as Chairman of the Blankenburg League, an immigrant political organization, urged city officials to find a location where push cart operators and store owners could both make a living. Besides S. 4th Street, push carts were located on S. 7th Street between Federal Street and Snyder Avenue in South Philadelphia. For Tierkel, see *New York Times,* May 30, 1948, and *Bulletin,* May 29, 1948. Tierkel's papers are located at YIVO. His published works include, *Shirei David* (New York: A. H. Rosenberg, 1904), a thin volume of Hebrew poems, including a poem about ancient Israel written in Philadelphia upon his arrival in 1893; and *The Juvenile Stage: A History of the Yiddish-Hebrew Dramatic Societies* (Philadelphia: The Federal Press, 1940). His most important work, the history of the Yiddish theatre in Philadelphia, was left in typescript format, and has never been published. Joseph Gross, who wrote for the paper, was

born in Kiev in 1880. He came to Philadelphia in 1890, and was a member of the first graduating class of Temple University Law School in 1901. Gross served as the solicitor of the Jewish Sheltering Homes and in his later years wrote for the *Evening Bulletin*.

100. Although the People's Bank (the immigrant bank of Charles Lipshutz) merged on October 20, 1923, to form the People's Bank & Trust Company and moved out of the area, on July 9, 1925, Frank E. Hahn & S. Brian Baylinson, Registered Architects, drew plans for the People's Bank to alter the bank at 701-703 Passyunk Avenue. Despite the plans, it does not appear that People's Bank moved back into the Jewish quarter.

101. Whether everyone in Local 306 was, in fact, Jewish was an investigation that the District Council was not anxious to make. According to a circular printed at the time of the revocation in 1939, non-Jewish paperhangers joined Local 306 even in the early years. The local argued unsuccessfully to the General Executive Board that on the application blank for new members there were no questions as to race, nationality or faith of the applicant, and, therefore, the charter should not be revoked. They also pointed out that in the general constitution of Local 306 there was no provision which forbade a non-Jew from joining. In analyzing this dispute in the 1970's, Maurice Cohen, the long-time business agent of Local 587, went through the records of Local 306 and wrote a short history. He learned that at the time the charter was revoked, a District Council election had been scheduled, and the outcome of the election hinged on the positions different factions took on the charter revocation question. Cohen found that internal politics, rather than anti-Semitism, drove the decision to revoke the charter. Maurice Cohen, *The History of the Paperhangers Trade Union Movement in Philadelphia*, typescript, 1974, PJAC.

102. Philadelphia journalists were fascinated by Levis: Hugh R. Thayer wrote, "the old Neighborhood, daily Levis duel: hot dogs at 300 paces," *Inquirer,* April 1957. James Smart, who wrote a column entitled "In Our Town" for the *Evening Bulletin*, published a long article on Levis: "'Old Original' Hot Dogs Sold At Same Stand for 75 Years," November 6, 1970; Richard Deasy, wrote for the *Philadelphia Daily News:* "Levis Dogs to Star at Playhouse," April 14, 1972; and William K. Mandel, "Original Hot Dog Purveyors Mark 75th Anniversary," *Evening Bulletin*, November 17, 1970. The newspapers could not get enough of Levis. In 1973, Joe Clark of the *Daily News* wrote a story about a decision at Levis' to charge 2¢ for a dish of pickles. Previously there had been no charge. The bookkeeper at Levis, who requested that her identity not be disclosed, defended the decision to charge for the pickles as if under cross-examination by the entire City of Philadelphia. In 1958, a customer who became unruly and would not behave, was shot in the foot by a quick-fingered manager. Smart's article also included a "Levis Inflation Index," which narratively and by chart traced the price of a Levis hot dog from 2¢ (until World War I) to 20¢ in 1966. In 1970, the price almost doubled, increasing to 35¢. Philadelphia's love affair with Levis continued for three generations.

103. The soda fountain was also called a "soda mixer." Levis acquired the property next door at 509 S. 6th Street, and in 1914 he cut a hole two feet high and eight inches wide in the party wall between 507 and 509 S. 6th Street, on both the first and second floors. Evidently, food was passed through these openings. Little is needed to convince the reader that Levis was an individualist. If more proof is needed, the building permits of the city and newspaper articles together contain another story. Levis got into a dispute with the Philadelphia Electric Company over electric charges. Levis stated that he did not need the company and would produce his own electricity. On July 31, 1915, Levis took out a building permit to build a concrete foundation for a seventeen-horsepower White & Middleton gas engine in the basement at 509 S. 6th Street (Permit No. 5729).

104. *Inquirer,* July 1, 1994.

105. Joseph L. Malamut, Editor and Publisher, *Filadelfier Idishe Anshaltn un Zayer Fierer* (Philadelphia, 1943), p. 33. The south-Russian town of Belaya Tserkov (White Church) was home to a large numbers of Jews. Among themselves, the Jews called the town *Shvarts-Tume* (Black Impurity). Euphemistic names for this town can also be found (e. g., White Field). For an excellent guide to Jewish Communities in Eastern Europe, see Gary Mokotoff and Sallyann Amdur Sack, *Where Once We Walked* (Teaneck, New Jersey: Avotaynu, Inc., 1991).

106. B'nai Reuben wandered throughout the Jewish quarter before finally settling at 615-621 S. 6th Street. In the late eighties, B'nai Reuben moved from Passyunk Avenue to 240 Monroe Street (Hitzelberger Hall). In the early 1890's, it purchased the former Union Methodist church building, a narrow row house at 620 Minster Street for $2,600. When the building was used by Union Methodist in 1857, the church had one hundred members. About the middle 1890's, B'nai Reuben moved to Pennsylvania Hall, 926-930 S. 6th Street, where it remained for the next ten years. When it was located there, the rabbi (in 1901) was Charles H. Kahana, and (in 1904), Rev. M. Chorny and Bernard L. Levinthal.

107. Building Permit No. 1671, dated April 8, 1904.

108. Doebley, C. Pennsylvania Historic Resource Survey Form 061-87920-00615, Harrisburg, PA, Pennsylvania Historical Commission, 1980.

109. Born in 1859, John J. Dull was an architect, a teacher and a watercolorist. Dull apparently did not attend college and became an apprentice in an architect's office. He may have been taught by his father who was a carpenter. In the late 1890's, Dull helped start the architectural department at Drexel College and taught there for twenty-six years. In March 1904, just about the time the plans were prepared for B'nai Reuben, Bolton and Dull formed a partnership that lasted a number of years. B'nai Rueben was one of their first commissions together. However, Dull is not remembered today as either an architect or a teacher, but as a watercolorist. His first watercolor was painted in 1873, and in 1934 he was awarded the Dana Water Color Medal at the annual exhibition of the Philadelphia Water Color Club. At that time Dull was an instructor in water color at the Pennsylvania Museum School of Industrial Art. He had a one-man show in 1935 and several years later he was honored by the Philadelphia Sketch Club. In the spring of 1949, shortly after his death, a memorial exhibition of his works was presented at the Pennsylvania Academy of Fine Arts. Dull painted many buildings in and around Philadelphia. He loved to paint his home town. A favorite subject was churches, but it is not known if he painted B'nai Reuben. *Bulletin,* November 5, 1934; December 26, 1939; January 18, 1949; and April 17, 1949.

110. "The main facade and entrance for the men was on the west. The woman's entrance was discretely placed on the south side of the western tower. This led to one of the two stair halls where the women could ascend to their balcony behind the majista [divider] unseen." Jasmine Chu and N. Moses Corrette, Synagogue B'nai Reuben, 615 South 6th Street, Philadelphia, submitted to fulfill a requirement in

Building Pathology, Program in Historic Preservation, Graduate School of Fine Arts, University of Pennsylvania, May 1, 1998, p. 6. I would like to thank Jasmine Chu and N. Moses Corrette for allowing me to quote from their study.

111. The galleries were not supported by pillars: "The most remarkable structural innovation, the balcony, was removed. This [the balcony] wrapped around the south, west and east walls, and extended some 12 feet into the room. This innovation was that this balcony was unsupported from below. Instead of using columns, Bolton & Dunn [Dull] suspended the balcony from the shallow barrel vaulted ceiling. This was done by employing two and a half inch diameter rods from the trusswork to the floor of the balcony. The iron rods remain although the balcony does not." Chu and Corrette, Synagogue B'nai Reuben, p. 6. The synagogue was built with no water system or heating plant. Two bathrooms were added in 1950. Ibid.

112. *Jewish Exponent,* April 22, 1891. B'nai Reuben was one of three synagogues that invited Rabbi Levinthal to come to the United States in April 1891. The other two were B'nai Abraham and Anshe Shavel.

113. *Jewish Exponent,* January 6, 13, 1905.

114. *North American,* January 9, 1905.

115. Cantors, like Rev. Abraham Solotist from B'nai Abraham, supplemented their salaries with other endeavors. Solotist, for example, stated on his business cards that he was a composer, teacher of music and singing, a first class *mohel,* and a ceremonial performer. Tickets to his concerts in 1902 were 25¢.

List of Abbreviations

ABHS................................American Baptist Historical Society
AJA...................................American Jewish Archives
AJHS.................................American Jewish Historical Society
AME..................................African Methodist Episcopal
APS...................................American Philosophical Society
AUC..................................Archives of the Unitarian Church
BEA...................................*Bibliothèque et archives de L'Alliance Israelite Universelle*
CJS....................................Center for Judaic Studies (formerly Dropsie College)
EBA...................................Elizabetgrad Beneficial Association
FLP....................................Free Library of Philadelphia
HEAS................................ Hebrew Emigrant Aid Society of the United States
HIAS................................ Hebrew Immigrant Aid Society
HLS...................................Hebrew Literature Society
HSP................................... Historical Society of Pennsylvania
JCA...................................Jewish Colonization Association
JPS.....................................Jewish Publication Society of America
JTA....................................Jewish Theological Seminary of America, Archives
LOC.................................. Library of Congress
NAP...................................National Archives and Records Administration,
Mid Atlantic Region (Philadelphia)
PAJHS............................... Publications of the American Jewish Historical Society
PHC.................................. Philadelphia Historical Commission
PHS...................................Presbyterian Historical Society
PJAC.................................Philadelphia Jewish Archives Center
PSA...................................Pennsylvania State Archives
UA.....................................Urban Archives, Paley Library, Temple University
WSJHQ.............................Western States Jewish Historical Quarterly
YIVO.................................*Yiddisher Visnshaftlikher Institute*
YUA..................................Yeshiva University Archives

Appendix A

ORGANIZATIONS MARCHING IN THE PARADE OF MONDAY, JUNE 2, 1919

Organized by the Philadelphia Federation of Ukrainian Jews[1]

Twelve Hundred United States soldiers, sailors and marines

Three Thousand members of the Ladies' Waistmaker's Union

Three Hundred Lodges of the Independent Order of Brith Sholom

Two Hundred Lodges of the Workingmen's Circle

Carpenter's Union, Local No. 1073

Good Friends Aid Society

Lomzer Beneficial Association

Keshenoff Ladies Beneficial Association

Sevastopoler Beneficial Association

Overall Makers' Union Local 199

Lodges of the Progressive Order of the West

Sochochover Beneficial Association

Home Beneficial Association

Independent Bertha Rawitz Lodge No. 1

Rumanian Workingmen's Beneficial Association

Young Men's Beneficial Association

Independent Keshenoff Unterstitzungs Verein

Bucharest Rumanian Beneficial Association

Rumanian Iassyer Beneficial Association

Young Rumanian Beneficial Association

Brith Achim

Jewish Progressive Order

Southwark Mutual Aid Society

Independent Lineth Hazedek

Independent First Prokurover Beneficial Association

Austrian Beneficial Association

Radical Zitomer Beneficial Association

Somach Noflim Ladies' Association

Wiminetz Podolier Lodge, No. 168, W.S.O.

Chevra Tilem Mishnaies Anshe Sfard

Resistchever Lushoner Beneficial Association

Woliner Ladies' Aid Society

Thepoler Beneficial Association

Resistchever Beneficial Association

Amalgamated Clothing Workers

United Hebrew Trades

Boslover Beneficial Association

Independent Woliner Progressive Beneficial Association

Pinsker Beneficial Association

Belzer Bessarabian Beneficial Association

Denenberger Beneficial Association

Tauben Beneficial Association

New Constantine Verein

Cloak Makers

Elizabetgrad Beneficial Association

Ladies Auxiliary Elizabetgrad Association

Egg Inspectors' Union

Vitebsker Beneficial Association

National Workers' Poale Zion

Jewish National Workers' Alliance;

Ida Straus Lodge No. 1

Ahavath Israel Congregation

South Phila. Hebrew Association

Women's Protective League of South Philadelphia

[1] For Appendix A, the spelling of names of organizations was taken from the newspapers. Some spellings differ from those contained in the charters issued by the Courts of Common Pleas.

Appendix B German & Russian Clothiers

I. GERMAN The beginnings of the Jewish Clothing Houses, or wholesale clothiers, are traceable to the German Jewish community and the Philadelphia Clothing Exchange.

I. MEMBERS OF THE PHILADELPHIA CLOTHING EXCHANGE, 1886

(Listed alphabetically)

Name of member	Location of Clothing House	Number of Cutters
Aronheimer & Baruch	14 N. 3rd Street	6
Blumenthal Bros. & Co. (B)	46 N. 3rd Street	30
Bacharach, Loeb & Co.	55 N. 3rd Street	12
A. Bacharach & Co.	409 Market Street	6
Frank, Bros. & Co.	51 N. 3rd Street	15
Fleisher Bros.	28 N. 3rd Street	50
Goldsmith Bros.	47 N. 3rd Street	20
Joseph Goldsmith & Co.	26 N. 3rd Street	10
Goldsmith & Co.	15 N. 3rd Street	3
Goldstein, Friedman & Co. (B)	354 Market Street	12
Goodman Bros.(B)	327 Market Street	15
Greenewald & Co.	9 N. 3rd Street	6
Hanauer, Kohn & Co.	235 N. 3rd Street	–
Hexter Bros.	16 N. 3rd Street	28
Hilbronner Bros.	35 N. 3rd Street	3
Hirsh, Frank & Co.	37 N. 3rd Street	7
H. Kohn & Bro. (B)	328 Market Street	5
Kohn, Rosenheim & Co.	312 Market Street	10
Ab. Kirschbaum & Co.	306 Market Street	35
Charles Klein & Co. (B)	246 Market Street	3
S. Leopold & Bro.	19 S. 4th Street	11
Lisberger & Wise	52 N. 3rd Street	6
Liveright, Greenewald & Co.	45 N. 3rd Street	16
Joseph Loucheim & Co.	314 Market Street	10
Daniel Meyers, Jr.	36 N. 3rd Street	8
D. Meyers & Co.	36 N. 3rd Street	36
Joseph Netter & Co.	12 N. 3rd Street	8
Schoeneman Bros. & Co.	18 N. 3rd Street	10
Emanuel Schwerin & Co.	26 N. 4th Street*	4
Shloss & Loeb	248 Market Street	16
N. Snellenberg & Co.	40 N. 3rd Street	40
Strouse, Loeb & Co. (B)	49 N. 3rd Street	30
S. Wilson & Sons	35 N. 3rd Street	5
		Total = 476

(B) = Boys clothing

* = Schwerin & Co., here before and after 1886, is presumed to have also been here in 1886.

Other German Jewish clothing houses or wholesale clothiers were located on the block of N. 3rd Street between Market and Arch and on the nearby blocks of Market Street in 1886, but it is not known if they were members of the Philadelphia Clothing Exchange:

Name	**Location of Clothing House**
S. A. Bacharach & Co.	313 Market Street
Bloomingdale & Co.	332 Market Street
Gans, Arnold & Co.	22 N. 3rd Street
Meyer Goldsmith *(see Goldsmith & Co.)*	15 N. 3rd Street
Isaac Harris & Son	7 N. 3rd Street
Emanual Katz	31 N. 3rd Street
Meyers, Goodman & Co.	43 N. 3rd Street
Saller & Newman	19 N. 3rd Street
Stern & Bros.	521 Market Street

As actuary, Mr. Israel Hecht handled the day-to-day business of the Exchange. Meetings were held in Hecht's office. By 1884, information was traded with New York, Baltimore, Rochester, Cincinnati, and Chicago. In that year the officers of the Exchange were: President, Herman L. Freedman; Vice-President, Leo Loeb; Treasurer and Secretary, S. L. Haas; Board of Managers, Benjamin F. Greenewald, Simon Fleisher, Joseph Goldsmith, Emanuel Schwerin, Joseph Loucheim and Joseph Stern. It had a credit bureau, regulated the time of labor, and established a board of arbitration.

The beginnings of the grand traditions of the German Jewish Philadelphia clothiers date from this period. Members of the Exchange were also members of the Mercantile Club, originally known as the Mercantile Reading Club. A literary association formed in 1853, the Mercantile Club grew into one of the greatest social and charitable organizations in the city. Members of the Exchange were also prominent in forming the Philmont Country Club some years later.

Appendix B continued

II. RUSSIAN Clothiers with Russian Jewish surnames did not appear until about 1892. It is not known if they had their own exchange. The Russians began their clothing houses on Bank and Strawberry Streets. Although most clothiers on these streets had Russian Jewish surnames, it is not always possible to determine nationalistic origins solely from a surname (some of these were obviously German). The following is an incomplete listing chosen for randomly selected years; it also includes a few factories.

1 Bank Street	(1897):	Benjamin Strauss, Woolen & Worsted Goods manufacturer
	(1900):	Brook & Leff, wholesale clothier
	(1908):	M & D Shilafsky, wholesale clothier
3 Bank Street	(1895):	Solomon & Aaron White, pantaloons
	(1900):	Abraham Dogulov; Lazarus Lemisch, wholesale clothiers
	(1906):	B. Zion, clothing mfg.
	(1908):	Benjamin Zion
7 Bank Street	(1896):	Fin & Ritch, pantaloon mfg.
	(1897):	Clothing cutting
	(1897):	William Eckstein, men's furnishings
	(1900):	Tisch & Yeagerman, wholesale clothier
	(1908):	William Eckstein, men's furnishings, wholesale
	(1910):	Adolph Rosenblum, clothing manufacturer
17 Bank Street	(1908):	W. Stomel & Son, wholesale clothier
19 Bank Street	(1897):	Boy's pants, cutting & sewing
	(1897):	P. Goodman Son & Co., pantaloon manufacturers
	(1900):	Jacob Blum, wholesale clothier
	(1906):	M. Winogradsky, wholesale clothier
20 Bank Street	(1908):	Edward Ziegler, wholesale clothier
21 Bank Street	(1897):	wrapper factory
	(1897):	Cooper & Levin, ladies & children's clothing
22 Bank Street	(1893):	Abram Rubin, wholesale clothier
	(1897):	Naramore Button Co., button makers
	(1900):	Mesirov, wholesale clothier
	(1905):	Morris Krichevsky, wholesale clothier
	(1908):	Samuel Blum, wholesale clothier
23 Bank Street	(1897):	shirt cutting & sewing
	(1897):	Simon Eichengreen, shirt manufacturer
24 Bank Street	(1897):	Edward T. Steel & Co., woolen & worsted goods
	(1903):	Guggenheimer & Co., clothing factory
25 Bank Street	(1897):	buttons
28 Bank Street	(1897):	M. Haber & Co., ladies & children clothing
30 Bank Street	(1897):	Reliance Shirt Co., Inc.

3 Strawberry Street	(1900):	Louis A. Schneyer, wholesale clothier
	(1908):	Michael Leaf, wholesale clothier
4 Strawberry Street	(1900):	Harris Hanapolsky, wholesale clothier
	(1903):	J. Berman & Sons, wholesale clothiers
	(1906):	M & D Shilofsky, wholesale clothiers
5 Strawberry Street	(1900):	Herman Mickelwitz, wholesale clothier
	(1900):	Edward Ziegler, wholesale clothier
	(1900):	Joseph Zion, wholesale clothier
	(1903):	Zion & Mamolen, wholesale clothiers
	(1908):	Joseph Zion & Co., wholesale clothier
6 Strawberry Street	(1908):	Herman C. Bernstein, wholesale clothier
7 Strawberry Street	(1896):	Genstein & Werblum
	(1900):	Joseph Benjamin, wholesale clothier
	(1903):	Simon Makransky & Co., wholesale clothier
9 Strawberry Street	(1896):	Lemisch & Langinger, wholesale clothiers
15 Strawberry St.	(1902):	Backerman Bros., wholesale clothiers
19 Strawberry St.	(1893):	Abram Yuckman, wholesale clothier
20 Strawberry St.	(1892):	A. Rabinowitz & Co., wholesale clothier
35 Strawberry St.	(1900):	Jacob Siegelman, wholesale clothier
	(1900):	Isaac Brodstein, wholesale clothier
	(1910):	S. Blum, clothing mfg.
	(1910):	Morris Rice, clothing mfg.
39 Strawberry St.	(1897):	S. Moskovitz & Co., mfg. of ladies & children's clothing
	(1900):	Barry Berkowitz, wholesale clothier
	(1908):	Samuel Maimon, wholesale clothier
41 Strawberry St.	(1908):	Bloom & Lazaroff

Appendix C

SMALLER SYNAGOGUES IN THE JEWISH QUARTER [1]
(In alphabetical order) (1884 - 1942)

Name(s)	Address(es)	Founded	Years at Address(es)
Adath Israel	843 S. 3rd Street	1902	1904-1942
Ahavas Israel	322 Bainbridge Street	1920's	
Anshe Polen	326 South Street	1908?	1908-1918
	523 S. 4th Street		1919-1920
Bet Hakeneseth	417 Monroe Street	1921	1921-1942
Beth Jacob-Anshe Lubavitz	414 Christian Street	1910	1910-1925+
Beth Judah	232 Lombard Street	1921	
B'nai David-Anshe Grodno	611 Lombard Street	1887	
B'nai Jacob-Anshe Sfard	438 Lombard Street1887	1887	
B'nai Joseph	525 Bainbridge Street	1903	1903-05
Chesed Shel Emeth	203 Pine Street	1894	
Chevra Ahwas Zion	815 S. 4th Street	1903	
Chevra Reim Ahuvim	343 Monroe Street	1892	1892-08
Chevra Wohliner-Anshe	322 Bainbridge Street	1919	1930
Kahal Adath Jeshurun	754-756 S. 3rd Street	?	1936-?
Kahillis Israel-Nusach Sfard	234 Bainbridge Street	1914	1917-1927
Kesher Torah-Anshe Lubliner	610 S. 3rd Street	1920	1920-1926+
Po'el Zedek	716-18 Lombard Street	1889	1889-1899
Porath Joseph	754-756 S. 3rd Street	1905	1905-1936
Prushzver and Shershiver Chevra Linath Hazedek	542 Queen Street	1920?	1920-?
Shomre Shabot	N.W. Corner 4th &Gaskill Streets	1894	1894-1900?
	518 S. 3rd Street	1900-?	
	230 Lombard Street	1908	
Shomre Shabot	414 Christian Street		1920
Tzirie Israel	335 Christian Street		1942

[1] Names of synagogues were taken from various documents. When names were taken from Yiddish documents, transcriptions into Latin letters do not follow YIVO standards. This listing is not complete.

Appendix D

YIDDISH NEWSPAPERS PUBLISHED IN THE JEWISH QUARTER [1]

(In chronological order) (1891-1914)

Name of Newspaper	Address(es)	Year Founded	Years of Operation
Dos Licht (The Light)	708 S. 5th St.*	1891	1891-1892
Di Yidishe prese (The Jewish Press)	708 S. 5th Street*	1892	1892-1894
Der Folks Vechter (ThePeople's Watchman)	310 S. 5th Street	1893	1893-1894
Di Filadelfia Stadt-Zeitung (The Phila. City Newspaper)	710 S. 3rd Street*	1894	1894-1895
Yudeshes Volks-Blatt (Jewish People's Paper)	708 S. 5th St.*	1894	1894-189?
Di Gegenwert (The Present)	824 S. 5th St. 522 S. 5th Street	1895	1895-1898
Der Telegraf un Filadelfia Post - (The Telegraph and Philadelphia Post)	339 S. 5th St.* 702 S. 5th Street	1898	1898-1899
The Philadelphia Jewish Evening Post	718 S. 5th St.*	1900?	1900-1913
Filadelfia Morgen Zeitung (Philadelphia Morning Newspaper)	718 S. 5th St.*	1907	1907
Die Philadelphia American	703 Passyunk Ave.	1908	1908-1910
The Philadelphia Jewish Herald	626 S. 3rd St.*	1913	1913
Di Yidishe Velt (The JewishWorld)	233 S. 5th St.*	1914	1914-1942

[1] An asterisk next to the address of the newspaper indicates that the newspaper was printed at the location indicated. It is not known at what address the *Genenwart* was printed, but it was printed in Philadelphia. The *Morgen Zeitung* may have been printed at 626 S. 3rd Street or at 718 S. 5th Street. New York papers have been omitted from this listing.

Appendix E

HALLS IN THE JEWISH QUARTER [1]

(From east to west and north to south)

Name of Hall	Address	Years used as a Hall
Library Hall	203 Pine Street	1887-1891
Caledonian Hall	214-216 Pine Street	1886-1904
Forward Hall	200 block Pine Street	1908-1913+
Knights of Pythias Hall	238 Pine Street	1881-1903?
Boslover Hall	701-703 Pine Street	1925-1965
Liberty Hall	716-718 Lombard Street	1885-1893
Howard Hall	322 Bainbridge Street	1883-1897
Hitzelberger Hall	240 Monroe Street	1883-1898
Market House Hall	725-735 Christian Street	1889-1906
Firehouse Hall (2nd fl.)	512 S. 3rd Street	1881?-1916?
Roumanian Hall	518 S. 3rd Street	1904-1913+
Cosmopolitan Hall	520 S. 3rd Street	1897-1906
People's Hall	520 S. 3rd Street	1906-1913
Connerton Hall	603-605 S. 3rd Street	1890-1900?
Central Hall	610 S. 3rd Street	1904-1906
New Central Hall	610 S. 3rd Street	1906-1918
New Arcadia Hall	610 S. 3rd Street	1918-1924
Eagle (New Eagle) Hall	611 S. 3rd Street	1893-1910
Star Hall	614 S. 3rd Street	1908-1913+
New Auditorium Hall	747-753 S. 3rd Street	1905-1912
Heartfellow Hall	754-756 S. 3rd Street	1895-1905
Washington Hall	521-525 S. 4th Street	1896-1907
New Academy Hall	521-525 S. 4th Street	1907-1917
Majestic Hall	521-525 S. 4th Street	1917-1919
Standard Hall	622-624 S. 4th Street	1897-1909
Central Hall	336 S. 5th Street	1900
Wheatley Dramatic Hall	511 S. 5th Street	1867-1891
Hall (name not known)	724 S. 6th Street	1887
Sampson Hall	733 S. 6th Street	1886-1908
Pennsylvania Hall	928-934 S. 6th Street	1895?-1906
New Pennsylvania Hall	928-934 S. 6th Street	1907-1910
Lyric (New Lyric) Hall	928-934 S. 6th Street	1910-1926?

[1] Some of the buildings that housed the halls were put to other uses. For example, New Auditorium Hall became the Franklin Theatre in 1912.

Glossary

A. FOREIGN WORDS AND TERMS

As a non-professional in the art of Yiddish and Hebrew transcription into English, I have struggled mightily. Happily, I have noted that our most gifted writers have also struggled. As far as I can determine, it is the one trait I have in common with these writers. The only known antidote for this malady appears to be humor. Accordingly, if the reader will approach the glossary with an open mind, a kind soul, and a song in his or her heart, one can cope with the reasoning that follows. I hope that any errors of mine do not grate too harshly on the minds and spirits of those who have expertise in this area.

I have divided Hebrew and Yiddish words into two categories: (1) words found in Webster's dictionary and (2) words not found in Webster's. For Hebrew and Yiddish words found in Webster's (e.g.,Chanukah, kibitzer, mikvah, Rosh Hashana, Succoth, Talmud Torah, yeshiva, Yom Kippur, etc.), I have not repeated them in the glossary and I have not italicized them in the text (there are a few exceptions). For Hebrew and Yiddish words not found in Webster's, I have used the standards suggested by the YIVO Institute for Jewish Research for the transcription of Yiddish into English, but I have not used these standards rigorously (Hebrew mistranscriptions into English do not appear to generate the emotion that Yiddish mistranscriptions generate). When it appeared that modifications to the YIVO standards should be made for Yiddish words, for various reasons, I made such modifications (e.g.,*Yahrzeit*; YIVO=*Yortsayt)*. My modifications are based on the idea that some words look better in English if the YIVO standards are not used, unimpressive reasoning I admit, but reasoning that has driven others to reach a similar conclusion.

Yiddish and Hebrew words not found in Webster's are defined either after their first use, or in the glossary, or both. Generally, I have italicized foreign words not found in Webster's (e.g., *bimah, Yidn, kaddish,* etc.). The capitalization of Yiddish and Hebrew transcriptions in Latin letters I found even more baffling than the question of transcription itself (*kaddish* or *Kaddish*?). I have generally opted to capitalize a Yiddish word transcribed into English if the word would have been capitalized in English.

To identify words in this glossary, a Y has been used for Yiddish; an H for Hebrew; an R for Russian; a G for German; and an A for American Yiddish.

Alte Heym: (Y) Old country.

Am Olam: (H) Eternal People.

Arbeiter Ring: (G & Y) The Workman's Circle.

Aron Kodesh = Ornkoydesh.

Balebuste: (Y) Homemaker, lady of the house.

Besmedresh: (Bet Hamidrash=H) House of Study.

Bimah: (H & Y) An elevated platform, traditionally in the center of the synagogue, where the Torah is read. (see, Kesher Israel and B'nai Abraham).

Bokher: (H) Youngster, bachelor.

Chassidic = Hassidic.

Cheder (Heder)=Kheyder.

Chevra Chevrah, Chebra): (H) A society, association or congregation (In English, written Chebroth in the plural in the early *Exponent)*. Also, Chewra.

Chevra Kadisha: (H) Holy Society (i.e., Burial Society).

Chinovnik: (R) Bureaucrat or clerk in czarist Russia.

Chumesh = Khumesh

Daven (Davn): (Y) To pray.

Der Ferder: (Y) 4th Street.

Ezras Noshim: (Ezrat Nashim = H) Women's section of a synagogue, a gallery (see Kesher Israel, B'nai Abraham and the Vilna Shul: for a women's gallery in a former synagogue, see church at 754-756 S. 3rd Street). Also, helping women. *Ezrath Nashim* was the original name of the Jewish Maternity Hospital, 532-534 Spruce Street).

Fareyn: (Y) Association.

Fatsheyle and Fatsheylke: (Y) Shawl and kerchief.

Frumigheit = Frumkayt: (Y) Devoutness.

Gabbai: (H) A synagogue trustee or manager.

Gaon(Goen): (H) Genius.

Gastrolarin: (Y) Used by those in the early Yiddish theatre world to describe a traveling company going from town to town. This was similar to the American term that referred to companies that played the "circuit," performing in different towns each night.

Goldene Medine: (Y) The Golden Land (The United States).

Gomel: (H) (Goyml = Y) Prayer of thanks, after crossing the sea or the desert (and at other times). Said by the immigrants after their safe voyage across the Atlantic Ocean.

Greener: (A) Greenhorn.

Guberniya: (R) Province.

Gymnasia: (R) Secondary school in Russia. An eight-year course.

Hakhnosses Orkhim: (H) Sheltering the transients. Hospitality.

Hakofes: (H) A circular procession with the Torah scrolls.

Haskala: (H) (Haskole = Y) Enlightenment.

Hassidic: (H) A member of the Hassidic movement, founded by Israel Baal Shem Tov in the 17th Century. Emphasis placed on joyful worship.

Jargon: (F) Used extensively in the English-language press at the end of the last century to describe the language spoken by the immigrants *(see Yiddish).*

Kaddish: (H) Prayer. Said at the death of a parent or loved one.

Kamarinskaya: (R) A popular lively Russian dance.

Kashrus: (H) Ritual lawfulness, especially of foods.

Katerinka: (A) Sewing machine (Harkavy tells us it is a "Jocular American" Yiddish word). Katerinka, one of the most popular words in the vocabulary of the immigrant, has, unfortunately, fallen out of use today.

Katorzhnik: (R) A galley slave. A convict.

Khaseneh: (H) Wedding.

Kheyder: (H) Elementary Religious School.

Khupa: (H) Wedding canopy.

Klezmer (Kley Zemer): (H) A musician. Here, a musician in the early Yiddish theater.

Kol Nidre: (H) "All vows," the most beloved prayer of the Jewish people. Prayer recited at the beginning of Yom Kippur.

Korobka (short for korobochnii sbor): (R) Box. Here, a Tax, or a Basket Tax.

Koved: (H) Honor

Kruzhok: (R) Circle (or as used by the early *Exponent,* a club).

Khumesh: (H) The Five Books of Moses.

Landslayt: (Y) Countrymen.

Landsmanshaftn: (Y) Hometown associations.

Litvak: (Y) Jew from Lithuania (and nearby regions).

Mekhitza: (H) Partition, dividing men's section from women's section of synagogue.

Mentshlikh: (Y) Human, humane, decent, honorable, and more.

Meydl (maidel): (Y) Girl.

Mikve: (Y) = Mikvah.

Mishpokheh: (H) Family.

Moyre Hoyroeh: (H) After the death of the Gaon of Vilna, the rabbis of Vilna bore this title.

Moyshev Zkeynim: (H) Old people's home.

Nakhes: (Y) Sweet joy.

Narod: (R) People. Used here as defined by Shlomo Lambroza, The Pogrom Movement in Tsarist Russia (1981), pp. 191-200 (workers and peasants).

Ner Tomid: (H) Eternal light. Traditionally, the light hanging on the eastern wall of a synagogue or above the ornkoydesh. In the Jewish quarter of Philadelphia not every synagogue had an eastern orientation.

Nusakh: (H) Rite in prayer.

Ornkoydesh: (Aron HaKodesh = H) Holy Ark, in the synagogue contains Torah scrolls.

Pale of Settlement (R = Cherta Osyedlosti): The Border of Settlements. Jews were required to live in the fifteen western-most Guberniyas (provinces) of the Russian Empire from the partitionings of Poland in the latter part of the 18th century until 1917. These fifteen Guberniyas made up the Pale of Settlement.

Parshe: (H) Parshe, weekly section of the Khumesh.

Patriot (Pl. Patriotn): (A) A fan of a particular Yiddish actor or Yiddish acting company.

Peysekh: (H) Passover.

Pogromshchik: (R) One who makes pogroms.

Poshete: (H) Plain.

Shabbes: (H) Sabbath.

Shames: (H) Sexton.

Shevues: (H) Feast of Weeks. Pentecost. Holiday commemorating the giving of the Torah.

Sheeny: (A) Although Sheeny is not defined by Harkavy in English, he does define it in Hebrew: "A disgraceful name for a Jew in America." Harkavy also gives a possible origin of the word.

Shnayder Boss: (A) The boss tailor.

Shomer: (H) Guardian. Here, a watch over the sick and over the dead. Sent to read Psalms.

Shund: (Y) Literary trash.

Shtetl: (Y) Town, townlet or village. Plural, shtetlyekh.

Simkhes Torah: (H) Rejoicing of the Torah.

Sukkah: (H) Booth; a wooden construction covered with branches.

Talis: (H) Prayer shawl, at that time worn exclusively by men. Taleysim (pl) = Y.

Tehilim: (H) Psalms.

Tfiln: (H) Phylacteries.

Treyf: (H) Ritually impure.

Vaad: (H) Board.

Vaad Hakashrus or Vaad Hakashruth: (H) Board of Dietary laws

Warheit: (G) Truth.

Yahrzeit: (Y) Anniversary of death. (YIVO = Yortsayt).

Yid (pl. Yidn): (Y) A Yid was an east European Jew. Pronounced "Yeed," to rhyme with "seed," not Yid, to rhyme with lid (pejorative).

Yiddish: (Y) The primary language of east European Jews. During the period of immigration often referred to as Jargon or Jewish.

Yiddishkayt: (Y) Jewishness. Jewish way of life. Also, Yiddishkeit.

Zamlbuch: (Y) A collection of articles about a scholar on his sixtieth birthday (sometimes issued for other birthdays and upon other celebrations). Only Zamlbuch used here is the one compiled for Moshe Katz, the editor of the Yidishe Velt. But see book for Harry Berger.

Zhenitba: (R) Marriage.

Zhid: (R) Jew (pejorative). See, John D. Klier, "Zhid: Biography of a Russian Epithet," in The Slavonic and Eastern European Review, vol. 60, no. 1, January 1982, pp. 1-15.

B. ARCHITECTURAL OR BUILDING TERMS

Attic Story: The space above the wall cornice (see 603-605 S. 3rd Street).

Balusters: Small posts that support the upper rail of a railing.

Balustrade: A railing held up by balusters. See the bimah at Kesher Israel and the Ezras Noshim at B'nai Abraham.

Balustraded sill: A Balustrade placed on the sill of a window. A feature of Beaux Arts type of architecture. Can be seen on the window sill of the second story of 603-605 S. 3rd Street.

Belt course: (see stringcourse)

Cornice: The projection at the top of a wall.

Cupola: A small dome or similar structure on a roof. Originally, cupolas were architectural features at B'nai Abraham; and above the staircase towers of the Hungarian shul and B'nai Rueben. Today, the only remaining cupolas are on the building at 615-621 S. 6th Street - formerly B'nai Reuben.

Flemish Bond: A decorative method of laying bricks where headers (laid with their ends toward the face of a wall) and stretchers (laid with their sides toward the face of a wall) alternate in each course. See the former bath house on the south side of Gaskill Street.

Gallery: A platform or projecting upper floor attached to the back wall or sides of a church or synagogue, theatre, etc., especially the highest of a series of such platforms in a theatre, with the cheapest seats.

Lintel: The horizontal crosspiece over a door or window, carrying the weight of the structure above it. See the building of the Hebrew Literature Society, 310-312 Catharine Street.

Lunette: A crescent-shaped or semicircular opening. See the Neziner synagogue.

Mansard: A roof where the lower slope is steeper than the upper slope.

Pilaster: An upright architectural member rectangular in plan and structurally a pier, but architecturally treated as a column. It can be load-bearing or merely surface decoration.

Parapet: A barrier to protect the edge of a platform, or here, a roof.

Portico: Here a porch, consisting of a roof supported by columns across the front of a building.

Stringcourse: A horizontal course of brick or stone set in the wall of a building.

Voussoir: A wedge-shaped stone used to form an arch. See B'nai Abraham, portico.

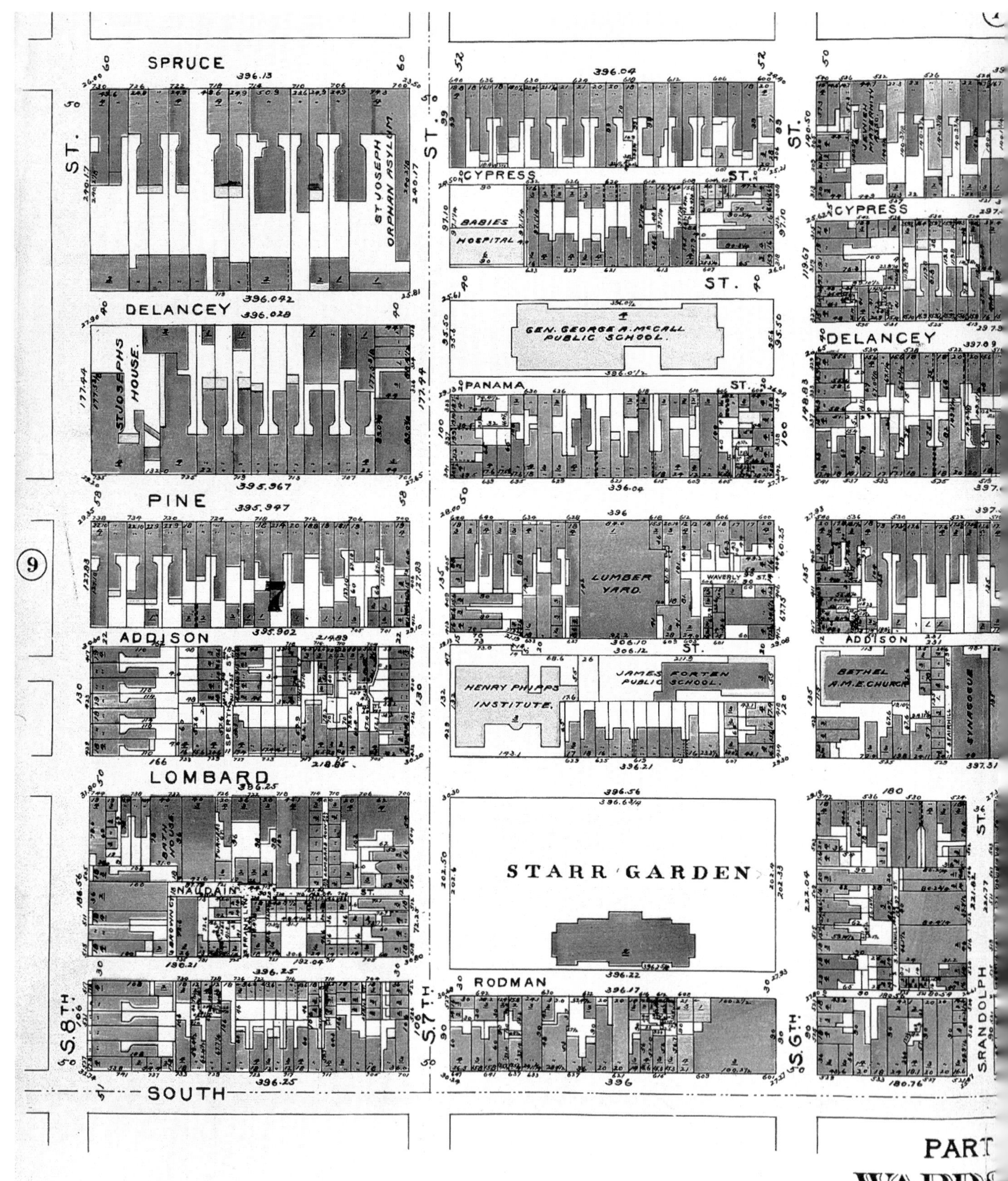
SPRUCE
ST JOSEPH ORPHAN ASYLUM
CYPRESS
BABIES HOSPITAL
DELANCEY
ST JOSEPHS HOUSE
GEN. GEORGE A. McCALL PUBLIC SCHOOL
PANAMA
PINE
LUMBER YARD
WAVERLY ST.
ADDISON
HENRY PHIPPS INSTITUTE
JAMES FORTEN PUBLIC SCHOOL
BETHEL A.M.E. CHURCH
SYNAGOGUE
LOMBARD
BATH HOUSE
STARR GARDEN
NAUDAIN
RODMAN
S. 8TH
S. 7TH
S. 6TH
S. RANDOLPH ST.
SOUTH
PART
WARDS

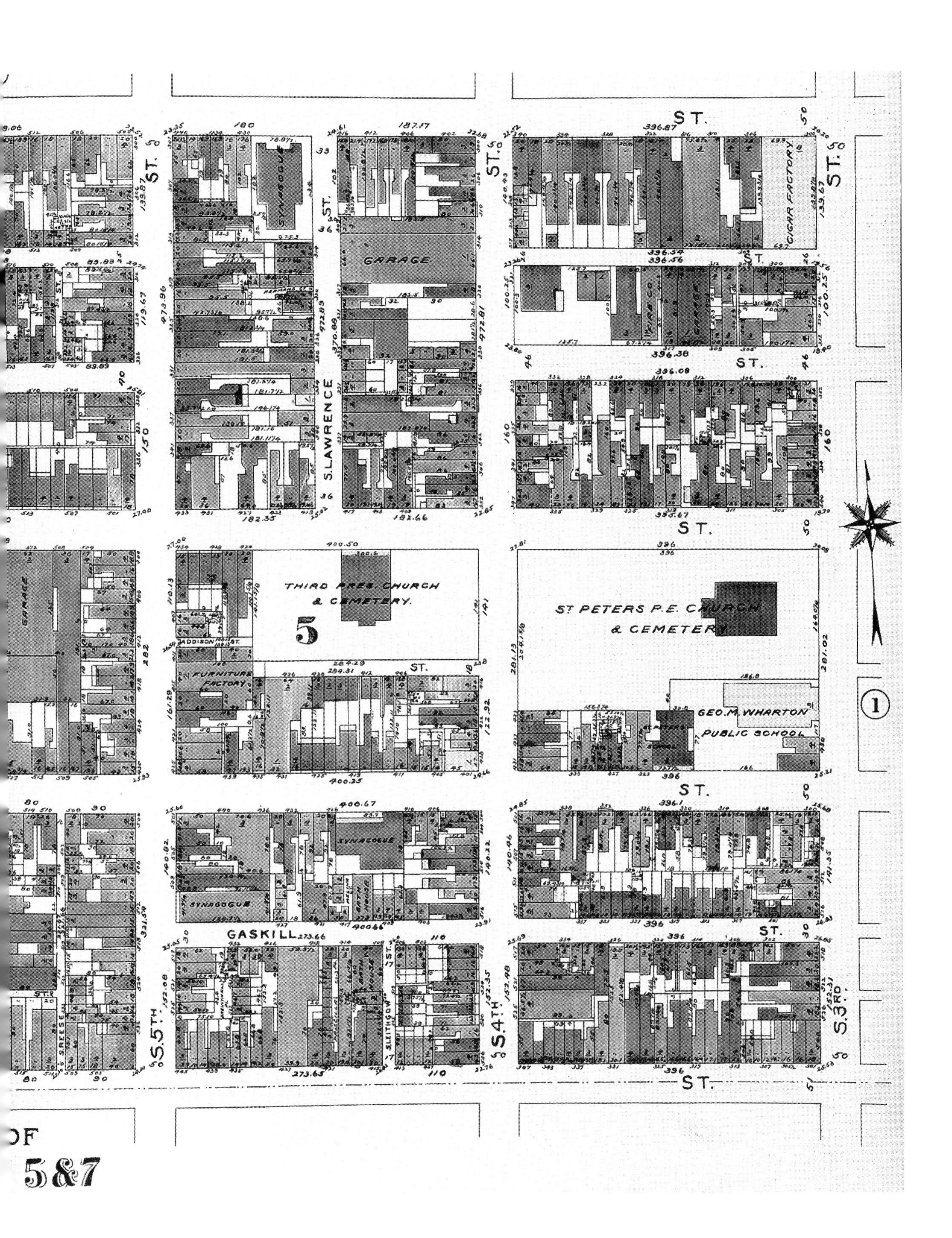
ST.
S.5TH
S.4TH
S.3RD
S.LAWRENCE
GASKILL
ADDISON ST.
SLEITHGOW ST.
SREESE
SYNAGOGUE
GARAGE
CIGAR FACTORY
FIRE CO.
THIRD PRES. CHURCH & CEMETERY
ST PETERS P.E. CHURCH & CEMETERY
FURNITURE FACTORY
GEO. M. WHARTON PUBLIC SCHOOL
ST. PETERS SCHOOL
BATH HOUSE
5
1
OF
5&7

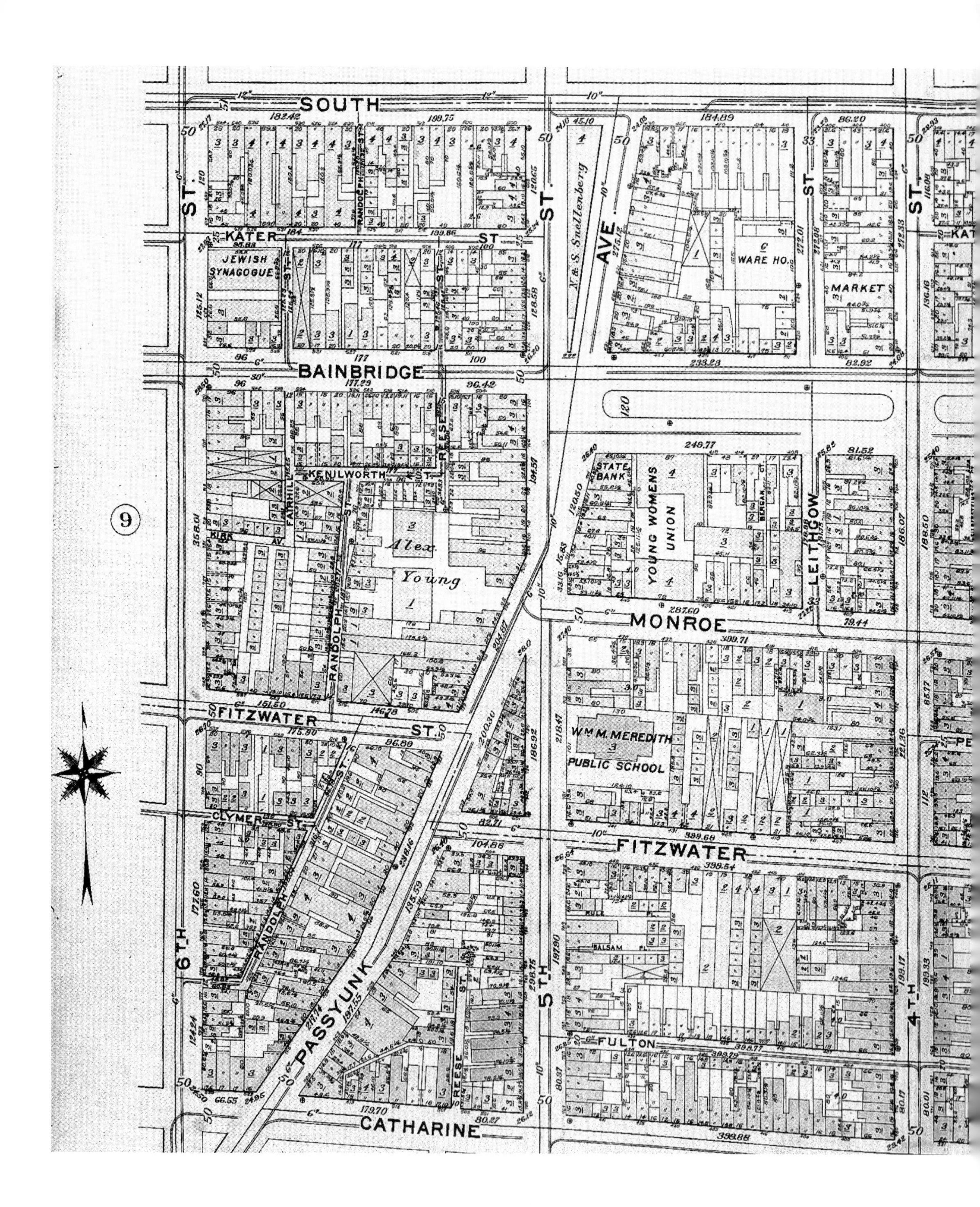
SOUTH
KATER ST
JEWISH SYNAGOGUE
BAINBRIDGE
KENILWORTH ST
FAIRHILL
KIRK AV.
REESE ST
RANDOLPH ST
Alex. Young
FITZWATER ST
CLYMER ST
PASSYUNK
CATHARINE
6TH ST.
5TH ST.
4TH ST.
AVE
N. & S. Snellenberg
WARE HO.
MARKET
STATE BANK
YOUNG WOMENS UNION
LEITHGOW
MONROE
WM M. MEREDITH PUBLIC SCHOOL
FITZWATER
BALSAM PL
FULTON
9

CRYSTAL PALACE THEATRE
HALL
ORIANNA ST
ST
3RD ST
AMERICAN ST
SOUTHWARK NATIONAL BANK
GUILFORD PL.
RALSTON PUBLIC SCHOOL
PHILIP ST
2ND ST
JEWISH SYNAGOGUE
DISPENSARY
GARAGE
LEVIS COURT
MBERTON ST
SAXON PL
WOOL PULLING FACTORY
FRANKLIN THEATRE
ST STANISLAUS R.C. CHURCH AND SCHOOL
JEWISH SYNAGOGUE
3
MT VERNON PUBLIC SCHOOL
CONCORD PL
FULTON ST
3

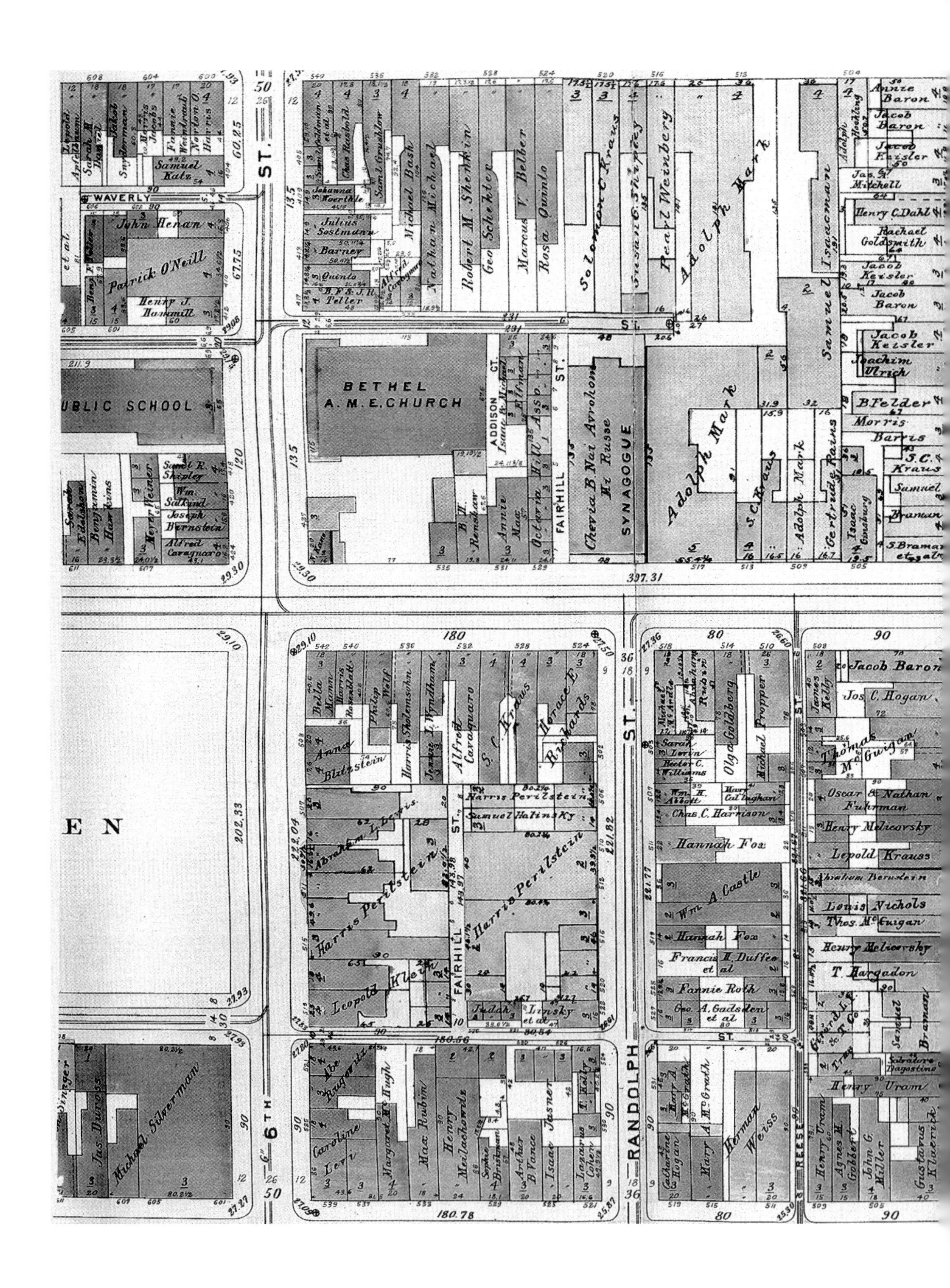

WAVERLY
ST.
John Henan
Patrick O'Neill
Henry J. Hammill
Samuel Katz
UBLIC SCHOOL
BETHEL
A. M. E. CHURCH
ADDISON CT.
FAIRHILL ST.
Chevra B Nai Avrohom Mi Russe
SYNAGOGUE
Julius Sostmann
Michael Bash
Nathan Michael
Robert M. Shenkin
Geo Schekter
Marcus V. Belber
Rosa Quinlo
Solomon C Kraus
Susan G. Shipley
Pearl Weinberg
Adolph Mark
Samuel Isaacman
Annie Baron
Jacob Baron
Jacob Keisler
Jas. W. Mitchell
Henry C. Dahl
Rachael Goldsmith
Jacob Keisler
Jacob Baron
Jacob Keisler
Joachim Ulrich
B Felder
Morris Barris
S. C. Kraus
Samuel Braman
S. C. Kraus
Adolph Mark
Gertrude Rains
Isaac Ginsburg
S. Braman et al
Samuel R. Shipley
Benjamin Hawkins
Meyer Weiner
Wm. Salkind
Joseph Bernstein
Alfred Caragnaro
Annie Max
Octavia Hill Asso.
B. H. Renshaw
E N
Bella Mann
Harris Rosenblatt
Philip Wolf
Harris Sholemsohn
Jennie L. Wyndham
Alfred Caraquaro
S. C. Kraus
Horace E. Richards
Anna Blitzstein
Abraham L. Lewis
Harris Perilstein
Samuel Halinsky
Harris Perilstein
Harris Perilstein
Leopold Klein
Judah Linsky et al
ST.
RANDOLPH
Olga Goldberg
Michael Propper
Sarah Levin
Hector C. Williams
Wm. H. Abbott
Chas. C. Harrison
Hannah Fox
Wm. A. Castle
Hannah Fox
Francis H. Duffee et al
Fannie Roth
Geo. A. Gadsden et al
Jacob Baron
Jos. C. Hogan
Thomas McGuigan
Oscar & Nathan Fuhrman
Henry Melicovsky
Lepold Krauss
Abraham Bernstein
Lewis Nichols
Thos. McGuigan
Henry Melicovsky
T. Hargadon
Samuel Braman
Salvatore Dagostino
Henry Uram
REESE ST.
6TH
Michael Silverman
Jas. Dunoss
Abe Rugowitz
Caroline Levi
Margaret McHugh
Max Rubin
Henry Malachowitz
Sophie Bristman
Arthur B. Vance
Isaac Jasner
Lazarus Cohen
Catharine Hogan
Mary A. McGrath
Herman Weiss
Henry Uram
Agnes M. Gobbert
John G. Miller
Gustavus Klaerick

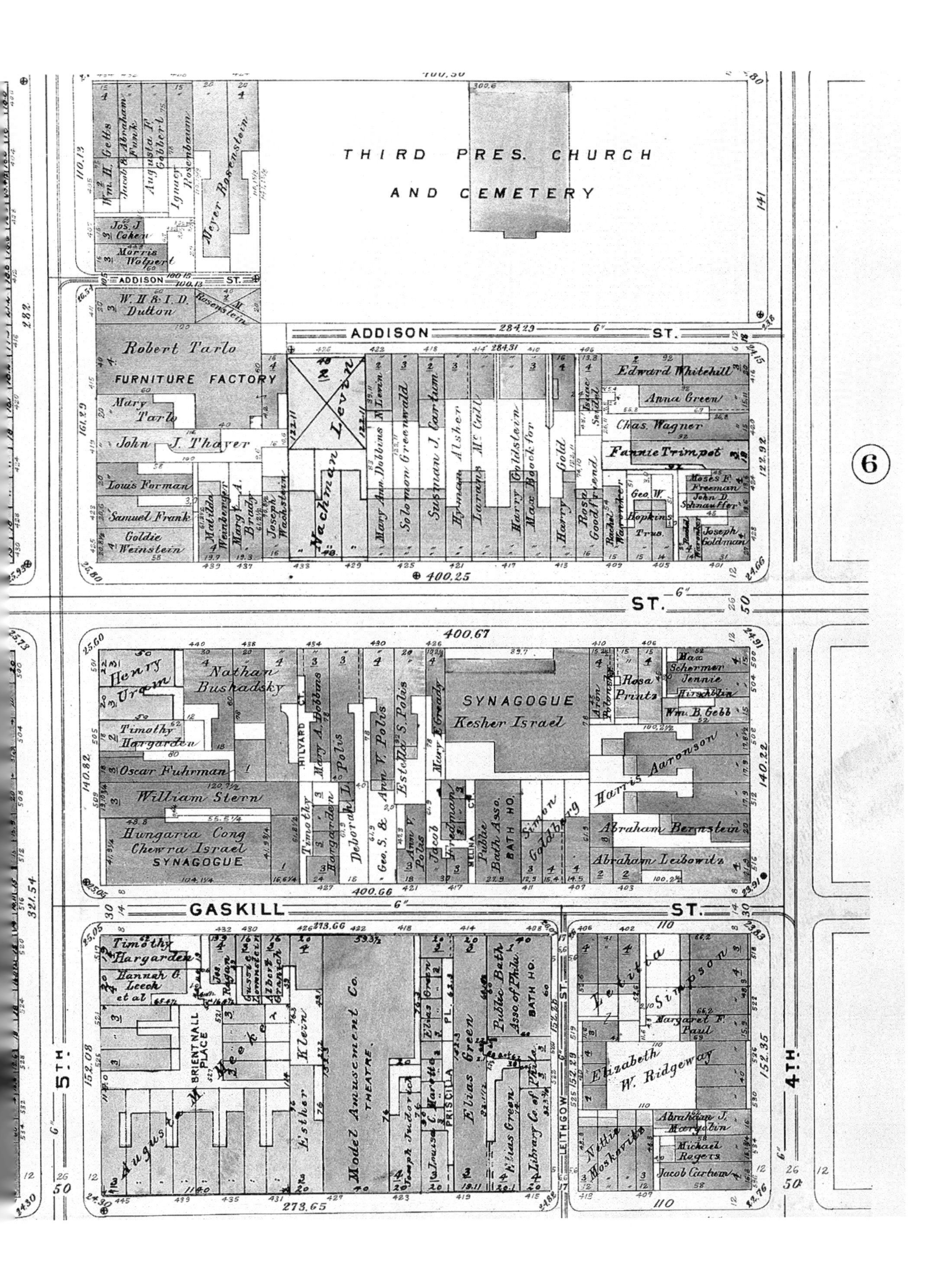

THIRD PRES. CHURCH
AND CEMETERY
ADDISON ST.
Robert Tarlo
FURNITURE FACTORY
SYNAGOGUE
Kesher Israel
Hungaria Cong
Chewra Israel
SYNAGOGUE
GASKILL ST.
Model Amusement Co.
THEATRE
BRIENTNALL PLACE
LEITHGOW ST.
5TH
4TH
6

Index